Legacy of the Prophet

Legacy of the Prophet

*Despots, Democrats, and the
New Politics of Islam*

Anthony Shadid

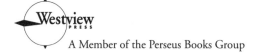
Westview
PRESS
A Member of the Perseus Books Group

Copyright © 2002 by Anthony Shadid.

Westview Press books are available at special discounts for bulk purchases in the United States by corporations, institutions, and other organizations. For more information, please contact the Special Markets Department at the Perseus Books Group, 11 Cambridge Center, Cambridge MA 02142, or call (617) 252-5298.

Published in 2002 in the United States of America by Westview Press, 5500 Central Avenue, Boulder, Colorado 80301–2877, and in the United Kingdom by Westview Press, 12 Hid's Copse Road, Cumnor Hill, Oxford OX2 9JJ

Find us on the World Wide Web at www.westviewpress.com

A cataloging-in-publication date record for this book is available from the Library of Congress.
ISBN 0-8133-4018-7

The paper used in this publication meets the requirements of the American National Standard for Permanence of Paper for Printed Library Materials Z39.48–1984.

10   9   8   7   6   5   4   3   2   1

For my wife, Julie,

a source of hope and inspiration

Contents

Note on Transliterations

Transliterating Arabic into English is typically a messy business. This book does nothing to make it less so. In nearly all cases, I have spelled names as they were given to me by the person interviewed or as they appear in common usage—Sadat or Nasser, for instance. When possible, I have avoided using dashes and apostrophes to represent Arabic characters in an effort to make the words less complicated for the unaccustomed ear. Occasionally, the same name will appear with different spellings, usually a reflection of its pronunciation in individual countries. The name Mohammed, for instance, appears in the book as Mehmet in Turkey and Mohammad in Iran. In other cases, names may have different spellings depending on the source in which they appeared. As for transliterations of my research in Arabic, I used a phonetic system that I can safely say is my own, and I am responsible for its inevitable inconsistencies.

Acknowledgments

It would be impossible to acknowledge everyone who helped me prepare this book. Many are colleagues and academics with whom I worked in the Middle East and the United States. Others are friends in Egypt, Lebanon, Palestine, Sudan, and Iran who helped me challenge my assumptions and question my beliefs. Two people who deserve special mention are Adel al-Buhairi and Abbas al-Tonsi in Cairo. I also want to thank Scheherezade Faramarzi, Mariella Furrer, Christine Hauser, Hamza Hendawi, Bassem Mroue, and Enric Marti for their unswerving support. The friendship they have shown can never be repaid. My work at the Associated Press would have been impossible without the help of my colleagues, in particular Earleen Fisher, Gerald LaBelle and Eileen Alt Powell. In the United States, I am especially grateful to James Bishara and his colleagues at *Middle East Report* who for thirty years have maintained a critical, honest and principled perspective on the region. I am also thankful for the insightful comments of Samer Shehata, Hosam Aboul-Ela, Arang Keshavarzian, Wadie Said and David Waldner on the initial idea for a book and its earlier drafts, although they are in no way responsible for the opinions that follow. Amal Ghannam was tireless in her help in researching the thesis, and Todd Rosenberg helped out with his usual artistic excellence. I could never say enough about my agent, Robert Shepard, who brought a singular determination in getting the book published and then offered the crucial advice in editing and expanding the ideas that made the book possible. Finally, I owe thanks to my proud family. Generations on, they have not forgotten their roots, taking pride in their heritage and the challenges they endured in making a successful life in America. Of course, I am most indebted to my wife, Julie, who listened patiently to endless passages and paragraphs, at all hours, as an editor and friend.

—*Anthony Shadid*

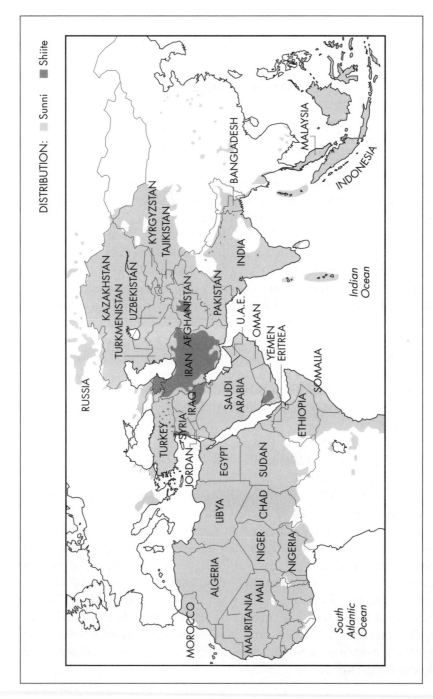

DISTRIBUTION: ▢ Sunni ■ Shiite

Muslim World

Introduction

HIS WORDS CAME SUDDENLY, delivered with righteousness. His concern was Osama bin Ladin. "A hero, that's the feeling of the people right now, that he's fighting to save the Muslim world," Mohammed Abdullah said. "When he dies, he'll be a martyr." His sentiments, unadulterated by sensitivity, left me with a sense I had felt often as a journalist in the Muslim world. In October 2001, as smoke continued to rise from the rubble of the World Trade Center and the ugly gash in the Pentagon lay bare, I traveled to Cairo, one of the Muslim world's greatest cities, to cover one aspect of a story that, by then, had become sadly familiar to me. Off and on, for nearly ten years, I had reported and written about the attacks, the strife and the bombings that had come to define, for much of the world, the face of political Islam.[1] Similar circumstances brought me here again, and much remained familiar. There was grief at the shedding of innocents' blood in the attacks of September 11 and over the death of more innocents in the war that followed in Afghanistan. There was disbelief at the spectacle that terrorism can unleash. And, no less troubling, there was the same misunderstanding, the same yawning gulf in perceptions that seemed to follow the scars left by the attacks.

Abdullah, I soon learned, was not alone in his beliefs. To the young men that had gathered around me at a sprawling bus stop in Cairo, their beards suggesting a fervent devotion, the Saudi militant exiled in Afghanistan was a symbol of an embattled religion, the very personification of the men's own frustrations at a faith overwhelmed by an omnipotent West. Their issue was justice, or a lack of it. Bin Ladin, they said, spoke of defending Palestinians, of ending sanctions on Iraq, of curtailing near-total U.S. sway over the region. An older man in a white peasant gown spoke up, raising his voice over the square's circus of vendors hawking fruit and buses barreling down the street, their exhaust stirring the dust carried by Egypt's desert winds. "He's a man

I

who defends his rights," the man insisted, as others nodded in agreement. "If someone tries to hit me, I have to defend myself. He's defending his land, his religion, his rights and himself."

How had we reached this point? As I stood amid Cairo's thriving chaos, I began to think about the divide that made two cultures, both defined to a great extent by religion, almost incomprehensible to each other. Many Muslims, whose disenchantment with the United States evoked an almost nihilist disdain, seemed to cast bin Ladin as militant rather than terrorist, dissident rather than executioner. His defiance of the West had assumed the mantle of heroic resistance. The world's affairs here were defined not by liberty, nor by freedom, but instead by justice, a concept that takes on greater importance to those without it. To the men at the bus stop, the United States and, by default, the West were the instruments for depriving justice across the Muslim world, a vast territory embracing one billion people who make up a majority in some forty-five countries.[2]

Passions were no less ardent in the West. The attacks of September 11 were the latest, most persuasive evidence of modern-day Islam's seeming penchant for senseless butchery. Before much of the world, and in a frighteningly short time, one of history's most sublime prophetic messages had become a faith defined not by the omnipotence of God and the need for generosity and justice but by a darker, more menacing side of human nature. Lost were memories of Islam's proud past: the Ottoman Empire's centuries of glory, Arab accomplishments in mathematics, astronomy and medicine, the conquests of an Islamic army whose domain stretched from Central Asia to southwestern France and Islam's heritage in preserving, tailoring and then transmitting Greek philosophy to medieval Europe. Instead, a new legacy had evolved in our lifetimes, and the messages of Islamic militants scrawled in blood were poised to leave a more lasting impression. The result, it seems, is yet another repetition of the fear, misunderstanding and hostility that have defined relations between Islam and the West since before Pope Urban II launched the crusades to liberate the Holy Land in the eleventh century.

The challenge of this book is to suggest another impression, to investigate a phenomenon with repercussions both for Muslims and the West and for our future together. It is a journey of sorts. Through the Turkish slums of Istanbul, the teeming neighborhoods of Cairo, the battle-scarred *wadis* of Lebanon and the austere Iranian seminaries of Qom, it seeks to shed light on a transformation that is far removed from the gloom pervading discussions of Islam in the West and, in particular, the United States. While this book was completed before the events of September 11 and the war in Afghanistan, its assumptions and findings remain accurate today, despite the impressions—some permanent and some doubtless temporary—that were left behind by the nation's nightmare. Most of the book's predictions, I believe, will survive intact.

My concern is democracy, or more specifically a transformation that I believe is under way across the heart of the Muslim world—Iran, Turkey and Arab countries—in both the style and the message of Islamic politics, even as much of the world grapples with the remnants of Islam's most militant currents. That transformation, only now emerging, is fraught with danger but will be of far-reaching importance, both for Muslims and for us in the West. In exploring this phenomenon, my focus is twofold: to see the way in which the adolescence of many of yesterday's militants has yielded to the maturity of a crucial segment of today's activists and to explore a new generation that is finding a more realistic and potentially more successful future through democratic politics. Despite recent events—and while wild cards undoubtedly abound—this movement toward democracy remains undeterred.

Appropriately enough, the transformation finds its roots in 1979, the year of Iran's Islamic revolution, an upheaval that seared itself into Western consciousness with its anger, its militancy and its excess. To many in the West, the revolution served as a wake-up call, signaling a new danger that until then few had recognized and even fewer had worried about. In the Muslim world, electrified by its stunning success, the revolution gave meaning to political Islam, or *Islamism,* a term that not only conveys a moral meaning but also suggests an all-embracing approach to economics, politics and social life.[3] More a critique than a program, political Islam aligns itself with the disinherited, who struggle with chronic joblessness, a widening gap between rich and poor, obscenely corrupt governments, heavy-handed repression and the desolation and hopelessness of daily life. The movement defines itself through questions of identity: What does it mean to be a Muslim in a world subservient to a West that seems predatory in its politics, economy and, most importantly, culture? And it addresses the faith's perceived decline over the past 500 years, blaming it squarely on Islam's eclipse from modern life.

In time, this ideology came to guide Sudan's leaders, to mobilize Palestinians in Gaza and the West Bank, to motivate activists in Turkey and to inspire poor Egyptians in Cairo's alleys and the country's long-neglected south. Since 1979, despite staggering failures in Sudan and Iran and setbacks in Egypt and Turkey, Islamism has become a part of mainstream life, a vibrant, diverse socioreligious movement that claims its own modernly educated intellectuals, cadres and institutions far removed from the militancy for which it is better known in the West.[4]

With that evolution has come maturity, namely in the politics of Islamism. In Jordan, Yemen, Egypt and Kuwait, Islamic parties that trace their roots to the once-violent Muslim Brotherhood, arguably political Islam's most influential movement, have all undergone a striking transformation, competing in elections and making notable gains through the ballot box. Few of these parties' demands have been met, but all have remained within the limits and confines of a democratic system. In Turkey, the Refah Party once preached a millennial vision of conflict with the West. And yet it became Turkey's largest party in parliament in 1995 not through confrontation but rather through a persuasive message of justice and equity. Its success was a tribute to grassroots, community work that flourished in an environment in which people could express their gratitude as votes. Turkey's generals, who view Islam as the biggest threat to the staunchly secular regime founded by Kemal Ataturk in 1923, forced Refah from power. But its influence, its numbers and its message seem destined to continue under the banner of the Virtue Party or in another incarnation under the guidance of a dynamic younger guard.

That interplay, between parties oriented toward Islam and the society around them, is one element of a phenomenon that is no less important than the bloodshed of militant Islam. As compelling is the transformation under way inside the movements themselves, a development that not only complements but also nurtures the democratic opening. Across the Muslim world, Islamic activists and their leaders are questioning their long-held goals and tactics, a rethinking that is independent of whether or not they operate in a democratic environment. Already, that search is taking root in Iran, where President Mohammad Khatami has urged the creation of an Islamic civil society in which the rule of law—not of the revolution—is paramount. He is aided by Abdol-Karim Soroush and other brave thinkers, who are questioning fundamentally the legitimacy of religious authority. Another example is Lebanon's Hezbollah, a group born of the death and destruction of Israel's 1982 invasion that has transformed itself from militia to movement, running candidates in elections for parliament, entering into alliances and preaching dialogue with the seventeen other religious sects that make up Lebanon's rich but troubled mosaic. And in Egypt, the Muslim Brotherhood began organizing as the first modern Islamic political movement. Now, new currents and even a new party have risen from its sclerotic old guard, forgoing its iron discipline for a new style of politics that has dared to welcome women and even Christians.

All of this sits uneasily with Islam's record in the West, which typically views political Islam—not without justification—as a menacing, destabilizing force. That view, at times, can be overwhelming, so much so that it seems to me to stand as the Western equivalent to the sentiments I heard about bin Ladin in Cairo. Not unexpectedly, political Islam enjoys a more balanced reputation in the Muslim world. There, it is often better known for its extensive welfare work that has made possible its viability as a democratic, grassroots movement. Through a mix of religion and social activism, Islamic activists have created a reservoir of good will, building the foundation for their success in recruitment, in gaining popular support and in winning elections. There are few better examples than the Palestinian territories, where Islamic groups in the refugee camps of Gaza, amid fetid streets a shoulder-width wide, run kindergartens, orphanages, sports clubs and libraries. Activists in Lebanon share that approach: hearts and minds, Islamic-style. In a country still reeling from a fifteen-year civil war, residents can count on dirt-cheap but quality treatment at hospitals and clinics run professionally by Hezbollah. It is the same organization linked to the 1983 bombing of a U.S. Marine barracks, which killed 240 Americans, and the kidnapping of more than fifty foreigners amid the war's anarchy.

Remarkable, though, is that—barring Turkey—no Islamic group has yet to come to rule through popular, grassroots work. Rather revolution has served as the path to power, bringing forth avowedly Islamic governments in Sudan and Iran, two regimes with divergent backgrounds and aspirations but both espousing the basic aim of creating an alternative to the West by turning the popular slogan "Islam is the solution" into reality. Zeal and intolerance have largely undone Sudan's experiment, a work that is still in progress. Frustration and disillusionment have begun to exhaust Iran's revolution but, oddly, in a way that may help chart an alternative. In the Islamic Republic, a realization is growing that Islam does not have the answers to all of societies' problems, that by itself it cannot handle every challenge, be it economic, social or political. That realization opens the door, however gradually, to the new equation, in which dissent, coalitions and even human rights can take their place in a more open playing field.

This nascent transformation represents one of our age's great ironies. The attacks of September 11 will define Islam in the West for years to come. Yet those attacks were launched by networks that, in the end, had little to do with the Muslim world. They sprawled across disparate countries, in particular the United States and in Europe, and their cadres were made up of different nationalities with few, if any, connections to their original homes in Egypt, Yemen, Saudi Arabia and elsewhere. The violent spectacle, as we will see, substituted for a rigorous ideology. These groups were effective because they could navigate in the West, exploiting its freedoms and resources for their visions of apocalyptic resistance. As the men hatched their plot, the militant Islam under whose banner they operated was in retreat in the Middle East and much of the Muslim world. In those countries, the new politics of Islam were beginning to take hold.[5]

Egypt is a compelling example of this shift. For years, insurgents bombed banks in Cairo, massacred European tourists and fought almost daily gunbattles with the government in a simmering rebellion that eventually claimed the lives of more than a thousand people, most of them police and militants. Today, that violence is on the wane, despite occasional outbursts that still scar the Nile Valley. The insurgents' leaders—in jail or exiled in Europe and Afghanistan—are at odds, their mounting disputes played out in competing leaflets faxed to Arabic-language newspapers.

In their stead new currents have emerged, most notably within the Muslim Brotherhood, a movement founded in the home of an Egyptian schoolteacher in 1928 that quickly became the most influential revivalist organization in the Muslim world. The 1990s witnessed a new leadership within the movement. It rebelled against secretive ways inherited from the Brotherhood's early years that emphasized iron discipline and unquestioning loyalty within its ranks. The disenchantment was not confined to Egypt. Across the Middle East, where branches of the Brotherhood have long exercised influence and power, activists voiced these same complaints. The most dramatic dissent came from the Center Party. It was founded in 1996 by Brotherhood outcasts in Egypt as an alternative, a group that stated its support for elections and the alternation of power but more importantly said it believed in dissent and coalitions with non-Islamic parties. Most strikingly, it surrendered a claim of representation: the traditional assertion of Islamic revivalist groups that their message represented Islam and that they, therefore, had the right to guide the *umma*, or Muslim community. As Essam Sultan, a Center Party founder, put it to me in an interview: "No one in Egypt can say that I speak on behalf of the people of Egypt or I speak on behalf of the majority of the Egyptian people, like some of the parties present now say. ... (A)ny person who says he represents the majority of the Egyptian people, he is a liar."[6] His statement is a far cry from bin Ladin's exhortations on behalf of all Muslims.

More so than at any other time in the past, the West has an essential role in this evolution, not least to cope with the kind of sentiments I heard voiced by Abdullah and the others at the bus stop in Cairo. From 1979 on, U.S. policy toward the Muslim world has been dangerous and remarkably flawed. Typically, it has been content to view political Islam as inherently threatening or as a target of sometimes cynical opportunity. The approach has helped bring about nearly two decades of enmity with Iran and conflict with Sudan. In Saudi Arabia, our blind support for the monarchy—and, by default, its corruption and repression—has cultivated an Islamic opposition that today threatens both U.S. troops and access to the world's largest oil reserves. U.S. policy toward Israel and the Palestinian authority has inflamed activists there, embroiling the United States in a conflict that need not be our own. In distant Afghanistan, on the cultural and political periphery of the Muslim world, the United States opportunistically armed and supported militias that drew on Islam to fight the Soviet Union in the 1980s. Today, many of those same militants are sworn enemies of America. Bin Ladin, of course, became their most influential graduate.

There is an alternative, one that will require a particular element of courage in the wake of the attacks of September 11 and the war in Afghanistan. The United States and the West face a strategic choice, and that choice will go far in determining the course of politics in much of the Muslim world. Egypt again may be enlightening. Since the Arab world's largest country signed a peace treaty with Israel in 1979, the United States has acted as its patron, wielding substantial, almost colonial, influence over its internal and foreign affairs. This influence, however, has not entailed pressure on its authoritarian government to enact democratic reform. Both Egypt and the United States recognize that such changes, in time, would give rise to an already popular Islamic current in Egypt's political life. That policy is shortsighted and clearly untenable. Repression has already failed in Iran and is soon to fail in the Persian Gulf and in countries like Egypt, where time and again the government has failed to stamp out the substantial support political Islam enjoys, giving rise instead to a generation of militants whose exploits still scar New York, Washington, Luxor, Islamabad and beyond. That leaves one viable alternative: The West must encourage democracy in places like Egypt with the realization that it is, in effect, encouraging Islamism by making room for its growth. It means governments might be elected that have no love for the United States. On the other hand, America's support for those same movements—the Center Party, for instance—could bring forth a new relationship in which U.S. policy and political Islam find common ground. To do so, the West must take further steps in ending the isolation of traditional enemies, giving countries like Iran an opportunity to evolve into more democratic states. In nations like Turkey, Jordan, Kuwait and Yemen, where democratic Islamic movements are now emerging or already in place, the United States must seek to make clear that their assumption of power is not in itself an adverse development. The choice is not sentimental, and without question, the risk of such policies is great. But the potential benefits are myriad—stability in an oil-rich region, democracy in authoritarian countries, a more viable weapon against the scourge of terrorism and the first step in ending a cultural conflict that, today more than ever, threatens to escalate. Both sides must take the journey together.

This book is my attempt to understand this crossroads. It is the product of five years of research and hundreds of conversations with religious sheikhs, students, activists and politicians, many of those interviews stemming from my time as a correspondent with the Associated Press in Cairo. My attempt to chart this evolution has given me the chance to explore a swath of the Muslim world—

Lebanon, Afghanistan, Sudan, Egypt, Turkey, Iran, Yemen, Syria, Jordan, Libya, Iraq, Pakistan, Israel and the Palestinian territories. At each locale, I have tried to understand as a journalist what the revival means not only to the faith and its adherents but also to the West, delving into the history and the tragedies that have brought us to where we are today. In addition, I have sought to convey the activists in those countries, as much as possible, in their own words, avoiding judgments and prejudices. The writing, though, is not unbiased and my own views will undoubtedly come forward.

In many ways, the book constitutes a personal journey as well. As a Lebanese American of Christian parents, I have long been fascinated by the power and pull of faith and, at the same time, disheartened by the stereotypes and prejudices so rampant in the West toward both Arabs and Muslims. Yet, despite my Arab roots and ability to speak Arabic, Islam has nevertheless remained sometimes foreign and all too often confusing and troubling—the attacks of September 11 being just one example. To understand it, I felt, was in part to understand myself and my fractured relation to the region, helping to unravel the nagging reality of most hyphenated Americans: the sense of being an Arab in the United States and an American in the Middle East. Within that struggle, I suspect, is a certain understanding of the difficulties posed by questions of identity, what I consider one of the most salient features of modern Islamism.

The geographical emphasis of the book is on the Arab world, Iran and Turkey. In many ways, I believe that region constitutes the heart of the revival, the arena in which political Islam will most strikingly develop, but I may be rightly criticized for ignoring a vast portion of the Muslim world—from West Africa to East Asia, including the Muslim world's most populous country, Indonesia. I can only say that I have done my best to differentiate between custom and belief, between tradition and faith, taking pains not to apply what I have seen in one country to the religion or to the Muslim world as a whole. Those other countries, perhaps, are better left to another book. As well, salient issues such as the changing role of women and the rights of minorities in Muslim countries do not receive the attention they deserve. In defense, I do not claim to have written a systematic or comprehensive work. Rather, I have sought to bring together selective interviews, travels and history into a narrative argument that is accessible and interesting both to the lay reader with a passing interest in politics and religion to policy-makers with a stake in the region's destiny. I expect many Muslim activists, journalists and scholars to disagree with my conclusions, but I hope that disagreement raises questions and prompts discussions that can take us a step beyond the stereotypes and misunderstandings that seem so common on both sides.

1

— ✦ —

A Question of Identity

From Afghanistan to Egypt,
Islam as a Refuge in
Troubled Times

IT WAS A LITTLE BEFORE DAWN, the lightning streaking and
shimmering over the Hindu Kush Mountains, when we arrived at the
camp of Afghan fighters outside the war-shattered capital of Kabul. I
came with a driver, Amir Shah, a burly Afghan[1] with little taste for
war or religion but a sensibility instilled by time and circumstance to
accept both. We were conspicuous—as any foreigner visiting
Afghanistan is—but no one seemed to pay attention. They were
instead preoccupied in an unsuspecting kind of way, moving in age-old
ritual that had become habit. The men washed their hands and feet,
figures illuminated by faint flashes of light, before they began their
prayers. The minutes passed, and the men, slowed by sleepiness, came
together on the soiled, ratty mats that served as their prayer rugs.
Clothes tattered and flowing turbans askew, they cast their heads
down, bowed, then kneeled before God, a sign of submission required
five times a day. Artillery thundered in the distance, the echoes of war
rolling over the lonely camp.

After prayers, one of the fighters, a man I would later know as Mirza
Khan, climbed up a sun-baked mud hut that served as their barracks,
opened a green, wooden artillery box and gingerly pulled out yellowed,

well-worn copies of the Quran, the Muslim holy book. He kissed each one as he handed them out to his expectant comrades. For another hour, he and the twenty men sat cross-legged, some rocking back and forth with blankets draped over their shoulders, and read the word of God. Their voices sounded like the murmur of an audience. Soon after the first rays of sun had snuck over the mountains, their day had begun.

I had left my home in Cairo, Egypt, for a monthlong assignment with the Associated Press that allowed me to spend time with these devoted young men of the Taliban, a militia of thousands, fired by faith, who had poured out of the religious schools of southern Afghanistan in 1994. Their campaign, both in its speed and severity, was nothing short of breathtaking and soon stunned the world. In less than three years, the fighters had overwhelmed the scattered remnants of armies known as the *mujahideen*, crusaders once adored by the West for their success in ending a ten-year Soviet occupation of their country.[2] The Taliban's offensive culminated on the night of September 26, 1996, with their entry into Kabul, a city that was seized by wanton lawlessness and brutality inspired by factional fighting. The victory was probably most remarkable for being so anticlimactic. Flying a white flag to symbolize their religious purity, they rolled into the city from all directions with barely a shot fired. Their erstwhile opponents had already abandoned the capital under the cover of darkness. Almost immediately, the Taliban acted with the confidence of conquerors. Within hours, they stormed the UN compound that had sheltered a former Afghan president. They hauled him away, then hung his beaten and bloated body by a wire noose from a lamppost outside the presidential palace from where he once tried to rule the country. It was still there after dawn, a macabre spectacle for thousands who studied his corpse with horror and fascination. The Taliban, in typically resolute fashion, had announced their arrival.

For the miserable inhabitants of Afghanistan, 2.6 million of whom had already fled abroad to Iran, Pakistan and elsewhere, the victory was more bitter than sweet.[3] Their city, once libertine by the region's standards, was wrecked by years of fighting. Rubble rested uneasily against still-standing walls and doorways, and abandoned homes were overgrown with weeds. Two-thirds of the city was uninhabitable, looking more like an archaeological dig than the capital of a country. The desolation was not only physical. For the city's residents, the best-paying jobs were those offered by aid agencies: a day shoveling

Afghanistan

rubble for fifteen pounds of flour. When I spent a month in the city in fall 1997, half of its one million people depended on food handouts. I had never seen nor imagined such misery.

Once in Kabul, the Taliban made a name for themselves in the West through a vindictive campaign of repression and harassment that seemed geared to making the capital's residents, especially women, pay for living under the Soviet-supported communist government of the 1980s. In a bizarre mix of Islam and tribal law, nightmarish in its intolerance, women were beaten for not cloaking themselves in a head-to-toe shroud known as a *burqa*, the traditional garb of Afghan village women. High heels were banned, as were cosmetics and white socks (lest they attract the attention of men), and most women were prohibited from working outside the home. Men were told to grow their beards as the Prophet Mohammed did or face lashings and a few days in jail. Music and televisions were declared off limits.[4] At Taliban checkpoints and intersections, glossy ribbons stripped from cassette tapes fluttered from poles in a not-so-subtle warning. It seemed effective: I never heard music while I was there.[5]

I had arrived in August 1997 to help out during the absence of our Afghan reporter, who had been arrested and beaten. Fearing more trouble, he left the country upon his release. At the time, I had begun researching the thesis that would later become the genesis of this book: the opening of Islam to democracy. Tied up in that phenomenon were questions of identity, issues that I had only begun to explore. In my years in Cairo thus far, my travels had been limited to the Arab world and countries like Iran and Turkey that bordered it. The assignment to Afghanistan was a rare chance to explore a region I saw as occupying the edge of the Muslim world, both physically and ideologically, and hopefully to learn more about the role of faith in people's lives, even in the most trying times. Here was a country in shambles, locked in medieval conditions. Its people had known nothing but war for a generation, and through a combination of poor health, poverty and fighting, were not expected to live beyond forty-six years (in the United States, life expectancy is nearly seventy-seven years). Of its 26 million people, one in ten had no access to water that would not make them sick.[6]

What could faith mean to people here? I saw that question as crucial to the debate over Islam and democracy. In the Muslim world, as elsewhere, identity and politics are intimately linked, a two-way path in which one helps define and shape the other. Islam's resonance in people's lives holds the potential for the faith's emergence as a moderating, democratizing force in the politics of the Muslim world. In Afghanistan, I hoped to explore the connection between Islam and identity—a specifically Muslim identity—and its attraction in times of unrest and change.

The answers, I soon learned, were not with the Taliban. Almost immediately upon arriving, I got the sense that they had no program or ideology, putting them beyond the purview of political Islam, which seems obsessed with its own modernity. Their goal was the imposition of Islamic law—a code they believed they exclusively understood—and the expulsion of women from public life.[7] They left the rest to God.

The answers, I believed, were elsewhere. I went to Bandi Khana, the soldiers' camp that was about a half-hour from Kabul, in an attempt to find them. I hoped for a glimpse of the role of Islam in the lives of these men on the front line, fighting in battles that rolled over Afghanistan's deserts, valleys and mountains like passing clouds.

Mirza Khan was one of those men, a fighter just twenty-two years old. As I walked into his camp with Amir Shah, he was one of the first to greet us, declaring simply and starkly: "This is the life I want." That life was along one of four fronts in the country, about twenty miles north of Kabul, where the Taliban, day after day, sparred with remaining units of the *mujahideen* grouped under Ahmad Shah Massoud, a legendary guerrilla commander. Khan's was the life of a soldier: bursts of violence punctuating long periods of boredom and idleness. In Bandi Khana, the men typically roamed around the mud-brick huts and simple stone bunkers of the camp, waiting idly for something to happen. The monotony was broken only by their camaraderie—there was no rank among the Taliban, only a commander and the fighters.

Like many of those young Afghan men, Khan was strikingly handsome, his chiseled, tawny face set off by a green turban striped with white. His slight body was cloaked in a gray tunic and he wore worn black sandals. His face had that haunting look of abbreviated youth: the beard of an adolescent, its hair still wispy. Of the young men, Khan was one of the more reserved ones. When they joked, he looked to the ground. When they laughed, he tried to do no more than smile. During the time I spent at Bandi Khana, though, Khan had a certain magnetism that seemed to attract respect, even adoration from his colleagues. More than one of the youths told me Khan could recite the Quran from memory, a sign of obvious devotion.

In his modest way, Khan was eager to talk to me, fascinated by a Christian and an outsider who spoke an unfamiliar language and inspired countless questions. With Khan and his friends, I often found myself answering more than asking: Do I drink alcohol? How many times a day do I pray? Do Christians burn their dead? Do I have a girl-friend? And, my favorite, what is the weather like in America? Throughout, even when answers unsettled them, I was treated with respect and warmth that made me think the often clichéd notion of hospitality in the Arab and Muslim world actually rang true on these parched plains outside Kabul. That generosity even extended to shar-ing their food. Around noon, as the sun arced overhead, a van flying the Taliban's white flag brought the soldiers' rations—bags of vegeta-bles, yogurt and an armful of *nan*, the ubiquitous Afghan bread that is a staple on the front. Our dialogue became especially festive as we pre-pared for an early lunch in a hut made of the surroundings: stones, mud, discarded wood, metal barrels and shell casings. For the soldiers, the truck's arrival was one of the more exciting moments of the day and lunch was surprisingly extravagant. Sitting cross-legged on soiled, gray blankets, we feasted on potatoes and okra, rice, onions, peppers, yogurt, bread and tea. There, I heard Mirza Khan's story.

Khan fell in the middle of a family of eleven boys and six girls who lived in Kabul through its darkest times. He spoke little of his child-hood, the hardship being part of his generation's upbringing during war (he was only four years old when the Soviet Union invaded Afghanistan, setting up its base in the capital). Like many Afghans, day-to-day survival engendered few memories he wanted to share. Those he did recall were of loss and anger. He remembered Russian soldiers in Kabul, and the fury that sights of non-Muslims eating, walking and laughing in the streets instilled in him. He remembered, too, his uncle and his cousin leaving Kabul in the 1980s to join the *mujahideen*. His father, he said, was too old to fight. Khan, of course, was too young.

"I had no power," he told me. "I could only hide."

In time, partly to flee the war, he made his way to a religious school in the Pakistani town of Mardan, but his stay there was short-lived. He said he soon felt a higher calling for sacrifice, prompted in part by the urging of his teacher, who told him: "Whoever wants to become close to God should fight in the *jihad*."

Khan left the school, known as a *madrasa*,[8] catching a ride in 1996 with other students in a truck to the Afghan border. They then found a rickety public bus with no windows to Jalalabad, an embattled city in eastern Afghanistan, where they joined the Taliban. As Khan remembered it, a friend had to teach him how to shoot a Kalashnikov rifle.

"When I left, no one knew I came here," he told me. "But I knew I had to leave. I gave my address to all my friends. If I die, I said, send my body to my family. If I live, I'll go back myself." He paused, then added with a mix of determination and commitment: "I got a Kalashnikov because of God."

Khan's friends joked that he, in fact, wanted to die, that he wanted to become a martyr, or *shahid* in Arabic, someone who gives his life for God.

"If I become a martyr, it's the will of God. If the fighting ends, it's the will of God, too," Khan said, his turban covering short-cropped black hair. "If I live or if I die, it's up to God because I know I am already on the right path."

His conviction, which I considered genuine, was startling. In a West often obsessed with self-indulgence, here was a twenty-two-year-old, already a hardened veteran of war, who took to heart the actual meaning of the word Islam—submission, submission to God and, for Khan, submission to a righteous path he felt he was already traveling. I probably would not want to share that conviction, but I had to admire it. It was the devotion that struck me time and again in my travels in the Muslim world—faith infusing life, defining it and directing it at a level outsiders often find difficult to comprehend. Typically, we in the West identify ourselves by race, gender or hyphenated ethnicity, placing religion squarely in the corner of personal belief. In the camp at Bandi Khana, and across the Muslim world, that personal belief is identity, often more important than race or nationality. There is room for misperception in missing the scope of that identity. To look at Islam only as a set of fixed beliefs and doctrine runs the risk of misunderstanding the dynamic of the faith and the way it appeals in our time to a young, jobless man in Egypt, a woman activist in Turkey or a fighter likely to die on the plains in Afghanistan. Dealt a sobering reality of misery, hardship and frustration, Khan knew he wouldn't be betrayed by his religion. His conviction was who he was.

In Jalalabad, Khan began his life as a soldier. He fought for five months in the region around the city, best known today for its rich harvest of blood-red opium poppies, the raw material of heroin that is grown by more than 200,000 families in Afghanistan.[9] He lost his half-brother Abdel-Rahman there and, even now, did not try to romanticize his time. Solemnly, Khan pulled out a black-and-white snapshot taken in Jalalabad, showing himself with a rifle, a World War I–style ammunition belt in front and the same turban he was wearing when I met him. In the picture, he was grimacing, much the same way he did when he recounted the story. I was struck by the gesture of showing me the picture, unsure if he wanted to prove to me the truth of his story or to demonstrate his record as a fighter for God. Eventually, I concluded that it was his way of showing that he had fulfilled his duty, that despite hardship, he had not wavered.

Jalalabad fell to the Taliban in September 1996, a key victory in their consolidation of control over the country. Afterward, Khan returned to his family in Kabul and stayed there for eight months. He soon grew bored with the business of trading wheat and flour and was eager to start fighting again.

"It was tough to spend night after night in the house," Khan said, running his fingers through his thin beard. "One morning, I woke up early to pray and just decided to go. I got my blanket and came here."

"What Islam commands is higher than the wishes of my mother and my father," he said matter of factly. "I'm happier here than with them."

After walking toward the front for about an hour, carrying only a gray blanket with a green and red border, a young Taliban commander spotted him, asked him what he was doing and brought him to the camp. He had arrived only three weeks before I met him.

Our conversation came to an end with another ritual. A little after noon, a lone soldier stood outside, giving the call to prayer. It began with "God is most great," a phrase repeated three times. Men walked off into the desert with pitchers of water to perform the ritual washing required before they pray. They then threw their tunics down, bowed toward Mecca, Islam's holiest city, and prayed in unison in a scene remarkable for its simplicity. A light breeze blew their turbans slightly in the wind, catching the heat from embers still burning in the fire that was used to prepare the lunch. After they finished, they shook their tunics out and threw them back over their shoulders, a moment of purpose that soon gave way to the dull routine of waiting.

We wandered outside, some men sitting on the ground, others leaning against the mud huts. Next to Khan was his Kalashnikov rifle. The Soviet-designed weapon has a romantic place in Third World militancy, celebrated as a symbol of Arab leftists and Palestinians in the 1970s and even today pictured on the emblem of Hezbollah, the Lebanese guerrilla group. Khan's rifle, however, had a mixed message. A white-and-pink paper flower was tied with green thread around the end of its barrel. It was an odd sight, I thought, a symbol of peace when neither Khan nor any of his friends, all in their twenties, could remember anything but war. Khan seemed aware of the irony. Even here, he told me, the flower represents peace, but in an Afghan way.

"Peace will only come through war," he told me. "If we're killed in the bus on the way to fighting, we're going to heaven. And if we live, we're heroes."

And the fighting itself, I asked him, how long will that go on?

"That's a question for God, not for us."

Before sunset, the men sat on mats thrown on the ground, sharing snuff, chatting or waving at the passing Taliban cars flying their white flags. Echoes of artillery rounds firing off in the distance drifted over the camp. As the last rays of sun lingered over the mountains, Khan stood up, looked out at the escarpment of the Hindu Kush and raised his hands to his ears. His voice carried the call to prayer, its plaintive affirmations mixing with the rumble of shells in the background. A flash of lightning brightened the soft horizon, and more thunder rolled across the plain. The men gathered again for prayer.

The simplicity of the scene overwhelmed me. Without the guns, the military truck nearby and the rusting water tank in the backdrop, Khan's call could have been uttered 1,400 years ago near Mecca, as the Prophet Mohammed gathered together his small following of outcasts. Distant were the edicts of Taliban leaders: the firing of bureaucrats for trimming their beards and the beating of women with canes for breaking the Taliban's rules against their vision of feminine excess—perhaps an arm showing from underneath a cloak. The petty battles in Kabul over whether Islam sanctioned music, soccer, photography, videos or flying kites seemed part of a nightmare remote and removed from Khan's reality. Here, in his realm, there was no culture shock, no corruption, no rich and poor. The West and its hedonism, worship of the individual and arrogance in its power were abstract ideas, no more than words tossed about in Friday sermons. On the war-scarred plain under a darkening sky, Khan had found purity, a sense of meaning and the security of destiny. He was happier here than with his family for a reason: His faith was his family, its love unconditional. For him, there was clarity in God.

It was a theme I would encounter again—in places like Afghanistan, on the psychological rim of the Muslim world, and in cities like Cairo, my home for five years. Individuals like Mirza Khan were not significant in themselves. Rather, in understanding the connection between identity and Islam, it was what they represented: Islam spoke with clarity, offered simplicity and served as a familiar refuge in troubled times. It absorbed rebellion from the smoldering embers of Third World nationalism and appealed to the identity of an already devout people. In some ways, I thought, it was like a signpost in times not all that unlike those of another era, a period of strife and rebellion that gave rise to the founder of a new faith, the Prophet Mohammed. It is perhaps impossible to understand the power of that message more than 1,300 years after the prophet's death without first understanding the conditions that originally gave such power to his ministry. The birth of Islam spoke similarly to another generation.

In the harsh, inhospitable and rugged climes of western Arabia, the kind of terrain from which prophets often spring, the dejected followers of Mohammed had gathered gloomily in the home of his favorite wife, Aisha. Their prophet had died a day earlier, on Monday, June 8, 632, a passing that came somewhat suddenly. He had left no arrangements, no instructions to his followers and no advice on what should happen next. In fact, his sole gesture to the affairs of the vibrant new faith and state he had founded had been to appoint Abu Bakr, the first convert to Islam from outside the prophet's family and long his chief lieutenant, to lead the community's prayers. Confusion reigned in Medina, the city that had given the prophet refuge during darker days, and fear gripped the haggard men who had assembled. The future of the faith seemed in danger.

To that anxiety and unease, Abu Bakr rose, looked out across the men and uttered words that so many Muslims even today can recount by heart.

"If anyone worships Mohammed, Mohammed is dead," he said. "But if anyone worships God, he lives and does not die."

It was a fitting epitaph for Mohammed's ministry, which began, according to tradition, when the archangel Gabriel appeared to him at the age of forty in a mountaintop cave called Hira. At the outset, Mohammed's message was to the people who inhabited the trading town of Mecca. Implicitly, however, it was addressed to all those who would listen, and it spread with the ferocity that only converts can bring. To many of the first Muslims, those men gathered in Aisha's home, its appeal was its simplicity and clarity: the goodness, omnipotence and unity of God and the need for justice and generosity among mankind—in that, the last and most perfect divine revelation.

Mohammed was born in the barren climes of western Arabia in about 570, spending most of his life there. Although remote, the town was by no means provincial. Unlike modern Arabia, which is almost entirely Muslim, the peninsula of Mohammed's day was a festival of faiths. Important Jewish communities were settled in Medina and other parts of Arabia, though their days were numbered. Christian Arab tribes roamed on its border with Syria to the north and in Arabia itself; others lived to the south in Yemen. Mecca, as a religious and commercial capital with an annual trade fair, no doubt attracted many, either as slaves, pilgrims or merchants seeking a piece of its booming trade. There were others who entered Mohammed's life even more directly. Waraqah, a cousin of his first wife, was a Christian and he was reported to have had conversations with Mohammed on occasion.[10] Legend also has it that during a caravan to Syria, Mohammed met Bahira, a Christian monk, who identified the young merchant as a prophet.

The winds of imperial power blew across Mecca, as well. The great powers to the north were the Byzantine and Persian empires, the first stretching across Asia Minor, Greece, Egypt, Syria and other parts of Europe and Africa, the latter extending through a broad stretch of land from Iraq into Central Asia. Wars between them raged through much of Mohammed's life, and their spheres of influence reached across the desert into Arabia. Adding to the town's eclectic influences was a cosmopolitan element: Mecca was somewhat of a boomtown. Although not particularly ancient, the town had become a key entrepot of trade routes that traveled along the Red and Mediterranean Seas and the Persian Gulf. Through the year, its caravans ventured south into mountainous, fertile Yemen (home to frankincense and myrrh), across arid Arabia and north to Gaza, Damascus in the Syrian hinterland and

on to faraway ports like Basra in present-day Iraq. The mercantile culture was developed, pervasive and rewarding, and in western Arabia,
Mecca had become preeminent, monopolizing the region's trade and,
as a result, transforming a town in a sandy, narrow valley surrounded
by mountains into a flourishing city whose name in English has come
to mean a center of activity.

The transformation had a side effect: Mecca began to feel that its
culture, traditions and values were under seige, a sense not unlike the
dislocation and alienation Westernization brings to much of our world
today. The source of that transformation was affluence, which was
shifting the nomadic life that long defined Mecca and its inhabitants
to a mercantile existence. Tribalism was giving way to individualism
and business interests—both power and influence—were becoming
more important, even to the extent of putting commerce ahead of
clan.[11] The shift was responsible in part for a far-reaching and momen-
tous social revolution, fertile ground for a reformer.

Little is known of Mohammed's youth, although his life was
undoubtedly difficult. His father, Abdullah, died before he was born
and his mother followed when he was six. As an orphan, he was cared
for first by his grandfather, then by his uncle, Abu Talib, who headed
the clan of the Hashim. Although not wealthy, the family belonged to
Mecca's most prestigious merchant tribe, the Quraysh.

Mohammed's early career seemed to be frustrated by his lack of capital rather than skill and, in time, he gained a reputation as an able
trader and organizer. The key to his moderate success as an adult was
Khadija, an independent woman and the widow of a wealthy Meccan
merchant, who hired him to lead a caravan of goods across the desert
to Syria. He did well and, on his return, she proposed they marry. He
was twenty-five. Khadija, who had been married twice before, was said
to be forty, although other accounts suggest the number was a guess
and she was probably younger. Together, they had six children, two
boys who died in infancy and four girls. Their life together was prosperous but undoubtedly defined by Mecca's restless times.

The ascent of Mohammed's ministry was a long one and, through
much of his life, he was met with skepticism if not outright opposition. Mohammed received his first revelation in 610 and began
preaching in Mecca three years later. His wife was his first convert
and a handful of others followed, but merchants in Mecca soon
resented him—some historians say feared him—and questioned his

claim of prophethood. Eventually, they boycotted his entire clan. He received a similar reception elsewhere. In one jarring episode, a rabble threw rocks at him when he visited the nearby town of Taif to propagate his movement. At times, Mohammed even suffered self-doubt. He always saw himself as a simple man, unsure why God had chosen him. Throughout his life, he never claimed divinity and, although acting as judge and messenger, never suggested that he had the power to perform miracles. Rather, he was a man, albeit one summoned by God.[12]

Mohammed delivered a message tailored to the time, ideas that emanated from the rivalries, disputes and wrenching changes of one locale but that are relevant to a broader world. In a changing Mecca, he preached religious and social reform. There was one god, he said, and believers in him had to reject the worship of others, whose shrines littered the desert town. Obedience to God and his prophet would bring new life to a lost and faithless community, creating a fraternity of believers whose identity built on and transcended traditional ties of tribe, clan and kin that were losing, however gradually, their strength amid the sweeping changes.

It was a message of defiance, too. The rapacity of Mecca upset Mohammed, and his message sought to create a new moral code. He condemned social injustice and exploitation of the poor, orphans and women. He urged help for the poor through alms and forbid corruption, fraud and cheating. Throughout his ministry he railed against the flaunting of wealth and arrogance and handed down strict punishments—some still in force today—for slander, theft, murder, drinking alcohol, gambling and adultery.[13]

The message was stern, austere and even ascetic, but its simplicity was obvious. There was right and wrong and good and bad, leaving little room for moral ambivalence. In a confusing time, when traditions seemed irrelevant and ethics were primarily to keep others in line, its clarity provided a secure refuge. That refuge—in a telling sign of the message's power—remains relevant for adherents of all faiths, as we will see later.

By 622, though, twelve years after his first revelation, the message had found only limited appeal. Probably less than a hundred had followed Mohammed's wife into Islam. Troubled by the failure of his ministry and burdened by the responsibility of his message, Mohammed was eager to find other ways to establish his faith. The road he chose became known as the *hijra,* one of the decisive events in world history.

The word *hijra*—or hegira as it is known in English—literally means emigration or exodus. It marks the time in 622 when Mohammed's followers made their way to Yathrib, a town about 250 miles north of Mecca that later became known as Medina.[14] Long under the shadow of Mecca, the town relied some on trade but was more prominent as an agricultural oasis that produced dates and cereals. In Mohammed's time, it was a troubled town, riven by long-standing and sometimes violent disputes among its tribes. The strife, in essence, resulted from a lack of leadership, providing a window of opportunity for Mohammed. Some of the residents of Yathrib had met him during a pilgrimage to Mecca in 620. A year later, another delegation came, this one numbering twelve and representing the tribes and factions of the city. They asked him to come and mediate and promised to abide by his decisions and accept him as prophet.[15] Mohammed, always a tactician, agreed and sent ahead deputies well versed in his message. They found success, and by the summer of 622 he was ready to send his followers to Yathrib. They made their way without incident and, in September, Mohammed himself departed with Abu Bakr, leaving a city that had always been hostile to his ministry. They took pains to avoid assassins and eventually arrived in Yathrib on September 24.

That summer would assume supreme importance to Muslims. Its beginning (July 16, 622) marks the start of the Muslim calendar and, in broader terms, signifies the beginning of the *umma,* or the Muslim community, a symbolic moment when Mohammed's followers began to look beyond their tribal and clan affiliations and see themselves foremost as Muslims, believers in God, the god of Abraham. The idea of the *umma*—from Indonesia to America—remains powerful today, a sense of fellowship and unity that stretches across borders and language.

The Mecca of Mohammed's time was not the only Arabian city in the throes of change. In Medina, too, Mohammed found a society in flux. There, tribesmen conditioned by an austere nomadic background defined by the desert were beginning to live a settled life. Like Mecca, a new lifestyle and the social system it brought began to emerge, throwing into question the norms, mores and traditions that had regulated Arabian life for generations. In that context, his message again found a responsive audience.[16]

Over the next decade, Mohammed would lay the foundation for a society that would conquer, in less than a lifetime, an expanse larger than the Roman Empire, assuring that his message would endure to the present day. In the beginning, he built his power gradually, slowly assuming rule as temporal and spiritual leader. Money came to his community through raids outside Medina, and Mohammed eventually won out over his antagonists through a mix of diplomacy and might. Even his Meccan antagonists fell to his authority, and in January 630, nearly eight years after fleeing Mecca, he triumphantly returned to the city of his birth. Although his victory saw some of its inhabitants executed—not so unusual for the time—he was generous with most, despite the long years of feuding. As a prophet, he destroyed shrines to the goddesses of Manat and al-Uzza that were outside town, and inside Mecca, he cleaned houses and the city's religious center of idols. As reformer, he abolished most of the old offices and privileges of the Meccans.[17] Soon, as general, he embarked on what would later be seen as the first Arab war of conquest, setting off along the road to Syria with an army of 30,000 men.[18]

Just two years later, in 632, Mohammed died. His passing was greeted with disbelief and anxiety, the questions immediate and far-reaching: Who could replace him? Who would lead the community? And, without his authority, how would the faith survive? There was not even a Quran, chronicling the revelations as conveyed by God to his prophet. Rather, Mohammed's years of preachings were scattered in writing among his followers or tucked away in the uncannily accurate memories of his contemporaries. Looking back, it is an odd idea: Islam without the Quran and the faith without a prophet. But it was testament to the strength of the nascent religion. Despite civil war, assassinations and power struggles, the community survived and less than twenty years later, by 653, the Quran had taken its present form, conveying what Muslims believe to be the word of God. It is seen by the faithful today as perfect and complete. The importance of its completion rivals the *hijra,* bringing the world the faith of Abraham unadulterated and uncorrupted, free of the misunderstandings that were believed added to God's message over the years by Judaism and Christianity. In more lasting terms, the Quran and the Sunna, the example of the prophet and his companions, provided the basis of society—a historical utopia of Islam's early years that Muslims today look upon as a type of salvation. To reestablish the righteousness of that era

as envisioned in the Quran and Sunna is to return to God, and
Islamists today believe that a renewed, modern application of those
texts contains the essence of their program, goal and answer.

The interpretation of the message, though, is as divergent as the
faith itself. And the simplicity that appealed to Mirza Khan is complemented by ambiguity, the same ambiguity that prompted Abu Bakr's
remark to the funeral. In essence, for the faithful, the same questions
remain in our time: What follows Mohammed's death, even today?
And in this modern world, an admittedly confusing time in which the
faith and the context are changing more rapidly than at any time in
the nearly 1,400 years since the prophet first began preaching, what is
the community's role in the modern world and what is the faith's relationship to modern life, whether in law, in government, in politics or
at home? In essence, Islamists ask, where do we go from here, and on a
more visceral level, what does the faith mean to us? These questions
define political Islam.

The sheer diversity of the faith complicates that definition, a
breadth that never ceased to surprise me. In Sudan, I met a group of
Sufi mystics in white robes who had come together on the sun-
parched banks of the Nile River. At dusk outside Omdurman, the
twin city of the capital Khartoum, the men swayed to a drumbeat and
chants of "There is no god but God." Within their circle, barefoot men
in ragged clothes, meant to symbolize their disavowal of worldly
things, jumped up and down, stomped the dirt and threw themselves
to the ground. Delirious with religious fervor, they shouted "God," as
the religious ceremony known as a *zikr* reached its wild, frenzied and
unpredictable climax. Afterward, a mystic named Zubair Abu Zeid,
who was dressed in lion skins and carrying a staff like Moses,
approached me.

"It is worship," Abu Zeid told me.

A few weeks later on another continent, in the long-tortured streets
of the Lebanese capital of Beirut, I encountered another interpretation
of that message. Organized by Hezbollah, the country's most impressive popular movement, a march drew tens of thousands of men and
women clad in black to mark the martyrdom of a revered grandson of
the prophet. Cadres shouted chants through megaphones to a sea of
humanity that stretched to the urban horizon. Overhead was a canopy
of flags testifying to their fight against an army that occupied their
homeland.

"Our battle will continue," promised Hassan Nasrallah, the respected leader of Hezbollah, to the wild cheers of the mobilized faithful.

Those two scenes were just a hint of a world so eclectic it sometimes seems unfair to group it together under the designation "Islam." From Mirza Khan to the Sufis in Sudan to Hezbollah in Lebanon, its territory stretches east to the Atlantic Coast of Africa and then west to the Philippines. Counted among its inhabitants are Sufis, Shiites and Sunnis, all with myriad subdivisions and other sects, some recognized as orthodox, others not. They make up a majority in some forty-five African and Asian countries, and virtually every nation in the world counts Muslims among its citizens, including a segment of the United States, where they represent one of the fastest-growing religions.

Their political breadth is remarkable as well: Activists who see in Islam an overarching approach to modern society have served in governments in Jordan, Sudan, Iran, Malaysia, Turkey and Pakistan. Islamic activists have achieved remarkable success in elections, one even being voted into the Israeli Knesset. Islamic groups are the main opposition in Egypt, Algeria, Tunisia and Palestine. Islamic-oriented governments in Saudi Arabia and the Gulf count as some of the closest allies of the United States, although Washington has accused the Islamic governments of Iran and Sudan of sponsoring terrorism. Some of these Islamic activists work through hospitals and clinics, others through schools and summer camps. Their books crowd for space on racks in downtown Cairo or outside mosques in Sudan. Across the region, their banks offer an Islamic alternative to Western institutions by finding ways to avoid the Islamic prohibition on usury, often interpreted as paying interest on loans.

Each locale is defined by often unique conditions of language, culture and ethnicity that determine the faith's ebb and flow over society. But on a broader level, the sentiments to which the faith speaks are shared across those borders, many having in common a wreckage of brazen corruption, searing poverty and relentless repression where leaders rule by the consent of their soldiers, regrettably at the expense of their people. To much of today's generation, religion infuses their activism as they seek to transform societies adrift and confused, the goal of renewal that so many espouse.

Perhaps most potent is their shared sense of loss. In the West Bank and Gaza Strip, Palestinians talk of a peace process that no longer struggles with issues of justice or its lack, but instead engages in the bargaining of a bazaar over percentages of land. In Bosnia and Chechnya, Muslims found themselves threatened by overwhelming odds and the world, despite proclamations of sympathy, seemed unable or unwilling to help them. Muslims in Central Asia struggle with the fading but still well-entrenched remnants of the officially atheist Soviet state. And in India, a surge of Hindu nationalism worries a Muslim minority that is more numerous than the populations of most Muslim countries. But rather than encountering sympathy, Muslims often find themselves the target of a hostile and, at times, uncomprehending West. Few in the Muslim world would deny that the barbarous slaughter of innocent villagers in Algeria or the massacre of tourists in Egypt are abhorrent acts of terrorism. But they see counterparts among Jews and Christians who have carried out equally insidious deeds. Still, they argue, few in the West would claim that David Koresh spoke for all Christianity at Waco, Texas, or that Baruch Goldstein represented Judaism when he gunned down twenty-nine Muslim worshipers kneeling at a mosque in the West Bank town of Hebron.

As powerful as the loss is the belief that the Muslim world is suffering from a decline, deformed by colonialism, misled by nationalism and wrecked by socialism. The sense of weakness and vulnerability is a painful admission for a glorious Islamic culture that long dominated the world. The generation of fervent converts that followed Mohammed, first under Abu Bakr and then his successors, swept across a land stretching from Central Asia through the Middle East and North Africa to southwestern France. Its scribes transmitted Greek philosophy and helped make way for the Renaissance. Its scholars developed astronomy and mathematics and invented algebra, the term itself an Arabic word. As late as 1683, its armies under the flag of the Ottoman Empire were at the gates of Vienna, in the heart of Europe. To many Muslims, the decline since then, and even before, can be blamed on a departure from Islam, a long movement away from the true faith and its principles in both personal and public life. A return to the simple but ambiguous legacy of Mohammed, they believe, will restore the prestige and power of a Muslim identity becoming increasingly important in the wake of the last generation's failure.

Sometimes, we can see even our own society reflected in those concerns.

Consider this episode: At a political rally, angry demonstrators complained of attempts by the state to keep their faith out of the public view. Freedom of religion does not mean freedom from it, they shouted, and religion should always be at the center of public and private life. It is a question of God, not of law.

"We are drawing a line in the sand and saying, 'Devil, you've taken enough from us,'" one angry clergyman shouted from the steps of a government building to the fervent cheers of a crowd. A judge under fire for promising to bring the faith into his courtroom—even if it meant breaking the law—told the thousands gathered: "Your presence today will send a message across the nation. That message is clear: We must—nay, we will—have God back." The rally was in Alabama in 1997.[19]

Then listen to Adel Hussein, an activist in Cairo. Substitute the word Christian for Islamic, and the parallels are evident.[20] He might be a Christian fundamentalist in America's Bible Belt, representing the kind of rhetoric that has entered our mainstream. "Most of what is shown on television, in films, in plays is not what we need if we are committed to Islamic values," he told me as we sat in his suburban Cairo home. "So if you change what is said in the media and what is taught in the schools, this will encourage families to bring up their children according to Islamic principles."[21]

Gilles Kepel, an Islamic scholar who lives in Paris, calls the phenomenon of revived faith, which he believes is shared by Christianity, Islam and Judaism, "the revenge of God," the religious response to a deep malaise in societies across the world.[22] The faiths appeal to identity, offering an almost holistic approach to the unease of the present day. Similarly, they provide an impetus to their politics, their message making it incumbent to act.

"It is arising in civilizations that differ in both their cultural origins and their level of development. But wherever it appears it sets itself up against a 'crisis' in society, claiming to have identified the underlying causes of that crisis beyond the economic, political or cultural symptoms through which it is manifested," he wrote.[23]

I always felt that malaise was most powerfully experienced in Cairo, the greatest of Arab capitals. Cairo is as much the heart of the Muslim world as Afghanistan is its frontier. The nuances of that city contrast with the starkness of Mirza Khan's life, but despite their distance, both offer insights into the evolution of political Islam: They cater to the appeal of a simple but ambiguous message. The force of faith there is another side to the relationship between Islam and identity, and understanding it took me across the city's Westernizing neighborhoods, booming suburbs, ramshackle cafés and the haunts of its tradition-bound trashmen.

———

July 26th Street is a thoroughfare that cuts through the chaos of Cairo's 15 million inhabitants like an urban chameleon, tying together in a desperate sort of way the city's contradictions, frustrations and sense of loss. The street takes its name from the 1952 revolution of Gamal Abdel-Nasser and, in a sense, speaks of that revolution's failure. In the wealthy enclave of Zamalek, it runs past boutiques, antique stores and the stuff of plenty: Rolex watches, designer sunglasses and Persian rugs. Fast-food restaurants, McDonald's, Pizza Hut and others whose names read like a roster of American capitalism open new branches along the road in a city once famous for its thousand minarets, catering to the conspicuous consumption of Western-clad, Americanized men and women.[24] But across the languid Nile River, the waterway on which Cairo is so perfectly perched, the street takes its travelers to another world, an altogether different reality. In the sprawling slum of Bulaq, snarled traffic paralyzes the street, saturated with incessant horns and choking exhaust. Half-paved roads branch off into desperate, dreary neighborhoods painted in yellows, browns and tans, the dull colors of poverty. In these crumbling houses, amid rotting trash and the stench of sewage, are the majority of Egyptians—and, in a way, the majority of all Muslims. Westernization makes them feel uneasy, even adrift. Most of them, tossed aside by the growing gap between rich and poor, have not shared in its rewards. They are fiercely conservative: suspicious of the West, fearful of materialism and uncomfortable with the sweeping changes it promises. For these Cairenes, Islam provides refuge from fears and frustrations and, as with Mirza Khan, a return to the faith confers a clear, almost Manichean Muslim identity.

At Friends Cafe, a shabby alcove along July 26th Street, covered with a generation of grime, I sat with Ahmed Hassan and Ayman Hamdan, two Egyptian laborers in their twenties, and our brief conversation stuck with me. Both drivers rented their cars out on a daily basis, making a few dollars a day. They eked out a living so precarious that a flat tire or engine trouble could spell disaster. Their hardships made them resentful of the excesses of their counterparts living across the river, whose alien lifestyle they associated with the West rather than with their own culture. That was the negative identity, what they were not. But beyond that I wondered, how did they see themselves? Who were they?

First, they were Muslims, they said, hardly pausing to think, then they were Egyptians. After that, perhaps, they were Arabs.

"Faith is the first thing," Hamdan said, his eyes narrowing. "It comes before community. It comes before everything."

Hassan looked on, then added a thought that at first seemed disjointed but, in hindsight, added context to Hamdan's declarations. "The world has changed," he said, as if trying to explain Hamdan's devotion. "Everything has changed."

Again, it was the idea of faith as a retreat, a haven that grew in appeal as Cairo went through its biggest changes in a generation in its lifestyle, its landscape and the way in which its people interacted. Not surprisingly, it came to the fore in unusual if complementary ways. One of my first assignments as a reporter in Cairo was covering elections for Egypt's parliament in 1995. It was a sobering experience. The government's vision of campaigning ran something like this: arrest hundreds of members of the main opposition, shamelessly stuff ballot boxes and hire thugs to intimidate voters. In that milieu, Adel Hussein, a prominent Islamic activist who ran as a candidate for the misleadingly named Labor Party, distributed a card that, to me, symbolized the appeal of Islam as a refuge. Across the bottom was an apocalyptic scene under a burning red sky, marked by the shabby, soulless concrete buildings built by Nasser that still dominate the Cairo skyline. A flag charred black hung limply on a cracked pole, an image of broken promises and failures of leadership. Across the top was another scene, Islam's version of socialist realism. The awesome minarets of medieval Cairo towered above a blue sky caressed by clouds. A flag that read "To God, thanks," fluttered before the words, "God is most great." Below was printed the enticing slogan, "Islam is the solution," a motto of Islamic activists today that says little yet speaks, in its simplicity, to the estrangement of modern Cairene life.

What is the nature of that alienation, the signposts of estrangement? In my time in Cairo, it went beyond July 26th Street with its Rolexes and restaurants; it was the attitude as well, sometimes a brazen, almost in-your-face taunting in a country where modest affluence probably includes no more than 5 percent or 10 percent of the population, probably less.[25] Near my apartment, a billboard broadcast the slogan of the country's cellular phone company, MobiNil: "A mobile in everyone's hand"—that, in a country where a phone's yearly subscription and one-time deposit cost the annual per capita income of $1,250. MobiNil was not alone in its divorce from reality. One Egyptian bottled water distributor proclaimed, "All of Egypt drinks Baraka"—another jarring suggestion when the homes of one out of five Egyptians have no running water.[26] A short detour away, tucked in a maze of streets in Mohandiseen, among Cairo's more fashionable neighborhoods, was the Fat Black Pussycat and Jazzy Dog Cafe, one of the city's hottest nightspots whose name, understandably, proved difficult to translate into Arabic. A $6 cover got you entry into the "The Big Lizard," billed by a local guide as "the best dance night in town." It also bought a Stella beer, the local Egyptian brand.[27] In just a few short years, the beer had gone from a game of Russian roulette with a three-day hangover to an eminently drinkable, even good beer. In the mid–1990s, a Stella Premium hit the Egyptian market, along with a "light lager" known as Meister, cans and draught. It was all part of a campaign, the company's spokesman once told me, with complete sincerity, to create a beer culture by tailoring "a taste for each pocketbook."[28]

Along with the attitude was the ostentation, a reckless move in a city that in 1952, 1977 and 1986 erupted in jealous anger, its streets seething with riots, protests and arson directed at symbols of the West and the decadence and wealth associated with it. The most memorable display of that ostentation was a twin-tower behemoth with a stone facade that rose over a Pizza Hut near the Cairo Zoo, providing a singularly choice view of the Pyramids and some of the rougher slums Cairo has to offer. Most apartments in the First Residence building, dubbed the "Tower of Power" by local newspapers, offered a small swimming pool, a private elevator, marble imported from Brazil and Italy and gold-plated door handles. (One had a staircase with bullet-proof doors to the building's helicopter pad.) The bare-bones apartment ran a cool $1.9 million. One went for $29 million, or so rumor had it, in a country where nearly one-third of Egyptians live in homes with dirt floors.[29]

Finally, over the years, the geography of Cairo seemed as though it was being remade. Of Islam's great capitals, Cairo is perhaps the most physically unremarkable, defined more by the Nile than its skyline, less by its avenues than its traffic, which runs like meandering rivers of steel through the low-slung neighborhoods. More than 600 years ago, the Arab traveler Ibn Battuta described Cairo as "boundless in the multitude of buildings." Today, it is one of the most crowded cities in the world. With nearly six times the density of Mexico City, it makes Manhattan refined and quaint.[30] On the outskirts of the city, sprawl washes over former farmland, and the blurred line between urban and rural never seems to end, spilling out past the Pyramids of Giza and into its desert environs. In another direction, redbrick and concrete apartment blocks flow like lava across dense groves of palm trees, interspersed with crops of clover watered by muddy canals.

Then, like an eclipse, Cairo ends, and the green gives way to brown hills—rolling, although not so romantic. A few trees, meager and scrawny, lean with the relentless wind, planted in either hope or delusion. Pylons of cemetery gray cart electricity to a faraway horizon. The only splash of color—and, for that matter, life—comes from a vendor hawking his watermelons, apples and oranges from the bed of a pickup truck on a lonely stretch of simmering asphalt. The expanse is even more startling in Egypt, more than nine-tenths of whose people are shoe-horned into a fraction of the land, the 1,000-mile-long oasis known as the Nile Valley.

A new city—or a vision of the old—was going up next to those rolling brown hills. Billboards for new desert developments called Garden City, Greenland and Elite pleaded for attention, competing with ads for Nissan and Toyota. Blue trucks passed, carrying sand and cement to other settlements that made up Cairo's land rush: Beverly Hills, Dream City and Monte Carlo, some of the developments conveniently near Crazy Water, an amusement park in the desert with three water slides and a wave machine. To the south, still in the desert, was Katameya Heights, a resort and community of 300 red-roofed villas spaciously surrounding a man-made pond next to a golf course of twenty-seven holes, carpeted by Georgian turf flown in from Atlanta in refrigerated crates. (Membership ran a tidy $7,350, then nearly $600 a month in fees.) Cairo's newspapers were full of ads for the suburbs, peddling "English-style" mansions or "chalets" that look more like Soviet-era copies of Spanish colonial. I remember one ad that promised a self-contained desert community with a park, school, sports club, business center, cinema, mosque, clinic, supermarket and Internet access, the latest symbol of what it takes to be modern.

Oddly, many of those developments were blooming on land that the late Anwar Sadat foresaw as a so-called satellite city for the people, a group often heralded in Egypt by those who care little for them. He christened it the 6th of October, the date of his army's surprise attack in the 1973 Arab-Israeli war. That city and others in the desert like it—at a cost of $5 billion to the government—were supposed to attract industry and, more important, 1 million people by 2000. Only 250,000 came. A decade or so later, the government admitted failure and happily turned over to private developers huge chunks of the desert land, along with the costly infrastructure.[31] By the late 1990s, those developers had sketched, broken ground or completed forty projects. Their vision was helped by a boom unleashed by economic reform that took hold after years of stagnant growth, placing in private hands as much as four-fifths of an economy once synonymous with heavy-handed state control.

The changes were bewildering and ominous. The Cairo of my years was perhaps more Egyptian than any time in its recent past, judging by its Arab ethnicity and overwhelming Muslim majority. That was not always the case. In the 150 years after Napoleon Bonaparte landed at the modern-day resort of Agami—his Army of the Orient dreaming of an empire in the East and soon vanquishing an outnumbered cavalry armed with carbines, pistols, scimitars and javelins—Cairo entered what historians describe as its modern age. Modern meant a disorienting array of foreign influences. Pharmacies and taverns went up, shops peddled manufactured imports from England, bankrupting their local competitors, and a European theater courted unveiled women. Max Rodenbeck notes in *Cairo: The City Victorious* that by 1927—a bankrupt Egyptian monarchy and a British occupation later—the capital "no longer aspired to be cosmopolitan; it already was." A fifth of its people belonged to minorities: Christians, Jews, Greeks, Italians, British, French, White Russians and Montenegrins. Arabic, a vulgar necessity, was the language to order servants. English and, to a greater degree, French were the preferred tongues. For its pampered, familiar elite, it all seemed to make sense of a remark by the nineteenth-century ruler, Ismail Pasha, that "my country is now in Europe; it is no longer in Africa."

Then came the 1950s, a time of riot and revolution. It was not the first instance of anger unleashed in Cairo's history. As far back as 1521, Ottoman troops had rioted because their favorite opium merchant was executed for dealing during the holy month of Ramadan. But the anger was, without a doubt, the most far-reaching. Decades of colonial rule and privilege—always chafing a Cairo that remained deeply conservative and traditional, if superficially Western—had swollen a reservoir of ill will that spilled into the streets in 1952. Cairo burned. The Cinema Opera went up as it played "When Worlds Collide." It took twenty minutes for the landmark Shepheard's Hotel, an icon bar none of British distinction, to never do business again. In all, more than 700 symbols of Cairo's sybarites—bars and nightclubs along tree-lined avenues, Groppi's, the Rivoli Cinema, the British Council, Thomas Cook's, car dealerships, the exclusive Turf Club—were wrecked by mobs and arsonists.[32] A picture I once saw of the riot has stayed with me: Egyptian peasants near railroad tracks watching smoke rise over the city, a bent metal sign advertising Dewar's Whiskey propped against a telephone pole in a rubble-strewn street.

A revolution followed and, on July 26, 1952, a corpulent, corrupt king named Farouk sailed his royal yacht into exile. Cairo was never the same. The Qasr al-Nil barracks that once housed colonial British soldiers were demolished, King Fouad Avenue, named for Farouk's father, became July 26th Street, and Ismailiyya Square, named after his grandfather, became Liberation Square. In time, the foreign community, which never felt quite Egyptian nor wanted to, would flee, en masse, and Cairenes would find unity in their poverty.

In walking along Cairo's modern streets, through the old-wealth neighborhood of Zamalek, the nouveau riche haunts of Mohandiseen and along the pulsing artery of the six-lane Arab League Street—a name recalling a headier day of anti-Western Arab nationalism and its catastrophic battles with Israel—I sensed that the same resentments, divisions, alienation and anger of that era were emerging once again, diverging only in style and symbol. The ostentation and estrangement were creating another vision of Egypt in Europe, or more accurately today, in the West, with far-reaching repercussions for the role of faith in modern life. One signpost of that was the *hanin* that seemed everywhere in my time in Cairo, a source of support for opposition politics. An Arabic word, it means both longing and nostalgia, and in Egypt, it had come to define a thirst for a time of romanticized brotherhood, a bond that was always more powerful in memory than in reality. The sense of community forged by collective deprivation in Nasser's years had given way to a yawning gap between poor grappling with a loss of crucial subsidies and the abysmal state of public education and health—in effect, the side effects of economic reform—and rich finding opportunity in its wake— in the capitalism of Mohandiseen and the speculation of the desert boomtowns. The unseemly materialism and the growing dislocation with an unfamiliar Western lifestyle were fertile ground for, in Kepel's phrase, "the revenge of God."[33] It was the personal side of political Islam's appeal, awaiting a movement that could speak to it. In Cairo, I found a trashman named Eid Rabia its most eloquent spokesman.

I first encountered Eid in 1996 when he came to my door for his $1.50, the monthly fee to collect my trash. He took the money, then paused—a feigned gesture to suggest he should be embarrassed. He wasn't. Eid was *ibn al-balad*, salt of the earth.

"You don't have a hat, do you?" he asked, his sheepish grin at odds with his staccato bursts of Egyptian slang. "I need one for riding my motorcycle around, you know."

Eid was the equivalent of a broker for a community known as the *zabbaleen*, literally the trash people, a name that dates back at least 300 years, when the city was ruled by the Ottoman Empire and its work—from bath attendants to butchers—was run by guilds ferocious about their turf. The *zabbaleen* were one guild—and a lucrative one. Cairo always had plenty of trash. Archaeologists have turned up scraps of papyrus and pottery that littered streets 3,000 years ago. For centuries, the city itself was ringed by fetid, ripening 100-foot-high walls of refuse, a medieval garbage dump and likely a more formidable barrier than any stagnant moat or stone rampart. There was money in those hills, too. One medieval scholar insisted that trash worth "a thousand gold dinars"—clay pots, straw racks, string and bags—was cast away every day in the capital.[34]

Eid's history is far more recent. It starts, in a roundabout way, at the end of the nineteenth century, when migrants from three villages in an oasis in the Sahara Desert made their way to Cairo. They became known, naturally, as the *wahiyya*, or people of the oasis. With the gangland zeal of their guild brethren, they soon cornered Cairo's market on collecting trash, selling it as fuel—then, as now, the city had few trees—to heat the waters for the steaming Turkish baths and to roast a bean known as *ful midammis*. In a practical stroke, both were boiled in the same establishment.

Kerosene came in the 1930s, threatening to put the *wahiyya* out of business. But they stumbled on a new market in immigrants like them, waves of Christian peasants from Egypt's wretchedly poor south. The Christians needed food to raise their pigs in the shantytowns on the outskirts of the booming capital. Obligingly, the *wahiyya* turned over the often-distasteful job of hauling and disposing the trash to the Christian *zarraba*, or pigpen operators. They, however, jealously guarded their role as the fee collectors: Even today, the men like Eid still collect the money from the tenants, charging about $1.50 a month.

The system that evolved then is the system that exists now, and nobody breaks the rules of the game. The *wahiyya* justify their racket by an age-old collection of rules known as *urf al-minya*, or the customs of the trade. Nothing is in writing, but to them, that doesn't matter. The *wahiyya* claim their monopoly by simple tradition: They have worked the neighborhoods for generations. They pass the rights to buildings from father to son, dividing new turf among families with a minimum of competition—the souk-style bargaining of a guild that remains the same 100 years on. Decoding the layered ties of kinship, ethnicity, custom and habit would be akin to mapping a miniature genome.

The Christian *zarraba*, more commonly known as the *zabbaleen*, don't object. They are stitched by the same tradition into the *wahiyya*'s fabric. Besides, a challenge to the monopoly might threaten their lifeline to the fresh, ripe rubbish their pigs rely on. That would mean disaster. Many of the *zabbaleen* are set up on a precarious sharecropping system, supplied with animals and sometimes money by Cairo's four pork dealers. Not so generously, the dealers split the profits fifty-fifty, a rewarding enterprise despite a Muslim prohibition on pork that leaves Christians—about 10 percent of the population—and the growing number of foreigners as their only market.[35]

Eid was one of the *wahiyya* and he ran his thriving business from the Hilal Café in Zamalek, working as a middleman between the *zabbaleen* and tenants of apartments rich in trash. The Hilal Café was where I joined him after accepting an invitation.

Eid was one of those characters who never fade too far away from memory. His skin was weathered and tight, and his nose and face were both long, features reminiscent of Egypt's pharaohs. Always, he exuded a sense of determined ease, sitting on the bench against the café's faded blue wall, dragging on a local Lite cigarette. On this day, his other hand was busy at work with the long cord of a water pipe, drawing on its sweet smoke in between drags of his cigarette. In an effervescent Egyptian way, he warmly greeted colleagues and acquaintances with Turkish titles of distinction, addressing them in a few short moments as "pasha," "bey," and, my favorite, "engineer pasha."

Then, as is his custom, he engaged them in conversation.

Eid always enjoyed talking, and a few words punctuated his mean- derings: morals, principles, values and traditions. Or, as he liked to put it, the Egyptian way of life.

"There are people who walk within the borders of God and there are people who walk outside the borders of God," Eid told me, a replay of a conversation he had countless times. "I am not against change. I'm against the change of principles."

He put a spoon of sugar in his tea, a rich brown, and went on.

"If you drink this tea and it's just right, then you add spoon of sugar after spoon of sugar, can you still drink it?" he asked me.

Eid's empire stretched over thousands of apartments, much of his route inherited from his father, Hassan, who inherited much of his route from his father, Rabia. None of it was in writing and none of it was formalized. The contract was held together by thousands of visits by Eid, his father and his grandfather—usually not more than a good morning to one tenant, a peace be upon you to another and the famil- iar, obligatory exchange of money.

"I have 100 years of experience," he assured me.

Eid was running late this day and, to avoid cutting our time short, he invited me to accompany him, to see his route. He quickly finished his tea, sweetened just right, and walked out to his twenty-year-old moped, a Vespa—known by Egyptians whose alphabet has no "v" or "p" as a "Fisba." A sticker of "God is most great" was plastered on front, and a weary spare tire hung near the seat cloaked in a blue cloth.

On a lazy morning, we puttered along Zamalek's wealthy but clut- tered streets, past Marlboro signs, a Korean restaurant, a shop called Signee with its suede jackets and men's suits and a women's boutique named Why Not. At each locale, Eid waved to the *zabbaleen* hauling trash in wicker baskets slung over their backs, Baraka bottles mixing with the scraps of last night's dinner.

"Have a good day, God willing," Eid shouted.

"You need anything?" one man, Gamaa, asked.

"No, have a good day," Eid answered.

Down the street, two more men were lofting bags of garbage into a white Toyota truck. Across from them walked two young women in black shirts and tight black pants. Eid assumed they were students at the American University in Cairo, a group he called *mitamrikeen*, a derisive term for Egyptians who have adopted American manners.

"I don't know how to deal with them," he told me, shaking his head. "They use Western phrases—instead of *mashi*, they say OK, they say sure instead of *muwafiq*. I don't understand their thinking."

We passed a man with a long white beard and a prominent *zabiba* on his forehead, the scar some Muslims earn by very diligently bowing their head to the ground in prayers five times a day.

"If you adhere to your values and morals, they call you *ibn al-balad*, a son of the country. In Zamalek, Mohandiseen, the high-class areas, you find all of them distant from one another, strangers to each other. They don't know who's that, they don't know where he lives. They don't know each other," he said. "The popular areas are different. They have connections. I know that's the son of the son of the son of so-and-so. I know that's the son of so-and-so, the son of so-and-so and the son of so-and-so."

"The *mitamrikeen*," he said, "they're lost. They're strangers in their own land. They're like a feather, floating in the wind this way and that. The people who stick with their values, principles and morals, they're like the Pyramids. Nothing shakes them. If I were to leave Egypt, I would feel I have died."

In Eid's words was the hint of *hanin*, probably the same sentiments shared more than thirteen centuries ago by the inhabitants of Mecca and Medina, two societies similarly being recast by forces that felt alien and unfamiliar. Like Mirza Khan, Eid found security in the idea of *umma*, a sense of community among Egyptians he romanticized and of a faith he celebrated. In it, he found an alternative vision of Cairo's changes, creating or perhaps retooling a language to enunciate morality and to express grievances. That reality, a utopia of memory, in turn spoke to alienation and *hanin*.

Albert Hourani, the late Oxford historian, once wrote that Islam provides an "effective language of opposition: to western power and influence, and those who could be accused of being subservient to them; to governments regarded as corrupt and ineffective, the instruments of private interests, or devoid of morality; and to a society which seemed to have lost its unity with its moral principles and direction."[36] For Eid, Islam—its systems of morals and ethics—was what made him Egyptian. It was the way he related to people, treated them and bestowed respect. It was what held his community together.

Through the morning, we passed other *zabbaleen* on their routes. One of them, Fahmi Salib, a Christian with bad teeth, came up and greeted Eid. He pulled out two cigarettes, placed one in his mouth and gave the other to Eid, offering a light.

"You don't want anything?" he asked.

"Say hello to your father!" Eid answered.

Eid turned to me, enjoying our dynamic of insider-outsider and relishing his display of a virtual neighborhood that was spread across his turf. Fahmi's father, he said, used to work with his father. Now, both sons work together, plying the same route a generation later, bound by tradition and history.

"He'll go back to his house and say what to his father?" he asked me, smiling and perhaps hoping. "He'll say Eid said hello."

Eid made his rounds and we returned to the café. He liked to do his business here—spending hours smoking and drinking tea, his version of *urf al-minya*, the customs of the trade, in a setting as timeless as the archaic rules that defined his livelihood.

To Eid, those customs, his reading of faith, were his security, a window on times that he remembered as good and a psychological buffer against a future that made him uneasy and uncertain. Alienation is perhaps the most personal of feelings, not brought on by poverty, repression or tragedy, but rather by a nagging sense that identity and reality seem somehow at odds. Like his profession, the Egypt he feels he knows—the layers of custom, kinship and habit, wrapped up in faith—was inevitably becoming another facet of nostalgia and myth, the very scene around him an anachronism. As Eid spoke, that older Cairo came to life: One man passed with an antique incense burner, swaying it back and forth. The aroma mixed with the pungent smell of cooked liver, the smoke of water pipes and cigarettes and the scent from tin buckets of shrimp and fish stacked in dirty ice on the corner.

"Fresh! Fresh!" the fishmonger called out. "Straight from the sea!"

Identity, I thought as I watched the scene unfold, is desire made real by memory, and Eid's words, in their rough sophistication, spoke to a phenomenon once termed "the reactivation of tradition," a gut, visceral response to a changing world.[37] One scholar called politics "a struggle about people's imaginations"—the conflict over their memories, their desires and the symbols that represent them—and in the contemporary Muslim world, that is the key to understanding Islam's response and its powerful appeal for Eid and others, the forces through which Islam has emerged as a successful political force.[38] Eid was the personal side, one of countless Muslims who have looked to faith and tradition for salvation and security. In that, Eid speaks for Cairo and Cairo speaks beyond Egypt's borders, where the struggle over imaginations represents the political side of Islam.

That conflict provided the Muslim Brotherhood, one of the Arab world's largest Islamic groups, the key to its success in Egypt and abroad, ushering in the dawn of the modern movement of Islamic activism.

2

Intersections and Messages

Islam Interpreted and Reinterpreted

THE STRUGGLE OVER PEOPLE'S imaginations has defined the political movements that swept the Muslim world in the twentieth century. Political Islam is one of them and perhaps the most lasting,
although it was overshadowed for years by secular ideologies that
flourished under the banner of anticolonialism, economic and social
justice, nationalism, and development independent of the West. They
were heady, idealistic promises that appealed to a new identity or, in
the case of the Arab world, reclaiming an identity that had been lost
amid centuries of foreign and colonial rule. Virtually all the ideologies
spoke to a reactivation of tradition, but with the pointed claim of creating every revolution's aspiration: a new man, a citizen that was
modern, progressive and secular. In various incarnations, particularly
after World War II, they offered answers, a program of action, in a
changing world. Those ideologies were the political side to questions
of identity confronted by a nascent Muslim *umma* or by men like
Mirza Khan in Afghanistan and Eid Rabia in Cairo.

Political Islam does not stand in a vacuum. Its evolution is indebted
to the ideologies with which it competed: They shared grievances and
goals and contested the same symbols and memories. Political Islam's
emergence as a modern movement is grounded in centuries of thought

and tradition, from reformers to intellectuals to revolutionaries, who reshaped the faith's formidable intellectual history to create an alternative that is viable in today's world. But it was shaped, too, by its intersection with the secular ideologies that captivated the region for decades. It is crucial to see their shared histories—their intersections—to understand its evolution.

The conflict with Israel is one starting point. The struggle inflicted a wound on the region far more severe than many Arabs and Israelis will realize. Its trauma was long in coming; the exhilaration of its early days is almost forgotten. The intersections that grew out of that conflict—the historic figures, their ideas and the interactions of secular and religious movements—were instrumental in defining contemporary politics today.

—

Plujot Junction is a lonely locale along tidy farms and rolling hills near the Israeli coast. The intersection today stands quiet, a simple crossing of roads that ties together cities both ancient and modern: Beersheba, Ashkelon and Hebron. But in 1948, during the first Arab-Israeli war, Plujot, better known in the Arab world as Faluja, became fodder for myth. There, through some of the war's fiercest days, a burly, broad-shouldered young Egyptian major named Gamal Abdel-Nasser fought against soldiers of a nascent Israeli state across strategic land that overlooks those cities of historic Palestine. His heroism in that battle brought him a shoulder wound and the nickname "Tiger of Faluja." But trapped for four months in a pocket of contested land, he was betrayed by a corrupt monarchy in Egypt that failed to provide his men with weapons, fuel and even food. Surrounded by a well-armed enemy and often under attack, Nasser and his men held out, against the odds and by sheer will at times, finally to venture out under an armistice agreement in which they felt they kept their honor.

In ensuing years, Faluja would become to Nasser what the Long March was to Mao and the Sierra Maestra was to Fidel Castro. It was at Faluja where he won a reputation for bravery that would give him legitimacy in the coming years of blood-soaked enmity between Israel and the Arabs. It was on the battlefield far from home where he called the first meeting of disgruntled soldiers known as the Free Officers. And, most important, it was where he plotted the revolution that just four years later, in 1952, would overthrow the teetering monarchy of

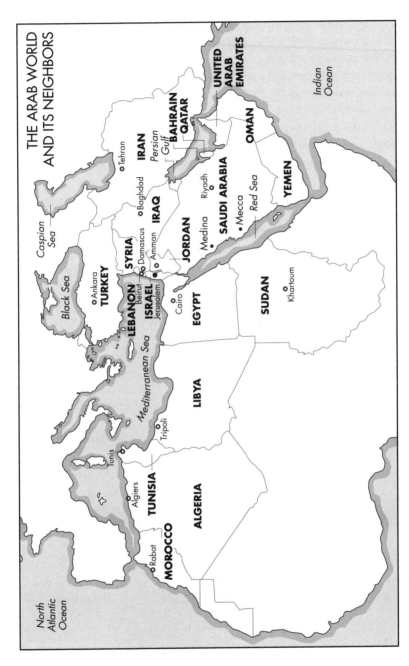

Arab World

King Farouk and deliver him power in Egypt. The event would lay the foundation for the high noon of Arab nationalism, inspiring—and later disappointing—a generation.

"Faluja was a symbol, a symbol of resistance," said Khaled Mohieddin, who in his late seventies is one of the few surviving Free Officers.[1]

Mohieddin, one of Nasser's earliest colleagues, hailed from a family with sizable land holdings in the Nile Delta but, through his life, played the not uncommon role of the well-to-do revolutionary. I spoke with him in his stately, tastefully decorated Cairo apartment, watching a man slightly bent with age in a dark suit too big for him reminisce about times that only a few could still recall. Despite his age, he remembered the potency of the battle. "Nasser always considered Faluja a case that showed if the people have the will to stand, they can stand," he said. "They were surrounded by the Israeli army, the Israelis had better arms than them, the Egyptians had a lack of food and ammunition and petrol, but they were able to organize themselves and defend themselves against any attack. That group of people in Faluja had the will to fight."

For many Arabs, the 1948 Arab-Israeli war stands as the *nakba*, a tragedy in which Palestine was humiliatingly lost. Its flip side, though, was a powerful impetus toward Arab nationalism, a call for unity and independence. Nasser, more than any other figure in modern Arab history, embodied that conflict, the struggle over people's imaginations. Much of the time that he ruled was heady, even euphoric, and despite the repression at home, the torture of dissidents and the arrests of his enemies, Nasser soon represented the aspirations of an Arab world that saw itself awakening from centuries of slumber. With his staccato cadence, he rallied, incited and cajoled with an eloquence that is still legendary—perhaps at no time more memorable than with his nationalization of the Suez Canal in 1956 or his union with Syria in 1958, the first step in what many hoped would be a united Arab homeland.[2] He brought inspiration to a region emerging from colonialism and rallied it for what many saw as an apocalyptic battle against Israel, whose very existence was stitched like a Gordian knot into the Arab fabric. As Nasser himself wrote in *Philosophy of the Revolution*, the Arab world was "wandering aimlessly in search of a hero. This role is beckoning to us—to move, to take up its lines, to put on its costume and give it life." He saw it as his destiny. As the historian Albert Hourani put it:

The personality of (Nasser), the successes of his regime—the political victory of the Suez crisis of 1956, the building of the High Dam, the measures of social reform—and the promise of strong leadership in defence of the Palestinian cause: all these seemed to hold out the hope of a different world, of a united Arab nation rejuvenated by genuine social revolution and taking its rightful place in the world. Such hopes were encouraged by skillful use of the press and radio, which appealed above the heads of other governments to the 'Arab people.' These appeals deepened conflicts between Arab governments, but Nasirism remained a potent symbol of unity and revolution, and embodied itself in political movements of wide scope.[3]

For much of that era, Nasser diverted the limited resources of his still poor country into martial endeavors aimed at securing his place at the forefront of the battle with Israel, imperialism and the West.[4] Variants of Nasserism and other secular ideologies such as Ba'athism in Syria and Iraq and Palestinian nationalism coincided with his ideas and aspirations to the degree that the former Egyptian soldier seemed to personify a region. For ten years or so, in fact, he was an unqualified success.

Disenchantment and disillusionment, though, soon followed. First, Nasser blundered with Egypt's misguided, five-year intervention in faraway Yemen that at one time tied up 50,000 troops in the Arabian Peninsula. Then, far more disastrously and with blinding suddenness, he brought catastrophe in 1967. He led the Arabs to defeat against Israel in just six days. His army was left in ruins, its commander committed suicide (some speculate that he was murdered) and Nasser himself stepped down, only to relent soon after when Egyptians, perhaps sincerely, poured into the streets shaken less by war than the prospect of their country without a leader who had so long embodied their hopes and dreams. Nasser returned a broken man. The year 1967 remains a synonym for catastrophe, in Arab nations and across the Muslim world. Israel had conquered Jerusalem, placing the city's Muslim and Christian holy places under Jewish control. Palestine's other vestiges from the 1948 war—the West Bank and the Gaza Strip— were also under Israeli rule, putting a conclusive end to Nasser's promises to liberate all its historic lands. As stunning, the rout pointed to the woeful limits of Egypt's political and military power and demonstrated all too clearly that Israel was far superior to any coalition of Arab states. The war marked more than a military defeat:

Nasser and his project, an endeavor shared by an Arab world that looked to him for leadership, was dedicated, both symbolically and practically, to the coming battle with Israel. The totality of defeat discredited it like no other setback could.

The resonance of that war was far-reaching: Through it came the symbolic demise of the secular philosophies of nationalism and socialism that Nasser had embodied and that had, until then, posed a convincing and persuasive alternative to the banner of Islam.[5] All at once, the heroism of Faluja, the promises of Arab unity and the solidarity of the Third World seemed to many a sham, a selfish and cynical manipulation of their feelings, passions and loyalties for what, in the end, turned out to be a failure. As Anwar Sadat, his successor, uncharitably noted in his autobiography, "Those who knew Nasser realized that he did not die on September 28, 1970, but on June 5, 1967, exactly one hour after the war broke out."[6]

The self-doubt and malaise from the defeat still pervade the thinking of that generation. For them, the promise of Arab nationalism, a path to progress independent of East and West and an army in the service of a state striving for justice and equality had come crashing down, revealing a landscape of corruption and cronyism, hollow slogans and misguided priorities. The nationalist answers themselves no longer seemed vibrant or progressive but instead came to be viewed as symptoms, distortions or incompetent copies of the cultural imperialism those ideologies were supposed to confront.[7] For those too young to remember it, including two-thirds of all Egyptians, Faluja, Nasser and his dreams of unity bear little consequence, a regrettable, somewhat irrelevant chapter of recent history, if that. Their lack of collective memory may be the greatest testament to the depth of the disillusionment those years now represent. To them, Nasser's project seems naive in an Arab world divided today by a lack of common interest, where the United States holds sway and Israel stands paramount. Failures are best forgotten.

I once asked a twenty-four-year-old named Magdi Samir, sitting in a café I frequented in the Cairo district of Bulaq, what he thought of Nasser's bravery at Faluja in the 1948 war. He looked at me, paused as if searching his memories, then shook his head doubtfully.

"I don't think Nasser fought in '48."

Those tumultuous years gave rise to divergent destinies, and none was perhaps as stark as another movement that rose, matured, collapsed and then rose again during the same era in which Nasser reigned. That movement was the Muslim Brotherhood, founded by Hassan al-Banna, an Egyptian schoolteacher, in the Suez Canal town of Ismailiyya in 1928. From just one of many religious societies in Egypt during that period, it quickly became among the most important political contestants in the country, the first modern movement defined solely by Islam. Its success in those years was a mastery of organization: weekly lectures in mosques and elsewhere, a vibrant press, outreach to students, civil servants, urban laborers and peasants and a message that addressed Christian missionary activity, Zionism, the British presence in the country and other issues of the day. Its growth was almost as spectacular as the rise of Nasser's Arab nationalism; its mission, in Banna's words, was to resurrect Egypt and "to give it life by means of the Quran."[8] And for many years, its destiny was tied intricately with the fortunes of Nasser's Arab nationalism, both in its meteoric ascent and more lasting fall. They both competed for people's imaginations with promises of rebirth and renewal and appeals to identity. Yet, today, only one still has currency, and their opposing fates offer powerful lessons for the state of political Islam, its viability, dogged appeal and ability to remake itself—in essence, mature—for successive generations.

Their first intersection came in 1948, in the same battle at Faluja, in fact. Brotherhood cadres had been involved in Palestine since the 1930s, their concern reflecting their identity as Egyptians, Arabs and Muslims, with a deep religious sense of Jerusalem's resonance in land they, like Christians and Jews, considered holy. From those years on, the movement had helped raise money, devoted time and resources to propaganda and organized demonstrations. More decisively, as the first Arab-Israeli war loomed in October 1947, the Brotherhood's leaders ordered its members across the country to start preparing for *jihad*, or a crusade, sending battalions of ill-prepared but zealous fighters to help the armies of Egypt, Transjordan, Syria and Iraq defend Palestine from the Zionists, who throughout the conflict maintained an edge in arms, training and, most important, clarity of duty.

Most of the Brotherhood fighters remained inactive during the 1948 war. Some, however, made their reputation, as Nasser did, at Faluja. Early on, they provided assistance to him and the other besieged

Egyptian soldiers, helping run supplies through the encircled forces. On the home front in Cairo, the Brotherhood joined with others in an attempt to press a corrupt and ineffectual government to send more volunteers to help the trapped garrison break out of the pocket. The government refused, but the Brotherhood's efforts did not go unnoticed.[9]

Mutual admiration came out of the adversity they had in common. As Richard Mitchell noted in *The Society of the Muslim Brothers*, the future Free Officers in Palestine were impressed by the willingness of the Brotherhood volunteers to fight and die, a determination that was not shared by many in the Egyptian army, particularly its leadership. Those impressions proved powerful, and the goodwill fostered by the camaraderie and shared aims—a strong and modern Egypt, independence from the West, an end to corruption and economic injustice and an abhorrence of the weakness that seemed to permeate the society in which they were raised—kept the two at peace. That truce continued into the first years of Nasser's reign, which began unofficially with the revolution in 1952.[10] The feeling of goodwill was so strong that, for a time, the Brotherhood came to see Nasser's success as "our revolution,"[11] an idea that the leaders of today's movement, hardened by their long years of mistreatment and torture in Nasser's jails, would probably find outrageous. The moment was telling, though. The grievances were shared, even if the ideology was not, helping to define a landscape of politics that remains in place in the Muslim world today.

Their brief honeymoon came to an end in 1954, ripped apart by personalities and policies. The Muslim Brotherhood, willfully or not, represented a threat to Egypt's revolution, claiming as it did 500,000 members in 2,000 branches and an additional 500,000 sympathizers across Egypt (from just four branches in 1929).[12] Nasser's Free Officers were wary of its influence, and they acted decisively against it in January, at a time when the Brotherhood was riven by internal disputes over both leadership and tactics. The government ordered the group to dissolve, contending the movement's leadership had tried to subvert the army and had not sufficiently supported the revolution, its land-reform program or its repeated overtures at coexistence. Tense months passed, and each side bided its time before the decisive blow came in October 1954 with an assassination attempt on Nasser. Eight shots were fired at the Egyptian leader as he addressed an outdoor rally in the Mediterranean city of Alexandria, allegedly by a Brotherhood cadre. Unhurt, and in dramatic fashion, Nasser continued his speech and, by default, sealed the Brotherhood's fate. Less than two months later, six Brotherhood members were hanged and thousands were imprisoned, many of them tried and sentenced.[13] To many in Egypt, the devastating crackdown had driven the Brotherhood into obscurity.

Its message, though, proved far more enduring. Despite the ebb and flow of repression that saw the Brotherhood crushed under Nasser, then allowed to revive only to be crushed again, its thought and ideology were able to blossom, typically in the cells of Egypt's jails. The intellectual currents defied the disappointment of Nasser's years and the failure of his movement, laying the groundwork for a political philosophy that, in one form or another, remains the most influential in the Muslim world. It was born of the anticolonial movement in Egypt and soon spread across the Arab world to Syria, Jordan, Palestine, Kuwait, Sudan and Yemen, more successful than any experiment in Arab nationalism.[14] It was based on identity and faith, a program of Islamic renewal that hailed action over ideology and activism over scholarship. Mixed in the message was a fierce nationalism wrapped in religion and hostility to an imperialist West. Throughout, it espoused a concern for the poor phrased in corporatist terms that self-consciously invoked the idea of a reconstructed, modern *umma*.[15]

The man behind the movement was Banna, whose influence was seminal, as leader and as ideologue. Banna was born the eldest of five sons in Mahmudiyya, a town in the Nile Delta. Raised in a religious family, he studied in a traditional *kuttab* school, then entered a primary school at the age of twelve, already showing the religious devotion and activism that would guide his life. It was a turbulent time in Egypt; anticolonial currents coursed through the country, and Banna was witness to its intellectual ferment and political upheavals.[16] He was shaped by the time: Banna later recalled with anger the sight of British soldiers occupying his hometown in the wake of a failed revolt in 1919, perhaps the same bitterness felt by Mirza Khan toward Russians in Kabul more than sixty years later. The sense of powerlessness reinforced his faith, which became stronger and more active as he studied first in nearby Damanhur, and then the capital, Cairo. There, he became even more politicized by the city's seeming obsesssion with secularism and its implicit break with a traditional past. He saw those forces in the universities, the quarreling political parties, literary and social salons and the media, whose books, magazines and newspapers he felt were determined to weaken the role of Islam. As he remembered it, he and his fellow travelers spent night after night pondering the problems and the remedies that faith could bring. At times, the predicament seemed so formidable that, he recalled, "we reached the point of tears."[17] Four years later, trained as a teacher and hardened as an activist, he accepted a government assignment to Ismailiyya, despite, he admitted, not knowing exactly where the city was.

Ismailiyya, the most picturesque of the Suez Canal cities, has various claims to fame: home to the French diplomat who was the force behind building the canal; named for the Egyptian ruler who went bankrupt trying to finance his share of the investment to build it; and site of a clash in 1952 between Egyptian police and British soldiers there to control it, a battle that left about fifty of the police dead and electrified an already restless Egypt (leading, a day later, to the burning of Cairo's Westernized veneer discussed in Chapter 1). Perhaps most important, though, is its role as witness to the birth of Banna's movement.

Standing vigil over the canal, the city was at the heart of British interests in the early twentieth century. Its employees lived in luxury in colonial villas on leafy avenues that overlooked the squalor in which Egyptian workers lived. Street signs were in English, and British military camps housed the soldiers who ensured that Egypt's independence was primarily in name. With his activism in hand from Cairo, and his anger seething at a British presence he considered an occupation, "he began to preach Islam in a new style. He taught young men not only in mosques, as was common, but in coffee houses, where he would give a weekly lesson about Islam."[18] Six months later, he gathered a close-knit group and, in March 1928 in his home in Ismailiyya, formed the Muslim Brotherhood. Banna's followers were reported to have said: "We have heard and we have become aware and we have been affected. We know not the practical way to reach the glory of Islam and to serve the welfare of Muslims. We are weary of this life of humiliation and restriction. Lo, we see that the Arabs and the Muslims have no status and no dignity. They are not more than mere hirelings belonging to the foreigners. We possess nothing but this blood . . . and these souls . . . and these few coins."[19] They had no idea what their movement would become and the impact it would have.

The Brotherhood and other activists working to return Islam to the daily lives of people are fond of quoting a verse from the Quran: "God changes not what is in a people, until they change what is in themselves."[20] To this day, that idea remains at the core of the Brotherhood's organizing. Banna's cadres made a conscious effort to eschew the theorizing of nineteenth- and twentieth-century religious modernizers like Jamal al-Din al-Afghani, Mohammed Abdo and Rashid Rida, all of whom had a tremendous impact on Islamic intellectual currents.[21] They favored concrete action, the type of activism that would change the lives of everyday Muslims. The way to do that was through *da'wa*, a concept embraced by the Brotherhood leadership from 1928 on.

Da'wa literally means call or appeal but also can be translated as missionary work and, for the Brotherhood, it was the essence of their program to spread a message of revival and renewal among a people who had grown distant from Islam and its principles. In essence, as Banna saw it, *da'wa* was the process of persuading Muslims to abide by *sharia*, or the code of Islamic law,[22] and apply its precepts in everyday life. Through that, the movement would change society and the world around it.[23] The message was a slogan in itself: Islamic law and faith in God will right a society adrift and dependent on the West. To Banna, that message would spread through society, transforming it from below.

In addition to the preaching of individual reform, the movement had the goal of creating Islamic space, another grassroots approach that, as envisioned by the Brotherhood, would lead to the gradual transformation—or, more appropriately, Islamization—of society. Each new branch Banna set up copied the blueprint conceived in Ismailiyya: an office, a mosque, a school, a workshop and a small sporting club. That type of activism, which will be explored in Chapter 4, has become the hallmark of today's Islamists. From Algeria to Palestine to Turkey, activists have delivered emergency aid to disaster victims, free medicine and cheap medical care, school equipment, nursuries and kindergartens, orphanages, summer camps and even potable water. Some have called those attempts part of an effort to create an "embryonic countersociety," a visible demonstration of the activists' ability to better provide for the people than the state itself.[24] For Banna and the Brotherhood, though, it was more an effort to create liberated space, providing a refuge from a godless society in which Muslims could be encouraged and supported in their return to the faith.

Both *da'wa* and the activism that came with the Brotherhood's welfare efforts point to a key characteristic of the movement's approach to society: Muslims would be changed from within, on a grassroots level, not through the imposition of a political system from above. If Muslims and their behavior are reformed, if they themselves return to the faith, then society will naturally follow. Consequently, education, or *tarbiyya,* was envisioned as the principal role of the Brotherhood. As Banna said, "Our duty as Muslim Brothers is to work for the reform of ourselves, of our hearts and souls, by connecting them to God the all-high; then to organize our society so that it becomes a virtuous community which calls for the good and forbids evil-doing, *then from the community will arise the good state.*"[25] For the most part, and with notable exceptions, changing the political system was not the goal of the Brotherhood's work, and the state was not the arena of contest. Rather, the community was, and the Brotherhood insisted it would only exercise power once everyday Muslims had come closer to the true faith and brought about a devout, Islamic society themselves. To bring about a change in government before the society itself was renewed would be misguided and, in the end, pointless. Banna's successor, Hassan al-Hodeibi, felt so strongly about the principle that he warned his followers: "Power corrupts the soul."[26] Although not always followed in practice, particularly during the violent, unstable years that preceded Nasser's revolution in 1952, the principle was to guide the movement until the ascent a generation later of a far more radical thinker named Sayyid Qutb.

The movement's activism was not the only influence on political Islam. Its internal organization was also important, a hierarchical structure that had a lasting influence on the Islamic movement. The Brotherhood was a group that stressed obedience as a virtue, be it obedience to God or obedience to *al-murshid al-amm,* the general guide of the movement. The concept of absolute obedience was known as *al-sama' wa'l-ta'a,* literally hearing and obeying. It began with the oath of loyalty taken of a member—who on induction in the society swore "complete confidence in the leadership, and absolute obedience in what one likes or dislikes to do"—and, in theory at least, continued through the person's life.[27] The authoritarian nature of the movement—iron discipline, secrecy and unquestioned loyalty to a leader at the center of the movement—yielded little room for dissent, and it worked in the Brotherhood's early years.

Why did it work? Banna was a man of obvious personal magnetism, with an ability to convey sincerity and selflessness and, more important, to appeal to all strata—both the clergy at al-Azhar, one of the Muslim world's esteemed seats of Islamic scholarship, and the shopkeeper in a teeming alley of Cairo's warrens. His followers spoke of speeches that would go on for hours but seem to pass in just minutes; of his gift of seizing the emotions and passions of men and guiding them in the direction he wanted. He was personally venerated, almost untouchable, a loyalty that some compared to mystical devotion. One Egyptian newspaper suggested that "if Banna sneezed in Cairo, the Brothers in Aswan would say 'God bless you.'"[28]

The hierarchy of such a movement, though, needed the magnetism of Banna to work. He was assassinated by Egyptian police in Cairo on February 12, 1949, an act believed to be in revenge for the assassination of Prime Minister Mahmoud Fahmi al-Nuqrashi Pasha by a Brotherhood member seven weeks earlier.[29] In the turmoil that followed, a lesser figure, Hassan al-Hodeibi, became the movement's next general guide. A former judge, he was a quiet man without Banna's eloquence or charisma. He abhorred violence and, through his tenure, sought to end the ability of the Brotherhood's covert branch, known as the "special section" or the "secret apparatus," to carry out violence. In a decisive setback, he also failed to win the overwhelming support of the movement's cadres.

The full extent of Hodeibi's ability was never determined since, as we saw earlier, the Brotherhood ran disastrously afoul of authority in 1954, when Nasser's government set out to crush it. The crackdown marked the beginning of the movement's prison years, a period the group has held up as a time of martyrdom and sacrifice when horrific repression, torture and ritual mistreatment were visited on the Brotherhood time and again. Into the 1970s, the movement was forced to retain its rigid discipline, particularly within the prisons, if it was to survive. As compelling was its need for loyalty by the rank and file: Decisions handed down by the general guide were not to be questioned, at least in theory, and political work with other groups was frowned upon.

Critics, however, painted a darker picture of the movement's prison years. In Nasser's jails the persecuted Brotherhood became a truly underground movement, a facet of the group's history that still plays itself out today. As Hassan Hanafi, an Egyptian scholar, put it: "A prison psyche began to develop and to impose itself on their minds. Their deep motivation was a hatred of reality, a need to revenge what nationalism, Arabism, socialism, secularism, and all that Nasser . . . stood for." The siege mentality led the Brotherhood to consider itself devastatingly alone and, as a result, it refused dialogue or to consider compromises. As its followers saw it, the Brotherhood itself would serve as the agent for change. "This division of the world into white and black, good and evil, right and wrong, belief and disbelief, pure and impure, made the Brethren mind highly Manichaean. They lived in permanent internal and external war."[30]

It was that environment that gave rise to Sayyid Qutb, a figure of singular importance to political Islam, both as a godfather of its extremism and, surprisingly after his death, as a guide to its transformation, a man who recreated the Brotherhood's Islamic ideology. In life, he was driven by faith and radicalized by persecution, a typically dangerous combination.

—

Qutb was born in 1906 in the village of Musha[31] in the province of Asyut into a family of southern Egyptian farmers with enough land to be prosperous but too little to be wealthy. His father, a figure of influence in the village, was married twice. Qutb had an elder brother Mohammed and two younger sisters, Hamidah and Aminah.

His path of education followed that of Banna and many other Egyptian youths, who by virtue of the country's rush to embrace Western reform were finding opportunities for an education long denied men of their class. Qutb briefly studied the Quran in a traditional *kuttab* school then attended a government school, moving to Cairo at the age of thirteen to enter high school. He, too, became a teacher, instructing in several schools and working for years in the Egyptian Ministry of Education. During that time, his life was perhaps most remarkable for how ordinary it was for an intellectual in the 1930s and 1940s, when under the colonial watch of the British, Egypt had a semblance of parliamentary democracy. He wrote short stories, poetry, novels, an autobiography and essays and literary criticism for newspapers and journals, his work usually reflecting the liberal, secular and nationalist currents of the age.[32] He was an *adib*, Arabic for a man of letters, living a life not unordinary for an educated man.

Qutb, however, soon experienced a religious transformation that would set him apart. It began in 1948, the year he was sent by the government to the United States to study the American education system. The visit was in part necessity: His increasingly political writings had alienated powerful figures in Egypt, even the king, and jail was a likely prospect. Qutb's time in America, though, only made him more political. He was disgusted by what he saw as the country's lax morality, its materialism, sexual promiscuity and racism toward Arabs, themes found in the writings of many Islamic intellectuals who, through education, work or travel, straddle both East and West.[33] To them, the United States is often a source of seemingly contradictory allure and disgust, evoking admiration for its technological accomplishment, economic prowess, military power and self-confidence, offset by a fierce resentment of its commercialism, materialism and arrogance in dealing with others. Qutb was no exception. He commented in a postcard written during his time there that "if all the world were America, it would undoubtedly be the disaster of humanity."[34] His resentment would stay with him the rest of his life. In a book that appeared just two years before his death in 1966, he wrote a scathing critique of his experience:

Behold this individual freedom, devoid of human sympathy and responsibility for relatives except under the force of law; this materialistic attitude which deadens the spirit; this behavior, like animals, which you call 'free mixing of the sexes'; this vulgarity which you call 'emancipation of women'; these unfair and cumbersome laws of marriage and divorce, which are contrary to the demands of practical life; and this evil and fanatic racial discrimination.[35]

Upon his return to Egypt in 1951, he so bitterly denounced American society that he was forced to leave his job in the government ministry, his politicization a liability. He soon made contacts with the Muslim Brotherhood and was recruited to join the movement later in the year, at the age of forty-five. Although the move would end his life prematurely, there was only a sense of optimism at the time. "I was born in 1951," he later said. As a Brotherhood member, he rose rapidly in the movement's ranks. He was elected a year later to the guidance council, one of the Brotherhood's top offices, and soon the group thrust upon him a leading role in crafting its propaganda.[36]

When Nasser's crackdown got under way in 1954, he was arrested, tortured and sent with his colleagues to jail. He remained a prisoner until 1964, when he was briefly released and in ill health. Soon after, though, he was rearrested, tried on charges of plotting a coup as the head of a vast, new Brotherhood conspiracy and tortured to the point of breaking him physically. On August 29, 1966, he was hanged with two others, including a beloved disciple. His death made him a martyr to legions of activists in Egypt and abroad.

In many ways, however, his influence had only begun to be felt. Like Antonio Gramsci, the Italian Marxist whose prison writings secured his reputation, Qutb was a prolific writer when he was a prisoner of Nasser's regime. He penned five works there, including *Signposts,* a small book that stood as his most decisive jailhouse message. In the years after his death, the book was to forever change the face of Islamic politics. "If you want to know why Sayyid Qutb was sentenced to death," wrote Zaynab al-Ghazali, a Muslim woman activist and colleague of Qutb, "read *Signposts.*"[37] He began the work in 1962, often writing from an infirmary bed, and it was published in November 1964. Some have called it the Islamists' version of Lenin's "What Is to Be Done?" an acknowledgment of the powerful influence it exerted on radical Islamic activists in the 1970s and early 1980s, most famously the Egyptian assassins of President Anwar Sadat. It remains influential today. *Signposts* is a forceful, uncompromising book, written with the passion and anger that come with absolute conviction. Its message represented a break with Hassan al-Banna and the traditional Brotherhood that still exerts a daunting and decisive influence on the Islamic revival.

Qutb's key idea, and the one that has alienated so many orthodox Muslims, is his belief that contemporary Muslim society is *jahiliyya,* evoking the time in the Arabian Peninsula that predated the prophet and the divine revelation that he received. The word is often translated as a state of ignorance, but in fact its meaning is much more powerful, connoting something more like barbarism. For Qutb, a society that recognizes God, but tries to secularize him or confine him to a certain sphere of life, is *jahiliyya.* To worship God means to apply his law—the legal system known as *sharia* that was codified from the Quran and the example set by the prophet. Qutb believed that no modern society had properly done so, placing the entire world, from his perspective, in a renewed state of *jahiliyya,* a condition perhaps more sinister than its pre-Islamic variant. Modern *jahiliyya*, he said, is more sophisticated than "the simple and primitive ways of the ancient *jahiliyya*" because it claims that "the right to create values, to legislate rules of collective behavior and to choose a way of life rests with men, without regard to what God has prescribed."[38]

It was a conception of the word that no modern Islamic writer had dared. In fact, it is doubtful that even Hassan al-Banna would have thought the Egypt of his day *jahiliyya*, much less declared it so. Yet in a bold intellectual move, Qutb took the argument a step further, a decision that would prove significant for his own and subsequent generations. If *jahiliyya* is a state in which Islam is not applied, a society that fails to adhere to its laws, ethics, morals or values, Qutb argued, then those people who live under its sway cannot themselves be Muslims. Even if they pray, fast and make the pilgrimage—sacred duties of every follower—they do not obey God's law and therefore must be considered unbelievers. "The question in essence," he wrote, "is whether one should choose unbelief or belief, *jahiliyya* or Islam, and whether one should worship rivals to God and to the Oneness of God. This ought to be made clear. Indeed, people are not Muslims, even if they proclaim to be, so long as they live the life of *jahiliyya*."[39]

That line of reasoning was another decisive break from the Brotherhood. Banna and others argued that through *da'wa*, observant Muslims would produce Islamic life. If someone insisted they were a Muslim, it would not be the Brotherhood's right to deny that. Their task would only be to persuade them on to the right path toward a "proper" Islam. Once enough Muslims returned to that path, an Islamic society would logically follow. Qutb saw the contrary. In his eyes, changing the hearts of men meant changing the society in which they lived. Once that was accomplished, Islamic life would produce Muslims who could truly live according to God's all-encompassing will.

Implicit in that reasoning was a call for revolt and, more subtly, a critique of the Brotherhood. To be a proper Muslim, Qutb argued, means to bring about a life that adheres to faith. To Qutb, that meant to rise up against that iniquity, fight against *jahiliyya* and put the Quran into practice, as the prophet and his companions did in western Arabia in the seventh century. That fight becomes a divine duty, Qutb argued, and the only path to God. As he put it,

Preaching alone is not enough to establish the dominion of God on earth, to abolish the dominion of man, to take away sovereignty from the usurper and return it to God, and to bring about the enforcement of the divine *Sharia* and the abolition of man-made laws. Those who have usurped the authority of God and are oppressing God's creatures are not going to give up their power merely through preaching. If it had been so, the task of establishing the *din* [religion] of God in the world would have been very easy for the Prophets of God![40]

It was a devastating argument and set the conservative clergy of Egypt and much of the Muslim world squarely against him, unsettled by his unorthodox interpretation of *jahiliyya* and the implications of overturning an order in which they were firmly entrenched. In essence, his was a call to arms. For Qutb, the regime itself was in question, and it had to be overthrown by a vanguard, guided by the Quran, which would transcend *jahiliyya* and fight to abolish it. In his writings, he emphasized a role for the poor in that vanguard, arguing that they had long been the first to join religious movements, even in Mecca and Medina during the prophet's ministry. He urged the poor again to reject "the arrogant and the oppressors," and called upon the weak, both men and women, to rise up against the iniquity of today's societies. In essence, he was preaching to the same people the Brotherhood saw as its own audience; but whereas the Brotherhood assigned them a passive role, calling upon them to become "good" Muslims even if the state was illegitimate, Qutb made the masses the primary agent of political change. The goal of the vanguard's work was to create a new destiny, in part by overthrowing rulers and a system Qutb found unjust. Without this active struggle, *jahiliyya* would continue to reign and the dawn of true Islam would be impossible.[41]

Qutb's message was nothing short of revolutionary and, to Nasser's regime, dangerous. A friend of mine, a devout Muslim in Cairo, tells a story to illustrate how alarming the government found Qutb and his message. He recalls that one of Qutb's earlier poems, a harmless ode to the Nile River and springtime, was part of an elementary school textbook collection for an Arabic class. One day in 1965, after Qutb had been arrested on the charges of plotting a coup, the elderly headmaster entered the dusty classroom and whispered into the ear of his teacher. Once the headmaster left, the teacher asked the pupils, aged nine and ten, to open their books to Qutb's poem, tear it out and throw it in the trash can. Qutb was no longer to be remembered, as an author or as a thinker. A year later he was sent to the gallows.

—

Qutb's message inspired a generation of radical Islamists from Algeria to Iran. It was a blueprint for revolution, an ideological justification for disavowing those in power and bringing about their downfall. To them, the very struggle became a sacred duty. Today, fitting the rough mold of Qutb's legacy is Hassan al-Turabi, the urbane ideologue of Sudan's experiment in Islamic rule. A figure more brilliant as a politician than as a religious scholar, Turabi takes pride in degrees from universities in London and Paris and converses comfortably in English, French and his native Arabic. His background has aided, in part, his reputation in the West as one of a new generation of scholar-activists who seek to reconcile political Islam with the modern world. He is an engaging speaker, with a wry sense of humor and a laugh that punctuates his speech, almost compulsively. To Sudan, he brought the zeal of a revolutionary impatient with people he considers too backward or too ignorant to commit themselves to his vision of a new society.

For Turabi, like Qutb, the state is the real field of action, where change, namely Islamic change, will come through control of the levers of power. Turabi put that long-held belief into action, over a generation transforming a small band of followers recruited at the University of Khartoum into a revolutionary elite that was nearly akin to Qutb's vanguard. In the 1970s and 1980s, the group, known eventually as the National Islamic Front, infiltrated the ranks of the bureaucracy and the military officer corps. It took advantage of tax breaks from a somewhat sympathetic government to consolidate an economic base through Islamic banks, which it used skillfully to exert influence in crucial sectors of the economy like construction, transportation and the media. Then the front bided its time, finally seizing power in a bloodless coup in 1989. As Turabi once said of the group during an interview at his home in the suburbs of the Sudanese capital, "It had a plan always."[42] Even Turabi's opponents, and they are many, expressed admiration for his single-minded pursuit of power.

Turabi, too, enunciates the break with the Brotherhood. "Hoping that out of a good society, a good government will emerge," he says, is foolhardy, an approach whose failure was proved in Egypt, Sudan and elsewhere. Rather, he endorses what could best be termed Islamic

Bolshevism, in which democracy is dismissed—or, at the very least, delayed—for the greater good that can be obtained through revolution from above. Islam, in Turabi's eyes, can be installed with the precision of religiously minded technocrats. His example is before us. Soon after taking power in Sudan, his government sought to Islamize universities, requiring them to teach in Arabic rather than English, made mandatory a course in Quranic studies and pressured women to wear the veil. All students were ordered to complete training in the Popular Defense Forces—a wildly unpopular militia that is short on military training and long on religious indoctrination. Space was set aside at all government ministries for prayer, and television indulged in religious programming: the call to prayer five times a day, Islamic quiz shows, films on Islamic history and propaganda-like documentaries on the civil war in the south, some of them shocking in their violence. To Turabi, it was Islam in the making, a far superior approach to the Brotherhood's revolution from below, even if it was despised by many in a country as diverse as any in the world.

"Look at the Brotherhood; they don't change society at all, they never detribalize society, they promote a traditional, sectarian Islam against a progressive Islam," Turabi told me in the interview, which was interrupted from time to time by followers who crowded his well-to-do villa to pay their respects.[43]

"They don't know about economic development, or economic justice or economic institutions today," he said. "They follow a sheikh who is followed by another sheikh, and society today has to manage itself better than that."

For Turabi, society will do better because it is guided to do better. Often in interviews, he refers to the government, its leaders and its cadres as "they." What he means is "we"—the vanguard, the guides, the religious engineers.

"They have a long-term program, for development of society, not only themselves, but for society generally, more than all other movements," he told me.

Sudan's failure is the story of another chapter. Turabi's "Islamic experiment" was one endeavor to adapt Islam to the modern world, to answer the frustrations of a generation that shares the longings of Mirza Khan and the alienation of Eid Rabia, the trashman. But at heart, Turabi's vision was Qutb's with a twist, and its absolutism and intolerance were, in the end, its undoing. Other activists, from Turkey to Iran to the Palestinian territories to Egypt, sense Sudan's failure and see in it justification for their own adherence to a new style of Islamic politics. Evolution over revolution is their call, tolerance over intolerance and change from within rather than revolution from above. They are descendants of Qutb in that the state remains the arena of battle, and they believe that those who rule have the singular potential to bring about change in society. As Essam Sultan, a young Egyptian lawyer and former Brotherhood member seeking to form an Islamist party, told me: "We have read Sayyid Qutb."[44]

But, in practice and program, their approach is a world apart.

—

This generation is the inspiration of this book, the activists who in time will transform Islamic politics. Although heirs of Qutb, they stop short of his call for revolution and the violence and turmoil that it entails (the hallmarks of the Islamic activism so well known to much of the world). They do not subscribe to his concept of *jahiliyya*, since to them change can be wrought from within, legitimately and successfully. But they mine the same vein of social resentment, cultural dislocation and ideological collapse that Banna, Qutb and their generation did. They, too, share a certain zealousness in addressing issues of identity, coping with modernity, creating community, reforming the faith and presenting an alternative to the West. In addition, they focus their activism on the instruments of the state. To these activists, democracy is the only path to follow to achieve those aims, a course they see as viable, legitimate and sanctioned by their determination to bring about a more just, devout society. To reach that conclusion, though, required another intellectual voyage of discovery. In essence, they had to build on earlier thought—from nineteenth-century Islamic reformers to Banna and Qutb—but redirect it radically.

The relationship between Islam and democracy is not a new issue. Scholars as far back as the nineteenth century grappled with its significance, implications and meaning for religion. In particular, Mohammed Abdo, the Egyptian reformer, sought to reconcile the two to demonstrate Islam's compatibility with reason and progress, and his thoughts and writings continue to exercise influence on democratic activists. His motivation was simple: Muslims had a responsibility to bring their fundamental religious principles in line with the modern world, one of changing laws and customs. In his time, that meant identifying traditional Islamic concepts with the ideas of modern Europe. Hence, he believed parliamentary democracy was justified by Islam's tradition of *shura,* or consultation, a term based on the Quranic injunction for Muslims to consult among themselves. *Ijma,* the traditional Islamic concept of consensus, was interpreted as public opinion. *Maslaha,* another principle of Islamic legislative interpretation, was seen as the collective benefit or interest. Others have added terms like *aqd* (contract), *ikhtiyar* (choice) and *ikhtilaf* (difference of opinion) as reinterpreted concepts. Abdo's writings were far more extensive than a simple attempt to devise a slavish Islamic imitation of Western political philosophy, but his interpretation of those concepts proved perhaps his greatest legacy. It entered the popular Islamic discourse, particularly the idea and relevance of *shura.*

Not all Islamists have endorsed those concepts, or even Abdo's reasoning. A significant and powerful minority of Islamic scholars has argued that democracy is an unnatural innovation, an imported concept from an alien West. Their argument largely revolves around the idea of ultimate sovereignty: Does it belong to God or man? These scholars argue that democracy, as it evolved in Europe, handed authority to the people, not God, and stands as a particularly Western legacy that is inherently alien to the Islamic world. In that system, the people themselves are the arbiters of law and justice. If applied, it would contradict the absolute authority of God's law as *sharia,* which constrains people's right to legislate. Whatever the people's will, God's commands are immutable. Although the argument is heard more often as an explanation of a possible objection to democracy rather than as an outright attack, no one disputes that God's authority is, in the end, paramount. Kamal Habib, a former Islamic militant jailed in Egypt after Anwar Sadat's assassination in 1981, put it this way: "We feel there is a supreme lawgiver, a supreme lordship, dominant and absolute and that is God. And it appears there is a contradiction. The absolute authority in democracy is with the people while authority for Islamists is what God gave as law to man."[45]

Some would argue, too, that democracy's very heritage makes it an illegitimate model for the Islamic world. As the product of centuries of Western history, with its sweeping changes and secular reforms, its procedures and principles are ill suited to a God-centered *umma* bound by *sharia.* Even Tariq al-Bishri, an Islamic intellectual in Egypt who supports Islamists' participation in democratic politics, makes the point that there remains "anxiety and unease" over its blind adoption. "The Western democratic ideal is based on the development of the secular ideal in the West and relies on a secular frame of reference," he once told me. "Democracy was seen as an organization and a system in Western thought."[46]

That heritage has two results, according to some interpretations. On one level, its tolerance and secularism provide for a free-for-all, a liberty and lax morality that contravene the restrictions in behavior and speech set up by *sharia*, which was designed by God to counter society's failings. Blasphemy, for example, would be beyond the pale; it could never be protected as freedom of speech. Party politics are also alien. The very existence of parties demonstrates that more than one ideology is present in society, they argue, when only Islam can hold sway. Beyond that, the Quran states that only two parties are possible in the world—the party of God and the party of Satan; hence the popularity of the term *Hezbollah*, which means simply the party of God in Arabic.

On another level, the track record of Western powers in the Muslim world—decades, even centuries of colonialism, imperialism and their aftermath, support for Israel at the expense of Arab countries and a latent racism perceived by Muslims in Western discourse—has done little to glorify Western institutions and values. It is hard to boast of self-determination, liberty and individual rights to a people often on the receiving end of the boot of military power. There is a latent suspicion, too, that democracy as prescribed by the West is available only for those who fit its definition of legitimate participants (secular, procapitalist and in line with Western foreign policy). There is precedence for those opinions. The West failed to act after Algeria's military canceled parliamentary elections that an Islamic party was set to win in 1992.

Many of those objections, though, are more tactical than ideological. The dispute is more with the West than democracy, a point that provides crucial space for Islamists to reinterpret its meaning in the context of the Muslim world. In fact, it is clear in the writings of many Islamists in the 1990s that the choice of democracy (albeit democracy typically on Islamists' terms) is increasingly seen as not only pragmatic but also sanctioned by Islam. The support has come to include the endorsement of concepts like citizenship, women's participation in politics and pluralism, which all happen to be shared by the

West.[47] Support for these principles is palatable as long as the concepts maintain an Islamic personality.[48]

This rethinking stands apart from the work of Abdo and other modernizers of past centuries. Islamists today are less inclined to look for similarities in Islam to prevailing Western values and principles. Although much of their thought and rhetoric may overlap, they are more inclined to demonstrate how democracy fits Islam and achieves its aims (Abdo and other modernists sought the opposite: to demonstrate how Islam could fit democracy). To them, democracy is an organization of government, not an expression of Western values and history, thus allowing them to avoid the baggage of the unpopular politics of the West. That insistence is one sign of Islamists' invigorated confidence and growing sense that their paradigm presents a legitimate alternative.

The shift, championed by a new generation of activists and aided by changing attitudes toward traditional sources of religious authority, is distinguished by the focus of its political work as well. Unlike past generations, Islamists today are under the still pervasive influence of Qutb: Those activists have added a focus on the state, essentially the capture of political power and the imposition of reform from above. They see the approach as the key to the truly successful Islamic reform of society—different means to the same goal espoused by the Brotherhood fifty years ago.

For these activists, democracy has several defenses, both pragmatic and idealistic. Often the endorsement is visceral, a radical vein of thought opposed to the authoritarianism that defines much of the Muslim world. Islamists since the Muslim Brotherhood's creation in 1928 have endured imprisonment, torture, harassment, assassination and exile at the hands of governments obsessed with the mantra of most post–World War II Arab regimes: security and stability. Prison time is part of their résumé, molding their opinions and actions.[49] Virtually all Brotherhood leaders have spent time behind bars, and for some of those activists, democracy has emerged as the most effective tool to resist despotism: "We demand democracy in its capacity as the most feasible and logical means to achieve our goals for a decent life," wrote one scholar, "a life in which we can call for Islam and work for God without being thrown into the darkness of prison or hung from the gallows."[50] Such rhetoric stands in stark contrast to centuries of Islamic thought and practice in which despotism—sometimes benign, usually not—was an accepted, even sanctioned form of Muslim government.

Democracy is also seen as the most effective path to power, a consideration that demonstrates Islamists' keen awareness of their own popular base in society. More often than not, they are vying with unpopular governments, a struggle that makes for compelling propaganda. If the society itself is Muslim, or if it is seeking a greater place for Islam in everyday life, or even if it is searching for a more pronounced spirituality, then what better way to reflect that than a system that endorses the will of the people? The Islamic concept of *ijma*, as was noted earlier, can be interpreted in this context as consensus, a principle that harks back to the earliest days of the prophet's ministry and is now seen as a powerful endorsement of majority rule. Under that idea, an undemocratic regime would be contrary not only to the will of the people but also to the intent of Islamic tradition.

The idea of a voice to the voiceless is a persuasive appeal and plays off the resentment and confusion of the young men in the Cairo slum of Bulaq. Turkish activists seeking to forestall the military's velvet-fisted coup in 1997 saw its logic, as well. In interviews and speeches, they often pointed out the irony, or even the contradiction, in the soldiers' declaration that democracy should run counter to public opinion. An Islamist mayor of Ankara, Turkey's capital, once made the point forcefully: "If the majority of the people wish to live as Muslims you have no option but to allow them to lead such lives."[51]

In more theoretical terms, these Islamists increasingly argue that the religion does not stipulate any particular political order. Neither the Quran nor the Prophet Mohammed handed down a specific organizational structure for the *umma*, the community of Muslims, to run its affairs. The form of government was left to the *umma*, and diverse choices were acceptable as long as they did not contradict Islamic principles. In the past, it gave the Islamic world a wide scope in choosing the systems of governance. "When Islam entered the land of the Persians or lands ruled under Roman law—Egypt and the Maghreb—there were customs, rules and systems," Tariq al-Bishri, the Egyptian intellectual, told me. "Those that agreed with Islam, that didn't contradict Islam, were given an Islamic attribution. They gave it an Islamic explanation and did it often."

What are the principles to which an Islamic government should adhere? Justice is one key element, and any system of government must ensure that the community enjoys it, be it by upholding *sharia*, Islamic law, or guarding against an abuse of power. The importance of justice cannot be overstated. Much more than liberty, justice in the

Muslim world is the concept by which policies, laws, rulers and even history are judged. As Olivier Roy noted in *The Failure of Political Islam*, the opposite of tyranny is not liberty, as in the West, but rather justice, which is "the watchword of protest."[52] That is in part the reason that virtually all Islamic thinkers would endorse the idea of a strong and independent judiciary in any form of government.

Another key principle is *sharia*. Most activists and thinkers (Ayatollah Ruhollah Khomeini, the godfather of the Iranian Revolution, being a notable exception[53]) would argue that no government can legislate or act against *sharia*, which sets the boundaries of the community and the society in which it lives. In addition, leaders are obligated to rule according to the principle of *shura*, consulting the people or their representatives in making decisions that affect the community. Finally, concepts like *ta'adudiyya* (pluralism), human rights and individual freedom are gaining currency, although their precise definitions remain fiercely debated.[54]

Islamists, particularly in Egypt, point to two thinkers for intellectual support, Sheikh Mohammed al-Ghazali and Sheikh Yusuf al-Qaradawi. They credit them with redefining the debate over democracy and Islam,[55] and in Egypt and elsewhere, their names come up in any forum or discussion on the future of politics. Their argument, by now, is familiar. Like other Islamists, Ghazali draws a distinct line between democracy as a means to govern and democracy as a product of a Western heritage. He sees it as the former, a way to organize the relationship between the rulers and those they rule. Through accountability, he views democracy as a way to prevent arbitrary rule and protect against the abuses of power, goals shared by Islam.[56] Qaradawi, who also enjoys a following, particularly among younger Islamic activists, elaborates a similar line. A *fatwa*, or religious opinion, that he issued in response to those who argued democracy was a form of unbelief *(kufr)* has become a key element in the debates over faith and freedom. In it, he argued that democracy as a value-free system gives people the right to choose their leaders without compulsion, to question them when they make mistakes and to depose them if they deviate from a contract with those they govern. Democracy's greatest strength rests in its ability to address those rights through protection against tyranny. Again, we see the ever-present Islamist motif of resistance to oppression.

On another level, Qaradawi argues that even though Islam does not specifically designate democracy as the form of rule, it offers a legitimate and effective way to institutionalize the abstract Islamic concept of *shura.* If it serves the community's interest, and does nothing to contradict Islam's values, ethics and ideals, then nothing should stop the community from adopting it as its own and employing it in its pursuit of freedom and justice. "Islamic *shura,*" he wrote, "approaches the spirit of democracy, or if you will, the spirit of democracy approaches the spirit of Islamic *shura.*"[57]

The rethinking of Ghazali, Qaradawi and others has gone beyond writings shared by intellectuals, and the popularization of the debate has guaranteed a far wider audience, making the discussion an argument over practice and politics rather than theory. Unlike the era of Abdo, when his audience was typically the intelligentsia of a nation struggling with colonialism, Islamists today have taken their beliefs directly to the people, and democracy often has become a preeminent part of party platforms across the region, from Jordan's Islamic Action Front to Yemen's Islah Party to Egypt's Center Party in its various incarnations. Ziyad Abu Ghanima, a prominent Islamist in Jordan, where the front lists as its priorities greater public freedom and democratic expansion, said that Islam itself encourages freedom of thought and freedom of action. In fact, he said, democracy is a form of *jihad,* a surprising use of a term better known in the West as the cry of Islamic militants engaged in violence, or of the Afghan *mujahideen* who fought Soviet troops in the rugged valleys of Central Asia.

"The sources of Islam encourage freedom of thought, freedom of action," Abu Ghanima said.[58] "Democracy is not a tactic for us, it is a strategy. The Islamic movement is not totalitarian. We believe democracy is part and parcel of Islam."

Nowhere is that strategy more evident than with the Center Party, potentially one of Egypt's biggest contributions to the Islamic revival since the birth of the Muslim Brotherhood. Like other activists, it views elections and political parties as the real path to success. Leaders like Abul-Ela Maadi, the jovial, engaging founder of the party (who is fond of Pierre Cardin suits), say they would prefer to work within a democracy rather than dream of revolution, recognize the system rather than fight it, and seek coalitions with other parties, even secular ones, rather than go it alone. They call the Brotherhood's clandestine style old-fashioned; its obsession with iron discipline and unity, they say, is better fit for another generation.

When I asked Maadi if I could use his phone, knowing very well that it was tapped by the government, he grinned. "There's nothing secret here," he said in a not-so-subtle swipe at the Brotherhood. "We're aboveground."[59]

For Maadi and others, the state remains the field of action, just as it was for Qutb and remains for Turabi. And like Qutb, they dismiss the Brotherhood's focus on change from below and its insistence on reforming grassroots society so that Muslims return to the faith in the belief that an Islamic government will inevitably follow. They envision a key distinction from Qutb, however. Their intention is not to organize a vanguard to destroy the state. Rather, they believe they can remake the state by competing within it, creating change by working inside the system, an approach endorsed by Qaradawi and Ghazali. Democracy, they say, is the most legitimate way to compete for people's imaginations and they, like others, have come to accept its tenets: pluralism, political participation, government accountability, rule of law and protection of human rights.[60]

"Most of the old guard now in the leadership have no conception of the future, what we need now; they have no answers. They repeat the old slogans: We need Islamic government, we need the Islamic caliphate, we need to preach our ideas throughout the world. These are old statements, what do they mean now? What about privatization, globalization, the peace process, nongovernmental organizations, tourism, terrorism? We have new things, and we are not ashamed of dialogue to deal with them," he said.[61]

Essam Sultan, the young lawyer familiar with Qutb, put it even more directly to me. Today's Brotherhood, he said, was locked in the battles of yesterday—the struggles with Nasser and the underground culture that thrived in the prisons. "The literature hasn't changed, the words haven't changed and the accusations haven't changed," he said. "The Muslim Brotherhood sees itself as an alternative to the regime, the Muslim Brotherhood sees itself as an alternative government and therefore you always see in the literature of the society phrases like 'an Islamic state, an Islamic state, an Islamic state and the state that is present is a kafir state.' We see in the Center Party that we are not an alternative to the regime, we are within the regime, the constitutional system, the legal system and the political system. By system, I mean in its broad meaning. We don't imagine creating a state outside of the constitutional system that is present now."[62]

The story of the Center Party and its rebellion against the Muslim Brotherhood is the subject of another chapter. But what it represents is symbolic of the choices movements in Jordan, Iran, Turkey and

Palestine are making—the popular application of changing intellectual currents within Islamic movements toward democracy. The Center Party and others are determined to reshape and redefine the state, to take part in its processes and to bring change from within. Some have already found success. In Lebanon, Jordan, Egypt, Yemen, Turkey, Tunisia and other countries, Islamic parties and their candidates have all won significant percentages of votes, although never a majority. In Egypt and Lebanon, Islamic groups have formed coalitions with non-Islamic parties, a striking divergence from the go-it-alone philosophy of years past. Beyond elections, activists have played a growing role in professional associations, labor unions, student and women's groups and sports clubs, practically any group in civic life.[63]

The entry of Islamic groups into mass electoral politics has had another effect on the faith. Over a generation, the Muslim world has witnessed a fundamental restructuring of religious authority, a democratization of a sphere of study once jealously guarded by a special class of scholars, known as *ulema,* and bound by centuries of tradition, dogma and refined rhetoric. The result has been to remove control over religious texts and religious interpretation from the traditional clergy and put it in the hands of the new generation, men like Maadi who have little formal religious training but now exercise as much influence as any Islamic scholar. This shift represents the last component of the changing face of Islam and democracy: from Abdo and the Brotherhood's pursuit of an Islamic revival to Qutb's focus on the state to Qaradawi and Ghazali's rethinking of democracy to the diffusion of religious authority. Taken together, they have made possible the reorientation of Islamic activism.

The revival of the faith has in part been shaped by the popularization of interpreting the Quran. For centuries, the power to do so was invested in the *ulema.* They were steeped in Islamic tradition, had mastered medieval philosophy and were charged with preserving and disseminating the faith to the faithful. Many of its members are venerated to this day, their intellectual achievements respected by both East and West. Some, like Ibn Taimiyya, have even been reinvented as revolutionaries. "The *ulema* are the heirs of the prophets" is a well-known phrase in the Muslim world.

But more often than not, in both medieval and modern times, the *ulema* have worked for the sake of those in power, supporting the status quo, even in times of despotism, currying favor with rulers for financial gain or otherwise. In contemporary Egypt, from Nasser to the present, the *ulema* are notorious for their creative ability to bestow blessings on policies dear to the government: peace with Israel, for example, or the paying of interest on loans, which was long thought expressly forbidden by Islam. Their collaboration has hurt their reputation. In Egypt, a 1988 poll of students at Cairo University found that three out of four of the students surveyed regarded al-Azhar, Cairo's preeminent center for training *ulema*, as "either partially or wholly ineffective in responding to the needs of young people."[64] In truth, resentment of their influence—or lack thereof—is nothing new.

Hassan al-Banna was shocked by their impotence, and other Brotherhood members loudly criticized their failure to inspire a living and dynamic Islam. They saw it, too, as a poor defender of the faith against Western ideas and values.[65] As a result, Banna and others argued, Muslims should take it upon themselves to understand the Quran and learn from the prophet's example. If they did so, they could decide what Islam meant to them, what it should mean and how it would order their lives. It was not a move to secularism, however, but rather an interpretation that could clear the way for a rethinking of society, a field of thought long the preserve of the *ulema*. Qutb was one proponent. To him, the *ulema* had completely failed to bring to Islam the dynamism and energy it needed in a modern setting and, as a result, they should be ignored. They would be circumvented by people rising up to interpret the text for themselves, in itself a revolutionary move. He saw such a reinterpretation as a particular duty for his vanguard, the elite group of Muslims who would be fired by faith to abolish *jahiliyya*.

In part, such thinking was made possible by a parallel move to dismiss much of the fourteen centuries of religious scholarship that followed the golden age of Islam, a time stretching roughly from the prophet's arrival in Medina through the reign of what are known as the four "rightly guided" caliphs who followed him. Banna, Qutb, and today's activists have found in the Quran and the prophet's example as preserved through history the guidance they need in applying Islam to the challenges of the modern world, and have set about making those texts work for them. This represents a stunning end-around: if the vast corpus of knowledge the *ulema* encompasses becomes irrelevant, why does one need the *ulema?* This argument has become particularly poignant in Iran, where thinkers like Abdol-Karim Soroush are, in effect, questioning the right of the clergy to interpret religion and therefore rule. In a larger sense, it represents the fragmentation of religious and social authority, giving legitimacy to numerous voices of interpretation.

Who are these voices? Many are part of a new generation of activists and intellectuals different in style and approach from any religious reform movement that preceded it. Abul-Ela Maadi is an engineer, not a religious figure, yet his party will play a key role in political Islam. In Turkey, Necmettin Erbakan and his associates with the now-banned Refah Party were anything but clerics. They were professionals and businessmen, and Erbakan himself was a professor of engineering. Some have questioned their knowledge of Islam, but the skepticism has had little perceptible effect on the appeal of their message to voters who at one time made them the single biggest party in Turkey's parliament. Adel Hussein, once one of Egypt's most respected Marxist economists, is another example. He now leads the Islamic Labor Party, which publishes *The People,* Egypt's best-known and most controversial Islamic newspaper. His transformation is one seen time and again: former Marxists and nonbelievers once captivated by Nasser's promises and the lure of ideologies like Ba'athism and socialism who have turned to Islam. In a twist, they are the same activists who a generation ago drew the ire of religious Muslims because their Marxist disavowal of God was not only seen as abhorrent but also as the biggest threat to the future of Islam. Now they bring yet another perspective, somewhat unorthodox, to its already eclectic currents of thought.

These thinkers are usually the products of a secular education, often fluent in English, French or another language and well versed in Western literature, philosophy and politics. They admire the West on a certain level, in particular for its achievements, its affluence, even its self-confidence. And they gain visibility by taking their ideas to mainstream newspapers, writing and addressing a general audience and speaking a language that is accessible not only to religious scholars but also to laymen burdened with issues of identity.

As important, though, is the effect of a popularized Islam on the makeup of the activists themselves. A democratized Islam is a more accessible Islam and this has brought legions of activists into the mix who would have been disenfranchised a century ago. One side of that is the emergence of activists like Maadi and his colleagues in the

Center Party. With the onset of mass higher education and the decline of *kuttabs* that educated Banna and Qutb, religious knowledge itself has become demystified. In many Muslim countries, it is more common to see an engineer than a turbaned cleric from al-Azhar explaining the need for *sharia* as a way to right society. "Because all knowledge is divine and religious, a chemist, an engineer, an economist, or a jurist are all *ulema*," Turabi, the Sudanese leader, said.[66] It is no surprise then that in Egypt, Islamists found some of their greatest success in the 1980s and early 1990s in competing in elections for leadership of unions of engineers, lawyers, doctors, pharmacists and professors. The young, ostensibly secular intellectuals who emerge from their ranks are the leaders of today's Islamic movement.

They represent, too, its maturity. They inherited a movement that was defined by the struggles with secular ideologies of Nasser and his generation, often sharing their aims and their protests. Shielded from the setbacks that devastated those movements, mainly by virtue of staying out of power, their ideology has endured. Over the years, it has been reshaped by the thoughts of Islamic modernizers, redefined by the Muslim Brotherhood and its ideologues, primarily Qutb, and redirected by a new generation that has sought to reconcile Qutb's focus on the state with the potential of democratic activism. Propelling forth the new activists was a democratization of the faith, a broad impulse toward a populist Islam that circumvented the *ulema* and the traditional centers of religious scholarship.

However, the flip side of that democratization, or more appropriately its popularization, is an impulse toward radicalism. That element of Islamic activism is fading as more and more activists pursue the promise held out by a democratic choice. But the success of that trend today could not have happened without the exhaustion and demise of its more radical current. From the same ranks of university-educated professionals aspiring to the middle class came a more dangerous idea: revolution inspired by Qutb's focus on the state but untempered by party politics. One example is Mohammed Abd al-Salam al-Farag, an electrician who heralded a militant phase of Islam and its fixation on the dramatic gesture and the decisive blow, inaugurating a generation of assassinations, attacks and insurgencies that came to mold Islam's persona in the West. Its history—occasional success overshadowed by failure—remains a crucial facet of political Islam's new directions.

3

～

The Hidden Duty

The Rise and Fall of Militant Islam in a War Without Borders

IN THE BELT OF MISERY that corrals Cairo, where sewage sometimes surges into pipes carrying drinking water and pirated electricity lines hang helter-skelter from buildings, an electrician who fashioned himself a preacher reigned over a private mosque built by his in-laws in a neighborhood of limp mud-walled buildings and narrow dirt alleys. The man was named Mohammed Abd al-Salam al-Farag, and his short life as a radical propagandist was an example—writ large—of popularized Islam.

Although little more than a handyman, Farag claimed insights into religious scholarship that the *ulema* had jealously guarded for centuries. And his demystified, blunt and rebellious take on Islam inspired the assassins of Anwar Sadat. His claim to the pantheon of modern Islamic militants was a tract titled *The Hidden Duty*, a pamphlet that positioned him as a philosopher-activist in Egypt's emerging radical religious movement in the 1970s. In it, he articulated a religion of revolution that impels its followers to sedition against illegitimate and unfaithful rulers. The movement that celebrated his argument would haunt the country until it receded in the mid–1990s through a mix of exhaustion, repression and backlash among the people it courted.

To understand the course of today's sea change in political Islam—
its maturity and mounting influence—it is first necessary to explore
the course of its counterpart, the militant movement that held sway
for years in Egypt, Palestine and other Muslim countries. The eclipse
of Farag's legacy, in many ways, made possible the nascent democratic
transformation. But Farag's earlier success still resonates among the
disenchanted of Cairo's slums, Gaza's refugee camps and Beirut's miserable sprawl. Although on the wane, undermined by its own viru-
lence, the violence inspired by Farag and others has left its mark in the
gulf that divides the West and its image of Islam from the hope that
Muslims have for their resurgent faith.

The Hidden Duty is not of the caliber of Qutb's classics. Farag had
neither the style nor the education of Qutb, a deficiency noted at the
time by some of his militant cohorts.[1] He did share, however, Qutb's
revolutionary zeal, which comes through clearly in the pamphlet. The
thrust of Farag's argument was that jihad, a religious crusade, was the
sixth pillar of Islam, an imperative of all Muslims.[2] They must resort
to armed struggle or revolt, he said, if the community of believers was
to end the decadence of modern society and bring about an Islamic
state. That duty, "the hidden duty" of his pamphlet's title, had been
obscured by co-opted or faithless ulema and by most Muslims themselves. His argument took Qutb's writings to their logical conclusion:
The state was ruled by illegitimate leaders who had defied God and
failed to implement sharia, Islamic law. Their transgression left only
one alternative, revolution. As Farag put it: "We have to establish the
rule of God's religion in our country first, and to make the word of
God supreme. . . . There is no doubt that the first battlefield for jihad
is the extermination of these infidel leaders and to replace them by a
complete Islamic order. From here we should start."[3]

For Farag, all other means to change were pointless. The Muslim
Brotherhood's da'wa, the approach to the reformation and resocializa-
tion of society as outlined by Hassan al-Banna, was a delusion, sure to
fail in the face of government power. Groups that sought to reform
the regime from within—or undermine it, depending on the perspective—could never overcome the authority of the overarching state.
And those who decided to flee a decadent society and form a pure
Muslim community in exile, as some in Egypt tried in the 1970s,[4]
were only delaying a battle that they could not and should not avoid.
As Gilles Kepel noted in his insightful history of Qutb, Farag and
their ideological descendants: "All this was of no importance so long

as power was held by rulers he characterized as apostates from Islam."[5] Farag saw the issue as a question of power and state, the same focus as Qutb. The overthrow of the irreligious leader was paramount. To him, reforming society, as the Brotherhood long advocated, was secondary.

Farag based his argument on a novel interpretation of Ibn Taimiyya (1263–1328), one of Islam's great medieval scholars, who lived under the Mamluk rulers of Egypt and Syria. Many activists today revere Ibn Taimiyya for his insistence on a purified Islam free of mysticism and worship of saints. Farag saw in his writings even more—a justification for revolution. In a lesser-known *fatwa*, or religious ruling, Ibn Taimiyya sanctioned the use of *jihad* against the Mongol rulers of his age because they administered some Muslim lands according to their own, non-Islamic legal code known as the *yasa*. The collection, codified by Genghis Khan, brought together Mongol traditional law and popular laws and customs. To Ibn Taimiyya, it was not God's law.

In his pamphlet, Farag drew a parallel between that system and the legal system in force in Egypt and other Muslim countries in the present day, a code that relied on Islamic law but was still in their eyes corrupted by Western influence. Egypt, in particular, seemed an ambiguous mishmash, basing its code alternatively on Islamic tradition, French law and British colonial regulations. Just as Ibn Taimiyya had sanctioned *jihad* against the prince who governed according to the *yasa*, Farag, too, saw a religious duty in leading a revolt against a regime that did not rule exclusively by *sharia*.[6]

The argument could have amounted to little more than the coffeehouse chatter of strident students had it not been for a twenty-four-year-old lieutenant in the artillery corps from the southern Egyptian town of Mallawi. His name was Khaled al-Islambuli, an unremarkable figure who would become legendary by virtue of zeal and circumstance. A member of Farag's group, Islambuli was determined to put Farag's words into action. His target, of course, was Anwar Sadat, a man they viewed as a vain, irreligious tyrant who had made peace with Israel and sought to divorce Islam from the state.

Looking back on those fateful days, it is perhaps most remarkable that his assailants actually pulled off the assassination. In reality, it should not have worked. The plan was ill-prepared, far too dangerous and opposed by ranking members of the militant movement that fell in and out of Farag's orbit. Luck, sinister as it was, won out, though.

Islambuli was the mastermind: He told Farag that he would kill Sadat during the parade celebrating Egypt's war against Israel in October 1973.[7] Islambuli had been placed in command of an armored transport vehicle that would drive in the parade and had managed to replace three of the soldiers in the truck with his accomplices. The driver was not part of the team, so Islambuli said he himself would pull the hand brake, stopping the truck. He and the three others would then jump out, throw grenades at the viewing stand and open fire with machine guns. They would kill Sadat and anyone else who crossed their path. Farag, the activist ideologue, took it upon himself to find the grenades and ammunition.

On September 26, Farag, Islambuli and other militant leaders from southern Egypt and Cairo came together especially for the occasion, although they were not yet in agreement on how to carry out the plans. Opposition was fierce. One of the older leaders of the move-ment, Colonel Abboud al-Zumur, an air force officer who worked in military intelligence, came out strongly against the attempt. It was poorly prepared, he argued, and the movement was not ready to capi-talize on it to usher in a popular revolution. That, he believed, would have to wait at least another two years. Zumur was ignored (which, in the wake of the assassination, probably prevented him from being exe-cuted) and the others went ahead with their plot. On October 5, Islambuli entered the barracks with the grenades and ammunition tucked in a duffel bag (as an officer, he was not searched) and joined his three accomplices. The following day, as planned, he stopped the truck, the men poured out onto the parade ground and, moments later, Sadat, dressed in a ceremonial military uniform, was dead, his corpse riddled with bullets. His assassin's words were soon immortalized: "I am Khaled al-Islambuli, I have killed Pharaoh, and I do not fear death." Six months later, Farag, Islambuli (who was wounded in the assassination but lived), and his three accomplices were executed for the crime.[8] During his trial, Islambuli credited Farag's thinking in *The Hidden Duty* for providing a justification for the death sentence of Sadat that he had carried out.[9]

The hoped-for uprising went nowhere after the president was killed. A brief but bloody uprising was launched two days later by the same group of militants in the southern city of Asyut. They stormed the police headquarters, beheaded the Christian commander and massa-cred poorly trained and badly paid recruits. The popular revolution, however, did not follow, and their revolt was crushed by Egyptian paratroopers flown in a day later. The most telling legacy, though, may have been the impact it had on the style and tactics of Islamic militancy. Many celebrated Islambuli's exploits. In revolutionary Iran, a busy thoroughfare in Tehran was named after him and even in Egypt, where mounting repression had made Sadat distinctly unpopular, people seemed fascinated, almost in awe of the temerity of the assassination. For other militants, it served as a lighthouse: One act, planned and executed by a handful of people, could change the course of history. There was no need for organization, no need for years of social activism in the slums of Cairo, Istanbul or Gaza, and no need for the discipline and ideological rigor that a modern political movement demanded. Rather, the sudden, blinding flash of violence could bring acclaim and attention. For some, that meant assassination and terrorism, for others armed struggle, and it came to define the Islamic movement in the years after Sadat's death. With a decisive blow, everything else would follow. As one former militant reflecting on those days put it to me: "There was no effort concerned with creating policy. The movement had turned to military activity, violence, and its opinion of strength was military strength only. Its perspective conceived of things in a limited fashion, narrowly or immaturely. It had the idea that it could change the political regime by relying on the force that it had."[10] The allure of that violence has only dissipated in recent years, its longevity propelled by another conflict—a decade-long struggle in Afghanistan that, for the Muslim world, served as the Spanish civil war, drawing a generation of Islamic activists from abroad to a battle they saw as righteous and just. To this day, their legacy, colored by vengeance and violence, stretches across the region.

—

In the world of militant Islam, Ali al-Rashidi was what you might call a soldier of fortune. With martial skills honed in fifteen years of war, he provided help to comrades in the far-flung reaches of the Muslim world: Sudan, Kashmir, Chechnya, Bosnia and Tajikistan. Some reports in the 1990s put him in Libya and others saw his hand in Eritrea. Even Burma was not beyond his reach, or so his comrades liked to boast. His obituary—dead with more than 550 others when an overloaded ferry sunk within sight of the shore in Lake Victoria in

May 1996—read like a road map for action. His training ground was the war against the Soviet Union in Afghanistan.

Rashidi was one of thousands from the Middle East who went there to fight, earning the nickname "Afghan Arabs" on their return home. With greater skill than design, they copied the blueprint of Sadat's assassination—the decisive blow—and their bloody exploits have scarred a broad swath of landscape from Pakistan and Afghanistan through Egypt to Algeria. The U.S. support in funding, arming and training them for their struggle against the Soviet Union has come to haunt Washington and its allies, as the veterans have fanned out across a region searching for a cause. They are an ephemeral enemy, an amorphous collection of fighters tied by a common experience but without a state, without a structure and without an ideology, bar the restoration of a romanticized notion of a bygone Islamic golden age.

Rashidi, also known as Abu Ubaida, was a policeman in his native Egypt in the 1970s—a time when the country dramatically opened to Western influence and the speculative investment it brought—but he was soon attracted to the militant circles that crossed paths with Farag's loose network of accomplices, disciples and like-minded competitors. His involvement led to his dismissal as an officer and he consequently spent three years in prison on suspicion of having a role in Sadat's assassination. Afterward, he fled Egypt for Pakistan, then across the border to Afghanistan, where his fate took a far different turn: He soon became a war hero, fighting in a battle near Jaji, a town about ten miles from the Pakistani border, where he and the other Arabs drove off a Soviet onslaught in their first major engagement. As important psychologically as it was militarily, the battle proved the Soviets could be defeated. He later made his name fighting near the fiercely contested town of Jalalabad in eastern Afghanistan.[11]

Oddly, his path was not unusual for a young Egyptian militant. In the 1980s, the war enjoyed fervent, almost giddy support across the Arab world, inspiring poetry, song and glowing accounts of courage and bravery in the name of Islam. Kamal Hassan Ali, an Egyptian defense minister, announced the training of Afghans in Egyptian army camps. In 1980, a year before Sadat's assassination and in an environment still permissive of the Islamic symbolism that he encouraged, the Egyptian parliament issued an invitation for Egyptians to enlist in the *mujahideen,* as the forces fighting the Soviet Union were known. The struggle there seemed pristine, unsullied by the bouts of Islamic opposition in Egypt to which few drew any connection, and government officials were eager to demonstrate their religious credentials. It went beyond the official. Newspaper advertisements invited young Egyptians to "join the caravan" traveling to Central Asia. Al-Azhar, one of the preeminent seats of orthodox Islamic scholarship, offered from its office in Cairo to help recruit youths and send them to Afghanistan as soldiers. Saudi Arabian airlines gave 75 percent discounts on flights to Pakistan to men going to fight with the resistance.[12] In courtrooms in Cairo, militants on trial for terrorism asked in vain to be sent to Afghanistan rather than waste away their youth in Egypt's miserable jails. Others, upon their release, took that very step.[13]

Rashidi was just one of the volunteers, and his history speaks to the reach that he and his colleagues had. He took his *nom de guerre—* Banshiri—from a victory over Soviet troops in Afghanistan's Panjshir Valley, a rugged independent-minded region that was often the scene of fighting.[14] In later years, he became the right-hand man of Osama bin Ladin, another veteran of the Afghan war and the scion of a wealthy Saudi family who has earned the reputation of a Muslim Carlos the Jackal. In recent years, he has had a reputed role in everything from Chechnya's war for independence to the bombings in 1998 of U.S. embassies in Kenya and Tanzania, in which 224 people were killed.

As bin Ladin's lieutenant, Rashidi was said to have left Afghanistan for Pakistan in 1993, then been forced to flee again when the Pakistani government began cracking down on the Afghan Arabs, under pressure from Arab governments who had begun to comprehend the danger posed by their brand of Islamic politics. Pakistan feared, too, that they might emerge as a threat to its own security. His home became Africa, and the legend began to blossom. In accounts that followed his death, he was reported to have set up training camps in Sudan at the behest of bin Ladin and led operations in Somalia against American soldiers, who had gone to stanch famine in 1992 but who had soon become combatants in that country's internecine conflict.[15] His organizing of a borderless *jihad* extended to Uganda and Eritrea, and the list only grew. His death was considered a blow to the wandering army of Afghan Arabs. One Egyptian militant group known as the Vanguards of Conquest mourned him in a statement as "a courageous hero and an eminent crusader," a loss of one of the Muslim world's true soldiers for the faith.[16]

Why was the Afghan conflict so important? Or, more appropriate, why did it become more significant after it had ended? As was noted in Chapter 1, it was a struggle that seized the world's attention, pitting the *mujahideen* against Soviet troops who had invaded in 1979. Anticommunists in the Reagan administration portrayed them as freedom fighters, with the solid, often fervent backing of Congress, although in reality they were some of the most Islamically minded, autocratic and anti-American activists the United States had ever dealt with. Those attributes were conveniently ignored, both by decision-makers and, with a few exceptions, journalists covering the conflict. Outside of isolated cases, Lebanon for instance, the politics of the Islamic peril had yet to decide policy. To the West, the fight was still on against Soviet aggression and it funneled in an army's worth of Soviet and Chinese weapons bought from friendly governments like Egypt and Israel. The Muslim world, on the other hand, saw Afghanistan as a fight for Islam, a religious crusade to protect a besieged Muslim country, and its call to arms attracted as many as 25,000 young, idealistic men, the biggest share of them from the Arab world. Frustrated by repression at home, bleak economies and a helplessness bred by the close watch of security forces, they went to Afghanistan to take a place on the front line of a war for Islam. In time, many would comprise a Who's Who of Muslim militancy: Hamas in Palestine, Algeria's Islamic Salvation Front, Egyptian organizations like the Islamic Group and Jihad and, of course, bin Ladin and his followers.

In Afghanistan, they were an Islamic International, and their network grew up in Peshawar, a wild Pakistani border town stocked with guns. Fused with militancy and mystery, Peshawar was the launching pad for the covert war organized by the Central Intelligence Agency, the Pakistani government and a host of Afghan guerrilla groups of varying integrity and discipline. The Arabs came, too, to this town, which is dominated by a fort first built by a Mughal emperor in the sixteenth century then rebuilt by a Sikh ruler in the 1830s. The town feels Old World—with its spice merchants and gold dealers doing business along its narrow lanes—but its location gave it new life in the 1980s. It stood near the Khyber Pass, a convenient route into Afghanistan.

Arab networks bringing men or money to the Afghan war flourished in Peshawar. The international Muslim Brotherhood opened an office there run by Abdullah Azzam, a Jordanian Palestinian who was assassinated in mysterious circumstances in November 1989. It helped ready Arab volunteers to fight, sending many to join the Hezb-i Islami camps of Gulbuddin Hekmatyar, one of the more strident of Afghanistan's Islamic guerrilla leaders and a favorite of the Brotherhood. As important, Azzam's office helped funnel the vast funds from Saudi Arabia—an estimated $3 billion or more, equal to the CIA's contribution—that were sent to support the *mujahideen*.[17] Not all of that money came from the government. Much of it was donated by foundations, charities and individual members of the 6,000-strong Saudi royal family, or collected by mosques and religious leaders across the kingdom. Saudi royalty was especially generous. Among the big contributors were Prince Salman, the powerful governor of Riyadh, and Crown Prince Abdullah, likely the next Saudi king, who donated dozens of trucks in the war's early years. Along with Pakistani and American intelligence, the Saudi money and organization made the war possible, and the Arab fighters took it with no strings attached. Most had little love for either the Saudis or the Americans but as the battle raged on, the Soviet troops were seen as the more immediate enemy.

The war changed the face of Islamic militancy. Few of the secular, Arab governments, or the United States for that matter, looked ahead to the war's conclusion with any foresight. The idea that the returning veterans might put their fervor and martial skills to use against governments they deemed un-Islamic was rarely discussed. If it was, the danger was dismissed as paranoia. Most naively expected virtually all of them to leave Afghanistan and settle down, matured by the youthful ordeal. "There was a belief that once this *jihad* was won, these people would go back home, to their families, to their jobs, to their normal lives," Mansoor Alam, a Pakistani diplomat who was in charge of Arab Affairs at his country's Foreign Ministry during the war's peak, told me. "No one expected them to change themselves after the war."[18] Most did not. But a handful of others did, and the connections they forged during the war, ties of faith and cause that transcended citizenship, held them together in a loose network that, for a while, became the scourge of these secular Arab regimes in the 1990s. With the Soviet Union defeated, a new, more mysterious threat seemed to lurk everywhere. As one of the leading Afghan Arabs, an Egyptian veteran of the war, said in 1993: "Some have died in battle, and some have gone to northern Afghanistan. Others are being kept in Afghanistan to be sent, when the time is ripe, to Egypt. Some have already been sent."[19]

The style of these men was familiar: the spectacular attack that would bring them attention and awe. Lurking underneath was a streak of nihilism. Violence in itself became meaningful. Even to a greater degree than Islambuli's assassination of Sadat, the Afghan Arabs who spilled out of the rugged valleys of battle plotted their strikes with little afterthought. The bombing of the World Trade Center in New York in 1993 and the Egyptian Embassy in Pakistan two years later, the twin strikes on the American embassies in Africa and even the attacks on U.S.-run facilities in Saudi Arabia were launched by different groups with different grievances with the sole intention of sending a message, which in hindsight amounted to little more than a vicious gesture at wrathful vengeance. The attacks and those who carried them out floated across borders and causes, divorced from the political movements that spawned them. The strikes, inconsequential in the cold logic of political change, were more often than not the full extent of influence or power the militants could wield, testimony to the superficiality of their tactics and ideology. Heroes to some, villains to most, their legacy may become more the stuff of myth in coming years, a Carlos-like phenomenon whose exploits spoke to a brief time that was brazen, even heady, in its reckless violence, but that were soon revealed as inconsequential, disappointing and disillusioning as the years passed. That bleak scenario is perhaps best encapsulated by the life of their titular head, Osama bin Ladin.

—

The men that make up the ranks of the Afghan Arabs are an improbable bunch: a doctor, brother of an assassin, students and *ulema*. None is more unlikely, though, than bin Ladin, who enjoys the greatest notoriety of graduates of the Afghan war. His itinerant lifestyle and lack of ideology beyond an ill-defined return to Islam and hostility for the West and his own Saudi government make him a model of the Afghan Arabs. His campaign is bloody, horrific in its arbitrary nature, but in the end, his crusade is more akin to a dark incarnation of Don Quixote, a would-be hero wandering from hoped-for battle to imagined contest, and his ineffectiveness speaks to the quandary in which he and the other Afghan Arabs find themselves.

Perhaps the most remarkable aspect of bin Ladin's life is the path he did not take. Born in the mid–1950s, the only son of a Syrian mother,[20] bin Ladin was raised in Jiddah, Saudi Arabia's commercial capital on the Red Sea, at a time that oil was changing beyond recognition a country long defined by the bedouin clans that roamed its expansive, unforgiving deserts. His father was Mohammed bin Ladin, a Yemeni emigrant to Saudi Arabia whose construction company made a fortune building during the boom, becoming a financial empire and making the family one of the country's most prominent. Among his fifty-four children, Osama soon gained a reputation as the most devout. Unlike many of his half-brothers, he chose to stay in the kingdom for his education, eschewing the West and an environment he regarded as un-Islamic. He graduated in civil engineering from Jiddah's King Abdul-Aziz University in 1979.

Despite his family's vast wealth, he was never known to flaunt it or boast of it. He married in his early twenties and chose to live with his wives in modest apartments. His three spouses—a Syrian and two Saudis—along with their fifteen or so children have followed their father through the different chapters of his exile.[21]

Bin Ladin came of age as currents of an Islamic revival swept through the kingdom. As home to Mecca and Medina, Islam's holiest cities, Saudi Arabia occupies a distinctive place in the religion as the birthplace of the faith, and its modern history has been shaped by a convergence of location and politics. The kingdom's birth can be traced back to an austere, revivalist movement known as Wahhabism, which rose in the peninsula in the eighteenth century. Its founder, Mohammed ibn Abd al-Wahhab, preached a return to the pure Islam of its earliest days and a fierce rejection of all that was considered innovation since then, namely the Sufi mysticism popular in many parts of the Muslim world and the culture and traditions of the West that were exerting influence on the region through trade, conquest and colonialism. The movement would have been a passing phenomenon, forgotten outside central Arabia, if it had not been for the alliance Abd al-Wahhab forged with the Saud family, a small tribal dynasty, before his death in 1787. The alliance's power surged and waned until the early twentieth century when a descendant, Ibn Saud, captured Mecca in 1924. Within years, the entire peninsula was under his control, minus the mountainous, isolated country of Yemen to the south and a handful of sheikhdoms on the Persian Gulf protected by the British. He was first recognized by the Soviet Union, then the British, and in 1932, he was proclaimed king of Saudi Arabia, the birth of the present-day country.

The changes that oil wealth brought, however, undermined the austerity that had bolstered Ibn Saud's image and long served as the basis for the country's social and political infrastructure. As the years passed, his family's reputation deteriorated and, by the 1970s, an amorphous collection of conservative Islamic activists had begun accusing the royal family of everything from vast corruption and sexual perversion to kowtowing to the infidel West, rumors of varying degrees of truth. The discontent reached a peak in 1979 when a group of Muslims briefly occupied the Great Mosque in Mecca. The seizure unsettled the royal family, which relied to a large degree on its role as a guardian of the faith for its political legitimacy.

The Soviet invasion of Afghanistan in December 1979 came at an opportune time, diverting the escalating frustration and discontent toward an external enemy. Bin Ladin was among those to go, taking several of the family's bulldozers with him to gouge guerrilla trails, tunnels and storage depots in the mountains and valleys of Afghanistan to move and shelter fighters and supplies. At times, he drove the bulldozers personally, exposing himself to strafing from Soviet helicopter gunships.[22] From Peshawar, he used his family's money, too, to build schools and shelters for refugees in Pakistan and to bring in and train, by his own count, thousands of Egyptians, Saudis, Palestinians, Turks and others to take part in the war against an ideology that spurned religion. His selflessness inspired admiration. "He has beautiful houses in Jiddah and Medina. He left all this behind and went into the mountains, suffering from bad food, water, tough climate, living in caves. He was badly hurt several times," said Khaled al-Fawaz, a bin Ladin follower who lives in exile in London and was arrested and questioned in the wake of the embassy bombings in Africa. "This made a lot of people willing to die for him."[23] It also set a pattern for his future activism, that of bankroller, not ideologue.

In time, bin Ladin picked up a Kalashnikov himself and joined the ranks of his recruits. His time as a fighter is most likely part legend, but it is nevertheless believed by those loyal to him and, hence, has taken on a truth of its own. To the men he fought with, he soon became a courageous and resourceful commander. He also gained a reputation for bravery that bordered on recklessness. In one instance, he was said to have been wounded by shrapnel in an attack on an airport. In another, he and his men faced near-impossible odds in the southern province of Paktia. Despite being outnumbered and poorly armed, they defeated the Soviet units in 1987. To this day, bin Ladin proudly shows off an assault rifle said to have been taken from a dead Russian general after that battle. He had become a hero.

On returning to Saudi Arabia, his credentials put him in demand as a speaker in mosques and homes, despite his soft-spoken, modest style. More than 250,000 cassettes of his speeches were distributed, and they typically sold out as soon as they appeared. In the now-banned tapes, the hints of his smoldering loathing of the West, particularly the United States and Israel, were already evident. "When we buy American goods, we are accomplices in the murder of Palestinians," he said in one speech. "American companies make millions in the Arab world with which they pay taxes to their government. The United States uses that money to send $3 billion a year to Israel, which it uses to kill Palestinians."[24] It is important to note, though, that his opposition to American foreign policy, particularly its perceived bias against the world's Muslims, did not, in itself, make him stand out. They were opinions shared by many in the Arab world. Even the Saudi royal family, despite its deep political and military ties to successive U.S. administrations, would have been reluctant to crack down on such dissent, attitudes no doubt espoused by a sizable number in the family. His determination since then has had the surprising effect of bolstering his popularity among the politically disenchanted, a powerful minority in Saudi Arabia and the rest of the Muslim world.

In Saudi Arabia, it took the Gulf War to end his stint as celebrity. He denounced King Fahd's decision to invite Western troops into the kingdom following Iraq's invasion of neighboring Kuwait in 1990. To the Saudis, the American troops were the last recourse to protecting the country and its vast oil reserves from a Saddam Hussein bent on expansion. To bin Ladin, the presence of infidels on Islam's holiest land was sacrilege, an unforgivable sin that he has not stopped condemning, in the most forceful language, to this day. Despite his status as a hero, the royal family was determined to silence his sedition and, in 1991, he fled to Sudan. When his denunciations continued, the government froze his bank accounts and his $350 million share of his family's multibillion-dollar empire, and then revoked his citizenship in 1994. Under pressure, his family publicly renounced him. He would never return home.

Exile was common for many of the Afghan Arabs. The most prominent Egyptian militants stayed in Pakistan and Afghanistan after the Soviet withdrawal or fled to Europe, mainly Austria, Holland, Denmark, Britain and Switzerland, where generous asylum laws allowed them to continue their opposition work abroad, to the chagrin of Arab governments.[25] A handful of them went to Yemen and Sudan, where bin Ladin had taken up residence. He maintained an ascetic life in the capital, Khartoum, despite his remaining wealth (he was said to have even refused air-conditioning in the scorching heat of Khartoum's desert environs), spending his days cultivating ties with Sudan's Islamist government and former comrades from the Afghan war. Throughout those years, the government described him as a businessman, which to a large degree was true. Bin Ladin's company, Al-Hijrah for Construction and Development, began building a desert road linking Khartoum with Port Sudan, more than 400 miles away on the Red Sea coast, as well as a modern international airport near the city. The U.S. State Department, in a 1996 profile of bin Ladin, said he embarked on other business deals with members of the National Islamic Front, the vanguard of Islamic revolutionaries led by Hassan al-Turabi who had seized control of the country in 1989. Among those activities, according to the profile, were ventures in exporting gum, corn, sunflower and sesame products, some of Sudan's major crops, and a $50 million investment in an Islamic bank, which sought to present an alternative to its Western counterpart by not charging the interest that is prohibited under Islamic law. As a wealthy veteran of the Afghan war, he also financed the travel of between 300 and 480 former Arab fighters to Sudan in 1994, according to State Department figures, after the Pakistani government began cracking down on those still residing there, under U.S. and Arab pressure.

What comes through in all the activities is bin Ladin's role as a paymaster—a man infused with the commitment of the deeply devout who is willing to spend his wealth to bring about change. His support has reportedly gone to groups in Egypt, Algeria, Yemen, Saudi Arabia, Chechnya, Somalia, Bosnia and Kashmir.[26] As an activist, though, he lacks the ideology or program to carry out that change or to elaborate a defined vision of a different future. As with many of the Afghan veterans, he knew what he was against: He opposed Israel, its occupation of Palestinian lands and its control over Jerusalem; he loathed American foreign policy and distrusted its intentions, even during the Afghan war; and he despised a Saudi royal family that would rely on tens of thousands of U.S. troops to protect land holy to Muslims. But what did he stand for? Beyond the slogans of Islam as a solution and a return to God's law, even his supporters would be hard-pressed to answer that question. Divorced from the countries they seek to change and often denounced by the groups they seek to represent, they are increasingly becoming marginalized, relying on the spectacle, the dramatic act, to make their presence known.

Turabi, no friend of America, once made that point to me in an interview after his government had pressured bin Ladin to leave the country.[27] He effusively praised bin Ladin's role as a *mujahid* and hero during the Afghan war and insisted, as other officials had, that he was in Sudan only as a businessman. He reminded the Americans, too, of their past support for bin Ladin's cause. "He was a hero in those days," he told me. "Even to the Americans, he was a *mujahid* in those days. Anyone who fights the Russians to you is a resistance *mujahid* but once the Russians are gone, he retroactively becomes a terrorist. You choose the words and you throw them at people. You're arrogant."

Yet for Turabi, who fashions himself as a scholar and an activist, bin Ladin was no more than a foot soldier, however heroic. He was removed from the endeavor to construct political Islam as a modern force that, in Turabi's vision, offered a viable social, legal and economic alternative to the dominant Western paradigm. "He's not in the current of Islamic movements in the world which are rising in public life, economic life, culture and so on," Turabi told me. "He's a *mujahid*, that's quite clear about him. He would assist anyone who is persecuted, whether it's in Bosnia or in the Balkans or in Asia or in Africa or in any place."[28] But, Turabi added, he's no visionary.

Bin Ladin might agree. A streak of martyrdom runs through his public statements, some of them seeming to express a death wish. His sacrifice would be the ultimate gesture to his devotion and he seems to savor the prospect of a heroic death. "I'm fighting so I can die a martyr and go to heaven to meet God. Our fight now is against the Americans. I regret having lived until now. I have nothing to lose," bin Ladin once told the editor of an Arab newspaper.[29] He left Sudan in 1996 at the request of the Sudanese government, which was under pressure from the United States and Saudi Arabia to expel him, and he returned to Afghanistan in a seeming attempt to fulfill that wish. He again took to living in damp caves infested with scorpions and rats, hiding from a feared strike by his enemies, be they Saudis, Americans or Israelis. He maintained his austere, disciplined life, waking before dawn for prayers and eating a simple breakfast of cheese and bread. From these remote locales, he was said to closely monitor world affairs and train in unsophisticated camps with his wandering army of Egyptians, Yemenis and Saudis, hurling explosives and firing weapons at imagined armies. The routine is a metaphor for their lives: on the outside looking in, destruction and violence the only means at their disposal.

Olivier Roy, an expert on Afghanistan, describes the phenomenon of bin Ladin and other militants in search of a cause, disconnected from the emerging currents, which were discussed in Chapter 2. His analysis is sharp and memorable:

The Sunni fundamentalist movements are capable of spectacular attacks and portray themselves as the vanguard of struggle against the U.S. But in fact they are largely disconnected from the real strategic issues of the Muslim world (except in Pakistan and Afghanistan). Their distinctive feature is their internationalism and lack of territorial base. Their activists wander from *jihad* to *jihad*, generally on the fringes of the Middle East (Afghanistan, Kashmir, Bosnia). They are indifferent to their own nationalities. They are thus disconnected not only from existing states (especially Iran), but also from the large Islamist movements, which have disowned their offspring. ... The large Islamist movements, such as the Muslim Brotherhood, the FIS [in Algeria], Refah in Turkey and Hamas in Palestine, place their struggles in a national framework and claim full recognition as protagonists in the political process. This approach, which is shared by Iran, might appropriately be described as Islamic nationalism. It is a far cry from the imaginary *umma* which Bin Ladin and his associates invoke. These are more like the urban guerrillas of Sunni fundamentalism which, without a genuine political project, recruit on the social and geographical fringes of the Middle East, where tensions are exacerbated by the political deadlock.[30]

The concept of Islamic nationalism is a compelling idea. It is a theme that will emerge time and again in both the evolution of political Islam in individual countries and the response of activists to the intensely local conditions that drive politics. The borderless careers of bin Ladin and the fighters shaped by the Afghan war are anything but local. From a distance, they demonstrated the inclination to the dramatic, the cataclysmic attack that would usher in change or, at the very least, serve a burning need for revenge. Their fate illustrates their disassociation from local movements that, in a different time and under different conditions, claimed them as their own—Egypt's Jihad and the Islamic Group, for instance. In less than a generation, the hidden duty conceived by Farag as a justification for revolution, or more specifically, assassination, had descended into an anarchic display of violence, wielded by militants whose slogans of *jihad* and Islamic law rang hollow from their retreats abroad. Despite appearances, the threat of the Islamic International is a sideshow, a peripheral contest that by its nature attracts attention but, by that same nature, remains ineffectual. We imagine these movements to be significant because the violent attacks are so wrenching and so visible. They force us to pay attention. But, in reality, their divorce from any coherent ideology or agenda makes them distinctly marginal. They have neither strategy nor goal in the attacks they devise, disengaged as they are from the countries in which they had originally sought change.

Another face of that militancy persists, though, an aspect that is still engaged in a local contest and still responds to local conditions. Two of the best examples are Egypt and Palestine. In Egypt, the defeat of an indigenous militant movement that grew up on the impoverished banks of the Nile River makes way for an alternate route of Islamic activism. The resistance in Palestine, meanwhile, returns to the question of identity, namely how Islam represents a powerful force that offers refuge to the most downtrodden and disenchanted. In this representation, it can reflect the anger and the frustration that fill the mosques of Palestine and reverberate in the slums of Cairo. In short, it speaks to the disinherited. The militancy of those movements is giving way to a maturity and moderation, but it still embodies the local conditions that gave rise to very local opposition that remains potent and influential. The disenchantment is far removed from the tactics and experience of the wandering Afghan veterans. In essence, the movements in Egypt and Palestine remain politically engaged with the community, seeking change—violent and otherwise—in the places where they live. The bleak circumstances at home shape these movements and create a reservoir of potential support. In some cases, it is evolving into viable political opposition. In others, it has become violent resistance, an enduring legacy of disillusionment.

The Hamads of Gaza are one such family defined by their conditions. I met them on a summer day in 1996 in Gaza, which is a baking, seething strip of fetid alleys, crumbling refugee camps and desperate, pitiful stabs at normalcy. It borders Egypt and Israel, and in a telling sign of how little its sandy flats are coveted, Gaza has changed hands three times in the span of a half-century. It went from the British to the Egyptians in the 1948 war, which led to the creation of Israel and the dispossession of three-quarters of a million Palestinians, who either fled or were driven from their homes in the fighting. For nearly twenty years, it was administered by Egypt but vulnerable to attack by Israel, which eventually seized it in the 1967 war and proceeded to carry out a brutal counterinsurgency to put down armed Palestinian opposition that had arisen there. Unlike the West Bank and its biblical sites, though, Gaza had little romantic value to Israel (the late Israeli prime minister Yitzhak Rabin once expressed the hope that Gaza would "sink" into the Mediterranean Sea[31]) and it was all too eager to hand it over to the Palestinians in a 1993 peace agreement that was a first but eventually fruitless step toward independence. It is not difficult to understand why the Israelis would want to let it go. One of the most densely populated regions of the world, Gaza is a swath landscaped in the dreary grays of poverty, cluttered with squat houses constructed of cinder blocks, the building bricks of refugee camps across the Middle East. The Hamads' house was one of those homes, perched near a blue crescent of the Mediterranean Sea that seemed scornful in its beauty.

Sitting lazily on cushions under a Quranic verse in a house of simple white walls and brown carpet, the Hamads took little time in getting to the topic that I had come to discuss: the decision of their youngest brother to blow himself up. Even now, a year after the attack, their memories were still framed by pride and defiance. Sorrow was nowhere to be found. As if describing a mystical scene, they told me about an orange left in his bedroom that turned brown but did not rot. A month and a half after his death, they said, a fragrance lingered in the autumn air as they laid a tombstone. They passed around pictures that show him dressed in white with a knife strapped to his calf. He holds a Quran in one hand, his other hand clenched in a fist. In other pictures, he poses with a Kalashnikov, part of the bravado and romanticized violence that came with his membership in Islamic Jihad, one of the smaller militant organizations opposed to Yasser Arafat's heavy-handed rule of Gaza and parts of the West Bank.

His death was chronicled as well. The brothers pulled out yellowed clippings of Hebrew-language newspapers that recounted the deed: with a bomb strapped to his body, twenty-one-year-old Hisham rode his bicycle past Palestinian police, veered behind the concrete blocks of an Israeli checkpoint outside the Jewish settlement of Netzarim and detonated the explosives, making himself a martyr. Three Israeli soldiers were killed with him. His mother heard the news as she was preparing a salad and fresh vegetables for his lunch. His brothers suspected Hisham was responsible even before anyone told them. Afterward, Islamic Jihad explained that the attack was in retaliation for the death of Hani Abed, a leader of the group in Gaza who was killed by a car bomb a week earlier, an act nearly everyone blamed on Israel.

The deaths of Abed and Hisham were part of a familiar story in Israel and Palestine: a high-profile assassination, the revenge attacks, the imminent crackdown and then another death, a ritual that claimed dozens of lives in bus bombings, suicide attacks and military raids in the mid–1990s. Hisham's death was one of those, and it brought the Hamads briefly and bloodily into the fray, the type of incidental involvement that has politicized virtually everyone in Palestine. To this day, as if a testament to the sacrifice of even ordinary people, the family holds on to the tattered articles from the Israeli newspapers and the front-page images they offered: a map that charted the route Hisham chose and pictures of the mangled wheel of a bicycle and a crying Israeli soldier.

Hisham Hamad was not unusual in himself. He grew up in Gaza, throwing stones at Israeli soldiers, as most Palestinian youths did during the *intifada,* or uprising, the mass revolt against Israeli rule that erupted in the West Bank and Gaza in December 1987. As the youngest son of eight boys and two girls, his family said he was spoiled. Food was plentiful, he had a room of his own and he rode a motorcycle through the sandy alleys that spun like a grim web around their home.[32] In 1993, that all seemed to change. He spent eight

months in prison—a typical stint for someone of his age and political
bent—where he passed long hours immersing himself in the Quran
and studies of the faith. Prisons in Palestine have a history of serving
as centers of indoctrination and education in language, religion and
politics, particularly during the *intifada,* and the detainees are often
autonomous within its walls and highly organized by party affiliation.
In the 1990s, the Islamists were especially so, using prisons as centers
for recruitment. Hamad emerged from his time there a determined,
devoted man. After his release, his family said, he spent his mornings
at a neighborhood mosque, later to become a young prayer leader
there.

In recounting his story, his brothers occasionally laughed, at ease
with Hisham's fate. They were casual in their talk, taking breaks to
serve orange juice and then dark, sweet tea. Their mother, Widad, was
the same—unfazed. She had said after the attack that talk of Hisham
being a suicide bomber angered her because it was wrong. "Those who
commit suicide drown themselves in the sea or shoot themselves. But
my son killed Israelis with his body. He's a martyr. Therefore, he
lives."[33] The brothers heartily agreed. As our conversation went on
into a sweltering afternoon, they hoped to provide proof of his martyrdom by bringing out a cassette for me that recorded his farewell.

"I swear there is no tear or sadness in my eyes in leaving you but
forgive me. Meeting God is preferable to living in this world," his
tinny voice says with urgency.

"Don't stand with your arms crossed in a line that has no hope.
Reject all the projects of humiliation and surrender. Resist and
become martyrs. Life is written for you because martyrs don't die.
Don't forget me with your prayers."

Fouad, his thirty-nine-year-old brother, interrupted and dead-
panned: "At least he got away. We're still stuck here." The remark
brought chuckles from everyone in the room.

Hisham goes on in the tape to extol martyrdom, condemn Israel and
its leaders, preach obedience to God and insist on the duty of Muslims
to fight *jihad* and resist the occupation. Then, he turns personal. "To
friends and family, forgive me if I've ever done you wrong. Finally, I
don't say goodbye. I say we will meet again in heaven. Pray that God
gives me the title of martyr and allows me to follow my martyred
brothers."

Another brother, Hassan, said afterward, "The words are beautiful, aren't they?" Nodding his head for emphasis, he looked at me, as if to reassure me that Hisham's death was, in fact, meaningful. "You have to have these actions," he said. "It's like a battery. It has the positive and the negative and that's what gives it power."[34]

Much is familiar in the conversation with the Hamads. There is the gesture to martyrdom, the faith in God, the desire for the dramatic act cloaked in faith that will send shudders through those responsible for oppression. But unlike the Afghan Arabs of growing fame, everything is cast in local terms. As I spoke to the family, I never for a moment suspected they were not touched by the conflict and shaped by its history.

In looking back, Hisham stands as the flip side of bin Ladin. He is a neighborhood militant whose transformation from disenchanted youth to Islamic martyr speaks to the appeal of the faith in places like Gaza. Today's activists there are imbued with a desperation born of a generation of occupation and a culture that celebrates violence. Their fury is inflamed by Yasser Arafat's Palestinian authority that arrived as a savior after the 1993 peace agreement only to become an autocratic, corrupt regime much like its Arab neighbors.[35] Add that betrayal to poverty only refugees can understand, made worse by a suffocating Israeli blockade that shows no sign of ending. Those conditions have given rise to Palestine's distinctly local movement, one that is unified by an overarching allegiance to religion and comprised of a generation of the disenchanted who differ from Hisham only in degrees of anger. They are Palestinian and they are Muslim, two identities that shape and define the other, creating a movement that is distinctly indigenous. Its program exploits the anger at Israel no longer claimed by Yasser Arafat's PLO and frustration with the prospect of peace that looks increasingly remote, if not unobtainable, and even treasonous to some.

Ibrahim Rashed is an example of the distinctly Palestinian mix. He is a student leader at an-Najah University in Nablus who speaks with an intensity that comes with not having to compromise. His office is decorated with the local, less-than-subtle taste of the devout: A mural on one wall shows an open Quran, imposed on a map of historic Palestine and the Dome of the Rock, one of the oldest mosques in Jerusalem and a potent Muslim symbol of the city. On another wall is a flag of Palestine and stickers with Quranic verses in green, yellow

and white. Nearby is a portrait of Yahya Ayyash, the mastermind of a
string of suicide attacks that killed dozens of Israelis and who was, in
turn, killed in 1996 by a booby-trapped mobile phone that blew off
his head.[36] Rashed, young and handsome, with a moustache more adolescent than his twenty-three years would suggest, speaks as if the
1948 war and Israel's birth were a recent memory. The conflict will
end, he promises, when Palestine stretches from the Mediterranean
Sea to the Jordan River. Like others, he insists America can never
understand the suicide attacks because it has not endured an occupation. And for every bombing, he points to the Hebron mosque massacre in 1994, when a Jewish settler gunned down twenty-nine
Muslim worshipers.

"There is the possibility for a temporary truce," Rashed told me, as
other students crowded around. "But in the end, there will be no compromise on Palestine. We are not able to compromise on one inch of
Palestine."[37]

When I asked him about other Islamic currents—in Egypt or Turkey,
for instance, where violence was eschewed in the name of political
participation—he offered a telling insight into the evolving nature of
Islamic politics and its local underpinning. "The West has to understand something fundamental about the Islamic movement," he said.
"The Islamic movement until now has differences, different perspectives, everyone understands Islam in a different way."

Violence, from his perspective, made sense, even in the context of
Islam. It was the answer to every humiliation at the hands of Israeli
soldiers, to every compromise the PLO has made and to every hardship
another day brings to a land convulsed with despair.[38] Unlike the
remote war of bin Ladin and his followers, this battle was real, and the
violence, however inexcusable, existed in an environment that encouraged it. This was war, blessed by God, against a historic injustice. "The
people in the West will never understand because they don't understand the occupation," he said. "If the people in the West were under
occupation, they would understand these responses. We've been in
prisons, refugees, humiliated. People will fight for their rights."[39]

Similar sentiments are echoed by the bored youths sentenced to life
in Jabaliyya, Gaza's biggest refugee camp, where half-eaten watermelon
litters dirt roads narrower than a car and houses hold eight to ten people
to a room. The maze of alleys, grim in their permanence, give off an
oppressive feeling of confinement, suffocation and seclusion. In these
streets, where poverty mixes with desperation, a youth culture of brava-

do reminiscent of urban America has grown up, a style that could be called "gangsta Islam," in which guns stand as a symbol and violence is exalted. Time in an Israeli or Palestinian prison is a badge of honor.

At a Hamas rally in 1995 in Gaza's Yarmuk Square, thousands of young men watched as activists reenacted the kidnapping in 1994 of an Israeli soldier who was killed in a rescue attempt. In the skit, men dressed as orthodox Jews and speaking Hebrew with heavy Arabic accents picked up the soldier, Sergeant Nachson Waxman. The crowd cheered when it heard his name. It went wild when the actor portraying him was beaten or cried out for his mother in Hebrew. Palestinian flags mixed with banners that saluted the suicide bombers and declared "there is no god but God." As was so often the case, it was a tense time in Gaza, the atmosphere pregnant with the threat of violence. The surreal reenactment seemed to thrive on that threat. In a conflict that had become so personal, so defined by historical grievances, I got the sense that the people at the rally felt the only way to get back at the Israelis they blamed for their plight was to hurt them emotionally. I doubted they really thought it was funny. They left it to the most militant among them—in this case, Islamists—to deliver to them the satisfaction of a response.

As Islamic movements in Egypt, Iran, Lebanon and even in Palestine move away from violence as an instrument of change, the example of Gaza remains a light on the glorified violence that persists, a tool of resistance by a movement cloaked in Islam and posited squarely in a local context drawing on misery, powerlessness and hopelessness. The violence does not come from Islam per se but rather from people's frustration with the inability of the established order to achieve serious political change. The frustration is elaborated in the language of Islam, and the violence finds a justification in its vocabulary. But above all, despite the trappings of Islam, the violence is political, not religious. It is not the program of mosque preachers or religious clerics, the image of the angry, bearded sheikh so familiar in the West; rather, it is the response of individuals and a movement grounded in the politics of persistent anger and historical grievance.

The legacy of violence is a face of the movement that cannot be discounted, however unsettling, and it stands as a reminder that the political evolution of the faith as a moderating force is still a two-way street. Palestine will seethe as long as injustice—perceived or otherwise—remains a constant. Whether it remains a defining element or an inconsequential sideshow like the Afghan Arabs remains to be seen.

One indication may be the fate of a similar struggle in Egypt. Far removed from the preaching of Farag and the plots of Islambuli in Cairo, another movement, this one in the country's south, drew on similarly bleak circumstances and employed violence to bring about change. After a nearly decade-long struggle, the insurgency came to an end. It surrendered the option of militancy in hopes of entering, at the least, a dialogue with the regime and perhaps an eventual political role in a system that it hopes will accept it. Its setting was the stark and troubled beauty of the Nile Valley.

A little after dusk, Train 136 shook and rattled out of Aswan in southern Egypt for an overnight ride to Asyut, a larger, poorer city halfway up the Nile River. Its third-class passengers, men in their sturdy peasant gowns and women in traditional black, paid 11.50 Egyptian pounds, less than $4, for an often scarce spot on board—perhaps atop the luggage rack, on a floor with ample dirt, next to an overflowing bathroom or maybe even a seat. I had already boarded, throwing my bag overhead and grabbing an empty seat, as part of a trip to Egypt's south, an isolated, traditionally neglected region never conquered by a colonial power. For years, it was the home of the country's simmering Islamic insurgency.[40] Fighting in that conflict had escalated in the 1990s along a 130-mile stretch of the Nile, prompting dire predictions that an impotent government in Cairo would eventually succumb to the spread of militant Islam. Although based in Cairo, I traveled to the south rarely and then only on assignment. Journalists in Egypt, particularly Westerners, tended to cover Lebanon, Israel or Palestine better than southern Egypt, the result of distance, unfamiliarity with the terrain and the difficulties caused by almost constant police surveillance and harassment. On this trip, I planned to take the time to ride along the river, hoping to learn more about the conflict, which had claimed more than 1,000 dead, many times that wounded and had led to thousands being imprisoned and beaten in a brutal, often arbitrary government crackdown that had lasted five years. As the sun set, I settled back in the worn, tattered seat, looking out at the oasislike vistas of the Egyptian countryside. A cool breeze came through one of those windows, blowing over a weary, seventeen-year-old Baha Hasabullah who sat across from me.

Egypt

Unprompted, he started to tell me his story, eager to speak with a foreigner in his native Arabic.

"I wouldn't travel anywhere if I didn't have to make a living," Baha said, heading home to his village near Asyut after a semester at a training school in Aswan.

Like many Egyptian youth, Baha looked to a future he believed was already determined: a stint in the army, working abroad in the Persian Gulf or Libya, then a homecoming with money enough to buy land, marry and raise a family. He had no desire to leave, but like migrants everywhere, "money is the main reason." It is even more so in southern Egypt, also know as Upper Egypt, where the average income is half that of Cairo and only a third of its inhabitants can read and write.[41] Faced with unemployment or jobs that pay next to nothing, hundreds of thousands of Upper Egyptians, many manual laborers but also legions of doctors, engineers and teachers, began leaving during the oil boom in the 1970s to work abroad. Then as now, the lack of jobs was most acute in the rural areas that dominate the region, where population growth is the country's highest. Only a fraction have jobs in industry, and the tiny plots of land so common in Upper Egypt can support only a few, if that. Peasants with an acre or more are considered rich. The poverty forces many to migrate for periods stretching over years in what has become a powerful, recurring theme in the literature of the region.

Hasabullah's father was one migrant. Now forty-nine, he took jobs in Iraq, Libya, Kuwait, Saudi Arabia and Lebanon, one to three years in each place, trying to earn enough to support seven children in a small village. That month, another son had joined him as a farmhand in Libya after finishing his service in the army.

Baha himself planned to follow them to Libya or maybe Saudi Arabia, working on a farm, as a butcher or in a store, despite signs that opportunities for work abroad were drying up as the oil boom became more a memory. He told me they are the countries Egyptians understand best, sharing language and faith. Besides, he said, he won't have to stay longer than a few years before he can return to his village, Sa'ula, where his mother and siblings tend to a small parcel of land growing corn, clover and garlic.

We sat in silence for a while, the train passing timeless scenes of peasants hoisting lush, green clover over their shoulders or families sitting under palm trees in fields of wheat that stretched to a sun setting on the horizon. At times, the region, known to inhabitants as the

Sa'id, can be a place of startling, unparalleled beauty, and my thoughts drifted off to the coincidence of so many countries sharing an underdeveloped south, a seeming curse of geography.

As darkness enveloped the scenery, we began to talk about Baha's future.

"What do I wish for?" Baha asked me, as the train jostled us in our seats. "To live in a small villa, next to a fountain, with a car."

"I want today to be like yesterday, yesterday like tomorrow, nothing new," he said, offering the antithesis of life for most migrants, himself included. "I'll go to work, I'll come back from work, I'll go to bed and then I'll wake up."

As he spoke, men hustled up and down the aisle of the train, hawking everything from crackers to razors to socks. "Pen for a pound," one shouted. "A lighter for a pound, a pair of scissors for a pound, four blades for half a pound." Nearby, someone banged on the bathroom door in a vain attempt to vacate a passenger who found room to sit in the stall. Other passengers turned their heads and stared as the knocking dragged on. Baha, clean-shaven and well-dressed for the sake of his family, had fallen asleep.

Baha's home province of Minya is among the poorest in Upper Egypt, embroiled in frustration over bleak circumstances and resentment toward a capital its inhabitants feel neglects them. The history of neglect and repression has given rise to rebellion and restlessness, and made the Sa'id a backwater for the richer north. It has also given rise to some of Egypt's most dangerous militants, men such as Islambuli. Virtually all the top leaders of the group that carried out Sadat's assassination hailed from the cities and villages of Upper Egypt: Abboud al-Zumur from Giza; Karam Zuhdi and Usama Hafiz, both from Minya; Nagih Ibrahim from Asyut; and Assem Abdel-Magid from Qena.[42] The Islamic Group itself, which has led the campaign against the government, usually with hit-and-run attacks on police stations, informers or Coptic Christians, was formed in the 1970s at Asyut University, which has campuses in three other southern Egyptian towns.[43] The presence of turmoil for so many years in the Sa'id has its explanations. Some analyses point to demographic changes, which saw the south's population explode after World War II, and the consequent migration to the more religiously conservative Gulf, in particular Saudi Arabia. On their return, they brought with them a more stringent version of Islam to the villages and cities of the south. The exodus coincided with President Sadat's attempt, which ultimately backfired, to cultivate an Islamic counterweight to leftists and Nasserists on the campuses and in the government.[44] Although reviled by Islamists later in his reign, Sadat early on tried to foster an image as a religious leader, appropriating the title "The Believer President." He sprinkled Islamic rhetoric in his speeches, increased Islamic programming in the media, built mosques and, in general, employed Islamic themes to legitimate key government actions, such as the 1973 war with Israel and the Camp David Accords that led to a peace treaty.[45] In the more religious atmosphere, some Islamists, particularly in the more conservative south, lashed out at "symbols of Western influence and immorality," such as churches, Coptic jewelry stores and property, cinemas, nightclubs, bars and video stores.[46]

In my time in southern Egypt, I always felt there was more to the conflict, an element that disassociated it from militant Islamic movements elsewhere. As in Palestine, it was inherently local, and it seemed to me another window on the idea of a specific identity under siege. Many in Upper Egypt set themselves apart from the rest of the country and seethed at the misery of their region, where a centuries-old tradition of lawlessness held sway. The more militant elements, grouped under the umbrella of the Islamic Group, lashed out at a sizable Christian minority that counted among its numbers large landowners or dominant figures in urban commerce. The conflict, colored by a modern-day feudalism, was far from exclusively religious, with important issues of class and identity helping it last as long as it did despite a ferocious government response.

Baha and I parted at Asyut, and I headed to Manshiet Nasser, a village of canals, mud-brick houses and littered streets beyond the grind of the provincial cities that I had visited several times over the years. With its ripe fields dotted by towering palm trees and trays of pita bread waiting to be baked behind wooden doors, the village was unremarkable except for one grisly moment in its past. In May 1992, Muslim militants, their faces concealed by scarves, opened fire with guns and pistols on Christians in the village's verdant fields and narrow alleys. Thirteen people were killed in what many call the beginning of Egypt's insurgency. Years later, the village had become quieter, but the bouts of solitude were still broken by anger, often directed at a government that villagers say has ignored them. The last investment, they pointed out, was an elementary school in 1989.

"There's no development here, and no one believes there will be," said Abdel-Rahim Abdel-Rahman, a forty-year-old farmer in white scarf and brown hat, standing under a hot sun near his fields of wheat and clover.

The village of Manshiet Nasser was another perspective on Baha's frustration on the train. It was the desperation, the festering resentment that is typical of countless villages. Through much of the countryside, the government long ago ceded control to the wealthy farmers and local notables, who effectively run the region's villages and hamlets. With more than a few acres, those farmers grow the lucrative vegetables, sugarcane and fruit. Wheat, maize and clover are left to their poorer neighbors, who farm with hoes and animal-driven plows that date back millennia. Many are without even those tiny farms. Villagers said that four out of five of Manshiet Nasser's young men had no work. Add to that a sectarian element: In the province, Christians made up 20 percent of the population, more than double the proportion elsewhere in the country, the vast majority of them living in the countryside.[47] Often large landowners, their prominence meant that struggles over land—the central source of conflict in Upper Egypt—took on a sectarian bent.[48] The divide between who has and who does not was especially sharp here, and the ill will made for a reservoir of potential support for militants seeking violent change.

"The people are worn-out," said Salah Mahmoud, a thirty-two-year-old villager who spoke to the vigorous nods of a crowd that gathered around him. "One person owns 100 acres, everyone else has a half-acre, and they have to support four people with that. What are they going to do? Eat from the street?"

"Listen to me," he said, gesturing in my direction. "There are no factories, even in the cities, and a huge portion of the people have nothing to do. In the delta, there are factories and companies and a lot of things and people can go work. Here, there's nothing. The people are sleeping. If there was concern, there would be companies, there would be work. I don't know the reasons. Until now, I don't know the reasons, really."

In the more cosmopolitan north, Upper Egyptians are met with contempt and jokes that cast southerners as innocent, simple or dimwitted are legion. The violence here is often blamed on tribal feuds, quick

tempers and a penchant for age-old vendettas.[49] The prejudices have
made it easier to treat Upper Egypt as a security issue instead of a
problem to be solved. That reinforces already solid anger at a north
seen by many Upper Egyptians as oppressive, deceitful or both.
Common is the phrase "cursed by Mina," a reference to the ancient
king who tradition has it unified Upper and Lower Egypt.

In villages like Manshiet Nasser, the last government representative was most likely a soldier behind a gun. After the massacre in
1992, security forces clamped a curfew on the village for sixteen
months. Soldiers were posted at its entrances, and young men were
randomly questioned or detained. Elsewhere in Upper Egypt, houses
were bulldozed, the relatives of suspects were arrested and security
forces resorted to torture to wrest confessions from members of militant organizations like the Islamic Group. Fathi Abdel-Mohsin,
another farmer I met in the dusty village, remembered the crackdown
bitterly.

"There was fear when you would see the police," the twenty-four-
year-old said. "We lived through a lot of tension and a lot of nervous-
ness with the security forces then. And until now, there's still no faith
in them. If I left my apartment, an officer could grab me and take me
to the station for questioning. Then they'd do an investigation. What's
my name, my address, how did I enter the village, what's my reputation like."

Egypt's war in the south was overshadowed for a time by high-profile attacks in the capital that drew headlines and dire warnings. For a
few brief but bloody years, the government seemed under siege from
all directions. In 1990, nearly ten years after Sadat's assassination,
Rifaat al-Mahgoub, the speaker of the parliament, was assassinated
near a luxury hotel on the Nile by four assassins riding two motor-
bikes (the real target was the interior minister). Then, three years
later, militants launched attempts on the lives of the information
minister in April, the interior minister in August and the prime minister in November, all of which failed. Abroad, Egyptians drawn from
the ranks of the Afghan Arabs tried to assassinate President Hosni
Mubarak in 1995 as his motorcade made its way through Addis Ababa,
Ethiopia. Later that year, a car bomb ripped through the Egyptian
Embassy in Pakistan, killing seventeen people and wounding nearly
sixty others. The battle seemed on, and hours after the attack,
Mubarak warned on Egyptian state television that "the hand of justice

will reach them sooner or later as a penalty for what their hands have committed in the bloodletting of innocent people."[50]

The attacks fit the pattern of the high-profile strike that was the legacy of Sadat's assassination. Those and others were blamed on the contingent of Egyptian veterans of the Afghan war who had stayed abroad: Rifai Ahmed Taha, the *emir*, or commander, of the Islamic Group; Mustafa Hamza, its military commander; Mohammed al-Islambuli, the brother of Sadat's assassin; and Ayman al-Zawahiri and Mohammed Mekkawi of Jihad, the group that assassinated Sadat. Another was Talaat Fouad Qassem, a thirty-eight-year-old Egyptian from Minya who worked as the spokesman abroad for the Islamic Group. He was the superior of Islambuli, but was arrested two weeks before the assassination and jailed in the high-security Tura Prison. He never talked, and security forces failed to uncover the assassination plot. In a later trial, he was sentenced to seven years and actually incarcerated for eight before escaping and making his way, via Sudan, to Peshawar, Pakistan. Following pressure exerted on Pakistan to extradite him, he fled in 1992 to Denmark, where he was granted political asylum, and subsequently took on a very visible presence.[51] In Copenhagen, he appeared on a local television station on Saturdays to preach and read the Quran. He drew thousands to his sermons at a Copenhagen mosque. Then, in 1995, he was on the move. He traveled to the Balkans, arriving in Croatia on September 12, 1995, en route to Bosnia where—his supporters said—he planned to write about the war there. Six days later, he was thrown out of Croatia because he did not register with police after his arrival. He has not been seen since. His family, including his pregnant wife, said he was abducted to Egypt and killed. To this day, his whereabouts remain a mystery, although it is strongly suspected that the Egyptian government had a hand in his fate.[52]

Qassem's case was a rarity, a secondary effort to abduct or win extraditions of militants abroad. The government's real war was in the south, along verdant fields dissected by mud barriers and canals fed by the Nile. It was a battle it eventually won, although for how long remains a question. The war entered its bloodiest stage in 1995, when 360 people were killed, most of them in forgettable hit-and-run attacks between police and militants that more resembled gangland vendettas than the armed struggle of a revolution. The toll dropped to less than half that the following year—about 170—and even further the following year.[53] By the end of the 1990s, the war was all but over.

What happened? The resentment remains, as do the very local grievances of a poorer and less populated region. But in this instance, rare
in such conflicts, the crackdown worked. From the early 1990s on, the
Egyptian government fought back with a ferocious blend of repression
and intimidation that used much of Egypt's mammoth bureaucracy.
The Education Ministry purged teachers in Upper Egypt and elsewhere who were suspected of bringing a religious agenda to Egypt's
16,000 schools. Education Minister Hussein Kamal Baha Eddin boasted at the Cairo Book Fair in 1997 that he had dismissed 1,000 teachers
and was ready to do the same to 10,000 more. A similar campaign was
carried out against Egypt's 55,000 private mosques, once a vigorous
source of support for Islamic activists, from militants to the nonvio-
lent followers of the Muslim Brotherhood. From the beginning of
1997, all preachers in privately owned mosques were required to
obtain licenses from the minister of religious affairs. The minister,
Hamdi Zakzouk, made clear that there would be no place in mosques
for preachers who held unorthodox views or engaged in political activity against the government. By the beginning of the next decade,
President Mubarak's government declared, it would take control of
every single mosque in Egypt for the first time in history.[54] The security forces, notorious for their lack of restraint, were just as blunt. In
addition to those killed, as many as 20,000 suspected militants had
been arrested and jailed indefinitely, often in miserable conditions.[55]
Meanwhile, Albania, Azerbaijan, Ecuador, Kuwait, Saudi Arabia,
South Africa, Jordan, Syria and the United Arab Emirates extradited
more than forty Egyptians suspected of aiding the militants with arms
and money from abroad.[56]

The actual end of organized violence came through an act more
spectacular in its horror than any in the country since Mohammed Ali
massacred hundreds of his Mamluk opponents to take power nearly
two centuries earlier.[57] Near Luxor, a city known to the world for its
pharaonic tombs and monuments, six men in black sweaters with
epaulets attacked sightseers gathered at the Temple of Hatshepsut.
When the bloodshed ended, fifty-eight foreign tourists and four
Egyptians had been killed, some by bullets, others hacked to death.
The massacre shook Egypt, with lasting repercussions on its militant
Islamic opposition.

Months earlier, there already had been signs of a retreat from the
violence, making that year a turning point. At a trial of ninety-eight

suspected militants that began on July 5, 1997, one of the accused, Mohammed Amin Abdel-Alim, read a statement that he said was written on behalf of the historic leaders of Egypt's Islamic movement, men who had been jailed in Tura Prison since Sadat's assassination.

"We appeal to our brothers to stop all violent activities inside and outside Egypt," he said to a stunned courtroom, "and to stop issuing statements calling for violent action."

He told those in the court that he expected no one to denounce the unilateral, unconditional cease-fire because it had come from "the legitimate leadership of the Islamic Group," including Abboud al-Zumur, Karam Zuhdi and Nagih Ibrahim.[58] Five days later, local leaders of Jihad, which was most active in Cairo, joined the statement.[59] But divisions within the ranks emerged quickly. The call prompted vigorous denials from the leadership abroad, mainly in Afghanistan. Through London-based Arabic newspapers, which at times seemed to be the best way for the two sides to communicate, it insisted the declaration was a fake and that the attacks would, in fact, continue.[60] For their part, the government's security officials dismissed the call as a tactical maneuver. Then came Luxor.

A day after the attack, the Islamic Group claimed responsibility for the killings, but said its gunmen meant only to kidnap hostages who would be freed in return for the liberation of Sheikh Omar Abdel-Rahman, the spiritual leader of the group jailed in the United States for his involvement in the bombing of the World Trade Center in 1993. Two weeks later, members in court said that their leaders inside Egypt had not ordered the attack. They claimed that it was carried out by a rogue faction. Then, in a spate of almost comical confusion, a flurry of statements purportedly by the Islamic Group followed, both claiming and denying responsibility for the attack or, increasingly, claiming or denying responsibility for what was said previously. On December 9, for instance, a statement attributed to the group's leaders abroad denied that they wrote a statement a day earlier urging a halt to attacks on tourists. The imprisoned leaders, for their part, again repeated their call, growing more frustrated by expatriates who were increasingly out of touch with the situation at home: "We tell our brothers abroad that if you are seeking the interest of Islam and Muslims in Egypt, you should call for an unconditional halt of armed operations in Egypt." The farce was played out in the pages of *Al-Hayat*, a London-based newspaper that is arguably the Arab world's best. Traditionally, statements printed in the newspaper were credible. This time, no one seemed to know what anyone else was saying, although deep splits had clearly begun to divide the Islamic Group.[61] Montaser al-Zayat was one example.[62] A lawyer in his early forties who had defended suspected militants through much of the 1990s, almost always unsuccessfully, he declared that in the wake of the Luxor massacre, he would no longer represent them. In January and February 1998, he went public with accusations that the Islamic Group's leadership abroad, particularly Rifai Ahmed Taha, its leader in Afghanistan, had undermined attempts at a truce:

> The most important thing about which they disagree is the cease-fire. Splits in the leadership exploded after the Luxor incident. The leadership in Europe began to understand the situation, maybe because of their moderate circumstances. They are less hard-line. Lately, they have accepted the initiative and condemned the Luxor incident. On the other hand, the leaders in Afghanistan . . . are far away, they are cut off from the rest of the world, they get no news, and all this led to their hard-line stand. All those here support the necessity for a halt to all kinds of armed operations, even those who have been sentenced to death.[63]

In the end, the horror of Luxor would prove too much, even for the leadership abroad, which had demonstrated its disassociation with the movement at home. Within a year, Abdel-Rahman would state his own support for the cease-fire and in March 1999, the group finally declared that it was ending all its operations, both within Egypt and abroad.[64] Even before that, from the beginning of 1998 on, Egypt had enjoyed quiet unprecedented that decade, and both sides appeared eager to sustain it. The government released thousands of prisoners and, in a more subtle but equally dramatic sign of an easing battle, sentences handed down by a military court against a group of suspected militants in May 1999 were remarkably light. Of the twenty-one men accused of planning attacks and assassinations in the Mediterranean port of Alexandria, no one was sentenced to death. One was even found innocent, a first for such a case. Since 1992, in similar cases, more than ninety people had been sentenced to death and about seventy of them executed. Across the country, arbitrary arrests occurred less frequently (although still in numbers unacceptable to international and Egyptian human rights groups), and the conditions of prisoners were improved. As the decade drew to a close, analysts were predicting a more formal rapprochement, and newspapers spoke of a new era as Mubarak began his fourth six-year term: "Islamists hope for a reconciliation with the state," one optimistic headline read.[65]

In hindsight, the uneasy peace was a product of heavy-handed repression that quieted the south without treating the sources of its historic resentment, a growing realization within the movement that two decades of violence beginning with Sadat's assassination had produced neither the Islamic state nor the revolution the Islamists had sought and, not to be underestimated, the popular revulsion over Luxor. In perhaps the most bitter irony, it took the carnage of that massacre to open the door for a new stage of activism. Kamal Habib, a former Islamic militant jailed after Sadat's assassination, called the massacre the decisive event in ending the violence that had wracked the country. "In my personal assessment, the future of the Islamic Group is in political work," he told me. "The initiative to stop violence which was announced in July 1997 and the repercussions that happened after it—the call by Omar Abdel-Rahman to cease military operations, then the unanimous agreement after the Feast of the Sacrifice that there shouldn't be military actions—confirmed that this is not a tactical position but a strategic one. What remains is entry into the political arena."[66] His initiative to form a party was one of a series of moves that remade Egypt's landscape in the wake of the cease-fire, inaugurating an era of hope—given government tolerance—in a country that has sorely lacked it for so long.

—

Although not the first, Islambuli's assassination of Sadat was the most spectacular act of violence in an Islamic arc of militancy. With it, a group inspired by an electrician who insisted *jihad* was a religious duty took center stage. In the years to come, the war against the Soviet Union in Afghanistan would draw those men and others motivated by a loosely imagined, common goal of an Islamic restoration, a borderless project more emotional than political. It would create an army of exiles disassociated from the struggles at home that gave birth to them in the first place. In these countries, opposition to authoritarian regimes continued, the repression and grievances creating support for movements that sought to address their long histories and specific concerns. In Egypt, the resolution of that battle demonstrated the degree to which the Afghan Arabs had been removed from the actual struggle itself. It pointed, too, to the ultimate failure of violence. Now, a window for political work has slightly opened, giving Islamic groups there, like others in Lebanon and Turkey, an opportunity for grass-roots activism that taps into a different vein of disenchantment, creating the popular support necessary for the success of a political movement.

4

God's Call

Behind a Backdrop of Violence, a Blend of Religion and Social Activism

VIOLENCE CAN BE A BLINDING backdrop. In the eyes of Westerners, many of the Islamic movements are defined by a violence and anger that overshadow the appreciation they have earned locally through their community work, social institutions and network of charities—a potent mix of religion and social activism. Mention the name Hezbollah or Hamas to Lebanese or Palestinians, and they are likely to bring up its clinics, legal-aid societies, schools, hospitals, dental offices or orphanages that dot the landscape where their own governments have withdrawn, either as a result of helplessness, as in Palestine, or through traditional neglect, as in Lebanon.[1] In those countries, as well as Egypt and Turkey, Islamic activists have moved in over a generation to fill the gap, identifying themselves with the poor and providing solace through their social activism, a style of welfare made famous by the Muslim Brotherhood along the Suez Canal in the 1930s. Their work creates a reservoir of goodwill, in all likelihood the most successful grassroots phenomenon to have emerged in the ascent of political Islam.[2]

For groups better known for their armed elements, Hezbollah and Hamas among them, the grassroots social activism is the flip side of the violence of the disinherited. It caters to the same realm of disenchantment, but is located squarely within a political movement. As that violence and militancy wane in the years ahead, this aspect of the movement's work will emerge even stronger, defining its reputation and positioning its elements as nascent political parties. Already, the groups' cadres hold up their work as the heart of the movement. To them, they are the ones working in the villages and slums, with the youth, unemployed and poor, work that they maintain will have a far more lasting impact for both the movement, be it Hezbollah or Hamas, and its role within the society. Elsewhere, those networks are a self-conscious substitute for armed action, a how-to for street-level organizing with demonstrated success. In Turkey, activists of the now-banned Refah Party have fashioned themselves as the most sophisticated representatives of political Islam, as organized and as efficient as any organization in the country. In their eyes, suggesting that they would resort to violence if barred from power would be akin to asking activists in the Democratic Party whether they would revolt if they lost an American presidential election. They portray themselves as a part of the country's common heritage, a member of its political system and, in a more permissive environment, a catalyst for a better society. Increasingly, in conjunction with a changing ideology and program of action, their social activism represents a maturing movement, a trend starting to be realized in Lebanon, Jordan and, to a degree, in Egypt.

On a more theoretical level, the activism demonstrates another transformation of traditional Islamic concepts into practical political programs, a theme witnessed again and again in the evolution of political Islam. It is a fascinating element of the movement—the way in which age-old tradition preserved in ideas like *shura* and *maslaha*, concepts as potentially foreign as Europe's divine right of kings, have become synonymous with one vision of modernity. In past generations, intellectuals have reworked those ideas to provide an explicit justification within religion for coexistence with democracy and individual rights, abstractions long thought the product of a Western polity. *Da'wa*, loosely the Arabic term for the social activism of modern Islamic groups, is another of those concepts, although it has come to play a role in politics through a slightly different evolution. *Da'wa* is Islamic reform from below, made real by activists on the ground in Palestine, Lebanon, Egypt and Turkey rather than through the writings of scholars.

Da'wa (literally, "call") is mentioned in the Quran as God's "call" to society to follow Islam, the true religion, and its messengers. Over the centuries, the word was elaborated as an ideology of proselytism. The Fatimid dynasty in Cairo, whose sway stretched east into Arabia and Syria in the tenth century, was famous for sending *du'a,* or missionaries, to propagate its "call," a sect of Shiite Islam. In less political terms, it implied education, namely the ability to recite the Quran, adhere to *sharia* and understand the faith as a part of daily life.[3] Today, with political and religious overtones, it has become more readily identified with the Islamist networks of welfare and charity, drawing again on tradition but reformulating the concept to embrace modern work. To them, *da'wa,* or following God's call, means adhering to a Quranic duty to create balance *(mizan)* and justice *('adl, qist)* within the community. Since Islam serves as a blueprint for a way of life, Muslims have a responsibility to work against social injustices and economic inequalities in everyday life. The activism of social welfare thus becomes religiously sanctioned, a tradition reformed, renewed, then made modern.[4]

This reformed tradition has most clearly developed in Palestine, Lebanon and Turkey, and the movements there are the subject of this chapter.[5] In the first locale, Hamas has created an embryonic counter-society, an alternative to traditional forms of politics and authority that has produced Islamized space. Within that space is a way of life that, at least psychologically, is beyond the purview of the state, ordered as it is by a different set of rules, ethics and hierarchies of power. Its success brings it influence and prestige, making Hamas a powerful institution in society. In Lebanon, the reformed tradition has helped transform Hezbollah, a zealous band born in war, into a political movement legitimized by the state and accepted, although not supported, by a wide swath of the population. With the end of its struggle against the Israeli occupation in southern Lebanon, its community work becomes the movement's most salient feature. Finally, in its most successful scenario in Turkey, *da'wa* has ceased to become *da'wa.* Rather, it was remade yet again, this time into no-nonsense political campaigning of the Refah Party, then its successor in the Virtue Party, where the institutions of social welfare—distributing to the poor, providing sanitation services or organizing disaster relief— have served the demands of electoral canvassing. In this case, social activism has become political activism, the helping hand of activists becoming an effective way to get out the vote.

In the previous chapter, the dissipating influence of violence was explored. Often, it has become a symbol of the desperation of Islamic movements. The Afghan Arabs are removed from the groups they once sought to represent, and their violence has become more spectacle than message. In some cases, Palestine included, it still reflects, however darkly, a community's frustration with the lack of change, be it a failure to end the Israeli occupation or to bring about a simple improvement in living standards. For Hamas, the violence remains part of the group's complicated nature. It sees no contradiction in attacks against Israel—what it views as legitimate resistance to the occupation—and the social activism it considers religiously sanctioned and necessary for the betterment of the community. The same applies to Hezbollah, which saw its armed operations against Israel as a right of self-defense. It claims a long-standing tradition of providing to Lebanese Shiite Muslims, the country's largest yet most neglected community. It saw, too, an imperative in resisting the twenty-two-year occupation of southern Lebanon that ended in May 2000. Rather than seeing the two features as contradictory, it might argue they are one and the same: a means to secure the dignity, rights and welfare of the community it serves.

Rather than defining the movements, though, the violence remains secondary and will become ever less important. Their true success comes through their *political* engagement, their ability to work within local communities defined by local conditions. That is what the movements in Palestine, Lebanon and Turkey share: a universalist message tailored to a specific community—the poor in Palestine's refugee camps, the neglected Shiites in Beirut and southern Lebanon or those newly arrived from the countryside in the slums of Istanbul and other Turkish cities. More than any other group or party in those countries, these Islamic groups are in touch with the people they serve, the true definition of a popular movement. As Ziad Abu Amr, a researcher who served in the Palestinian legislature, described it to me, "Social institutions provide an environment, a milieu, a support environment for the movement. It's a context." In coming years, the context of their community work will be key to their emergence as viable political organizations, creating and cultivating support that will serve them if and when a democratic opening permits them entry into broader political life.

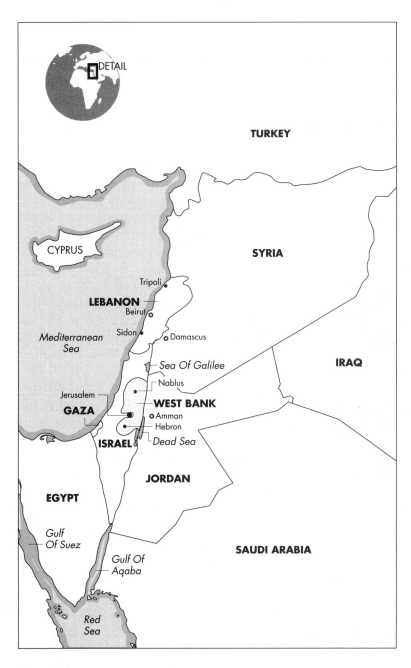

DETAIL

TURKEY

CYPRUS

SYRIA

IRAQ

Tripoli

LEBANON

Beirut

Sidon

Mediterranean
Sea

Damascus

Sea Of Galilee

Nablus

Jerusalem

WEST BANK

GAZA

Amman

Hebron

ISRAEL

Dead Sea

JORDAN

EGYPT

Gulf
Of Suez

Gulf Of
Aqaba

SAUDI ARABIA

Red
Sea

Near East

Israel and Palestine today are awash in flags. They flutter from the chiseled stone buildings of Jerusalem, along the snarled, matted electricity and phone lines of Gaza's refugee camps and in the protests in both over varying degrees of grievances, from dispossession to arbitrary detention. Perhaps in no country do they mean more. The six-pointed Star of David, a symbol of Judaism since the seventeenth century and, since 1897, the emblem of Zionism, speaks to a claim to a land, a national home for a diaspora. Palestine's flag, with its lines and triangle of green, red, white and black, was long banned by Israel and celebrated by Palestinians for the same reason: It spoke to the aspiration for statehood and the collective identity of a people. There are the UN flags that identify the charges of the world body, displaced Palestinians, and there are the green flags of Islamic activists, the color itself delineating a political profile. I have always found Israel and Palestine alluring yet uncomfortable places, inspirational for what they can represent yet claustrophobic in their contest over space and borders, of which flags are one symbol. There is an unending, grinding struggle to lay a political, social and psychological claim to everything from a nation to a schoolground, and the question of space—whose it is, who it serves and what it represents—is the real conflict in Palestine.

In my visits there, I wanted to explore contested space and the role of religion, particularly as it played out in the battle for political support, the proverbial hearts and minds, between Yasser Arafat's Palestinian Authority and his Islamist opposition, Hamas. The contest is everywhere, and Hamas typically prevails. One of the more memorable examples of that success was a summer computer camp I visited in Gaza, which employed a telling mix of modern and traditional in its approach. As I stood in a sun-drenched courtyard, 200 boys raised in the desperation of Gaza's alleys shuffled through the gate, leaving a trash-strewn lot behind them. Inside, they pushed, shoved, teased and laughed in boyhood exuberance until they were brought together by the clear authority of the camp's counselors. The men organized them, and in a few minutes, set them off on a round of ungainly calisthenics to a familiar cadence of one-two. The air was already tinged with humidity drawn from the Mediterranean Sea, but as summertimes in Gaza go, it was tolerable, even pleasant, with a soft breeze seeming to animate the giggling youths. Still early in the morning, a day of proselytizing, politics and charity had begun.

The monthlong camp of Quranic reading and computer classes was in its fifth year, run under the aegis of the Islamic Society. Its presence was clear: The boys wore green shirts with "The Islamic Society, Gaza Section" printed in black on the back. Overhead fluttered a flag for Palestine and another for Islam in its traditional green. Inside the building, meanwhile, counselors with the distinctive beards often worn by devout Muslims planned the day's extra events: a trip to the sea, maybe, or a visit to a hospital. Scattered on tables nearby were manuals for running programs on IBM-compatible computers, deciphering commands in English or learning the intricacies of Windows' Arabic version. The summer tuition ran just $15—a T-shirt, hat and two sandwiches a day part of the package. And at the camp's end, the boys received a diploma certifying their computer literacy, a crucial skill in a land where the money one worker makes must provide for an average seven people. The society called the camp a link between "the newness of today and the steadfastness of Islam," a poignant phrase that seemed to me to suggest a goal of becoming more modern while staying the same.[6] Taken together, the flags, the T-shirts, even the curriculum expressed the identity and ambitions of the Islamic Society. In this instance, space—a summer camp—had become Islamized. The society's vision of a modern, yet religious milieu had become reality in this remote stretch of the otherwise dreary landscape of the Gaza Strip.

That idea of Islamized space struck me again at a mass wedding in the West Bank. At that ceremony, in a bus depot turned open-air wedding hall, fifteen beaming grooms arrived on horseback in the town of Nablus to the sound of Islamic chants. In black suits and ribbons of green, they took their seats beneath a banner decorated with a Quran and two hearts, listening as Muslim clergymen dispensed advice over a microphone on how to make marriages succeed. Interspersed in their homilies were chants of "Islam is the solution," its meaning more political than religious. Almost 10,000 well-wishers looked on from red plastic chairs. They were offered coffee and orange juice in line with Islam's ban on alcoholic drinks. Hamas had partly subsidized the event, the public donated electronic equipment. In trying economic times in the West Bank, with an economy stunted by occupation and almost completely dependent on Israel, that meant the grooms had to part with the equivalent of only $110 each, a sum that would not cover the food at traditional, often lavish Arab weddings.

The wedding's appeal was multifaceted, pointing to the support the movement enjoys. To older, socially conservative elements, it suggested an austere moral code, stressed pious conduct and offered a way for Islamic values to serve as a framework for civic life. To its followers, it demonstrated Hamas's capacity to mobilize, the fruit of a thoroughly modern political organization. To the young and the disadvantaged, the audience of Islamists in Palestine and elsewhere, it made possible something that would have not been possible otherwise. In this case, it was a wedding; in other cases, it is an education, training, a loan or a costly operation. Perhaps most important, and on a more subtle level, a bus depot filled during the day with the cacophony of horns, traffic, vendors and taxis had become the territory of Hamas at night. In the contest over territory, another small patch of Palestine had, for a time, become Islamized space.

Although the devastating acts of violence by Hamas have commanded the greatest media attention, the bloodshed is, as with the Afghan Arabs, a sideshow to the movement's real history and potential. In the more than ten years since it emerged from the Palestinian Muslim Brotherhood, it has defined itself less by armed action, although important, and more by social welfare—in its vision, reclaiming space vis-à-vis Israel *and* the Palestinian Authority. It is the Brotherhood's work with a twist: Although Hassan al-Banna and his followers were quick to see the potential of social activism, they saw in it mainly a way to create a new man. He would be a reawakened Muslim who would help transform society gradually from below. Hamas drew from the Brotherhood's legacy but added to it and reshaped it: It abandoned the Brotherhood's quietism toward the Israeli occupation and began building an assertive, engaged alternative to the state—economically, politically and morally. Its brief history can be read as a methodical march toward that goal, creating an identifiable reality. The transformations it underwent in the process—making its religious agenda more militant and aggressive while deepening and broadening the more important social activism—shape one manifestation of *da'wa*.

As with Islamic movements in other Arab countries, the state (in Palestine's case, the occupation authorities) implicitly backed the growth of the Brotherhood. The support was for good reason: The movement has always had a troubled relationship with Palestinian nationalism. It bristled at its secularism, opposition that grew as

Arafat's movement tended toward corruption and materialism with an authoritarian bent. In divide-and-conquer fashion, Israel allowed the movement to flourish, particularly in Gaza, and covertly extended some financial aid through mosques and religious schools, fostering a group that would balance the PLO's leftist forces, which it deemed the biggest threat.[7] By 1986, the Brotherhood controlled 40 percent of Gaza's mosques and its sole Islamic university, which enrolled 7,000 students, the most in the territories.[8] Throughout that growth, the movement, under the leadership of Sheikh Ahmed Yassin,[9] eschewed the political and military work of the PLO, namely opposing the Israeli occupation, and instead focused on efforts designed to construct the social infrastructure that would become more important in coming years.[10] Even today, the biggest charity in Gaza is one founded by Yassin, *al-Mujama al-Islamiyya*.

The movement's development in the 1970s and, in particular, the 1980s did not come in a vacuum. It enjoyed clout that was derived in part from the growing disenchantment across the region with such failed secular ideologies as Arab nationalism and Nasserite socialism, as seen in Chapter 2, and the painful, typically unproductive experiments with capitalism, particularly in Sadat's Egypt. Virtually no country in the Middle East escaped the aftermath of those failures and, in many cases, it seemed the farther from the halls of power the better. Among Palestinians, meanwhile, the PLO itself was growing more unaccountable, dictatorial and, from its base in southern Lebanon in the 1970s, divorced from events in the villages, cities and camps of the West Bank and Gaza. The divide between the diaspora and the homeland exerts to this day a powerful influence on the movement. The PLO's standing suffered even further in the wake of the 1982 Israeli invasion of neighboring Lebanon, a defeat that eventually forced it to withdraw across the Mediterranean Sea to the North African country of Tunisia, a distant, isolated headquarters.

In Gaza and the West Bank, the once-feverish, romanticized support for the PLO and its guerrillas known as *fedayeen*, inspired most notably by the success against the Israeli armed forces in a skirmish in Karameh in the Jordan valley in 1968, had long since faded.[11] In its stead was a growing mood of religiosity, as elsewhere in the region, in part reflecting the desperation of wretched economic conditions and a seemingly permanent Israeli occupation. Though a purely anecdotal measure, the number of mosques in Gaza nearly tripled in the twenty years after the 1967 war, from 200 to 600, offering another form of sheltered, Islamized space.[12] As the 1970s drew to a close, the religious mood was bolstered further by the Iranian Revolution, a cataclysmic event that saw a popular movement overthrow a despised, pro-Western shah and mitigated, albeit to a small degree, the acute disillusionment that followed the 1967 war. The revolution's appeal was more in the means than the end. Few in the Arab world would share the idiosyncratic vision of a Shiite Muslim state elaborated by Ayatollah Ruhollah Khomeini, but many embraced the success of the revolution's religious mobilization, an empowerment of politics grounded in Islam. Coupled with people's frustration with the inability of the PLO to achieve serious change at the same time that it degenerated politically and ideologically, the Palestinian Brotherhood and then Hamas found themselves in an opportune environment of discouragement and disenchantment.[13] Their message, a critique as much as a program, became increasingly attractive. As Khalil Shikaki, a Palestinian academic whose brother, leader of the rival Islamic Jihad, was assassinated in Malta in 1995, said, "Hamas is the alternative in the absence of a better alternative."[14] The idea is perhaps overstated, since its religious message remains potent, but it is a compelling point. As Shikaki put it:

> Hamas is a grass-roots organization, first of all. It's very well organized, its message is a traditional message which finds fertile ground in societies like ours that are traditional, poor, lower middle class or middle class, and the organization has excelled throughout in delivering services under the Israeli occupation when you had no government to speak of to provide a lot of these services. . . . When you look at it, that's where Hamas really is. In a traditional society, in a society like ours, the message of Hamas is basically in the hearts of the people already. All they have to do then is package it in political terms.

The packaging evolved in the 1980s. The Brotherhood's quiescence, an accommodation with the occupation that had allowed its charity to flourish, ran the risk of alienating most Palestinians once the revolt against Israel known as the *intifada* got under way in 1987. Before that, armed action was foreign to the Brotherhood and its leaders. They saw themselves as reformers, not revolutionaries, and placed piety over the call to resistance. In the end, as the uprising mounted,

Sheikh Yassin resolved the dilemma of losing support or staying pure by setting up a separate wing that would engage the occupation and eventually overshadow and largely subsume the parent organization. He named it Hamas, an Arabic acronym for the Islamic Resistance Movement, which also means "zeal" in Arabic. Its military wing was called the Izzeddin al-Qassem brigades after a Muslim preacher who led armed resistance against British Mandate rule and Zionist settlement in the 1930s.[15] The decision made clear that the group had moved toward armed opposition to the Israeli occupation. Yet Israel, in a testament to its early support of the group, did not act against it until more than a year later, when it first imprisoned Yassin and other Hamas activists then formally banned the group in September 1989. That rupture in relations would come to haunt it, as Hamas's military operations—from ambushes of undercover operatives to kidnappings of soldiers to the suicide bombings of the mid–1990s—became the hallmark of its resistance, often displaying a sophistication, ruthlessness and political awareness that its secular counterparts in the PLO never matched in more than thirty years of armed resistance.

The shift toward a more engaged political organization followed a change in ideology as well. In the movement's early years, as was noted, resistance ran high toward the idea of nationalism, which it saw as, at best, another way to divide Muslims and, at worst, a form of atheism that put race or ethnicity before faith. To the Brotherhood, the land of Palestine was neither Jewish nor Arab, Palestinian nor Israeli. It was considered a *waqf,* entrusted to Muslims as a part of Islam's abode. To describe it as Palestinian would mean it was usurped, particularly as conceived by the PLO for much of its history: a land that would be home to a secular, democratic state. To the Brotherhood, that was no better than describing it as a land of atheism. By 1988, with the *intifada* in full swing and Islamists under pressure to take a more political stand, the outlook changed. The movement sought, unconsciously or not, to co-opt secular nationalism within an Islamist tradition, an idea that played well to the militant young cadres who were entering the group's ranks. Their priority was not just the implementation of *sharia* (that being difficult when you have neither a state nor a government to impose it), they also sought the end to the Israeli occupation, and at least in rhetoric, the liberation of all of Palestine, from the Jordan River to the Mediterranean Sea (the PLO sought to establish a state only in the West Bank and Gaza).

However unlikely, Hamas conceived that goal as a religious duty, making resistance an obligation of faith.[16] As Graham Usher, the author of an insightful survey of Palestinian politics after the Oslo accord, described it,

> The presence of this younger strata in Hamas signals not the demise of nationalist ideology, but its transformation, imbuing it rather with a religious soul that secularism is felt to lack. Hamas accommodated the PLO's secular nationalism ideologically by inventing for it an Islamist tradition that is now being experienced as an integral part of Palestinian national identity, especially by those generations politically forged by the uprising.[17]

Through the years of the *intifada*, Hamas succeeded in ideologically becoming a distinctly Palestinian movement. Its call for religious reform appealed to society's socially conservative elements and its elaboration of *jihad* courted younger, more desperate ranks. The attraction of the message was that it offered a promise, to those who accepted it, of both change *and* resistance to change.[18] The conception that evolved, though, was not necessarily welcome, and in my time in Palestine over the past ten years, the charged rhetoric seemed to me to have altered. Hamas had discarded the framework in which the conflict with Israel had been fought for fifty years. No longer was it a struggle between Palestinian demands for statehood and the Zionist vision of a Jewish home on historically Arab land. To Hamas, Zionism—a specifically political and ideological program—played little role in the equation. Instead, the conflict pitted Muslims against Jews, a contest that dated not to 1948 or even to the evolution of Zionism in the nineteenth century. It was the latest fight in the path of God that extended back to the prophet's time and his interactions with the communities of Jews that he courted, then banished in western Arabia in the seventh century after they refused his revelation. Hamas emphasized ethnicity and religion, both of which offer little room for compromise.[19] The movement, in becoming more involved in politics, had almost incidentally reshaped the conflict into a zero-sum game. In an odd way, another form of space, this time a distinct reality, had become Islamized, defined by its own codes and its own rules. In laying claim to the conflict, each party framing it in its own terms (for Israel security; for the PLO, a fight between nationalisms), Hamas succeeded in reconstructing Palestinian grievances as a historic clash of religions. The repercussions of that change are still unclear: It may merely tap prejudices already felt by many in the Arab world or, more dangerous, it may reorient the conflict in a messianic direction, mirroring and supporting the all-or-nothing visions of some Jewish settlers in the West Bank, who have amplified the religious face of Zionism by linking the land ideologically and spiritually to Judaism, making compromise altogether more difficult. With the land itself seen as sacred by both sides, the latter has become far more likely.

On a more tactical level, though, and perhaps more important to the evolution of political Islam, Hamas's transformation of Brotherhood ideology demonstrated a compelling pragmatism, an approach that saw political gain taking precedence over ideological rigor. Despite the Islamization of the conflict with Israel and the repercussions of its bloody, expedient attacks, elements that are removed from the day-to-day bargaining that defines the movement's position within Palestinian society, Hamas has proven itself above all a movement of the time. Its positions are popular and pragmatic: It defends its right to resist the Israeli occupation and demands a bigger role in Palestinian political life. While those two features may appear contradictory in the West, they can coexist in Palestine, even within the same movement. In interviews, some leaders defend electoral politics with the fervor of born-again democrats, stress their pragmatism, denounce extremism and offer scenarios for compromise. Others, in speeches and sermons, deliver the language of *jihad*. Both represent the movement.

A glimpse of that dichotomy—of how those currents coexist—came in a visit to Sayyid Abu Musameh, a Hamas leader in his late forties who appeared much older, and a younger colleague, Ghazi Hamad, at their office in Gaza, a concrete block colored the same gray as much of the territory.[20] A map of Palestine on the wall was the only dash of color. Abu Musameh started off and I soon noted that although he had spent thirteen years in prison, he still knew how to deal with journalists. He appreciated the value of a quote and the impact of a statement that seemed to break with tradition.

"We are indeed an Islamic movement from the perspective of our ideology, but this is a realistic movement," he told me. "When I say that I want to go and occupy Tel Aviv, this isn't realistic. But as an aspiration to return to my home from 1948, this I can desire." Urging patience over the pace of change, Abu Musameh added, "Every person in the Islamic movement believes that Islam will be victorious. If it isn't victorious tomorrow, it will be victorious after 10 years, after 20 years, after 100 years, after 200 years, after 1,000 years. We don't have any doubt about this."

For a while, Hamad seemed to go along with Abu Musameh's line of reasoning. At thirty-five, he was obviously junior, though his five years in prison and credentials as a veteran of the *intifada* conveyed respect. He had the impatience of someone who felt he had little time to waste and better things to do. Eventually, he spoke up. Hamad bristled at some of Abu Musameh's statements, interpreting them as passivity. Questions about attacks on Israelis, tensions with the Palestinian police and the poor relations with Arafat's government annoyed him. "Governments use force against the Islamic groups. They put them in the corners, they put them in the prisons, they arrest them, and after that, they ask them to respect their freedom and respect the government," he told me.

Abu Musameh cautioned him for being too direct, a dynamic that would persist through the interview. At that time, the tensions from a series of suicide bomb attacks in 1996 that followed the assassination of Yahya Ayyash, a Hamas bomb-maker, and killed dozens of Israelis still hung over the territories. Hamas activists were in jail and the organization was under one of its periodic spells of repression at the hands of Arafat's Palestinian police—social services were shut down, leaders were questioned, and the usual suspects were arrested. To Abu Musameh, the Hamas attacks had done irreparable harm to the cause. "The truth is that it did a lot of damage to Islam's image in the West," he said. "Any time you kill civilians, that happens."

Hamad interjected. "Israel opened the door of the civilian war. Israel started this war against us." He went on, his voice rising. "Both people are struggling for one land. Both of them, for one land. And the conflict will go on, maybe more bloody in the future. It is very difficult to accept Israel here in the Middle East. I am telling you what is a fact. It is not solved by signing an agreement. It is very difficult."

Abu Musameh started arguing back. It is the occupation, he said, not Israel itself that we oppose. Hamad became more strident. He dismissed his statements, insisting that an armed rebellion was imminent and that it would draw all Palestinians into it. He railed against Israel's control of Gaza's borders, ridiculing the Palestinians' plight and their failure to act. "What is happening now is death for the Palestinian people. We live in Gaza, surrounded everywhere. When we export something, we are at the mercy of Israel. 'Please open the doors of the checkpoint to allow the bread to come in, to allow the laborers to work inside Israel,'" Hamad said, his voice dripping with ridicule. "It is killing the people."

The interview broke up soon afterward, in part to keep Hamad from saying more to me. It was an enlightening experience. Although it would be possible to dismiss the statements of both men as somewhat contrived, there is a more telling insight in their words, and the anger that erupted inside the room was a window on a certain reality within Hamas. The organization, despite its loathsome reputation abroad, still must act as an umbrella. At times, it must balance its agenda of *sharia* and opposition to what is euphemistically called the peace process with the political realities of coexisting with Arafat's authority. Throughout the 1990s, it has had to balance the more moderate stands of its cadres within Palestine with the more militant program of its exiled, but financially important leaders abroad. At all times, it must juggle the priorities of the disparate generations within its leadership: a conservative, old-school Muslim Brotherhood generation with younger, more militant elements—the "gangsta Islam" of Chapter 3.[21] To do so, it must be practical.

From abroad, Hamas appears monochromatic. It stands as the vintage stereotype for an uneasy West: unflinching, unyielding, dedicated to violence and impervious to reason. In Palestine, the story is far different. Hamas is seen as shifting its priorities according to time and place. Its rethinking of nationalism is one example; its desire to participate in Palestine's troubled political life another. As Iyad Barghouti, a Palestinian professor of sociology in the West Bank, pointed out, "One thing that the rise of Hamas has proven is that it is above all pragmatic. Whereas there might be an ideological opposition to the mingling of men and women at universities, for example, they realize that it is impractical to demand such a separation and therefore do not do so."[22] Far more than the militant Islamic groups in Egypt, Hamas leaders are quick to call for "a national dialogue" or insist that the movement is "an integral part of Palestinian culture."[23] In the cold, often repugnant logic of *realpolitik*, even the suicide bombings can be seen as a carefully orchestrated *political* maneuver. Unlike the Afghan Arabs and their fondness for the decisive blow, Hamas's attacks on Israel have aimed

far more modestly: to derail an election or to bring to an impasse negotiations. They are often successful.

Part of that pragmatism, though, is the realization, in political
terms, of the setbacks incurred by those same attacks. By the end of
the 1990s, Hamas began to place far less emphasis on its military
wing. Israel and the Palestinian authority had exerted immense pressure on it through arrests, imprisonment, torture and execution, making armed attacks treacherously difficult, though not impossible.
Meanwhile, others within the movement, Abu Musameh for instance,
saw that violence was bringing diminishing returns, each new attack
inflicting higher costs on the movement and the people it sought to
help. Although they were not ideologically opposed to the right of
Palestinians to resist the occupation, doubts began to grow over
whether the attacks were worth the toll they took on the organization. In their stead was a renewed emphasis on the social and political
agendas of the movement that had emerged over the past generation.[24]
It fashioned itself as a legitimate opposition and sought to earn support from the mistakes those in power make.

To a large degree, Hamas has become a nascent political movement,
one that has a program of political action to cultivate support but, like
any movement, that must also maintain a flexibility to balance the
different demands and objectives of its disparate members. In that, it
has matured, and its growth is becoming grounded less in military
action and more in social activism, the infrastructure of charity, welfare and benevolent foundations that it constructed to make it a player
in Palestinian politics. That activism has allowed it to Islamize
space—to elaborate a program to a specific audience, shape its agenda
and recruit its following in areas it holds sway. Its emergence in the
1990s was the fruit of twenty years of creating the framework, often
silently, in which it could mature.

—

Across the West Bank's rolling hills, studded with olive trees, and
the sand and dune-covered coastal plain of the Gaza Strip, divided by
the invisible border of Israel, the schools and the clinics of Hamas are
considered far better than the meager alternative provided by Arafat's
cash-strapped authority. At least, that was what I had heard from
friends who knew Palestine far better than I did. I had come to report
on one of the periodic eruptions of religious and nationalist fury, this

one sparked by an Israeli decision in September 1996 to complete a tunnel near one of Islam's most sacred shrines in Jerusalem, stretching from the Western Wall to the Via Dolorosa, the street Jesus Christ is said to have taken to his crucifixion. Four days of bloodletting would follow, pitting Israeli soldiers against Palestinian protesters and out-gunned police. In time, over those violent days, the reporting would take me to Hebron, a city at the heart of the struggle between the competing nationalisms of Israel and Palestine and the competing agendas of Arafat and Hamas.

Hebron is a city of borders within borders. One hundred thirty thou-sand Palestinians call it home, as do 500 Jewish settlers in five heavily guarded compounds near the Tomb of the Patriarchs, a massive, fortresslike stone edifice built by King Herod and at the center of the city. The crypt has meaning for all faiths: It is the site where the Bible says Abraham purchased a cave and field for 4,000 silver shekels to bury his wife Sarah. Abraham, Isaac, Jacob (Ibrahim, Ishaq and Yacoub to Arabs) and their wives were said to be buried there, too. In the Christian era, a Byzantine church was built on top of the Jewish holy site, and after the Arab conquest of the city in 638, the building became a mosque. More than a millennium later, Jews and Muslims still pray in the tight quarters of the tomb, but in separate areas divid-ed by a chasm of mistrust and anger.

Those scars are more recent: In a 1929 massacre, Arab rioters killed sixty-seven Jews in two days and ended the Jewish presence in the city that had lasted hundreds of years.[25] The most recent massacre was car-ried out by an Israeli, Baruch Goldstein, who killed twenty-nine Palestinian worshipers in the tomb in February 1994 before being beaten to death by survivors. Those memories vivid, the borders between the communities mark every corner, every alley, every door-way in a city whose white stone houses radiate out across a valley and its rolling, rocky hillsides.

The mix in Hebron makes for fertile ground for any movement and, in my time there, Hamas in typically astute fashion had taken advan-tage of the opportunity. Islamic groups ran four medical clinics—all of them in poor areas—sports clubs that offered soccer, karate, judo and table tennis, welfare societies and two schools that could educate a child from the age of six to the end of high school. Indirectly, I had come across a graduate of one of those schools, by way of his family. His name was Ibrahim Sarahneh, a twenty-six-year-old unemployed

construction worker who killed an Israeli soldier when he blew himself up in 1996 at a hitchhiking post in the coastal town of Ashkelon.
He was disguised as an Israeli soldier, wearing an earring and carrying
the explosives in a green army duffel bag so as not to raise suspicion.
His home, about forty miles away in another world, was the refugee
camp of al-Fawar, near Hebron. It was a desolate place of corrugated
iron and cinder blocks, where milky sewage trickles down the center
of alleys in shallow gutters. Sentenced to life there, he and his family
were the products of the desolation and hopelessness that poverty
brings, the cactuses that grew up in the camp feeling like a testament
to the bitterness of their life. Their father died in 1978, and the mother, sixty-year-old Maryam, raised her five sons and four daughters by
herself.

I met Maryam a few months after her son had died. At first she was
relaxed, sitting in a long blue peasant dress and a brown scarf under a
hot sun just feet away from the tangled mess of stone and wire left
after the Israeli army blew up her house in retaliation for her son's
attack. She joked with me, pointing to my beard and telling me to be
careful. "If you weren't a journalist," she said, "they would think you
were Hamas." As we talked about her son, though, she understandably got grimmer, becoming less animated and starting to roll the
worry beads through her fingers. She knew his history: He had been
arrested twice in 1992, two years after graduating from Hebron's al-
Shariyya Boys School. He was devout, close to her (she said he liked to
cook chicken-and-rice dishes) and defined by the camp's grinding
poverty. He could go no further than high school, so he started working in hopes of making enough money to put his younger brother
through college. With him gone, she said, her life had become even
bleaker. Crying and muttering *la illah ila Allah*, there is no god but
God, she looked out across the rubble of her home shrouded in the
sickly yellow of the camp. "What do I have now?" she asked me.
"Sand. People can't eat sand."

How important, I wondered, was Hebron's Islamic school to her
son's fate? The school's construction and the society that built it
seemed to chart the Islamic movement's history, a gradual development, step by step. The society was formed in 1962, the high school
opened in 1968 (a year after Jordan lost the West Bank to Israel) and an
orphanage in 1972, an elementary school followed in 1977 and a workshop to teach girls sewing started in 1987, the first year of the *intifa-*

da. Today, the compound stretches out across a lot, hosting a mosque, two floors of beds and dormitories, a kitchen, a huge dining room and a courtyard where young boys in green baseball caps play at the "Young Believers Camp." The girls are in another building, sitting at their desks in white veils known as the *hijab*. The vision is one of uniformity and discipline. In a way, I thought, it was a world unto itself, self-contained and, within the walls, independent. "Our main concern is to provide an upbringing so that the children can stand on their feet and get into the street," Mohammed Eid, a somber man who had directed the society for six years, told me during my visit. As for Sarahneh and his time there, he skirted the question. "I don't think he was a student here," he said disingenuously. "I don't think."

Sarahneh was, though, and the world in which he matured was ordered by a different code than that followed outside its walls. He went there for a virtually free education, taking advantage of a facility considered better than its counterparts, and he was raised in its religiously defined milieu. Faith was foremost, sacrifice was celebrated and the fundamentals of religion, memorization and recitation of the Quran and Islamic history were interspersed with the modern trappings of education—computers, math and science. Within Palestine, it was the only infrastructure in which one ideology was shared, a concord of belief that infused a generation raised first under the occupation then under the arbitrary authority of Arafat's government. Foremost, it was accessible. A private kindergarten might cost $500 a year, a fortune for a family of refugees. Palestine's Islamic schools were free or very inexpensive, made possible by as much as $70 million in funding, much of it donated by governments and individuals in Qatar, the United Arab Emirates, Saudi Arabia and other sparkling emirates in the Persian Gulf.[26] Their reach was expansive. In Gaza, *al-Mujama al-Islamiyya*, founded by Sheikh Yassin, ran workshops to teach fifty girls sewing, medical clinics and a youth club. It operated seven preschools adorned with cut-out animals that hung from the ceiling, flags of Palestine and an occasional Quranic verse. In all, they cared for 1,500 children.[27] That work was noticed and it played well in the streets, an impression that was almost inescapable after spending any amount of time there.

On one visit, I sat with a friend at a coffee shop in an alley in Hebron that was quieted by tension. Arafat's forces were carrying out one of their periodic crackdowns on Hamas, arresting the usual suspects and shutting down some of its affiliated institutions. The news of 800 Hamas activists detained had upset him. Although not particularly devout, his loyalties were clear. He saw Arafat as a stooge, working hand in hand with the Israelis to police the Palestinians, and he was thankful for what Hamas had done in his city. A simple equation, but in a town in a cold war, the relationship was effective. In the battle for support, Hamas's evolving style of social activism meant tangible allegiance, and if true democracy ever visits the squalor of Palestine, Hamas will have laid the groundwork for tangible support. "Arafat's men are good with words, but they never do anything. They have never built any worthwhile institutions," my friend Nasser told me as we sat in the alley. "Hamas, they have built so much."[28]

The work to Islamize space, to claim territory, does not come through social institutions alone. It also relies on the movement's self-confidence, its perceived ability to offer all the answers, speaking with an assurance that only moral certainty brings. "Building a Muslim Family" and "Caring for Children" were titles on the shelves of the Gaza Islamic Bookstore. Outside the Palestine Mosque, young men crowded around a cart stacked with hundreds of cassette tapes selling for less than a dollar, their titles suggesting a comprehensive view of the world: "On Women," "On Adultery," "On Freedom," "On Salman Rushdie," "On the Veil," and "On Sound Marriage." That all-embracing approach has generally endangered the movement, as we will see later in the case of Iran, but in Palestine, it has served to offer a viable alternative to the secular nationalism of the PLO. In scope, political ideologies borrowed from the West cannot compete. They are limited by their failures, their context and their narrowness of vision. In political Islam, its advocates believe, there is a critique, a program and a solution—be it in schools, in bookstores, in orphanages or in mosques in a place that, more than any other country I have visited, lives through unease as the status quo. In essence, you belong to that order or you do not. When everything from wardrobe to diet to gender relations is defined and explained, there is little ambivalence. The Islamic movement is even more distinct when the promises of Arafat's authority are nonexistent: Talk of democracy is tailored to Western aid agencies, a capital in Jerusalem remains the stuff of rhetoric and human rights are reserved for criticism of Israel but not his own abusive police. In the 1990s, only one group in Palestine could claim to stick to its principles.

It is an overstatement, however, to draw too direct a connection between social activism and support for Islamists. Islamic institutions comprise anywhere from 10 percent to 40 percent of all social institutions in the West Bank and Gaza. In education, the number is much higher.[29] Not all the charitable institutions, schools and orphanages are run by Hamas, though. In fact, the majority may not be. The relationship is more subtle. These institutions create an environment and milieu that is distinctly Islamic, and Hamas does not have to run them to gain the support of those who benefit. Since it fashions itself as the standard-bearer of Islam in the West Bank and Gaza, elaborating a program of Islamic law, resistance to the Israeli occupation, a critique of Arafat's authority and defiance of the West, institutions that cater to that platform, or even parts of it, cultivate support. Because Hamas is the only significant political group elaborating that ideology, it by default receives the political support the institutions generate. As Ziad Abu Amr, the Gaza-born Palestinian academic, said to me, "There is a mosque in every city and every village. What do you make out of that? Can we say this is a Hamas institution or what? It depends. It depends on how influential Hamas is in that mosque or in that institution. You can't really draw a demarcation line between what Islamic institutions are operated by Hamas or on behalf of Hamas." What it comes down to, he said, is that "religiously oriented institutions feed into the general Islamic orientation and provide a conducive context for a popular and influential Hamas within the country."

I had the same sense in Egypt, where I lived. It is perhaps the most devout country in the Middle East. The call to prayer sneaks into every recess of Cairo's chaos,[30] worshipers spill out onto straw mats in the dusty streets on Friday (honking taxis navigating among them) and physical appearance—usually a beard or veil—is powerfully suggestive of the fervor of one's conviction. In the 1980s, there was a dramatic increase in the number of mosques that were not under the state's supervision—from 40,000 in 1981 to 70,000 in 1989. The space within those mosques was beyond the reach of the government and often served to air dissent or religious messages the government would unlikely endorse (criticism of Christians, for instance). It mirrored a general increase in religiosity: The publication and sale of Islamic books exploded, religious programming flourished and religious cassettes were among the most popular.[31] Perhaps the biggest explosion was in Islamic associations, which accounted for at least half of welfare groups in the early 1990s. They offered charity and health services to millions of Egyptian poor, and their profile seemed to grow as the government withdrew its subsidies, overturned rent control and undermined peasants' rights over land they rented, all moves that were part of liberal economic policies endorsed by the International Monetary Fund. One typical association in Ezbat Zein in Cairo offered classes on the Quran while providing a sewing center, day care, medical treatment, remedial tutoring, a food cooperative and septic tank cleaning.[32]

As in Palestine, those groups delivered. One of the most vivid examples was the response of the Muslim Brotherhood to the earthquake in October 1992. After it struck, killing 550 people, injuring 10,000 and leaving thousands more homeless when their shoddily built concrete hovels toppled in Cairo's slums, Brotherhood cadres poured into the streets with blankets.[33] Tents sprouted in the shadow of the Sayyida Zeinab mosque, offering food and medicine to the hardest hit and sporting bright green banners that read "Islam is the solution." The Doctors' Syndicate, a professional union controlled by the Brotherhood, arranged the makeshift settlement, distributing T-shirts bearing the logo of the syndicate's humanitarian relief project.[34] In those first few days, as the Egyptian capital reeled from the devastation, the government was often nowhere to be seen.

The professional unions themselves, many of them taken over by Islamists in the late 1980s and early 1990s, also delivered to their members. The leadership pioneered a new and effective plan of health insurance that provided for tens of thousands of families. For the same middle-class audience, always a traditional source of support for the Brotherhood, the syndicates made possible a pretense of prosperity by sponsoring sales of consumer goods on an installment plan, allowing Egypt's legions of modest earners to buy refrigerators, washing machines and video recorders.[35] They set up social clubs and, crucially, helped find jobs for unemployed members.

The vast majority of the groups, though, have no link to the Brotherhood or the more militant currents in the Islamic Group. They are Islamic in the loose use of the term: they see themselves as performing a religious duty, a reinterpretation of the concept of da'wa. As in Palestine, groups like the Brotherhood do not have to run these groups to receive the support they create. The support is more general and broader, an endorsement of the role of faith in political life and a return to Islam as a source of strength and identity. Whatever group captures the values and ethics adhered to in that space will benefit from the support. The institutions have created an atmosphere in which political action can occur.

—

Hezbollah is an example, par excellence, of social and political action. To much of the world the group, whose name in Arabic means Party of God, remains a shadowy band of militants suspected in the kidnapping of more than fifty foreigners amid the anarchy that defined Lebanon during its ghastly 1975–1990 civil war. More dramatically, it was the group blamed for two attacks on the American Embassy in Beirut and the 1983 bombing of a U.S. Marine barracks, which killed 240 soldiers, the American military's biggest loss of life in a single incident since the Vietnam War. The attacks brought it the notoriety abroad that still makes its reputation in some quarters, despite its steadfast denials of any role; the U.S. State Department, for one, insists it continues to engage in terrorism. In Lebanon, removed as it is from the Western demonization of the movement—a caricature tinged with racism—Hezbollah is most notably a social movement, enjoying a robust image as a defender of the poor. In the unruly tumult of Lebanese politics, a free-wheeling mix of partisan democracy, fierce sectarian affiliation and heavy-handed government repression, Hezbollah has taken the social infrastructure and grassroots move-ment of Hamas to another level. It has formally entered politics, with the aim of working within the system toward its still-resolute goal of an Islamic state.

Hezbollah's home turf of Lebanon is an oddity, and only in its tor-tured landscape of eighteen religious sects could such a movement exist and then prosper. France took control of the country after World War I when it carved up the defeated Ottoman Empire in concert with the British. The French had historically sought to act as the protector of the country's Maronite Catholics, who were concentrated in the area of Mount Lebanon, a rugged region of terraced hillsides and soar-ing vistas that enjoyed special privileges in Ottoman times. To make their region viable as a state, France added to Mount Lebanon the port cities of Beirut, Sidon and Tripoli, the fertile lands of the Bekaa Valley and the south and north, areas with a predominantly Muslim population. Many of the inhabitants of the annexed regions considered themselves Syrian, not Lebanese, and were not eager to join the French or the Maronite Catholics who then, as now, reluctantly saw themselves as Arabs and alienated their countrymen by occasionally treating Lebanon as their God-given right. In hindsight, those fears were warranted. To maintain Maronite authority, an arrangement known as a confessional system was adopted under the French, and again instituted after independence in 1943, dividing power among the country's religious groups. The Maronites, at one time the country's largest single community, got the presidency. By convention, the prime minister's office went to a Sunni, and the speaker of parliament to a Shiite. At least one Greek Orthodox and one Druze were to be in the cabinet and all public offices, including Parliament, were to respect the rule that there should be six Christians to every five Muslims. The system would not be changed until the civil war came to an end following the Taif Accord of 1989. That agreement, still in effect today, heeded the country's changing demographics and made equal the number of Christian and Muslim deputies in Parliament. It also reduced the powers of the Maronite presidency, transferring its once-sweeping authority to the council of ministers. In the decade since the war, the arrangement has kept a precarious if troubled peace, although virtually no one in Lebanon thinks much of it, least of all the Shiites.

To call the Shiite community historically underprivileged gives it too much credit. It was historically rural, illiterate and dominated by a small traditional elite of large landowners and reactionary clergy.[36] The community's leaders were feudal, more interested in their own power and profit than in bringing Shiites out of their medieval conditions. Into the 1970s, some of their regions had no roads, hospitals or schools (education was discouraged by the leading families). Running water was a luxury. Those conditions gave rise to a man who in time came to be seen as a liberator of the community. His name was Musa al-Sadr, a cleric born in Qom, Iran, who arrived in Lebanon to serve as a religious leader in 1959. His career was the story of a Shiite awakening. More an activist than a cleric, Sadr gradually expanded his efforts to help a sect whose numbers had increased from 225,000 in 1948 to an estimated 750,000 in the mid–1970s.[37] He came into his own with the founding in 1974 of the *Harakat al-Mahrumin*, or Movement of the Deprived, a campaign that at times sought to speak specifically for the empowerment of Shiites and, at other times, worked to shed its explicitly sectarian character, speaking on behalf of all citizens deprived of their rights. (That aspect of the movement can still be seen within Hezbollah.) The civil war, which erupted in 1975, interrupted his campaign and forced the community to take steps to defend itself amid the growing anarchy of zealous Christian militias, Palestinian fighters who had carved out a state within a state, intervention by a Syrian overlord and pressure from an opportunistic Israel. Sadr's followers started their own militia, Amal, which means "hope" in Arabic,[38] but his own efforts were cut short in 1978 when he suddenly vanished while on an official visit to Libya. Moammar Qadhafi's government, the leading suspect in his disappearance, has insisted, somewhat incredulously, that he left the country and took a plane bound for Rome. To this day, the reasons for his disappearance are little more than rumors, but the mystery remains a powerful symbol for Lebanese Shiites. To some, it echoes a central figure in Shiite theology, the twelfth imam, a descendant of the Prophet Mohammed considered the rightful leader of Islam, who vanished in the ninth century. For Shiites, the Day of Judgment will bring his messianic return.[39] Sadr's disappearance also came at a time that events abroad were shaping the community's destiny. His departure preceded by a year the Iranian Revolution, an event that catapulted a radical Shiite Islam to the forefront of world politics and invigorated a Shiite community in Lebanon that was becoming more politicized each year.

Hezbollah was conceived in that environment. As with Hamas, it was nurtured under the circumstances of strife, responding to a specific threat—in both cases, Israel. With the avowed aim of wiping out the Palestinian resistance in Lebanon, Israel once again sent its tanks across the border of its northern neighbor in 1982. The invasion extracted a terrible toll: Thousands were killed and tens of thousands more were wounded en route to further wrecking an already wrecked country. The fighting that ensued against the Israelis gave birth to the movement, which started as an offshoot of Amal cultivated by Iranian support. It would not announce its existence until 1985, but by then, its presence was already known, largely through the suicide attacks on Israeli and American targets.

Through much of the 1990s, Hezbollah's military operations against the Israeli presence made its reputation abroad and, to a degree, inside Lebanon. Across the war-scarred wadis of southern Lebanon, it fought a guerrilla war to dislodge the demoralized Israeli army and its allies in the vaingloriously named South Lebanon Army, a proxy militia of 2,500 funded, armed and trained by Israel. In its early years, Hezbollah was notorious for sending waves of zealous fighters in reckless, frontal assaults on Israeli positions. Most were simply mowed down. In later years, the movement became far more sophisticated, fielding an army of anywhere from 300 to 1,000 divided in cells and armed with night-vision equipment, Sagger antitank missiles and several variants of the Katyusha rocket.[40] Everyone seemed to notice the change, most of all the Israelis. As Timur Goksel, the spokesman for the UN forces in Lebanon who had served there since 1979, once told me, "These guys learn from their mistakes. One thing I think that makes Hezbollah stand out from other militias in Lebanon is that they are good students. They take their lessons very carefully."

By the 1990s, Hezbollah had thoroughly infiltrated the South Lebanon Army, gaining advance word on Israeli and SLA patrols in the uneven buffer area, which was about nine miles wide, roughly one-twelfth the total area of Lebanon.[41] Above all, it remained elusive. Its soldiers carried weapons by hand, motorcycle or in pickup trucks over the ancient, terraced hills of olive trees and cedars. It was rare to see a Hezbollah fighter in the open anywhere in Lebanon, a sharp contrast to the wartime tradition of other Palestinian and Lebanese militias, which seemed to exercise under the principle of the more checkpoints the better. And its confidence seemed to soar as the conflict dragged on and an Israeli withdrawal became imminent. Its television station, al-Manar, broadcast footage of the operations, the shaky videotape captured by fighters carrying handheld cameras. (Afterward, the tapes were delivered to the Associated Press and Reuters, which transmitted them internationally.) In one tape, the footage showed an Israeli soldier in a pillbox on a rocky hilltop. He was within range of a Hezbollah rifle, yet there was no firing and no attack. The suggestion was psychological: We can get you, it seemed to say, and that was enough for them. In May 2000, Israel completed the withdrawal of its 1,000 soldiers from Lebanon, all but acknowledging defeat. The SLA had already crumbled, its members turning themselves in or fleeing to Israel. Hezbollah guerrillas and jubilant civilian supporters then swept into village after village. In many of those locales, the guerrillas were granted a hero's welcome. Fighters were met with rice, rose petals and goodwill. The war, as Hezbollah well knew, was coming to an end.

Hezbollah understood the popularity that the Islamic Resistance, known in Arabic as *al-Muqawama al-Islamiyya*, delivered it in Lebanon. Of all Lebanese, only its guerrillas had taken up arms against the Israelis in the south and, throughout the struggle, they enjoyed a reputation as fearless, devoted fighters willing to sacrifice themselves before an army considered one of the toughest in the world. But in a telling example of how impressions in the West can diverge from the reality on the ground, Hezbollah was even better known in Lebanon for its social services, their development mirroring a conscious decision the group made after the civil war's end to become more Lebanese, shedding some of its Iranian trappings. (Its political and ideological transformation will be addressed in Chapter 8.) For a constituency of 1.2 million Shiite Muslims in southern Lebanon, the Bekaa Valley in eastern Lebanon and the poor southern suburbs of Beirut, it devoted most of its resources and its organizational ability to run nine schools, three hospitals, sixteen pharmacies and thirteen dental clinics, spending millions of dollars a year, made possible by Iran, under the auspices of the Relief Committee.

The committee is a paragon of organization, and Hezbollah has distinguished itself in Lebanon by its lack of corruption, its ability to mobilize its cadres and its success in delivering what it sets out to do, be it health services or armed attacks. An example of its sophistication is its targeting of resources. The committee divides people seeking its services into three categories: those without a breadwinner in the family, those with health problems and those with unexpected financial burdens. In addition to food, clothing and household supplies like blankets, mattresses, kitchen utensils and furniture, it delivers them money, too. In 1992, more than 21,000 families received $2,915,000, far outdoing the Lebanese government's meager abilities.[42] The aid went beyond simple welfare and the provision of health services. Hezbollah also set out to provide families with equipment to start their own businesses such as knitting machines, livestock and even beehives. In a first for Lebanon, it opened an employment office as well.

The war remains a defining feature of life in Lebanon, particularly in the predominantly Shiite areas of Beirut and southern Lebanon. At the height of the fighting, Hezbollah's Jihad al-Binaa, or Construction Crusade, began delivering water to the neighborhoods, setting up dozens of water tanks. They were supplied by seven huge water tankers twice a day.[43] The organization also dug wells, repaired sewers, collected garbage, built power stations and laid electricity cables. Its teams were always on call in the south, which bore the brunt of the fighting. After a ferocious Israeli campaign in April 1996, known as "Operation Grapes of Wrath," Hezbollah claimed to have repaired 5,000 Lebanese homes, rebuilt roads and provided compensation to 2,300 farmers.[44] It doesn't avoid the personal touch, either. After shell-fire by the Israeli-allied militiamen tore up a house in the village of Hadatha, one of the teams plastered gaping holes in the front stairs, plugged a smashed sewer pipe and shored up a delicate trellis holding aloft the gnarled branches of a grapevine.[45] In the wake of the Israeli withdrawal, teams sprayed insecticides in thirty-five villages and dispatched veterinarians to check up on cattle. Mobile clinics were sent to outlying villages. Hezbollah also took over the only hospital in the village of Bint Jbeil, and doctors soon began performing operations and delivering babies.[46]

None of the aid could exist without the largesse of Iran, Hezbollah's patron. The movement's leaders are famously reluctant to speak about how much they receive.[47] The estimates run from anywhere to $10 million to $20 million a month, although much of that money may not be directly from the Iranian government. As in Saudi Arabia and other Gulf countries, money is provided by individuals performing the religious duty of paying alms. For Shiites, that includes *zakat*, a tax on assets, and *khoms*, a tax on income. A portion of that comes from individuals in Iran but also Lebanese who leave money in donation boxes carried by young boys in yellow caps at virtually every Shiite mosque in Hezbollah strongholds. As with Hamas, those donations make possible support that would not be available otherwise. The movement also has secured income from other sources that are becoming more important as the movement matures, in part out of the belief that Iranian funding will not last forever. Hezbollah runs cooperative supermarkets in the Beirut suburbs and other areas of the country. Revenue also comes from school fees, as well as bookshops, farms, fisheries, factories and bakeries. In addition, it manufactures Islamic clothing, which it exports to expatriate Lebanese Shiite communities in Africa, the United States and South America, in themselves another source of donations and support.[48]

It takes little more than a skeptical view of Hezbollah to suggest the vast services they provide are geared mainly toward the movement's recruitment and support. With a battle against Israel in the south, the movement needed the support of the people in the war zone and, in typically enlightened military fashion, it set out to win the hearts and minds of the noncombatants. Hajj Nayef Kraim, a Hezbollah spokesman, suggested as much to me. I met him at the group's office in south Beirut, a neighborhood that nearly ten years after the war remained a dreary convocation of soiled, cement buildings more akin to Cairo's slums than the ritzy hubs of restaurants, bars and night-clubs of a more prosperous, libertine Beirut just miles away. Like other Hezbollah officials, he endlessly sounded the theme of the fight against the Israeli occupation, a struggle that virtually no one in Lebanon would condemn, at least publicly. To him, everything was tied into that crusade. "We are carrying out a struggle against the occupation," Kraim told me, as cellular-toting functionaries walked in and out of the Hezbollah office.[49]

> This struggle demands sacrifices, sacrifices that are coming from the people. If the people are going to be able to keep sacrificing, they need support, aid and help. This of course helps to solidify the popularity and the support of Hezbollah at a basic level, and it helps to bring additional support to the movement's fundamental project and that is the resistance project. People support Hezbollah because at the same time that it resists the occupation it is concerned, too, with the mass-es that it helps. It is concerned with the masses and the people.

In my time in Lebanon, though, I came to doubt that help was sole-ly a strategy. More than self-interest was at work in the hospitals, schools and clinics. There seemed to be a duty as well, an acknowledg-ment of the historic neglect of Lebanon's Shiites (although the facili-ties were open to all Lebanese, Shiites were their main beneficiary) and a determination born of religious loyalty and devotion to lift the community out of its woeful circumstances. In doing so, they had wholeheartedly pursued the reinterpretation of *da'wa:* To a large degree, they were acting out of an Islamic obligation to help the poor and provide assistance to the less fortunate. It was a theme sounded time and again by the low-ranking officials who ran the schools and hospitals that Hezbollah had set up.

Ali Bazzoun was one of them. A tall balding man with a beard and dressed in green and black, the colors of Hezbollah, he showed me

around al-Mahdi School in Beirut, which had gone from a kindergarten in 1993 that served 350 students to an elementary and middle
school that now served nearly 1,000 students. It employed 60 teachers
and 20 administrators, who helped provide scholarships to 1 out of 5
students. On the clean, green walls were pictures with captions
penned inside drawings of bees: "be honest," "be kind," "be careful,"
"be fair," "be polite" and "be prompt." Outside in a cement play-
ground, children in blue smocks played under the supervision of
women in full black veils. For the forty-three-year-old Bazzoun, the
war in the south was distant.

"Schools are necessary, hospitals are necessary, social services are
necessary. Everything complements the other and makes the whole,"
he told me. "Hezbollah provides water, fixes streets, opens schools
and runs hospitals. This is not the responsibility of Hezbollah. It is the
responsibility of the state, but it's not present here. The government
hasn't done these things." He paused for a moment, then added
earnestly: "We can't be patient, we can't sit around and wait."

I heard a similar sentiment from Adel Ollaik, the handsome director
of al-Janoub Hospital in the southern town of Nabatiyeh, within eye-
sight of Israeli positions. Just twenty-three years old, his beard and
wire-rimmed glasses giving him the look of an intellectual, he had
directed the facility for three years. The prices were cheaper than the
market—"we intend to serve, not to gain money," he told me—and its
sixty doctors were considered part of one of the best emergency staffs
in the region. He eagerly anticipated the day the war would end, when
the movement would have the opportunity to become even more
mainstream, legitimized as just another actor in the Lebanese political
arena. "After the war," he told me, "Hezbollah will succeed more
because the role of the social institutions, health institutions and education institutions will become stronger. There will be more interest
in the social services. We are a tough competitor in every field."

That attitude is one of the most remarkable features of today's
Hezbollah. It is already a political actor, accepted by the government
and tolerated, although not actively supported, by a vast majority of
the Lebanese public. In addition to the popular television station, it
operates a twenty-four-hour radio station (al-Nur, or the Light), a
weekly newspaper (al-Ahd, or the Pledge) and a Web site (www.hizbol-
lah.org). To a government it once vowed to overthrow, it now pledges
respect—an important acknowledgment when its services outperform

the government's programs among the increasingly prominent Shiite population. The group's secretary-general, Hassan Nasrallah, an impressive figure who was elected to lead the movement at the age of thirty-two, made that intention clear in an interview in 1998: "Hezbollah, whatever its capability, ability and institutions, is not a state and not a state within a state, either."[50] The Lebanese government, for its part, has had far less problem with Hezbollah's social activism than its military operations, which drew an occasionally devastating Israeli response as far north as Beirut. The government has registered the Relief Committee, the Islamic Health Committee and Jihad al-Binaa, sanctioning their work as well as business ventures, health services and educational programs. The group is licensed to construct clinics, hospitals, schools, research institutes, orphanages and centers for the disabled. It is authorized to make school and university loans, provide financial assistance for housing and give money to help start businesses.[51] Hezbollah may remain a guerrilla group, but it is that type of welfare that makes the organization. In that way, the movement is one step beyond Hamas. It shares with it the reinterpretation of *da'wa*, a religiously sanctioned activism for the betterment of the community, and the popular support it draws. Yet unlike Hamas, it has succeeded in using that same instrument to gain widespread legitimacy, to shed its confrontational stance vis-à-vis the government and other actors in Lebanon, entering into the mainstream of political life and positioning itself for the years ahead when armed action will have become no more than a chapter in Hezbollah's evolution.

The best example, I thought, of Hezbollah's coming of age in Lebanon was a story about soccer, a virtual religion in much of the Arab world. As with most everything else in the country, the fourteen soccer teams in Lebanon's national league are colored by faith. The Druze have a team and so do the Maronite Christians. The Sunni Muslims have their own, which was loyal to Rafik Hariri, a wealthy Sunni who served as prime minister (it was the league's best). Even the Armenians, long a presence in Lebanon, have a stake. They claim two teams—Homenmen and Homentmen—which took the idea of sectarian loyalty a step further. One was faithful to Armenian leftists, the other's fealty went to the community's right wing. Then, as if just another team in league play, there was al-Ahd, competing for the first year in the national league. The team, it turned out, was the standard-bearer of Hezbollah. This Hezbollah, though, was a very civilian Hezbollah: The team played down its connections to anything militant or, for that matter, political. Instead, it was all about soccer, a point that the club's president insisted on making clear to me.

"Any movement in Lebanon—be it sports, politics or economics— will have political implications," said Hajj Amin al-Shiri, whose office in south Beirut had a box marked for donations to Hezbollah guerrillas. "But it's our goal to keep politics away from sports. The goal of the club is soccer, nothing else."

Players, too, were reluctant to talk politics. If they spoke of Hezbollah, they referred to their responsibility to play with the proper attitude of devout Muslims. That discipline meant the team had not a single red or yellow penalty card in 1997 and the fewest of any team in 1998. The players made clear their code to me: Don't argue with referees, don't pick fights and always take heckling in stride. As for the fans, most of them from Beirut's southern suburbs, they were the best behaved. I went to game day on one Saturday, the match itself a microcosm of Lebanon: al-Ahd played al-Hikma, a Christian team, in a Druze neighborhood at a stadium plastered with slogans for the Druze political party. Al-Ahd fans turned out in droves. Like Hezbollah, they were well-organized and ardent, waving flags and placards and beating a drum to chants blared through a megaphone. Most of the way, the match was scoreless, but fans kept up their fervor, gasping at each missed goal, applauding each save. Occasionally, they shouted to the goalie, "God be with you!" Perhaps he was, I thought, as the game ended. Al-Ahd won 1–0.

In fifteen years, Hezbollah had gone from suicide bombers to soccer players.

—

Earthquakes, in the catastrophe they bring, have often shown Islamists at their best. In Algeria, Islamic activists responded quickly and effectively when a quake struck in 1989. It was no different in Egypt in 1992 when the first assistance victims saw came not from the government but from the Muslim Brotherhood. A similar story happened in 1999 when a devastating earthquake with a magnitude of 7.4 struck the industrial heartland of Turkey, killing at least 17,000 and injuring more than 40,000. Tens of thousands of buildings tumbled down, leaving 600,000 people homeless, forced to fend for themselves

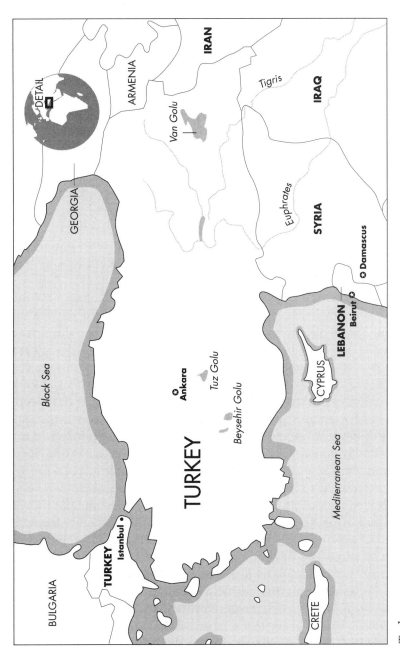

Turkey

in the chaos of the calamity's aftermath. A successful model before them, Islamist groups answered the need. The Virtue Party, the leading Islamist political organization in historically and staunchly secular Turkey, mobilized quickly, funneling millions of dollars into relief efforts. Within days the party plastered posters around Istanbul's poor outskirts showing the crescent moon of Turkey's flag—plus a heart—and a reassuring message for the dazed populace: "Let's heal the wounds together."[52] The Virtue Party mayors of more than twenty municipalities attended to their own towns then fanned eastward into the worst-hit areas, bringing tents, hot meals and baby formula and demonstrating once again the degree of organization the party enjoys. In some areas, mobile telephone stations went up, enabling people within the quake zone to call relatives free of charge. Elsewhere, mobile health clinics began treating the injured and the weary. As the days passed, the party sent wooden bungalows with blue waterproof plastic sheets, a vast improvement over the leaky tents the state had delivered to the area.[53]

The well-organized help was motivated by goodwill, undoubtedly, but there was a political message as well. "Citizens were waiting for help from the people they voted for," said Huseyin Burge, the Virtue Party mayor of Bayrampasa, a suburb of Istanbul. "They wanted to see their politicians alongside them. But they did not see it. I'm sure the response will be seen at the ballot box."[54] The government likely thought the same thing. Its efforts in the catastrophic first days were woeful, and its officials appeared at a loss about what to do in the face of such a disaster. As anger rose at local corrupt administrators for permitting shoddy housing construction, the entire political system, for a while, seemed under indictment. Yet the government responded like so many others have in the face of Islamist success—stop the help, even if it aids the people. The government froze the bank accounts of two Islamic organizations active in quake relief, ostensibly because they had failed to get permission to collect aid money. When asked why the government had cracked down, Murat Yilmaz, an official with one of the groups, said sarcastically, "We were probably targeted because we are devoted Muslims who pray five times a day."[55]

The work of Turkey's Islamists represents the most striking transformation of *da'wa* in a context where it is most unlikely. Like Russia before the Bolshevik Revolution, Turkey would seem one of the least probable places to witness the emergence of one of the Muslim world's most successful Islamist movements. Russia was thought to have no workers; Turkey was thought to have no Muslims who weren't thoroughly secular and Westernized.

During its short history, the Turkish Republic has borne the very distinct imprint of Kemal Ataturk, an almost mythical war hero who fought the Allies at Gallipoli in World War I, turned back invading Greek armies from Anatolia in 1922 then set out to deliberately destroy the discredited multiethnic, multireligious Muslim caliphate of the 600-year-old Ottoman Empire, once one of the world's most powerful. He sought to replace it with an unremittingly secular, pro-Western nation state that would draw together its disparate elements—Kurds in the East, Muslim refugees from the Balkans, peasants displaced by war from the Anatolian hinterland—under the banner of Turkish nationalism. To a degree he was successful. For decades, Turkey was considered the most secular of Muslim states. The sultanate and the caliphate of the Ottoman Empire were abolished in 1924. The Ministry of Pious Foundations, religious courts and religious titles followed and, by 1926, a secular civil code of law from Switzerland was in place. The Arabic script that Ottoman Turkish used was replaced with Latin script in 1928, and the Turkish language was purged of its substantial Persian and Arabic influences, a move that not only distanced the country from the Arab and the Muslim world but also from the language and script of the Quran. The shift took on symbolic importance when, a year later, the provision that Islam was the religion of the state was dropped from the constitution. Sunday instead of Friday was made the day of rest and, for a while, even the call to prayer from mosques was ordered to be in Turkish. In 1937, still in the heyday of a Jacobin secular onslaught, the philosophy of absolutist secularism in the Turkish Republic was enshrined in a constitutional amendment, at a time that Turks were forbidden from performing the *hajj*, the pilgrimage to Mecca that is an obligation of Muslims.[56]

Ironically, in my time in Turkey, a neo-Ottoman revival of sorts was under way, particularly in Istanbul, a city that speaks of empire with its awesome vistas of domes, minarets and crescents. I sensed almost a longing for a romanticized imperial past, and there seemed to be a fascination with all things Ottoman—from academic inquiries to television sitcoms and film. Bookstores were selling histories of the Ottoman Empire, anecdotes from an Ottoman military commander, a

survey of Turkish Sufism and an account from the life of a janissary,
the once elite imperial troops. Many saw a political element as well:
An identity forged by faith rather than ethnicity could serve as an
umbrella for Kurds and Turks, Circassians and Bosnians, creating a
new sense of self that would play down the Turkish nationalism of
Ataturk and play up the shared history of the Ottoman Empire and its
underpinning of Islam.[57]

Many of the people I spoke to traced that revival to the influence of
the country's military coup in 1980. The generals, looking for a more
conservative, traditional bedrock for state legitimacy, drafted a constitution that deemed religious courses obligatory for all levels of preuni-
versity education and set up religious seminaries, the first steps
toward a more religiously tolerant atmosphere. As the time
approached for handing over power to a parliamentary government,
the military junta went further, trying to modify the state ideology of
Kemalism with a "Turkish-Islamist synthesis." The concept was
designed to allow a greater state emphasis on Islamic values, in part to
curtail the still potent influence of the left. The program was picked
up by Turgut Ozal, the prime minister who took over the government
in 1983, became president in 1991 and died in office in 1993.[58] He, too,
created a more permissive environment for Islamists in the 1980s,
allowed Muslim foundations and charities to flourish and made possible Islamist access to broadcasting, a jealously guarded preserve of the
governments in Iran and most Arab states.[59] Ozal, in particular, saw in
"moderate Islamism"—a mix of capitalist norms with Islamist mores
and culture—a means to appeal beyond Turkey's borders, particularly
to the newly independent states in Central Asia that had emerged
from the Soviet Union's collapse.[60] Despite the talk of high politics,
the ideas were remarkably similar to the neo-Ottoman umbrella that
would group disparate identities within the country—Turk and Kurd,
for instance—under the banner of Islam.

It was in that environment that the Refah Partisi of Necmettin
Erbakan came into its own, a political party whose legacy still shapes
Turkey's political life. For me, it was the most impressive look at the
how-to of *da'wa*-turned-political campaigning. When I arrived in
Turkey in 1996, Refah, which means welfare in Turkish, was the
largest single party in Parliament and had recently entered a coalition
government, a stunning feat in the historic context of Kemalist
Turkey. Its activists, with a remarkable lack of religious fervor, were

self-confident and assured. They had found a striking degree of success and were not bashful in touting their accomplishments in Istanbul, Ankara and other large towns where their leaders had taken power through elections. Their program was not unlike those of Islamists elsewhere: neither ostensibly capitalist nor socialist. Rather, Refah crusaded for social justice, offered an argument against Western dependence, encouraged cooperation with the Muslim world and railed against inflation that could turn a life's savings into a week's paycheck. Like other Islamists, they won respect for their air of virtue and cleanliness, yet another example of a party succeeding with a searing critique of government corruption and the failure to achieve economic development and social justice. (*Sharia*, given that its abolition was a founding principle of modern Turkey, did not play as prominent—or clear—a role in the Refah Party program as it did in the platforms of Islamic parties in Egypt and much of the Arab world.)[61]

Most effective was the way in which it turned the charity, welfare and aid of Hezbollah and Hamas into the substance of electoral canvassing. Nowhere was that more evident than in the *gecekondu*,[62] the vast shantytowns of winding roads and houses built of cinder blocks that surround Istanbul, Ankara and other Turkish cities. There, candidates accompanied local cadres on visits, offering advice on how to deal with bureaucracies or providing support for weddings and funerals. Women activists took an especially important role, helping to gain access to homes and to establish female networks. So did Kurdish cadres, bringing the message to a marginalized community in its own language, a poignant gesture in the charged ethnic politics of Turkey, where Kurdish guerrillas had fought a devastating fifteen-year insurgency for autonomy in the southeastern part of the country.[63] In municipalities that the party controlled, well-organized foot soldiers efficiently distributed coal, clothing and soup to the neglected and the have-nots, creating a powerful and very visible ethos of community service.

Especially striking was the role of women. At one time, I was told, Refah had more than 2,000 women working in Istanbul, making house-to-house visits, attending funerals and visiting hospitals, schools and prisons. The goal of the party was ambitious: five women working every precinct, every voting booth, making a powerful statement for a movement often maligned for its record on women.[64]

Gulnihal Guldemler was one of those women activists. I met her at a serene park on the Bosporus, where the party had organized a day-long picnic to mark the traditional circumcision of young boys, making possible the coming-of-age celebration for those who could not afford it. Over a plate of yogurt, drinks, pilaf and dessert, courtesy of the party, she told me how her committee was organized in her neighborhood. Each group had a secretary and a president as well as a staff that dealt with local government, public relations, the press, education and economic and social issues. Her group brought coal and wood to the poor in the winter and provided secondhand clothes. It organized seminars on health and education and sponsored flea markets of handmade crafts, activities repeated by similar chapters again and again across the country.

During speeches by party delegates sharply dressed in very Western jackets and ties, I asked her how she separated her religious and political work. Guldemler looked at me quizzically. She considered the question and dismissed it.

"They are not two different ideas," she explained, her gracious brown veil misleading in its powerful suggestion of passivity. "They are one and the same. We are a political party but at the same time we have a philosophy of life."

Turkey's Islamists probably talked about Islam less than any other religious activists I met in the Middle East. Instead, they spoke about action, projecting a can-do mentality that reminded me of the young minds behind a startup company in the Silicon Valley. Their enthusiasm proved intoxicating. At one local headquarters in Istanbul, I met Selami Caliskan, a party activist dressed in yellow tie, blue shirt and slacks. His style was dizzying. In his office, one of the very few without a picture of Ataturk on the wall, he kept moving from the couch to the chair, back to the couch, then every few minutes, he would elect to stand up. "We work as if there are elections tomorrow," he told me, a statement that explained in part his hyperkinetic style. God rarely came up.

What we have accomplished is what we show the people. We don't really have to explain ourselves. Every day since we've come to power, we've opened new roads, new highways, new bridges. In the past, the city's garbage was never collected but we're collecting it now. Until Refah was elected, Istanbul's main problem was water shortages. Now, no one mentions the problem. Now, everyone talks about air pollution and traffic problems. By introducing natural gas for heating, we're going to solve the air pollution problem. What's important is that the job gets done, regardless of whether you're veiled or have a beard, regardless of whether you're a Muslim or a Christian.[65]

Secularists in Turkey were often in awe of Refah's organization, as were many of those who voted for the party, a sizable portion of them not overly devout.[66] Binnaz Toprak, a professor at Bosporus University, told me that part of its success could be traced to the fact that Refah was there when the state was not. "The Refah organization works incredibly well, incredibly well," she told me. "When there's a funeral in the neighborhood, there's a Refah guy there, when there's a wedding, they take a present, when there's an engagement, they do the same. When there's somebody sick, they find a hospital bed. It's this whole network of delivering to their voters." In that, I thought, she spoke to Refah's evolution of *da'wa*. The work was not seen as a religious duty; it was seen as a political campaign, opportunistic perhaps but in the end extremely effective.

After Friday prayers at Sultan Mehmet II mosque in Istanbul, I visited shopkeepers in the neighborhood. Many of the residents I spoke to had supported Refah in the election, citing its cleanliness, its vision of morality and justice and, above all, its effectiveness. One of those residents was Muammer Demir, a twenty-eight-year-old accountant standing outside a grocery store within earshot of the mosque. "We tried all the other political parties," he told me, "and we saw what a mess they've made of Turkey. We also tried Refah and saw how they handled the municipalities. What's not important so much is the religion, but what the parties do for the country. Refah has come here to work, not to change the order, not to change the constitution. It has come to serve the people."

After its string of successes, Refah ran afoul of Turkey's military, the single most influential institution in the country and the guardian of Turkish secularism. Refah had gone from the 1995 election in which it won more seats than any other party to a member of the ruling coalition. In 1997, though, the government fell and the following year the party and its leader, Erbakan, were found guilty by Turkey's top court—on trumped-up evidence and under severe military pressure—of trying to impose religious rule on the country. The party was shut down and Erbakan was banned from politics for five years. Its successor was the Virtue Party, which did not match the success of Refah but employed the same mix of justice and equity backed by an activist, inspired campaign of social work. Although still held in suspicion by the government, it seemed assured of helping shape Turkey's political life. Like Refah, Hezbollah and Hamas, it speaks the language of the street, tapping a current of identity with the ability to deliver effective, grassroots help. In that, it marks the culmination of a striking evolution in Islamist social activism from its origin on the banks of the Suez Canal, directed by Hassan al-Banna. The idea has been transformed into a political tool and sanctioned religiously by being ground in a modernist interpretation of Islam—a religious duty to achieve justice and equality. Politics are local, an adage Islamists know well, and their ability to tie their infrastructure to the needs of an often deprived population sets them apart from both governments and other movements.

Da'wa also provides a clear contrast to the movement's greatest failures: the attempt to impose Islam in an absolutist, intolerant form from above. Although *da'wa* has been the most successful, that style of revolutionary change has been the most visible, and Sudan is its greatest example. Across that country's jarring landscape, where a revolutionary vanguard seized power in 1989, a study in the defeat of an old-style Islamist movement is under way, one that has disavowed the grassroots success of parties in Turkey, Lebanon and Palestine as well as the emerging democratic trends in Egypt so that it could take power. Its authority became reason for its existence. Ironically, though, its defeat has charted a new path for the same movements.

5

Faith and Fatherland

The Monopoly of God and Sudan's Experiment with Islam in Power

THEIR PAUNCH STRETCHING COARSE cotton smocks and their beards peppered with age, middle-age men stand in lines under a scorching Sudanese sun clenching Kalashnikovs with no bullets. A terse "God is most great" calls them to attention, the start of another day of training in Sudan's Popular Defense Forces, a two-month ritual required of students, civil servants and the party faithful on this suffering frontier of the Muslim world. Under a watchful eye, the sweaty bureaucrats double-time in heat that easily surpasses 110 degrees. Chants of devotion to God punctuate their seven hours a day of drills, those chants interspersed by proper time for prayer. At night, after their drills are done, revolutionary cadres half their age and with twice their enthusiasm lead the bone-tired militiamen in sing-alongs that celebrate Islamic valor and self-sacrifice. Across the dusty lot stand four lonely portraits of *shuhada,* young martyrs who lost their lives in a seemingly endless civil war against Christians and animists in southern Sudan that the Islamic government declares a religious crusade.

Sudan's propagandists showcase the militia as the front line in a crusade for faith and fatherland. It serves, they say, as the fist of a revolution instilling zeal in its followers to adhere to the camp's motto: holy war, victory and martyrdom. The properly zealous—and there are more than a few in this country—stand eager to comply.

"When I get the chance, I will go and fight," declares Ali Mohammed Ali, a balding banker standing in formation, a month of camp already behind him. The drills, he says, "prepare me well for the enemy"—something of which his government has no shortage.

Only here in Sudan, Africa's largest country, among its poorest and one of its most diverse, did an Islamist group achieve its greatest ambition—seizing control of a government, setting out to transform a society and fashioning itself as a model to emulate. In opposition, its savvy, Western-educated leaders offered a textbook lesson on taking power—a single-minded vanguard pursuing power, something akin to Islamic Bolshevism. Then, after assuming control in a coup in 1989, they sought to turn the shibboleths of their activist days into action, remaking the traditionalism of mystical orders and powerful families that have long dominated Sudan. Their example was Islam in power. Here, activists no longer had the luxury of making promises. Rather, their clique of reformers, revolutionaries and putschists had to deliver, going beyond the appeal the faith offered to Muslims in Cairo, Gaza, Istanbul or Beirut and leaving a record on which they could be judged.

In earlier chapters, Islam was seen in opposition: as a sometimes violent force of the disinherited and as an effective network of charity and welfare with a grassroots message and appeal. In Palestine, for example, a movement tailored a universalist message of faith to a long-standing but, in many ways, very local conflict over land. It worked in the community and was shaped by the community's grievances. In Turkey, a similar community-based approach evolved into mass-based party politics. Sudan, on the other hand, is the inverse of this style of activism, a program of revolutionary change from above that sought to create an ideology of government rooted in religion and appropriate to the modern world. Its approach was elitist and intolerant; its legacy dangerous. A decade on, it serves best perhaps as a window on old-style Islamic politics, in which the tight-knit vanguard of Egypt's Sayyid Qutb acts as an agency of change, controlling the levers of authority (in Sudan's version, irrespective of the popular will). The Islamic state is then devised, sometimes gradually, sometimes abruptly, by all-knowing technocrats who set out to create a modern Islamic alternative. By example, Sudan has offered a powerful and compelling

Sudan

contrast to today's changing politics and their potential success. It is also a study in the failure of one particular incarnation: a how-to in what not to do with political Islam.

Soon after arriving in Sudan from Cairo, I met one of its architects, Ghazi Salah al-Din al-Atabani. Like many of his colleagues, he was educated in England, where he went for a medical degree and a Ph.D. in endocrinology. He returned home in 1985 and, in revolutionary fashion, left the profession to join Hassan al-Turabi's National Islamic Front, rising through the ranks after the government came to power. Intelligent and articulate, he was described by the American ambassador as "a formidable opponent" and considered one of the government's most prominent intellectuals and spokesmen.[1] In my interviews with him, I thought he suffered from the arrogance of power—and the resistance to criticism that brings—but to be at times persuasive and remarkably accessible. In our first encounter in 1996, he seemed to relish the idea of describing the rise to power of he and his cohorts—in his eyes, "an Islamic state in the making."[2] Like Islamists everywhere, he elaborated a concept of a modern, viable Islam.

At work, Atabani told me, was an attempt "to break the mold of traditional Islam and create a modern state whereby you have Islam addressing questions of democracy, questions of human rights, minority rights, women's rights, questions of economy—in a nutshell, addressing all the questions pertaining to a modern society and a modern state, that is, trying to marry the ideals of Islam to the needs and challenges of modernity. . . . It is the basic cultural question of a traditional society facing up to the realities of the modern world, which is primarily Western in its outlook, in its ways, in its attitudes."

Then, with a hint of defensiveness, he held up their experiment as a model. "We are builders, we are constructors, we are not destructive in our attitudes," he insisted. "You have a very constructive model and no one denies it, even our enemies don't deny that we are trying to build a model. Their quarrel with us is they don't like the model."

En route to building the blueprint of an Islamic government and symptomatic of the approach it took in realizing its ambitions, Sudan angered virtually all its neighbors—Egypt, Eritrea, Ethiopia and Uganda (even mercurial Libya became uneasy with its politics).[3] President Hosni Mubarak of Egypt blamed its leaders for an assassination attempt on him in Addis Ababa, Ethiopia, in 1995, accusations that prompted gunbattles over a patch of acacia trees, jagged mountains and flat, sandy coast along the border that was claimed by both countries. The United States, at times unfairly, lambasted Sudan's leaders throughout the 1990s. It added the country to its list of nations sponsoring terrorism, making it ineligible for U.S. support in seeking assistance from international financial institutions like the World Bank.[4] In January 1996, the State Department withdrew American diplomats from the capital, Khartoum, and nearly two years later, in November 1997, the Clinton administration imposed severe economic sanctions that included a ban on bank loans, an end to imports of goods from Sudan and the seizure of Sudanese assets in the United States. The following year, it attacked Khartoum with a barrage of Tomahawk cruise missiles, hitting a sprawling pharmaceutical plant on the outskirts of the capital that produced medicine to treat malaria and tuberculosis, had a contract to export veterinary antibiotics to Iraq under UN approval and, not unlikely, was the wrong target. The United States maintained it was making precursors to chemical weapons.

The government had few friends at home as well, the population estranged by the program of Islamization that was orchestrated by the coup's clique of junior army officers and, in the background, well-organized Islamic activists. After a period of consolidation, when resistance of unions, students and professionals was systematically crushed, the program went into full swing in 1991, seeking to impose religious orthodoxy in a country whose diversity is striking even by the standards of Africa.

Sudan sprawls across a territory equal to the United States east of the Mississippi, bordering nine countries, from Egypt in the north to Uganda in the south. The Blue Nile flows, at times in torrents, from the Ethiopian highlands into eastern Sudan, and the White Nile meanders from Lake Victoria in Uganda through the swamp and savanna of Sudan's south. They join in the relatively young city of Khartoum, a former nineteenth-century military outpost whose name in Arabic means an elephant's trunk.[5] Across the territory, the country's 26 million people, impoverished by the bitter civil war and wretched economic conditions, are divided into more than 450 ethnic groups and speak more than 130 languages.[6] Only about 60 percent—or three of every five—call themselves Muslim. The country is culturally Arab in the north, and the south is tied more to the countries of sub-Saharan

Africa. In between, the shades of coloration speak to politics and faith, a reality the government, blinded by the purity of its vision, steadfastly refused to recognize.

—

Religion has defined Sudan's modern history to a degree unseen in other Arab countries, with the possible exception of Saudi Arabia, and understanding the history of its arrival is crucial to grasping the nature of today's Islamic government. Islam was slow to reach Sudan, first making contact more than three centuries after the prophet's death when a representative of the Fatimid dynasty, based in Cairo, visited the Nubian king at his court in Dongola. He sought to convert him to Islam, but failed, although a small Muslim presence was established. The conversion that followed was slow. Despite the image in the West of the faith being spread by the sword, the growth of Islam in much of the Muslim world was an often reluctant, at times imperceptible process. Egypt, for instance, likely had a Christian majority centuries after the Arab general Amr ibn al-As arrived in the Sinai Peninsula in 639 at the head of a conquering force of 3,000 cavalry. Even today, as much as a third of parts of southern Egypt is still Christian. In Sudan, conversion was even more gradual, largely through the peaceful spread of Sufi orders, which brought the religion and language of Islam and still exert a powerful influence over Sudanese society.[7] Sufism is a form of Islamic mysticism that began to develop as early as the first century of Islam, stressing the personal, emotional relationship of the individual to God and providing a contrast to the more austere Islam propagated by the orthodox clergy of places like al-Azhar in Cairo.[8] Often embracing folk customs and pagan practices, fraternities of Sufi adherents gathered under a sheikh, or religious leader, hastened the spread of Islam throughout Asia and Africa. It comprises an eclectic insight into the way Islam transforms and, in the process, is transformed by the communities it converts. That reality struck me in nearly every country I visited. In Sudan, for instance, on the desert plain outside Omdurman, the sister city of Khartoum, I met Sufi dervishes dressed in red and green, the colors of the sect, swaying in a circle to the escalating beat of a drum that sounded African to Western ears. A trace of incense mixed with clouds of sand and dust kicked up by the dervishes, cloaking their circle against the backdrop of a setting sun. A continent away in

Afghanistan, I met another mystic who almost lost consciousness as he listened to the slow, melodic recitation of Persian poetry in a second-floor lodge on the outskirts of Kabul. Both considered themselves Muslims and Sufis, but they shared little other than their belief in God.

The Sufi orders (individually known as a *tariqa*) became a firmly established part of Sudan's religious identity during the period of the Muslim Funj sultanate, which lasted from 1504 to 1821 and maintained its capital at Sennar along the Blue Nile. Under its tutelage, the religion flourished, establishing ties with the Hejaz, the rugged, western part of the Arabian Peninsula that is home to the two holy cities of Mecca and Medina.[9] To this day, that influence can be heard in the distinctive Sudanese dialect of Arabic, and migration still crosses between the two countries, though the traffic across the Red Sea is almost exclusively by laborers from poorer Sudan to richer Arabia (or those returning laden with televisions, video recorders, refrigerators and other consumer goods). Another legacy is the relative failure of the Sufi orders and of Islam in general to penetrate deep into the south of Sudan, largely the reason that Arabic remains the language of just half of Sudan's people. The division was later made formal under British colonial rule that only ended in 1956. The divide still exists today, and many in Sudan blame it for the country's chronic civil strife.

Modern Sudan took shape in the nineteenth century, often through wrenching turmoil and epic conflict brought upon it by Egypt, Britain and its own mystic warlords. In 1820, forces under the Egyptian khedive, an Ottoman governor who was all but independent of the fading empire, crossed the border south into Sudan, an invasion horrifying at times in its brutality. The Turkish-Egyptian conquest, which in addition to regular troops relied on mercenaries and European adventurers, reached as far as present-day Uganda by 1870,[10] and the Egyptian troops imposed a harsh colonial rule on Sudan that still resonates in the often-tense relations between the two countries. At the time, Britain was strengthening its hold on Egypt, in part a result of the country's financial woes, and began exercising greater influence south of the border. Its representative was an English soldier named Charles George "Chinese" Gordon, who was appointed governor general of Sudan by the Egyptian khedive in 1877. In a short time, his fate would be inextricably tied to a Sudanese mystic and nationalist with pretenses of prophethood named Mohammed Ahmad ibn Abdallah, a boat-builder's son from northern Sudan.

Mohammed Ahmad was regarded by his Sudanese followers as the *mahdi*, a sanctified figure guided by God to restore the reign of justice in the world. He called his followers *ansar*, a term that refers to the "helpers" of the Prophet Mohammed, and consciously modeled his community on the early *umma* of seventh-century Arabia. An ambitious figure, he saw himself as a reformer and successor to the prophet and campaigned against the corruption of the faith that he saw around him. In 1881, as Sudan bristled under a foreign overlord, the Mahdi turned his words into action. He led a revolt that swept away often incompetent Egyptian rule in a series of startling victories that put most of Sudan under his unique religious and political movement. In it were the first stirrings of Sudanese nationalism and a distinct identity within the country began to emerge. Four years later, his war culminated in the conquest of Khartoum after a legendary but foolhardy defense by Gordon, who was under British orders to evacuate the city rather than defend it. In the decisive battle, the Mahdi sent 40,000 followers through a breach in the city's wall created by a Nile flood, and they quickly overwhelmed the English soldier's defenses. Gordon, fighting with revolver and sword in his celebrated last stand, was speared, shot then speared again before he died. His severed head was brought in a bloody cloth to an enraged Mahdi, who had given strict orders that Gordon be taken alive. Gordon himself, a deeply spiritual but unhappy man, probably anticipated dying as a Christian martyr, and his passing left a lasting imprint on Britain, where a demand for revenge contributed in part to a ferocious reconquest years later.[11]

The Mahdist state, known as the *Mahdiyya*, lasted for fourteen years, although the Mahdi himself died soon after Khartoum fell, probably of typhus. Its brief tenure sought to create a new identity that transcended tribal and local boundaries, namely by focusing a restored Islam on the Mahdi's veneration. Because he was the Mahdi, for instance, devotion to him meant that the *hajj*, the pilgrimage to Mecca, was no longer necessary. In fact, after his death in 1885, the *hajj* was replaced by visits to his tomb in Omdurman.[12] It brought, too, a new vision of Islam or, more specifically, a *reformed* vision. *Jihad*, the key to the movement's spread, was extolled. Despite the movement's origins in Sufism, traditions that had evolved over hundreds of years were banned, such as the practice of magic processions, marriage and circumcision feasts and visits to saints' tombs. Like many revivalist movements, it was high-handed, self-confident in its authority and vision and, above all, puritanical.[13] But in a foreshadowing of present-day Sudan, the austerity of its program sat uneasily with the marked eclecticism and divergent beliefs of a population chronically suspicious of authority.

In time, the state was undermined, too, by forces beyond its control. Famine made life hard, and the imperialist designs of Egypt and Britain made it remarkable that it survived as long as it did. The beginning of the end was in April 1898 when Major General Horatio Herbert Kitchener attacked the Mahdist army outside Omdurman with a force of British, Egyptian and Sudanese troops and wiped it out in fifteen minutes. The remaining forces retreated and the two sides dug in. Six months later, Kitchener entered Omdurman after another brief but horrifically bloody battle. He razed the Mahdi's tomb and, in a vengeful, humiliating gesture, scattered his bones in the Nile. From that time until independence in 1956, Sudan was ruled by a colonial arrangement known as the Anglo-Egyptian condominium. Although the British and Egyptians were to share authority, it was the British who ran the show, their influence still visible in the capital's architecture, and, until recently, the education at Khartoum University.

An even more lasting effect of their rule was the so-called "Closed Door" policy, under which interaction between the Arabized, predominantly Muslim north and the African south was restricted. Resources went to the north, where a Sudanese, English-speaking elite began to emerge. In the south, a separate education system run by Christian missionaries evolved and, at the expense of Arabic, the use of English was taught and encouraged. At the time, with the end of imperialism yet on the horizon, the British had wanted to keep southern Sudan separate so as to attach it to their colonies in eastern and central Africa, and the policy prevented the development of ties that might have bound together the fractious country after independence. The repercussions have devastated the country. Except for a ten-year hiatus, the army has fought southern rebels since the British left, a civil war that stands as one of the longest and most destructive in the world. The numbers fluctuate wildly, but it is no exaggeration to say that at least one million southerners have died in the fighting and in famines and poverty created by the war, which has been fought almost exclusively in their region. Many times that number—estimates by

the United Nations put the total at 4 million—have been driven from
their homes. A depressing number of them have settled in huts of
mud, sticks, cardboard, sacks or plastic that ring Khartoum in a moon-
scape of misery.

—

Sudan today is an Arab country by language (at least in the north)
and a Muslim country by faith (in the aspiration of its government),
yet it remains on the periphery of both worlds, drawing the lion's
share of its attention by virtue of its disasters of biblical caliber—
droughts, famines and conflict—and its program of political Islam that
has embroiled it in war at home and bouts of tension abroad. Sudan,
however, is no police state nor is it a bleak outback. Despite the distance, I visited Sudan more often than any other country outside
Egypt, and I found it one of the easier places in the Arab world to work
as a journalist. Its people are outspoken and forthright, often fearless
in what they say about the government, its leaders and the programs it
tries to impose. They rarely shy away from giving a reporter their full
name, a gesture almost unheard of in countries like Iraq and Syria, and
they cherish a long-standing tradition of tolerance and dissent, particularly among the educated and cosmopolitan elite. That pluralism
made Sudan's program of Islamization so striking. The model heralded
by Ghazi Salah al-Din al-Atabani was a stringent one.

The conception and execution of its Islamic experiment revolved
around a small wry man with an immaculately groomed beard and a
well-nourished ego named Hassan Abdullah al-Turabi, who has
emerged as a proponent of a modern Islam. A scholar, lawyer, ideologue and operator, Turabi has moved back and forth from Sudan's
political stage for more than a generation, sometimes in jail, sometimes in power, but always a presence on its turbulent landscape. His
career dates to the 1950s when, as a student at the University of
Khartoum, he joined the Muslim Brotherhood, an underground group
inspired by its namesake in Egypt. The son of an Islamic judge, Turabi
was by all accounts a brilliant student, and he soon emerged as a
leader of Islamic activists at the university. He went abroad to earn a
master's degree at the University of London, then a doctorate at the
Sorbonne in Paris. On his return to Sudan, he served as dean of the law
school at the University of Khartoum and became dissatisfied with
the more traditional approach of the Brotherhood to politics. As in

Egypt, Palestine and elsewhere, the movement disavowed an overt role in politics, choosing instead to focus its *da'wa* on the population at large. Once society had returned to the fold of Islam, the Brotherhood believed, an Islamic government would naturally follow. Turabi, as we will see later, broke decisively with those ideas. In the colonial-style, brown-brick buildings of the university, where many of Sudan's leaders today were classmates at one time or another, Turabi formed a group that would become the National Islamic Front (NIF), the key player in Sudan's Islamization.

The NIF enjoyed a reputation of playing politics better than anyone in Sudan. From the 1960s on, working under various names, it operated in the open and underground, choosing its moves deliberately and skillfully. Turabi was its public face. Under the regime of Colonel Jaafar al-Nimeiri, who seized power in a bloodless coup in 1969, Turabi spent time in prison, under house arrest and in exile then, in a turn of events not all that unusual in Sudanese politics, he returned to favor when Nimeiri made an overture to the Islamists in the late 1970s and early 1980s to broaden his faltering support. As Sudan's attorney general, Turabi had a role in the decree in 1983 of the so-called September Laws, which imposed *sharia* on the entire country, helping reignite the civil war, which had been dormant for a decade.[14] The laws included the more stringent criminal punishments of the Islamic legal code—flogging for alcohol consumption, amputation for theft and execution for apostasy. Unlike Libya or Pakistan, where the punishments are on the books but rarely carried out, amputations became disconcertingly common in Nimeiri's Sudan, the victims sometimes visible in Khartoum's streets. Abuses were common. The execution of a prominent, unorthodox Islamic thinker on the grounds of apostasy under the code brought revulsion from a public that saw the act as contradicting Sudan's tradition of political tolerance. Upholding the laws brought moments of the flamboyant and the bizarre, too. In one episode, Nimeiri released 13,000 prisoners to give then a "second chance" under Islamic law. In another, staged before local and foreign journalists, he poured $11 million worth of alcohol into the Nile River, with untold effects on the fish.[15]

Turabi fell out of favor again in March 1985. Nimeiri arrested him as part of an attempt to deal with opposition to his staggering regime. It was too late to salvage it, though. Nimeiri was overthrown in a military coup the following month, eventually going into exile in Egypt, and a year later, a civilian government returned to power along with a renewed parliamentary life. Turabi was freed and, with his National Islamic Front, began to take part in the sometimes chaotic, usually unstable coalition governments that followed under the leadership of Sadiq al-Mahdi, the Oxford-educated great-grandson of the Mahdi. In the election after Nimeiri's ouster, the NIF captured the third-highest number of seats.[16] Despite failing to win a seat in Parliament in that election, Turabi himself went on to serve as justice minister and, in 1989, deputy prime minister and minister of foreign affairs. That same year, the civilian government came to an end when the military moved out of the barracks and back in charge.

Before the coup, the NIF had infiltrated both the bureaucracy and state institutions, setting the stage for a decisive moment. Through the 1970s and 1980s, it took advantage of tax breaks to consolidate an economic base through Islamic banks, particularly in construction, transportation and the media. Nimeiri's government, meanwhile, appointed Islamists to teach "Islamic ideology and instruction" classes to top army officers, providing access to the all-important military.[17] Throughout those years, its support was strongest in urban areas and, like the Brotherhood elsewhere, it drew to its ranks academics, lawyers and doctors as well as traders, financiers, landowners and military officers who benefited economically from their association with the party. At all times, though, it remained at heart an elite movement, plotting the steps that would deliver it power. That moment came with the coup on June 30, 1989, when Brigadier Omar Hassan Ahmad al-Bashir overthrew, without bloodshed, Sadiq al-Mahdi's elected but ineffectual government. To this day, there is debate over the precise role of the NIF in the coup, but it is clear that an Islamist vanguard within the front guided the new regime in its first days and soon played a preeminent role in its policies. Its consolidation of power was a lesson in realpolitik.

Within eighteen months, the front had gone after the institutions that had generated popular opposition in the past. Twenty thousand judges, professors, soldiers and civil servants were fired and replaced with the front's supporters.[18] Military officers said to be involved in coup attempts and likely motivated by their opposition to the Islamist program were executed. Students unions, professional associations and trade unions, groups that had a hand in the overthrow of Nimeiri in 1985 and an earlier military regime in 1964, were shut down or taken over by NIF supporters through tactics that included the detention of rival leaders, dirty tricks and violence.[19] The unions were especially targeted. Labor has a long history in Sudan, which was home to the most powerful communist party in Africa and one of the strongest in the Arab world, and the country's unions often played a role in politics that went beyond the defense of workers' interests. In the transition period after Nimeiri's fall and under Sadiq al-Mahdi's regime, unions served as mediators between the government and the southern rebels. The NIF feared the unions' still sizable influence and, soon after taking power, banned them and confiscated their assets. The new government dismissed hundreds of their leaders from the public sector and ordered the detention without charge or trial of hundreds of activists who had begun to strike in opposition to the military coup. Human rights groups said these activists were systematically tortured in ghost houses, secret places of detention in Khartoum that are outside the prison system and beyond supervision.[20]

Khartoum University was another victim. Built in 1902 by the British along the Blue Nile and originally named Gordon Memorial College after the general who had lost both the battle and his life to the Mahdi in 1885, it figured into every power struggle since Sudan's independence. Like the unions, the university had a hand in the rebellion against two military strongmen as well as years of unrest and dissent, and the NIF was in no mood to leave a potential field of opposition unfettered within its walls. One former professor told me that he felt the newly installed government was vindictive in its crackdown, as if it was determined "to break the mystique of the university." There was certainly irony in the fact that the very men who started their activist careers on campus, exploiting the university's role as a vibrant political arena, would in time turn around and crush the same academic freedom that gave rise to them.[21] As another professor put it to me, "The university was a ladder to power. Now that they've arrived, they've thrown it on the ground so that no one else can climb it."

The assault was quick and decisive. After the coup, and before the year was out, Bashir decreed that the number of students in the universities be doubled, that new public and private universities be created (and, with a lot less history, better controlled) and that Arabic replace English as the language of instruction.[22] Dozens of professors were forced out, and police carried out periodic sweeps to arrest people deemed campus agitators. The government began appointing the universities' administrators, despite protests from staff and faculty, who had elected them as part of their cherished independence from the state. Students, meanwhile, were required to complete training in the Popular Defense Forces, receiving a healthy dose of Islamic indoctrination to go along with their school orientation.[23]

The university I visited during the 1990s was a wreck. Arabization had forced professors to read aloud from English-language books and translate into Arabic because there were not enough texts in translation to distribute. Lecture halls had no chalk and photocopying paper was in short supply. One administration official speculated that the university had lost two-fifths of its professors. Those remaining were paid the equivalent of $30 to $60 a month and the money increasingly did not arrive on time, a testament to Sudan's crumbling economy as much as to government neglect. There were signs of faith and the zeal the regime was supposed to inspire. At the university entrance, a yellow sign was graced with a lamp, one of the few modern touches on a campus that was not just colonial in its appearance. The sign urged women students to wear the veil. Outside the campus' main walls were amateurish portraits erected by the government spaced every ten yards or so of students killed in the civil war. Under the picture was their name with the appellation *shahid* (martyr), his school of study and the date of his death. On more than a few, there were scratch marks as though disgruntled students had scraped keys across the portraits to demonstrate their lack of appreciation for what the Islamic government celebrated as religious sacrifice. Student zeal, in fact, was hard to find there. During a visit in 1997, a rebel offensive had scored successes in eastern Sudan, at one point threatening the dam that supplied Khartoum its electricity. The government slammed shut the doors of the university, exhorting its 20,000 students to the front. "A million martyrs for a new era" was the slogan. In the end, students and professors told me, only about 250 heeded the call.[24]

Adlan al-Hardallu was a professor at Khartoum University whom I visited often during my trips to Sudan. His discipline was political science and he had done graduate work in Germany and the United States. In the 1960s, he began teaching at the university, his thirty years giving him an enviable perspective on Sudan's defining moments. His office, off a dirt road a short walk from the main campus, was a sad reward for that experience. He had no phone or computer. There was an old air-conditioner on the wall but it was broken, its frayed parts looking beyond repair. His lecture halls that once held 100 students were crammed with five times as many, sometimes more, some of whom were forced to sleep outside on the dusty campus grounds because they could not afford rent. (After the coup, the government did away with free housing for students, another source of regular campus protest.) As if to ridicule his plight, his wristwatch didn't work.

"Khartoum University in the minds of these Islamists is the citadel of secularism in the country," Hardallu told me soon after we met. "And some of them have called for dismantling this citadel. The future, as I see it, is rather bleak."

"They say they intend to remold the Sudanese personality in an Islamic form. They want Islam to penetrate all aspects of life. This is what they say, 'Islam should not be kept or restricted to saying your prayers and reading your Quran at home or in the mosque. It has to be part of every activity of every person.' I'm not going to say they've reached this, but this is the program." Hardallu spoke to me as if he had tired of the politics and partisanship that disrupted his once-proud university.

"You can do things with political power more than you can do them with the Quran," he said, summarizing succinctly the NIF's program from the start. "This does not mean a rejection of the Quran. But in order to apply the word of God in society, in many cases it is better first to have political power then, after that, to preach the Quran."

The ruthless pursuit of that political power would have made Lenin's cadres in the Russian Revolution proud. Even the NIF's critics seemed to be in awe of its success. I once asked Abdallahi al-Naim, a lawyer and human rights activist from Sudan who now teaches law at Emory University in Atlanta, about the NIF's ability to take control. "They know their terrain well," he told me, echoing nearly every other critic with whom I spoke.[25] "They know their opponents, they know the political parties and they know how to manipulate them and how to defuse their threats. Credit goes to the NIF as a political machine and to Turabi and his group as effective politicians." In hindsight, the movement was clear-sighted, determined and skilled in choosing the timing and means to capture the instruments of the state that it needed to accomplish its objective. To many, that means the NIF was no different than any other repressive, military-led grab for power in the Third World.

Naim, who taught law at Khartoum University for nearly ten years, saw it that way. "Turabi's project has always been a power-seeking project," he said. "I don't think it was ever a genuinely revolutionary vision. It is not modernist in content. It is modernist in tactics." The repression seemed to worry him. He expressed more disgust than anger with the future of his country, and he feared the implications and repercussions of such a well-organized and ideological police state on religion. It was a criticism I would hear repeated in Iran, another experiment in Islamic governance. To him, the NIF trivialized religion and made it mundane. The movement, he said, was "a certain failure."

"It did not achieve any of its objectives but it has at the same time destroyed something else. It destroyed the wider society's belief in religion as a positive force in their life. It has made them very cynical of any positive role for religion," Naim said. "That streak of pride and self-esteem and open resistance as opposed to whispers that distinguished the Sudanese people, I worry that has been lost. It will take time, energy, imagination and creativity to return to 1989."

I felt Naim's criticism was too strong. The Sudanese I met were devout, despite the government. But the cynicism he spoke of was apparent. In my time in Khartoum, a somnolent city whose streets were often swallowed by waves of sand carried by hot winds off the desert, jokes about the pseudo-Islamist credentials of opportunists were rife. Beards, often a sign of devotion in the Muslim world, became more popular after the coup and, just as quickly, emerged as a favorite object of ridicule among the less religious. A trimmed beard that might help in a job interview was called *min ajl awladi* (for the sake of my children). A bushy beard that might deflect the suspicion of the secret police was nicknamed *ana aiz aish* (I want to live). The intensity of Islamic programming gave rise to another joke: A man takes his television to the repair shop and asks the technician, "Can you fix this mosque for me?" Even repression came in for a ribbing. Years after the coup, as the number of security forces and their auxiliaries multiplied (police, security, popular police, friends of the police, military police), one friend of mine cracked to me that when police officers came to his door, he had to ask them, "Well, which police?"

Yet unlike Naim and others, I never doubted the intentions of the government's leaders. Although seeing Sudan from a distance, I took them at their word—that they were committed Islamists—and I believed that they were sincere in their desire to create an alternative through Islam that would be viable in the modern world, which had educated and socialized many of them. More doubtful was their style, the tactics that Naim loathed. There were worse examples of an Islamic authoritarianism: Afghanistan under the Taliban stood out, and even Iran was a more sinister place in its revolutionary heyday. What made Sudan so disturbing was the degree to which a small clique of leaders had become so assured in their program that they felt confident in imposing it on a population (a population, incidentally, that had already made clear its support for them in the 1986 election, giving the NIF less than a fifth of the seats in Parliament). They were committed to making a revolution without the fervor and creating a new man without the zeal. Even more so than the Brotherhood, Turabi and his colleagues were antidemocratic at heart, eschewing the popular work of Islamists in urban slums, bypassing the proselytizing among the middle class and disaffected professionals and deeming the *da'wa* of other Islamic groups too feeble to deliver them the power they needed to make their vision real. The people only stood in their way. Their message was clear: We will tell them what they need to know and create for them the society in which they need to live. In the Muslim world, there was no better example of Islam from above, a scenario of the faith that was doomed from the start.

—

The architect was, of course, Hassan al-Turabi, who arguably has had the greatest impact on political Islam in the 1990s. In a land of extraordinary contradictions, his contrasts still stand out: a shrewd, even devious politician who makes himself accessible to any and all journalists, particularly from the United States and Europe; an Islamist who speaks the language of a modern, democratic faith but who helped preside over an elitist, repressive Islamization forced on his diverse country; a self-admitted product of the West and its universities who once told me that the United States was "the incarnation of the devil, of evil."[26] Turabi has received lenient treatment by Western journalists attracted to his remarkable dexterity with languages (in addition to French and Arabic, he speaks perfect idiomatic English, if in a somewhat rambling and disjointed style) and his ability to converse on their level and in their cultural context, with references to American presidential scandals, racial tension in the United States and even Louis Farrakhan's Nation of Islam.[27] Not to be underestimated, and perhaps a result of his years studying abroad, he knows the importance of public image. He never fails to try to win over his guests—and there are many—with his pitch that, to a degree, "I am one of you." In one conversation in his spacious house adorned with Quranic inscriptions in a neighborhood upscale by Khartoum's standards, he referred to Ronald Reagan as "a fourth-rate actor." In another, he dismissed Bill Clinton as "an adulterous liar" and ridiculed his home state—"Arkansas is nothing"—later saying that next to Sudan, he would choose to live in America. "I know America very well," he proceeded to tell me, in his knowing, confident manner. "I know America very well, actually." My favorite example was the over-the-top welcome he gave me and other journalists visiting him after the United States attacked the pharmaceutical plant in 1998. He started the interview by asking which we would prefer, "English or Arabic?" When someone answered in English, he quipped: "In English English or American English?"

Worldly perhaps, savvy yes, determined most definitely. Turabi long fashioned himself a philosopher-king, coy about the influence he wielded in Sudan for years after the coup and confident in his determination to put forth a modernizing, reformed Islam that could withstand any alternative.[28] At heart, religion is his message. Like others, Turabi sees no division between political and religious life. Islam, he believes, is all-encompassing, an identity and way of living rather than a set of beliefs as it is often interpreted in the West. And on many points his aims are probably compatible with those of the vast majority of Islamists today: a revival of the *umma,* adoption of *sharia,* social and economic development and trepidation about the West's cultural, economic and political influence. His starting point, like theirs, is that secularism must be turned back.

"Do you believe in God?" Turabi asked me in our first interview in 1996. He was dressed in a white turban, white scarf with gold embroidery and a starkly white traditional Sudanese gown that, as usual, was impeccably pressed. "If you believe in God, is he just somebody sitting inside a mosque or a church and he's locked up like a prisoner? Is he an omnipresent being, watching me everywhere, his omniscience, his science, his wisdom all over? Does he reward me everywhere and punish me everywhere? Do you believe in such a being? If you don't believe in it, okay. If you do believe in it, he must be like that. Is he simply something to tell you what to do inside a church or a mosque? Oh, that is very stupid. That is irrational."

"Religion is a whole way of life," he said. "God is omnipresent everywhere, omniscient and omnipotent so he guides us all over the world. It's not one particular aspect of life, it's all life. Unfortunately, religions tend sometimes to deteriorate and become confined to private life. It certainly happened to Christianity and Islam and Judaism. But in Islam, there are always cycles of revival, renewal which integrates all light that has escaped from God and into religion once more."

For Turabi, Sudan's ambitious revolution was a cycle of that revival, and it was a process that worked two ways. Islam was transforming Sudan, and Sudan was transforming Islam, or more appropriately, it was creating a political and religious example in a country stunted by war, famine and poverty. The model, Turabi insisted, could be replicated elsewhere by Muslims seeking an alternative. Although never admitting it outright, he seemed to believe that Sudan's experiment, the change he sought to engineer, was a turning point in the history of Islam. To him, Sudan, a country on the fringe of the world's consciousness, was a window on its future. As Turabi put it to me, emphasizing the term he and his colleagues preferred, "We want to develop something better for humanity, and I think it will be a social model."

"The Sudan is changing, the view to religion is changing, to education is changing, to tribalism is changing. People are detribalizing because they are mixing through communications systems and roads. The economy is changing, politics are changing," he said. "Everything is changing and changing fast."

Beyond his boasts and gestures to the dramatic, Turabi left his mark as an ideologue by putting forth his design of an Islamic state and often raised issues that are pivots of Islamic thinking today. Some are theoretical, such as the centuries-long struggle to determine who has the right to interpret Islam. Some are legal—the rights of Muslims and non-Muslims in an Islamic state, for instance. And some are practical, the arena in which he probably had his greatest influence, a rethinking that, at one level, was independent of the fate of his country. Namely, Turabi, a disciple of the Muslim Brotherhood in his early career, explored the means through which a religious movement can achieve its aims. Is the model revolution, evolution or theocratic dictatorship? The change in his ideas over the years represents a decisive and broad shift in Islamic thinking.

Before taking power, Turabi had expressed the now familiar ideology of the old-guard Brotherhood, that once society itself became suffi-

ciently Islamic, an Islamic state and government would naturally follow. In essence, the Brotherhood forefathers of Turabi—Hassan al-
Banna and his cohorts—disavowed the idea of political work, believ-
ing that their efforts should be focused on activism, or *da'wa*, among
the people, not the assumption of power by seizing the government.
With the fate of Sudan before us, a country in which an Islamic elite
did, in fact, take power and seek to impose its will on a reluctant population, it is remarkable to hear the words of Turabi in the 1980s,
thoughts akin to Banna that he would disavow through action a
decade later.

"The state is only the political expression of an Islamic society," he
wrote at the time, outlining the shape of an Islamic government. "You
cannot have an Islamic state except insofar that you have an Islamic
society. Any attempt at establishing a political order for the establishment of a genuine Islamic society would be the superimposition of
laws over a reluctant society. This is not in the nature of religion; religion is based on sincere conviction and voluntary compliance.
Therefore, an Islamic state evolves from an Islamic society."[29] He left
little room for equivocation. An Islamic state cannot be imposed, and
it cannot be a revolutionary program, particularly that of an elite
removed from the society at large. A resurgent faith in itself will
resolve the problems that the *umma* faces. It is not the task of a government. "In circumstances where Islam is allowed free expression,"
he wrote, "social change takes place peacefully and gradually, and the
Islamic movement develops programs of Islamization before it takes
over the destiny of the state because Islamic thought—like all
thought—only flourishes in a social environment of freedom and public consultation."[30]

I was shocked the first time I read those remarks. They were a perfect, well-worded expression of the Brotherhood in the 1930s. The
thoughts were palatable to a larger audience and, more important,
acceptable to most governments in Muslim countries. They also comprised an argument that, at least by the time I met him in the
mid–1990s, Turabi no longer believed. A decade on, he was prone to
ridicule and dismiss his former Brotherhood colleagues, rather than
serve as a spokesman for their beliefs. He had turned his back on their
ideas. "We don't think that it is the model," Turabi told me in 1996
when I asked him about the group and its ideology. "I mean, look at
what happened to Egypt. It has been there for how many years? It has

been there since 1930. No progress, no progress at all, actually. They never change society."

Part of his disgust came out of the bitter battles he fought with other Brotherhood members who had disavowed his new brand of politics. His former cadres, many of whom see Turabi as a political opportunist, were unsparing in their criticism. Like most Sudanese, they spoke freely and openly, none more so than an Islamist named Hibr Nour al-Daim. A big, burly avuncular man with a gray beard and a deep voice, Nour al-Daim met me at his office at Khartoum University, where he taught Arabic and Islamic studies. He was unreconstructed Brotherhood and a diehard critic of Turabi.

"You can't build this room with the ceiling first," he told me. "Out of the Islamic society is the state and not the other way around. So the Islamic society should be built first and then comes the state later, as the Prophet Mohammed did. In Mecca and Medina, he built his community and then the power came to him afterward."

As for Turabi, Nour al-Daim had nothing good to say about him and, as the conversation went on, he seemed to delight in the range of attacks he could muster.

"He is fond of the Europeans, in spite of his criticism of some of the European ways of life. He admires them, actually," he said, a personal failing in Nour al-Daim's view. "I don't think he's truthful. He is an opportunist, I have no doubt about this, and he thinks the ends justify the means. He thinks he's the only one who understands Islam and that he's the most intelligent, the most able. Very conceited, actually."

Half joking, and taken aback by the ferocity of his views, I asked Nour al-Daim if he thought Turabi was a *kafir*, an unbeliever. "To some extent," he answered. He looked at me seriously for a moment, then began laughing boisterously at the thought.

Why Nour al-Daim's anger? Turabi's break with the Brotherhood of his generation was no less than the rupture Sayyid Qutb authored in the 1960s from the bleak confines of Egypt's jails. Turabi, in fact, is Qutb matured—he took the Egyptian militant's fixation on the state and turned it into reality, the only example of its kind in modern Muslim history. Although loathe to acknowledge the elite nature of his movement outright, Turabi nevertheless admitted to its record as a revolution from above, instilling Islam, a modern Islam in his eyes, into a traditional, backward society. To him, he was leading a government of intellectuals, a religious equivalent of technocrats, who were building his coveted "social model." Turabi is Qutb's revolutionary vanguard brought to life.

I asked him about the path to power. I was curious as to what he believed he had to overcome, who was qualified to take part and what kind of plan they had devised. He began his answer vaguely, finding pleasure in a question that he said he had never been asked. "Knowledge is wide," he told me, "but there are people who are more knowledgeable than others, and they take the lead." The lead, he said, was a movement to assume power. "They," he said, meaning his vanguard, "had a plan always, not just a program for the elections and then forget about the program and enjoy power. . . . It began as a religious movement, educated people in schools, universities, but it did not remain just a superstructure. It spread downward into society generally." At first, he said, it faced almost impossible odds and persisted in its vision at times through sheer will. "The outside is against you, the traditional inside is against you and your country itself is heavy, a heavy weight. It is poor, decadent." He added: "We knew it was going to be very difficult, it's going to be resisted, we knew that our own society is very traditional, all its culture is based on books written hundreds of years back."

Part of that imposition of will was the circumvention of the other centers of authority in Sudanese society. They had to be broken if his program was to succeed. The Sufi orders were one. They posed the biggest challenge to Turabi before the coup and continued to test his hold on power through the 1990s. The Ansar and the Khatmiyya were the two most important of these orders—legacies of Islam's gradual spread into Sudan—and their allegiance transcended religious boundaries. Over the years, they had transformed in part into political parties, and identification with them stretched across generations. Both parties had outpolled Turabi's National Islamic Front in the 1986 election, and loyalty to them would not be broken easily, however stringent Turabi's attacks, both through rhetorical flourish and the hand of the police.[31] The Sufi orders also still had the important religious identification, representing a defined, traditional set of beliefs to their followers that mingled with and enhanced their political identity. Understandably, the government banned all parties shortly after the coup, including those that sprung from the two Sufi orders, and officials consistently treated them as rivals at best, fifth columnists at worst.[32]

Turabi's other fundamental criticism was directed at the *ulema*, the class of religious scholars steeped in centuries of intellectual work who many religious reformers blame, en masse, for Islam's perceived stagnation. The denial of their legitimacy is a powerful theme in political Islam, and as noted earlier, their reputation has suffered as more and more Muslims take it upon themselves to interpret the Quran and find their own personal meaning in the faith. The result is a fragmentation of authority and, at another level, the democratization of the faith as more people decide the meaning of Islam for themselves. Banna endorsed the process, as did Qutb, who saw it as the key to unlocking a revolutionary rethinking of Islam. Turabi was another proponent, though his criticism may have been more geared toward eliminating potential competition with his ideas than democratizing the religion. His *ulema,* those who would direct Islam, were not limited to students in the halls of scholarship.

"What do I mean by *ulema?* The word historically has come to mean those versed in the legacy of religious (revealed) knowledge *(ilm).* However, *ilm* does not mean that alone," he wrote in an article published in 1983. "It means anyone who knows anything well enough to relate it to God. . . . So the *ulema* in this broad sense, whether they are social or natural scientists, public opinion leaders, or philosophers, should enlighten society."[33] It was a useful argument. By broadening the definition of religious knowledge, he thereby broadened the definition of *ulema.* They were not only religious scholars; they were also the men Turabi had recruited into his political movement. His technocrats then were *ulema,* and his definition conveyed on them a certain legitimacy, religious and political, to carry out his vision of an Islamic state.

In thought, that vision was utopian. He saw an Islamic state assuring a fair distribution of political power through the concept of *shura,* or consultation, and an equally just distribution of economic wealth. There would be no theocracy or religious dictatorship akin to Iran because the *ulema* would not be a defined, recognized class. Women would have rights as well, he said, pointing out that they had a considerable role in public during the life of the prophet and even contributed to the election of one of his earliest successors. "In principle," Turabi wrote, "all believers, rich or poor, noble or humble, learned or ignorant, men or women, are equal before God, and they are his vicegerents on earth and the holders of his trust."[34] Even Christians would prosper in his model of an Islamic state. Although he admitted that there might be "a certain feeling of alienation" because the legal code to which they would adhere would be *sharia*, or Islamic law, they would appreciate its wisdom and fairness. At heart, he argued, *sharia* is closer to Christian values than any secular law, what he called "Caesar's law," and it would not interfere with the way they practiced their religion.

"The individual has the right to his physical existence, general social well-being, reputation, peace, privacy, to education and a decent life," he wrote a decade before having the power to bring it to reality. "These are rights that the state ought to provide and guarantee for a better fulfillment of the religious ideals of life. Freedom of religion and of expression should also be guaranteed and encouraged. . . . If government becomes so alien as to transcend the *sharia*, he has the right and obligation to revolt. This is the revolutionary element in Islam. A Muslim's obedience is to God alone."

The rhetoric rang disturbingly hollow in the Sudan I visited, Turabi's prescription of an Islamic state violated at almost every turn. In those years before taking power, Turabi envisioned an Islam bubbling up through society, a grassroots awakening that would sweep an Islamic state into place and inaugurate an Islamic renaissance in one of the most unlikely places. In power, he did the opposite. Unlike the street-level work of Hamas, Hezbollah or Refah, Turabi looked for an all-too-easy shortcut. He bypassed those dogged efforts, dismissing the need for popular support, so that he could hasten the onset of his Islamization. His band of Western-educated intellectuals sought to engineer the revival from above, forcing their vision upon a people that, like in the Mahdi's time more than a century ago, were not willing to forgo their established lives for a high-handed system to which they were ordered to adhere. He saw no need to appeal to the disenchantment or frustration that even violent groups in Egypt and Palestine sought to exploit. He saw no urgency in formulating a program that would appeal to the poor, to a disenfranchised middle class and to those searching for an identity distinct from the West, the message that groups in Turkey and Lebanon were so successful in creating. In the end, he seemed to think that he simply knew best, condemning to failure the only instance of Islam coming to power by a coup. His tenure left a sorry if enlightening legacy: He proved that society cannot be forced to become more devout.

The messianic aspect of his tenure seemed to mount over the years, even as the failures inspired by his policies piled up. In the 1990s, Sudan was almost always under siege, alienating its neighbors, at odds with the United States and beset by a coalition of opposition forces that included everyone from the southern rebel movement to the patriarchs of northern Sudan's leading political families. At home, discontent ran as long as the Nile River that courses 1,860 miles through the country. With that unease came the always abundant rumors of a coup, a topic of almost every conversation I had on every visit to Sudan. A successful overthrow did not materialize, but the sense of time running out appeared to nag at Turabi. In interviews, he was often difficult to read, prone to an incongruous, seemingly uncontrollable giggle when he made some of his strongest statements. At other points, he let off an animated, high-pitched sigh. Often, he came across as clearly impatient. Like every revolutionary, he was unhappy with the revolution, desperately hoping for a Sudan that would never exist. I got the feeling that he believed if he said something often enough, it would somehow become true.

"Sudan is history developing," he told me in 1998, his usual levity turning serious, with an edge in his voice. "It's not just a system or a regime, it's history, history. Okay? Deal with it. And we want to deal with the world—by dialogue, by exchanging ideas and by trade and please don't give us anything, any aid. It's not a government. It's a system of life. How can people understand? We have to wait another century for historians to write respectfully about what is happening?"

I once spoke with Sadiq al-Mahdi, the former prime minister, about that dissonance between the urbane Turabi's thought and his government's repressive action. Sadiq, as he is known to nearly everyone in Sudan, had firsthand experience with the darker side of Turabi's rule. He was imprisoned for three years after the 1989 coup. Following his release, he was periodically interrogated and, at all times, a police guard kept up surveillance at his home. Then, in 1995, he was arrested again and imprisoned for three months. The following year, under the cover of his daughter's wedding, he tricked security guards into thinking he was going for a horseback ride and then fled overland to neighboring Eritrea in an escape worthy of a Hollywood cliffhanger. Once in exile, he joined the broad coalition aligned against the government.[35] All this despite the fact that Turabi and Sadiq, two of the country's bitterest rivals, are brothers-in-law. Turabi was married to Sadiq's sister, a telling insight into the interlocking nature of Sudan's elite. I met Sadiq a few months before his escape, visiting him in Omdurman at his luxurious home. It was a walled compound lined with palm trees and landscaped with a well-watered garden of flowers, the delicate scent of blossoms wafting in the stultifyingly hot air. Our hourlong conversation quickly turned to politics and, of course, Turabi. Sadiq spoke with the air of a political veteran, perhaps a little cynical.

"Although he has said enlightened things, he has acted in unenlightened ways," he said, his tall, massive build lending a sense of authority to his words. Turabi, he told me, has a singular fondness of speaking the language of a progressive Islam. Peppered through his speeches are references to democracy, women's rights, peaceful international relations and human rights. But in the end, he said, "it is a Third World dictatorship."

The Sudan that I encountered over several years—in the universities, in the lonely desert camps of its religious militias and in the words of its proud people—was far closer to Sadiq's bleak judgment than to Turabi's utopian vision.

—

My last visit to Sudan was in August 1998 to report on the U.S. missile attack on El-Shifa Pharmaceutical Industries Co., a compound of three one-story factories and a four-story administration building in an industrial area on the outskirts of Khartoum. The Clinton administration launched the strike in retaliation for the bombings of U.S. embassies in Kenya and Tanzania, and its destruction by cruise missiles unleashed a debate between the two countries over the true nature of the plant (and, for that matter, Sudan's purported role in terrorism believed to have been carried out by Osama bin Ladin). The Clinton administration insisted that the plant was manufacturing precursors for chemical weapons, namely the deadly VX nerve agent. As evidence, it said it had analyzed a soil sample collected by a field operative recruited by the CIA that showed the presence of the chemical EMPTA, or O-ethylmethylphosphonothioic acid—a material said to be a key ingredient of VX that has no commercial uses. It also claimed there was a connection between bin Ladin and Salah Idris, the Sudanese owner of the plant who has homes in Khartoum, London and Saudi Arabia. Days later, that link was described by U.S. officials as "fuzzy." In May 1999, although not acknowledging it had made a mistake, the administration quietly freed $24 million in Idris's deposits at the Bank of America (plus $1 million in interest), assets it froze after the bombing.

Although the plant's true nature may never be known, I had the impression during my time there that it was not what the American government had made it out to be. I traveled to Sudan with Enric Marti, an AP photographer, the day after the bombing on a plane chartered from Cairo by Reuters, BBC and other media organizations. Arriving after midnight, we left the airport and headed straight for the plant, entering the compound without hassle as the guards lounged on the ground and chatted. The missiles had wrecked the factory in a stunning example of a surgical strike (many of its walls were still standing). Inside, melted packets of pain relievers and bottles of antibiotics were strewn among the rubble of crushed red brick, splintered wood and white plaster. Brown glass jars sat in piles amid twisted sheet metal. For a supposed security installation, there was virtually no security, even as the smoke and pungent fumes of burning plastic from the attack still lingered in the nighttime air. Two prominent signs along the road pointed to the factory, and I ended up visiting the plant on several occasions at various times of the day, always unfettered. Coming from Egypt, where a bridge across the Nile is considered so sensitive to military security that photographing it is banned, I was surprised by the degree of access. The plant obviously produced pharmaceuticals, too, despite initial American suggestions to the contrary. It had a $199,000 contract to ship to Iraq cartons of Shifazole, a drug to treat parasites in animals, under a UN exemption to sanctions on that country. Its antibiotics and medicine were available at most pharmacies in the capital that I visited, always packaged in the company's distinctive blue-and-white cartons.

To me, Sudan's response to the attack rather than the target itself was far more illustrative of the nature of the regime. The plant's destruction had come after what seemed to have been a string of setbacks for the government. The country had just been hit by the worst floods of the Nile River in ten years. Electricity that in good times lasted half a day had been cut after six hours, often fewer, a result in part of the floods' effect on hydroelectric power. Blackouts and dire economic conditions (as many as nine out of ten Sudanese struggle with poverty) had sent people into the streets of several cities, including Khartoum. Disenchantment with the civil war, meanwhile, was everywhere and mothers had staged angry demonstrations over the drafting of their sons into the Popular Defense Forces. Then came the government's mobilization after the U.S. attack, a dramatic demonstration of its ability to turn out well-organized and dedicated cadres. The first time electricity had gone on for longer than six hours was on the night of the strike, allowing Sudanese to watch live footage into the morning of the factory and a protest organized at the U.S. Embassy. Days afterward, protesters encouraged by the government still poured into Khartoum's muddy, desolate streets. Boys were let out from high school and government bureaucrats were urged to attend on a government-mandated break. The grand jury investigation into President Clinton's relationship with former White House intern Monica Lewinsky seemed to be on everyone's mind. Signs carried at protests read, in English, "No war for Monica." Sudanese leaders saturated the airwaves—in Arabic for consumption at home and English for an audience abroad. Even the opposition, never reluctant to voice its grim assessments of the government, was disheartened. One of its members was Ghazi Suleiman, a leading Sudanese dissident in and out of jail. Suleiman was among the country's more recognizable figures, a tall man with heavy eyelids and bloodshot eyes set off by a full head of silvery gray hair.[36] Like other opponents of the regime, he feared that, in the end, the government would be the one to gain from the attack. "It would have been better if they had not done it," he told me sincerely when I visited him at his home. "The danger of such attacks is that it keeps people looking toward the sky and not toward the actual problems."[37]

The actual problems were everywhere, though. The government could mobilize its network of support, as it did during the 1989 coup and countless times afterward. It could dispatch its leaders the same night of the attack to distant locales in Sudan—Atbara, Gedaref and Wad Madani—to organize protests and mobilize its followers. But, as the years dragged on and the problems multiplied, its rhetoric rang increasingly hollow. Nowhere was there a spontaneous eruption of Islamic self-sacrifice, and in no place did the government and its supporters appear to be anything but a well-organized, disciplined elite dedicated solely to the idea of keeping power at all costs. Religion, in that equation, was a desperate reach for legitimacy when no other legitimacy existed. At heart, I felt, it was a Third World dictatorship, perhaps mild in the dissent that it would tolerate, but still a dictatorship imposed on a people that gave it little support. Turabi's vision of an Islamic renaissance had become a nightmare of political manipulation.

The most nightmarish aspect of the vision was the Popular Defense Forces, the militia the government held up as the vanguard of its religious crusade and, in more Machiavellian terms, a counterbalance to a 115,000-man military that even after the purge of up to 1,000 senior, non-NIF army officers was still seen as too secular and only reluctantly trusted.[38] The government had cast the war with the Sudan People's Liberation Army, Africa's longest, as a *jihad*, a crusade or holy war. Its aim, to varying degrees of vehemence, was a military victory in which a vanquished south would join the north in a brotherhood of Islam with Arabic as the lingua franca.[39] The PDF was held up as the ideological rigor behind the war and during my visits it was ubiquitous in Khartoum—in newspaper headlines, on television, in not-so-spontaneous demonstrations and in volunteer outfits the government hurried toward the front. The government saw the force as its primary tool for indoctrination of students and civil servants (volunteers were also accepted), and the training camps were always a demonstration in immoderate religious fervor. For maximum effect, one camp was in the city's downtown, ensuring that sleepy residents in Khartoum's concrete and adobe homes would be awoken by the recruits' chants of "there is no god but God" shortly after dawn.

Inside the lot, about 100 recruits from Khartoum, dressed in street clothes, thongs and mismatched camouflage, went through a day of perfunctory military training and much more zealous religious conditioning. On one wall was a poster with five columns that listed the names of martyrs who had died in the distant and increasingly unpopular war. Underneath a tent, a band with an accordion, violin and drum played songs exhorting the recruits to battle: "March forward holy warrior and do not worry about what you leave behind." A short distance away, near the presidential palace, other recruits in camouflage and headbands colored red for sacrifice turned out for one of the daily protests organized after the American attack. "We are ready! We are ready!" shouted the *dababin*, the term for recruits who fashioned themselves as kamikazes ready to blow up the tanks of rebels. It all seemed a little surreal to me, an impression bolstered by a remark by Sudan's chief of staff, General Ibrahim Suliman, that was remarkable for its callousness. Being sent to the south, he said, was considered "advanced training."[40]

The force seemed another metaphor for the government's approach to society—a top-down imposition of its will—and for the lack of popular support it enjoyed outside its own network of cadres. Islam was its rhetorical tool, perhaps even believed by the men who orchestrated its use, but repression was its result. After high school, men not attending university had to have two months of training in the militia and then serve eighteen months. University students had to finish a year of service after they graduated. In some regions considered strategic, whole villages were required to undergo training in the militia.[41] Not all volunteered. Residents and diplomats told me that when the civil war flared security forces were prone to take youths of draft age off the streets, from buses and at traffic roadblocks, press ganging them into service under cover of darkness without telling their families. Other youths were barred from entering universities, taking jobs, particularly in the government, or receiving an exit visa to leave the country until they served. Such measures probably seemed necessary from the government's perspective, since no one I met outside officialdom seemed to like the militia or tolerate the indoctrination it promised. Reports of desertions were rife. During riots over bread prices in 1995 in Gedaref, in northeastern Sudan, militiamen were said to have fled the barracks at the first word of trouble. Two years later, rebel leader John Garang claimed that nearly 1,000 militiamen had defected to his side and "more were joining daily."[42] In one of the most disturbing incidents, at least fifty-two recruits died when their boat capsized in the Blue Nile in April 1998 as they tried to flee a camp named Aliafoon, about fifteen miles southeast of Khartoum. Opposition groups claimed the death toll had been much higher, at least 129, and that soldiers beat and shot the recruits as they tried to escape.[43]

The bankruptcy of the force struck me most vividly when I met the women who had bravely organized protests against it in the months before the American attack. At first, mothers were seen helplessly wailing in Khartoum as their sons boarded trucks bound for the camps. Later, they became organized, hundreds of them taking to the streets in Khartoum and Omdurman, its sister city across the Nile, to protest conscription for the war. Some fought battles with police, who fired tear gas. In one such confrontation in December 1997 in front of the UN offices in Khartoum, security forces kicked and hit women and beat them with hoses and bamboo sticks. Thirty were carted off to jail.[44] In another incident in May 1998, mothers stood in front of buildings in the capital where final exams were being administered to prevent security forces from taking their sons after they had finished. Mothers who could afford it sent their sons out of the country on tourist visas to dodge the draft. I found their activism remarkable in a country where the government had dismissed women from the civil service, tried to force them to wear veils and sought to subdue, rather unsuccessfully, their political work. Their resistance, it seemed, was too strong to suppress.[45]

One of the women leading the protests for nearly a year was Suad Ibrahim Ahmed, a frenetic, in-your-face firebrand of an activist in her sixties, whom I met in 1998. When I arrived, she came to the door with a bowl of dates and, despite having no appointment, graciously welcomed me inside. Her intoxicating enthusiasm belied her age. Her gray hair pulled back and her eyes hidden behind glasses, she was the type of person who enjoyed talking, about anything, and we soon found we had at least one thing in common. We were both graduates of the University of Wisconsin, albeit thirty or so years apart. That was the starting point for a conversation that went from the militia to the government to Islam and back to the militia. Every so often, she would stand up, her back hunched over in age, then shuffle across the room in her black slippers to grab another piece of paper, a letter, a picture or a map that might help illustrate the point she was trying to make. She would return to the chair, prop her leg up on the table—a very masculine gesture in a very masculine society—and take another drag on her ever-burning cigarette. Over and over, the point she made was the need to do something about a government and war colored by faith that no one seemed to like.

"They hijack people in the streets, and you won't know where your child is. You don't know whether he is alive, dead or missing," she told me.

"It's very clear that people are tired of the war. And what is this war? It's a war over accumulated grievances. That can't be called a religious war." The country, she said, was falling apart, and the government and the fifteen-year conflict were responsible. "Half of Sudan are beggars and the other half have left the country."

"You are talking about a government that has decided to transform the society into its own image," she said, the delivery of her words slowing for emphasis. "It has permeated our arteries and veins; only the NIF has the right to move or work."

Ahmed was a longtime activist and a veteran troublemaker. Like Adlan al-Hardallu, the professor at Khartoum University, she conveyed the sense of having seen it all. She boasted that no other woman in the country had been detained in prison for political reasons longer than she had (from February 1971 until May 1973) and she bragged about her jail time the way a general would tout his medals. She was proud of it and prepared to do it. When both she and her husband were detained, she said, they sent their son to stay with neighbors. Since the coup, police had arrested her three or four times and taken her in for questioning, mainly to harass her. Security forces also had searched her house "two or three times" and kept her under surveillance. In one of her more recent detentions, Ahmed spent two and a half hours at the police station after the confrontation in front of the UN offices. She said she had mixed it up with police.

"I have rheumatism, and I wasn't strong enough to fight with my hands," she told me. "So I used my elbows."

And still she enjoyed talking. To her, the Sudan of today echoed the nineteenth-century Sudan of the Mahdi when another movement grounded in religion had sought to impose its blueprint on society. That short-lived state, which General Kitchener brought to a bloody end in 1898, sat uneasily with a Sudan that even then was eclectic and imbued with divergent faiths and heterodox doctrines. She believed that same high-handedness and intolerance, an elite philosophy imposed then, was evident again today.

They have made it into a religious war and Sudan is known as a very tolerant country. Our Islam is a very tolerant Islam. Islam took over 800 years to spread peacefully and that is why Islam is very, very different. It's almost unique. It has never been extremist in any form. People came to Sudan and mixed and intermingled peacefully, rather than by force. This kind of extremism is unknown in Sudan. We had it for a few years in the Mahdist period and it resulted in famine and isolation from our neighbors and the national unity of the Sudan was torn apart. When Kitchener came, half the country had disintegrated. We lost half our people because of that continuous war and now we face the same circumstances.

"At the end of every century, we suffer this," Ahmed declared, finding humor in the absurdity of the statement. She looked at me, smiled, then let out a thundering laugh scarred by years of unfiltered cigarette smoke.

Ahmed's age probably saved her from much harsher treatment by the government. It was unsavory to mistreat women in Sudan in public and even more so to harass elderly women. She seemed to sense their reluctance. Lately, she told me, guards had been hassling her about not wearing a veil in public, particularly on the bus. Whenever that happened, she would shout at them, "I'm the age of your mother!" Then she would deliver her angry assessment of the government's program: "I don't want to go to your paradise by force! God didn't ask you to come and reform my religion!"

In the bus, she said, people would begin to clap.

—

I met Gassim al-Badri on each visit to Sudan and, in time, came to see him as a man whose impressions were usually understated but always insightful. Our first introduction was while I was reporting a story on Sudanese education in 1996. I was interested in Al-Ahfad University, a private institution that had nearly a century of history, first as an elementary school, then a secondary school, a college and, in 1995, a university. It is the only women's college in the Arab world and, situated in Omdurman, it had generally managed to avoid the attempts by the government across the Nile in Khartoum to rein in the big universities. Its curriculum had a decidedly activist bent. Many of its students said that after graduation they planned to return to their villages, help rural women or work with development and aid groups. The college still taught in English, even though the government had instituted Arabic elsewhere in higher education as the medium of instruction. And unlike at other Sudanese colleges, the women students sitting outside in a campus courtyard shaded by date palms and eucalyptus trees seemed under little pressure to wear the veil.

Their freedom was credit to their simple maxim: No politics. This stood in contrast to other Sudanese schools, particularly Khartoum University. Although that school had weathered badly under the Islamic government, many of its students were still outspoken, often recklessly so. Inside the campus, signs of their opposition seemed to be everywhere. One poster destined soon to be ripped down proclaimed, "Down with the merchants of religion," a pejorative reference to Islamists. After clashes between Khartoum University stu-

dents and police in 1998, a law student was arrested and died in custody. According to students, his skull was crushed and his leg was broken. When I visited the campus later in the month, the memories of
his death were still vivid. One twenty-five-year-old law student
approached me on his way to class, gave me his name then proceeded
to tell me, "Not only students but most people are against the regime.
But I can refuse the government only with my tongue. It's the one
with the weapons." On another visit to the university, as rebels were
scoring successes in eastern Sudan, a twenty-three-year-old graduate
student gave me his name as well and declared that he was willing to
join the rebels. "If the people were sure the war would get rid of the
government, they would be for the war," he said. "But I don't think
the war will get rid of the government."

Al-Ahfad avoided the bravado, owing in part to the calming affect of
Badri, who served as the university's president. He was a tall, lanky
man, carrying himself with an air of dignity that I found common to
many Sudanese. In our first talk, he was loathe to discuss politics. He
hardly knew me and, besides, his concern was more the university and
its 4,000 students, making sure that enough girls applied and that he
could find new sources of revenue to keep the school afloat. When I
finally cajoled him into saying something about the government, he
remarked simply that Turabi was neither mad nor an opportunist, but
rather a pragmatist.

"All politicians," he told me, "want to go down as having accomplished something, so now Turabi has his chance."

In time, his ideas changed. When I visited him a year later in 1997, a
time when the civil war had intensified and the economy wilted even
further, he was far more outspoken. He talked with passion and anger,
condemning a government that sought to impose its will on a disenchanted population. It was the idea I heard time and again in Sudan:
The failure was not Islam since many of the country's people were
already devout Muslims, desiring that religion to shape and guide
their lives. Instead, the problem was the government's dictatorial
approach of instilling its vision—the entry of Islam into public and
private life, rendering of the civil war as a *jihad*, citizenship based on
faith, forced participation in the Popular Defense Forces and even the
insistence of women wearing the veil rather than the traditional *tobe*,
an elegant, sari-like gown in various colors that only loosely covers
the hair. The idea behind the vision was that only one Islam held the
key to God, that only one Islam was proper and correct. Like other

Sudanese, he was growing more and more disenchanted with the concept.

"Islam has never been asleep in Sudan, in the hearts and minds of the people, so we don't need these people to tell us about it. It's an insult, actually," Badri said. "Why should they have the right to tell us what is right and what is wrong?"

"*Khallas*, enough, they have tried their best to hang on to power and now they're running short of fuel. They have tried their best and they have ruled now for almost eight years and they have not convinced the ordinary person in the street that they are better than the others. They have made life harder for the people. Any government that fails to satisfy the needs of the people must go. *Khallas*, enough, what else are they going to do? It's a government by deception and you can't go on deceiving the people."

In our last conversation, I felt he hit on the essence of the failure of Sudan's Islamic experiment. In a country so diverse, so proud of its tradition of tolerance, so ready to defend its rights, a government that was both authoritarian in its use of power *and* in its use of ideology was bound to fail. It might remain in power through an apparatus that wielded the power of a police state, but it would not formulate Turabi's coveted social model nor would it inspire the people it sought to convert.

"The Sudanese people are antigovernment and antiestablishment," Badri said in 1998 after the American attack, speaking slowly as if he was depressed or, I thought, perhaps just weary of the tension. "Any establishment that comes, they are against it. It's something in their psyche. It's a problem for people who want to govern Sudan. I think many of the people in power are coming to this conclusion. They tried hard to change the people, but the people are not responding. What are you going to do in this situation?"

Then he delivered one of the lines I found most memorable in my time covering the Middle East. It spoke to the arrogance of power. "They have tried to monopolize Him," he told me, "but as Muslims they should know that they cannot monopolize God."

If there was a lesson in Sudan's bleak record, it was the compelling argument that it offered, by default, for political Islam's more democratic alternatives in Egypt, Palestine, Turkey, Lebanon, Jordan and even Iran, where activists were taking up compromise as opposed to Sudan's going-it-alone and searching for coalitions as opposed to the fondness of Turabi and his cohorts for a tight-knit group that acts as a vanguard. Turabi left the scene, at least temporarily, at the end of 1999 when he lost a long-running power struggle with President Omar al-Bashir.[46] No longer willing to run affairs from afar, Turabi had sought a more formal elaboration of his power. The underestimated Bashir struck back, declaring a state of emergency, suspending parts of the constitution and sending troops to take over Parliament. Some of Turabi's former colleagues and disciples—among them, Ali Osman Taha and Ghazi Salah al-Din al-Atabani, once among the most fervent of his students—sided with the president. As Sudan's political winds blow, he seemed the safer bet. Turabi was left to formulate the government's ideological direction but removed from the day-to-day politics and administration of the country. I suspected, though, that his career was far from over.

About a year before his departure, he provided me a long-winded description of why his government had lasted as long as it did, despite the enmity of its neighbors and many of its own people. What he told me seemed to be more his longing for what could have been. In his mind, he had somehow made his dreams reality.

Governments in Western Europe and the United States say, oh, it won't take more than one month, a few months and this government will collapse. They don't understand history. What's happening here is not just a slice of elitists at the top of society who control power, a few elitists who have taken power. This is social change, this is historical change. I mean, society is changing, all of it. . . . This is not something transient. This is a culture that is growing from below, into the economy, into politics, into culture. It is not spreading by imperialism but by its influence, all over the Arab world, the African world, the Muslim world.

In the end, it could claim none of those accomplishments. It would be left to another Islamic government, one that came to power through a popular revolution rather than a coup and one that had the capacity to reform itself rather than self-destruct, to chart a more viable society ordered by faith. In Iran, the young, a new generation of clergy and a brave class of reformers and leaders led by Mohammad Khatami sought to remake an exhausted revolution into a civil society ruled by law. The success of their experiment holds the key to a more practical future for political Islam.

6

Iran's Lesson

The Iranian Revolution and the Rebirth of Political Islam

HASAN YUSUFI ESHKEVARI, in so many ways, was the very picture of the glowering Iranian mullah whose brooding, unbending image is seared in the consciousness of the West. Like other devout Muslims, he wore a bushy beard, imitating the style of the Prophet Mohammed in Arabia more than 1,300 years ago. His white turban sat neatly atop his head, and his gray robe draped itself over a body made soft by years of religious study. He smiled only rarely, and even then, it seemed more a gesture of hospitality than cheer. I had come to interview Eshkevari on the recommendation of several young Iranian intellectuals, visiting him at his modest house in a neighborhood that, like many in Tehran, had been ground down by years of austerity. His son politely escorted me upstairs and, after an exchange of pleasantries that put neither of us at ease, we sat cross-legged atop a sprawling Persian carpet, its design of geometric shapes, passionate colors and intoxicating intricacies as puzzling as today's Iran and as complicated as the religious thinker a few feet away from me.

Eshkevari, it turns out, was a revolutionary. He languished in jail twice under the despotic rule of the Shah in the 1970s and then took to the streets in heroic protests that captivated a world still oblivious to the horrors that would follow. With the Shah in exile and Ayatollah Ruhollah Khomeini in power, he was elected to the first parliament

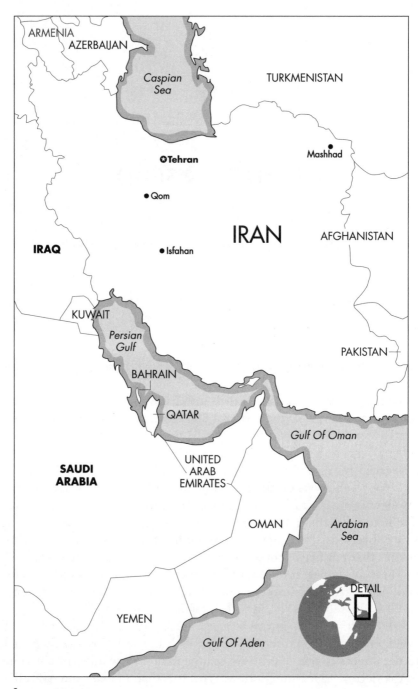

Iran

convened in the Islamic Republic. Its inception was a bold move that many Muslims at the time saw as the initial step on a path that would be distinct from both capitalism and communism, ideologies they associated with the West. More surprising, and unlike many of his fellow citizens in Iran, he withstood the disenchantment and hardships of eight years of war with Iraq or the disgust at hundreds of thousands of young lives lost, many of their graves cluttered together in a junkyard of sacrifice and sorrow outside the capital. Through it all, somehow, he kept his faith in Islam and his belief in justice.

No longer, for Eshkevari was still, in an odd way, a revolutionary, taking part in the far-reaching changes in Iran today that may very well determine the course of Islamic politics in the rest of the Muslim world. As I sat with him, picking at a plate of grapes, plums and peaches, I listened, with growing disbelief, to complaint after complaint of the way things were, a litany recited with barely a show of expression, accented only by his fingers running languorously over a string of worry beads.

"I'm one of the critics of the way of religious thinking in the Islamic Republic," he said to me, with not a hint of fear or irony.[1]

Islam in itself was not meant to rule a country, he said, and its tenets cannot alone solve the economic, social and political problems of a modern society. Like other clergy, he said he feared what the growing disenchantment with the Islamic government would mean for the clergy, who for centuries as guardians of the faith had built a reservoir of support, respect and goodwill among Iranians of all backgrounds, often raising the black banner of rebellion in the face of arbitrary oppression and reckless autocracy. Again and again, he told me that—in words similar to a phrase made memorable by former Iranian prime minister Mehdi Bazargan—the main threat in Iran today to Islam as a faith is the experience of people under the Islamic government.[2]

"We say under the banner of religion that there will be equality, under the banner of religion, there will be development, under the banner of religion, there will be a successful economy. But if there is not, this failure of the religious state will be a failure of religion," Eshkevari said, leaning back on red pillows against the spartan wall. "The failure of the government, therefore, becomes a failure of the faith."

In a rapid-fire succession of surprises, he went on to talk about the Arab world and its Islamic movements, groups like the Muslim

Brotherhood in Egypt, the Islamic Salvation Front in Algeria or the National Islamic Front in Sudan, all of which have boldly offered to take the religion and create a renaissance in regions that had lost their dynamism, pride and self-confidence centuries ago. Expecting an answer in the abstract, a quality so common to his fellow clergymen, talented as they are in the art of obfuscation, I asked him what message Iran offered these movements.

"Not only does Iran have no message for them," he told me, "the movements themselves in Algeria, Sudan or Egypt have no message either."

So much for abstraction, I thought.

As he spoke, I was struck by the tenor of his answers, the way in which he came across. Eshkevari was, in many ways, a child of the revolution, but he seemed exhausted by it, disenchanted with it. The revolution, to him, had entered its Thermidor, the month in the calendar of the French Revolution that symbolically marked the fall of Robespierre and the end of the Reign of Terror. Like the France of that period, the zeal was gone, the answers were missing and the once unmistakable message was corrupted. The revolution had become unfamiliar, even unrecognizable, and disenchantment and failure were in its wake. In the end, he believed, the example it had left was idiosyncratic at best.

"There is one problem and that is that the governments of these Arab countries cannot solve the problems of the people or the nation. It means that they cannot solve the problem of backwardness and create an independent and modern government and country and not be dependent on the West or others. In any Muslim country, if the government can provide these fundamentals, it will be successful," Eshkevari said.

His were the complaints of many a Third World revolutionary, struggling to embark on a path that would lead to a still undefined modernity independent of the West, a future that would mean a life free of poverty and disease, a modern society ordered by technology and an indigenous culture and faith, and a government accountable to those it governed. Iran's revolution promised one vision; to Eshkevari, it had failed to fulfill it. Other Muslim countries, he felt, still had a path to choose.

But, Eshkevari believed, they should not look to Iran. "In these countries," he said, "a religious government is not necessary."[3]

Iran, today, is a startling place, and its surprises offer the most telling insights into the future of political Islam, a movement in the throes of a transformation in the place, many believe, where it began. I had come to Iran to look for the legacy of the revolution, a movement that had left a decisive impression on me and others of my generation who were raised amid the images of blindfolded hostages in the American Embassy, burnings of the U.S. flag in protests of angry, bearded men, their fists punching the air, and the glowering portrait of Khomeini featured on so many magazine covers and in *Nightline* cutaways. Even today, his face remains haunting: an intimidating visage that seems to convey revolutionary ardor suppressed by the cold logic of determination and commitment. As I left Cairo for my first visit in 1996, I hoped to find out what a revolution that promised to create a new society had actually brought about, and what had a government's promise to use the faith to solve society's problems done to Islam itself. Was there, in fact, an Islamic order in Iran? More important, what did that Islamic order mean today, how could it change and what did those changes promise for the future?

In the early 1980s, Islam was conceived in Iran as a complete social, economic, political and moral system—the almost clichéd reference to "Islam is the solution." That monopoly on truth meant there was no room for competing views or systems. As one Iranian scholar put it, "Islamism was exclusivist and intolerant of pluralism."[4] The message that I found in my time in Iran was that Islam was, in fact, not the solution, that the faith by itself could not provide the answers or, perhaps more important, different answers—neither for the economy, nor for spirituality, nor for a morality that would replace the allure of Western materialism and the predominance of Western culture, commerce and politics. The example of the revolution to which Eshkevari dedicated his life had reached a turning point; its symbols, energy, appeal and sources of legitimacy that drew from the climactic days of the Shah's overthrow seemed exhausted.[5]

That was the easy conclusion. Almost always, it seems, failure is far easier to gauge than success. I was in Iran at an opportune time, having the chance to witness some of the greatest changes to sweep the country since the revolution itself: the emergence of thinkers like Abdol-Karim Soroush and Mohsen Kadivar, the flourishing of a vibrant, skeptical newspaper culture and the breathtaking electoral participation that brought President Mohammad Khatami to power in

1997 and ushered in a parliament of deputies in 2000 who were dedicated to sweeping social and political reform. What I found during that visit and those that followed was that Iran, despite its failure, could still chart a new style of Islamic politics, one in which dissent, democracy, human rights and even coalitions could take their place in a more wide-open playing field. In Iran, the thoughts of Egyptian thinkers like Sheikh Mohammed al-Ghazali and Sheikh Yusuf al-Qaradawi and the experiments of Egypt's Center Party and similar attempts in Palestine, Lebanon, Jordan and Turkey were beginning to be realized. Here, there seemed to be an attempt to secure greater freedom *and* keep allegiance to God, creating a generation whose commitment to pluralism was matched only by its duty to Islam. The equivalent of that vision, I thought, was the transformation of Soviet communism to European socialism, a brand of politics that lost its revolutionary exclusiveness and often blind dogmatism for a more palatable and eventually successful pragmatism and pluralism. In my time in Iran, I had the sense that people did not want to necessarily overthrow the Islamic Republic or undo the revolution. Rather, they wanted their republic to be more democratic, to reconsider its relationship to religion, to provide security and adhere to the law and to choose an order born of a stable democracy instead of an unsettled revolution. After years of disenchantment and sullen anger, taking shape in Iran was an example of how a government grounded in religious principles could reform along democratic lines.

There was an irony in that lesson. Here was a country that was the inspiration for the coming of age of political Islam a generation ago. Now, it was demonstrating the potential to be the inspiration for its successful rebirth. The road to that realization, though, was long—a path cluttered by terror, war, alienation, apathy and even nihilism. Its success was by no means guaranteed. The evolutionary change of the revolution was unfolding, and there still existed in Iran two contrasting faces of one revolutionary vision. A religious society was a given. More important was the meaning of an Islamic democracy.

To many in the West, the Iranian Revolution was Islam incarnate—dramatic evidence that a new force had surged on the world scene, promising to remake politics, alliances and even governments. The Shah's Iran was an oil-rich Western ally, its military the generous recipient of American largesse and its society, from the vantage point of the capital, distinguished by a Western, modern veneer. Foremost, it served U.S. interests, providing oil to Israel, policing the Persian Gulf and Indian Ocean and serving as a bulwark of an American-orchestrated military alliance (and the lucrative arms contracts that entailed). The Shah's unpopularity and repression were less visible abroad. But by early 1979, eighteen months of strikes, bloody clashes and mass protests that brought waves of humanity into the streets had toppled the Shah in a revolution that electrified the Muslim world like no other event this century. The upheaval seemed heroic; the empowerment of a people unprecedented. And its dramatic climax—the Pahlavi dynasty's demise—came with the arrival of Khomeini on February 1 aboard an Air France Boeing 747 jetliner from Charles de Gaulle Airport outside Paris. His return, after fifteen years in exile, was greeted by 3 million people in the streets of the Iranian capital[6] and marked the symbolic and decisive end to 2,500 years of Persian monarchy.[7] Less than two weeks later, Tehran's radio station would declare: "This is the voice of Tehran, the voice of true Iran, the voice of the revolution."[8]

Perhaps no Muslim country escaped the rumblings of the upheaval. Here, in its all fervor and excitement, was an example of a Muslim people rising up to take their destiny into their own hands. For the revolutionaries in Iran, many of them hailing from the clergy, Islam would fulfill that destiny, a complete system for a modern society. It was an example in which others found inspiration, if not guidance, and it stands today with Cuba's revolution, Algerian independence and the Vietnam War as one of the Third World's seminal moments.

Iran's revolution was critically guided by one man, Ruhollah Musavi Khomeini, a figure as compelling as any in Islam's history whose life mirrored the intense passion, emotion and sacrifice of the Shiite faith he sought to reshape into a modern ideology of government. He was born in 1902 in Khomein, a provincial town from which he drew his name. His father, Sayyid Mustafa, was killed shortly afterward, possibly by government agents; his mother and father's sister died when he was sixteen.[9] After an initial religious education, in which he was said to have memorized the entire Quran by the age of six, he was sent to the famous Fayzieh *madrasa* in Qom to study with Ayatollah Abdol-Karim Ha'iri, the leading Shiite theologian of the time.[10] He completed his education there, then began teaching Sufi philosophy and Islamic jurisprudence at the Fayzieh. It was also rumored at the time that he wrote Sufi poetry and had mystic experiences, behavior that was frowned on by orthodox clergy but that added another nuance to a complicated, layered personality.[11] (Some speculated that Khomeini's asceticism, monotone delivery and lack of humor were intentional devices to dispel any suggestion that he had lost himself in mystical practices.) In his first major religious work, a now famous text known as *Kashf-e Asrar* (Revealing the Secrets), he criticized the Shah's father, Reza Khan, for mistreating the clergy, but in general, Khomeini remained aloof from the political struggles of the 1940s and 1950s. His emergence as a leading opposition figure only came during mass protests against the Shah in 1963 that served as a prelude to the revolution. Khomeini was already in his sixties at the time, but endowed with an intuition that would distinguish his activism for the next twenty-five years. He understood mass appeal. Even in 1963, the issues he chose resonated with a people that lived uneasily under the Shah's rule and his modernization program known as the White Revolution, which brought land reform, women's right to vote and a vast expansion of the state throughout Iran. Khomeini, as a populist, railed against corruption, the rigging of elections, violating the constitution, stifling the press and political parties, neglecting the needs of merchants, workers and peasants, undermining the country's Islamic faith, selling oil to Israel and aping of the West, known in Farsi as *gharbzadegi*.[12] In his years in opposition and later at the helm of the revolution, he never lost the knack for gauging popular indignation and anger.

In November 1964, after a brief stint in prison, Khomeini was exiled to Turkey and then allowed to go to Najaf in neighboring Iraq, one of Shiite Islam's holiest cities, where he spent the next decade and a half. It was during this time that, as one of the clergy's highest-ranking figures, he delivered lectures on Islamic government that later developed into his idea of *velayat-e faqih*, or "guardianship by the jurist," a formula in which the clergy were not only charged to participate directly in the political process but, in a bold reinterpretation, to actually govern the state.[13] The monarchy, Khomeini argued, was an illegitimate institution that usurped the rightful authority of the supreme religious leader, the *faqih*, who should rule as both spiritual and temporal guardian of the *umma*. The idea would become the framework for the Islamic Republic.

Already by the 1970s, Khomeini had become a lightning rod for militant religious opposition to the Shah. His writings on Islamic government and other speeches circulated clandestinely. (When Khomeini was in Iraq, his elder son mysteriously died or was killed in 1977, many believed at the hands of the Shah's secret police, another instance of the sacrifice and tragedy he seemed to endure through his life.) As opposition to the Shah grew, Iraq expelled Khomeini in 1978. He was refused entry to nearby Kuwait, then persuaded to locate in Paris, where he had access to the international media and to printing and tape recording facilities. The instruments would be important in getting his message to revolutionary forces inside Iran. Finally, on February 1, 1979, with the Shah already in exile and his caretaker government under siege, Khomeini returned triumphantly, ready to create what he would describe as a government of God.

In the West, Khomeini was seen as one-dimensional, a revolutionary with a cold but fanatic hatred of the United States and Israel, an almost comic-book figure in his religious zeal. At home, he was far more complex, a man with a mixed relation to his homeland, a martyr and a populist despite himself. Khomeini's great-grandfather had moved from Khorosan in Iran to India (many accounts suggest Kashmir), and his grandfather returned to Khomein. The history was a part of Khomeini's identity and, as a young man, he used the surname "Hindi" to sign his poetry. He shared the notion of distant roots with other revolutionaries and nationalists—the Corsican Napoleon, the Austrian Hitler, the Georgian Stalin—and his weak link to a specifically Iranian nationalism came through in his determined adherence to an Islamic universalism. Iran was where the revolution began, he believed, not where it would end, and he rarely, if ever, mentioned its name in public.[14] To him, the insistence by many that the *faqih*, the religious and temporal leader in his Islamic government, would be Iranian was unimportant. If it was politically necessary, so be it, but a national requirement had no grounding in religious doctrine.

Throughout his life, he also conveyed to Iranians a strong sense of sacrifice. His father was killed, he was forced into exile, he lost his son, yet he seldom wavered from his pursuit of Islamic justice—be it the Shah's fall or the imposition of a truly Islamic government. That pursuit was part of his singular sense of popular appeal. Consciously, he sought to speak in a language of the ordinary man, attacking intellectuals, the rich and the pampered. At all times, he eschewed the scholarly, measured language common to other clergy immersed in study.[15] As he said in a speech in 1979 marking the anniversary of a massacre a year earlier, "A nation which had nothing broke a force in such a way that nothing remained of it. . . . Empty-handed, a monarchical empire of 2,500 years, 2,500 years of criminals was done away with."[16] As always, he brought to his words simplicity, directness and fervor, the rhetoric of a revolutionary.[17]

He acted as a revolutionary, too, a role he would play with enthusiasm until the end of his life. After eliminating nationalist and leftist forces that might compete with his theocratic vision for the country, and with the religious wing of the revolution firmly in the ascendancy, he proceeded to fashion the *velayat-e faqih*. He foresaw an ideal polity in which the clergy would be engaged in all aspects of society, acting as guardians of the community. They would interpret and implement law, shepherd the nation and oversee the politicians. Importantly, his vision was not just that of an Islamic government; it was, in fact, a clerical Islamic government, the clergy, in this instance, acting as a vanguard. For Khomeini, to succeed, the clergy had to gain actual control of the state and use its political power to impose Islamic law and create a truly Islamic community.[18] As in Sudan, it was a vision imposed from above, although by a different set of actors, and a variation of Qutb's obsession with the aim of controlling the government to engineer an Islamic state. More important, it assumed the ability of one class—the *ulema*—to interpret a single, true Islam. There could be no other vision of the religion, no competing ideas and no multiplicity of views. Islam was in the hands of the clergy, and the clergy were in control of the government.

In the heady, ensuing months of the clergy's consolidation of power, ministries and public institutions were purged and staff were replaced by mullahs and their protégés. To enforce religious zeal, revolutionary organizations were put in place to keep an eye on all aspects of government, society and the military. Across Iran, the government appointed in every city an *imam jomeh*, a preacher who led prayers on Friday, the Muslim sabbath, and delivered sermons on behalf of the revolution and its leaders. At the same time, prayers were enforced in the workplace, the veil was made mandatory in the early 1980s and religion—in particular, the symbols of Shiite sacrifice—became the discourse and framework in which politics were played out in daily life.[19]

Those same symbols and rhetoric served as a powerful ideology to mobilize for war, justifying for many a brutal, grinding conflict with neighboring Iraq that began in 1980, after small border clashes, and lasted until 1988, causing a staggering $650 billion in damage and resulting in more than a million casualties for Iran alone. In its scope, the sacrifice spoke volumes of Islam's ability as a faith to mobilize a people for revolution and war. It also served to further consolidate the young revolution, uniting the military's nationalism (as an institution, it was consistently under suspicion as potentially counterrevolutionary) with the devotion and zeal of the Islamic government. Demonstrations and protests faded amid wartime necessity and bitter repression ended potential challenges to the Islamic government, which remained a work in progress throughout the conflict.

What was that government? Khomeini's vision of a theocracy was straightforward enough, but in practice, it had to make compromises and concessions along the way. Always, its survival was paramount, taking precedence even over Islamic law, an idea that many clergy would consider wildly blasphemous. To Khomeini, the revolution's mission was nothing less than the creation of a government and community blessed by God and nothing, not even God's law, could stand in the way of that task. As he said in response to a statement by the country's president in 1988:

> [Governing] is a primary principle of Islam, overriding those that are secondary in nature, including even prayer, fasting and pilgrimage. The ruler can order the demolition of a mosque. . . . The Islamic government can unilaterally rescind any contract with the population, even one formerly approved and conforming to *sharia*, if it is deemed to be against the interests of the country and Islam. The government can forbid any act, religious or non-religious, when it is against the interests of Islam, for as long as necessary. It can temporarily forbid pilgrimage, one of the pillars of Islam, if it happens to be against the interests of the Islamic country.[20]

His government was a theocracy but one with representative institutions, a simmering contradiction between autocracy and democracy. In Khomeini's conception, the government's supreme authority was the guide of the revolution, a position he occupied until his death. (He was replaced by Ali Khamenei, a cleric with substantial revolutionary credentials but who lacked the popular stature and influence of Khomeini and, with a far less rigorous academic and scholarly background, was not generally held in high esteem by the country's clerical elite.) The guide, a position for life, is appointed by an elected body known as the Assembly of Experts, which can dismiss him only in the case of grave infringements on his duties. The guide, in turn, can dismiss the president, acts as commander-in-chief and appoints the heads of the media, revolutionary guards, military and the judiciary, all among the most important institutions within the government. He is expected, however, to refrain from interfering in day-to-day politics and affairs of state, although the degree of that interference is still fiercely debated today. The Council of Guardians, a body of six clerics and six jurists, keeps watch over Parliament,[21] ensuring that all legislation is in conformity with Islamic laws. The president, who is limited to two four-year terms, has the greatest popular mandate. He is popularly elected and appoints a cabinet whose members must be approved by Parliament, which can impeach them. The government, though, is designed with the clergy in mind, each popular institution with a religious counterbalance—the supreme leader and the president, Parliament and the Council of Guardians—with all key institutions, including the courts, firmly under the sway of the supreme leader.[22] Yet although the clergy keeps control, there remains room for popular expression and discontent, a feature of the government that has proven responsible for dramatic social and political change and, in the end, may be responsible for its successful reform.

—

Under the revolutionary government, Iran witnessed sweeping changes in education, political participation, even in the field of women's rights. Higher education, which was a luxury of the rich under the Shah, saw its enrollment rise in the twenty years after the revolution from 175,000 to 1.3 million. On the eve of the Shah's fall, only half of people between the ages of six and twenty-four could read and write. Today, in an achievement that speaks for itself, more than 90 percent of Iranians are literate.[23] Traditional women found the Islamic setting of educational institutions more palatable and hence comprised a larger and larger portion of their ranks. Across society, women continued to participate actively in the workforce and other spheres of public life. Although the economy became lethargic at best, beset by war, isolation and unstable oil prices, income distribution improved: the top fifth of society earned substantially less than it did during the revolution and the bottom fifth earned slightly more.[24]

The popular mobilization of the revolution and war remain, if weathered by middle-aged weariness. Although less frequently than in the revolution's early days, the country's powerful leaders still pay tribute to the revolution's populist legacy by occasionally visiting very public mosques on Friday to deliver sermons to audiences that number in the thousands. I found it remarkable that, in conscious opposition to the Shah's remoteness and ostentation, those politicians continue to feel an obligation to mix it up with the people, paying homage to the events that brought them to power. The commitment to the revolution remains a symbol, I thought, as I watched Hashemi Rafsanjani, the former Iranian president, speak casually with worshipers gathered at Tehran University, where in the days of the revolution the crowd would spill haphazardly and chaotically into the surrounding streets. In fact, if seen without the lens of the West, and the impression a religious government makes, Iran seems, in many ways, a more just, equitable and democratic society than it was in 1979.

Twenty years on, however, the fervor of that revolution was hard to find. Achievements aside, faith in modern Iran more and more resembled a defeated soldier returning from the front—weary of the now-clichéd slogans, blind to the symbols and desperate for an ordered life void of the revolutionary gusto and the tenacious disorder that brings. As I wandered through the streets of Tehran on my first visit, I was struck time and again by a sobriety that had left only faint echoes of the passion the revolution had once inspired. Along Teleqani Avenue, the martial mural that washed over several stories of a building was more a curious relic than an exhortation—painted was an American flag, its red stripes the streaks of missiles, its white stars a well-ordered fifty skulls. It seemed lonely to me, overshadowed as it was by the newly painted garden scenes and abstract geometric designs brightly splashed on walls and buildings throughout the city. They mixed well with the purple and pink buses careening through the streets as part of a conscious and, to a large degree, successful effort by Gholamhosain Karbaschi, the former mayor who tried to remake a city left dour by years of war and, in the process, created a new, distinctly un-Islamic aesthetic.

Tehran, the capital of the Islamic Republic, is a tantalizing city, full of the contradictions that collide and coexist in Iranian society itself. Oddly, it is not an Islamic symbol—it speaks neither of the faith nor of the revolution. Rather, in many ways, it reminded me of a pleasant European city: sharp confectioneries, clothes and shoe stores advertising in English, the all-too-American hamburger restaurants and canals carrying water along elegant, tree-lined avenues. Its freeways suggested Los Angeles as did its commercial billboards, which seemed irreconcilable with a movement that posed itself as an alternative to Western consumerism. In fact, only the veil, a somber mantle that dates to before the Prophet Mohammed and, its proponents say, is mandated by the Quran, distinguished Tehran as somehow Islamic. To this day, it remains the most visible legacy of the revolution, although the dark, alluring hair that often falls playfully from beneath its sad colors and formless shape signals creeping dissent against even that accomplishment.

I felt those appearances in Tehran suggested a deeper malaise, one that touched the very essence of the republic and its avowed mission. I wondered what the government that Khomeini created and the exhausted revolution he oversaw had done to the faith itself. Did others, in fact, share the fears of Eshkevari, the disenchanted cleric? Those were the questions I took to a friend of a friend, a strikingly beautiful literature professor who like many others in Tehran was reluctant to let her name be published since our visit came during one of the recurring bouts of repression that occasionally gripped the capital. Many Iranians saw the campaigns as an attempt by self-proclaimed defenders of the revolution to keep off balance real and potential opposition in and outside government. I would see that menacing, unpredictable nature of Iranian life played out again and again—on Stalinesque television programs that maligned prominent thinkers as stooges of the West, in death squad–style executions of intellectuals, in arrests and harassment of writers and journalists and in the fear I found so often in interviews. The unease rarely silenced people—Iranians are remarkably forthright—but it was often enough to hang over conversations in Tehran like a sleepy sentry, and no one seemed to know what might bring the guard out of his slumber.

As we sat over small cups of tea sweetened with hard candy, the professor recalled the Islam of her youth, during the Shah's time, when she considered faith sacred, an element of her culture and beliefs that went unquestioned. It was a religion that, reshaped and redefined by the enforced orthodoxy of the revolution and its defenders in government, no longer resonated with her. Islam, she said, had lost its spirituality and its identity. In her words, I heard the distinct echo of my interviews in Sudan, where people under similar circumstances had persistently questioned the audacity of those in power to determine what they would believe spiritually.

"It's not sacred anymore," she said firmly, in tones marked more by anger than by regret. "No shah could ever de-Islamize Iran the way the Islamic regime did."

Faezeh, as I will call her, was in every respect a critic of the regime. She was an intellectual and a professor, educated in America and, like most of Iran's intelligentsia, despondent over the limited freedom she found in the country in which she was raised. That melancholy, at times, turned into tears as she painted a picture of a people thirsting for what she called "color and beauty." Her grief struck me. She was an independent woman with a doctorate from America and a reputation among literary critics in Iran, yet she yearned for the sanctuary and simple solace that Islam had at one time provided. The changes wrought by the revolution had deprived her of that retreat and, with it, the emotional force that Islam in Iran had once meant to her.

In her mind, Islam, particularly Iranian Shiism, had long defined itself as an otherworldly faith that spoke to the people, even at times embodying their opposition to oppression. Across the Muslim world, Shiism is a minority, overshadowed in most countries by the orthodox Sunni sect of Islam. The division between the two major branches dates to a debate over the selection of a successor to the Prophet Mohammed. At the time of his death in 632, the majority believed that the prophet had not designated a successor and accepted the decision of his closest companions to choose a follower as the community's political leader. To them, no one could succeed the prophet as a spiritual guide. A minority, however, insisted that Mohammed had chosen his son-in-law and nephew, Ali, to lead the community as a spiritual and political successor. Their name is drawn from that support. *Shi'a* means partisans in Arabic, in their case, partisans of Ali. They believed leadership of the Muslim community stayed in the hands of Ali and his descendants, and their legitimacy as imams, or spiritual leaders, is a central doctrine of the faith. The dominant Shiite belief, Twelver Shiism, which holds sway in Iran, stipulates that there were twelve imams, the last one disappearing in 873.[25]

The legitimacy of the prophet's descendants is what makes so painful to Shiites the martyrdom of Hussein, who was the second son of Ali and the prophet's grandson. He was killed in 680 in a battle at Kerbala near the Euphrates River in modern-day Iraq, and his enemies, despite having no claim to leadership of the *umma*, were afterward accepted by most Muslims as the rulers of the new Islamic empire. The Shiites defiantly rejected the claim, and Hussein's tragic death gave rise to an elaborate literature of prose, poetry and song that even today brings worshipers to tears and stands as a pervasive element of Iran's rich and enduring culture. It can be read as a revolutionary calling, as well. Within its stories are powerful currents of martyrdom and injustice, a skepticism of temporal authority and an ongoing battle against the illegitimate tyranny embodied by Hussein's killers. The power of that memory and its ability to inspire sorrow and grief struck me almost immediately after my arrival in Tehran, as I watched images on Iranian television of men listening to verse that told of Hussein's death and the legendary sufferings of his family. The force behind the pictures surprised and shocked me. In them, I saw the spirituality, the pain and the personalization of the faith. Men were sobbing, their heads buried in their hands, as they again endured the anguish of his death more than thirteen centuries later. Unlike the more austere, orthodox Islam in the Arab world that always seemed distant to me, this was a passion, emotion and conviction inspired by faith with which I could identify, one that recalled to me the sufferings of Christ and the tragedy and redemption of his crucifixion, even down to a shared fixation on blood. It was a death laden with symbolism and mysticism, and it can resonate today as it did 100 years ago, or even 1,000 years ago.

But to Faezeh, and to many others in Iran today, the faith had lost that mystique, surrendering the majestic for the mundane. She once saw religion as otherworldly, but now she complained that Islam in Iran had been made crass by, for instance, naming streets after imams. Who, she asked, could take seriously a highway named Imam Hussein? In her eyes, the government had brought Islam down to earth, where it could be questioned, doubted, blamed and maligned. No longer could it embody protest or even offer, as it had for centuries, a spiritual refuge for those who were oppressed.

"As soon as the government came to power," she said, her voice heavy with sorrow, "the faith lost that attraction."

What Faezeh alluded to was part of a greater phenomenon that served as a damning verdict of the revolution's legacy. Simply put, many Iranians had lost faith, at least the faith propagated by the Islamic government. In bookstores, in homes and in the streets, I felt people searching for spirituality, seeking a way to fill a void left by Islam's gradual transformation into an ideology. Islam, it seemed, had become shackled by a single interpretation brought to bear on people day after day through laws, edicts, pronouncements and even government policy. The clerical government had become Islam, Islam had become the government, and there was no longer any in between. Its exalted essence had been sacrificed for ideological purity. It was the opposite of what would become the rallying point for the reformers grouped around Khatami: pluralism, tolerance and the range of religious and political views that entails.

During one evening I spent with a young couple in Tehran, we spoke about that changing role of Islam in people's lives. They, like other people I met in Tehran, insisted that people had become less religious since the revolution or, perhaps, more reluctant to rely on Islam to fulfill their spiritual needs. They said this with sadness, as if they as Iranians had lost part of their culture or even their heritage. Some, they told me, had increasingly turned to alcohol, hashish or opium, evidence of a growing problem of abuse, particularly among the young, that was increasingly visible in Iranian streets. Nearly everyone, the young wife told me, had black market liquor tucked away in their cabinets, and I found it offered, with no hint of guilt, nearly every time I visited someone's house in the evening. There was the suggestion of subtle, unspoken defiance in the gesture, as if traditional hospitality had somehow become dissent.

Disillusionment, it seems, has a tendency toward nihilism, and in Iran, it was no different. About two-thirds of Iranians are under twenty-five, with no memory of a revolution that, despite its aftermath, remains popular among the vast majority of older Iranians. The government has long known that the indoctrination of those youth, through the media, through education, through cultural centers and through the military, is the key in deciding whether the Islamic Republic is a short-lived experiment, little more than a historical footnote, or the permanent face of a modern Iran. Without their support or, at the very least, good-willed acquiescence, the Islamic Republic has no future.

With that in mind, the government in the early 1980s launched a cultural revolution with the intention of completely overhauling the education system, at one point even shutting down the country's universities. Nothing would be left untouched, neither higher education nor preschools. The idea was to set up a religious curriculum, employ instructors committed to Islam, the revolution and the republic and create after-school activities that would help produce and reproduce that vision of every revolution—a new man, or, in Iran's case, an Islamic citizen. In my time in Iran, talk of Islamizing education, two decades after the revolution, still dominated newspapers, sermons and the speeches of Ali Khamenei, the country's supreme leader. A faithful example of that vision was put forth by Ali Akbar Nateq Noori, the powerful Parliament speaker and hard-line presidential candidate, who insisted that teachers should adhere to a certain standard of "Islamic values and religious dedication."

"If professors teach in universities who are indifferent to Islamic values, they could divert the minds of students with various tricks," he warned a meeting at Tabriz University. "Islamic values must be complied with in selection of professors, admission of students, employment of staff and even in textbooks."

But after all that time, what was the effect of the campaign? The positive side was the impressive gains the government had secured in higher education and literacy. The downside, at least for the Islamic Republic, was the failure of Islamization. Even official surveys seemed to suggest that, at best, the government had failed to instill religious fervor. At worst, it had actually turned youth away from Islam, ironically making the young in the Islamic Republic less religious. One such survey by the Supreme Council of Youth put it in stark terms: more than 83 percent of young people spent their leisure time before television sets, but only 5 percent watched religious programs; of 58 percent who read books, less than 6 percent were interested in religious literature.[26] What I was to find in a park in fashionable north Tehran gave me the feeling that those surveys told only half the story.

Shuan was one of those youths, Iran's version of a slacker. I found him sitting lazily on a bench in Qaytarieh Park along one of the pleasant, well-lit concrete paths that hem in the palace of a former Iranian prime minister. Families chatted at a *chaykhaneh*, a traditional teahouse, as the scent of homemade bread mixed with the soft strains of traditional Persian music and the ripple of water cascading down cobblestone canals. It was a remarkably tranquil scene, one that I found was not shared by Shuan.

"Iran is heaven for those who are not living here," he told me, as he dragged on a locally made cigarette in a pose of studied disregard.

Shuan, a handsome man of twenty-five, had no job. The future held neither promise nor dread; it simply awaited him. With his friend, Nouri, he spent most evenings at the park, playing chess, he said, or trying to pick up women, always on the lookout for patrols of young, religiously committed men who considered flirting an offense worthy of a little time in jail or maybe a few lashes.

"You grew up in America with hope," he told me in a way that suggested he was eager to talk to someone about it, "but here we don't have any hope. In America, if you get sad or down, you can go into the street and shout as loud as you want."

It was an idea repeated over and over in my meetings with young Iranians: that they were suffocating and that they, somehow, had to break out. It was the atomized nature of Iran that I would see time and again—a powerful current that reformers have sought to stanch and then redirect into political participation. As it was, many of the people I encountered, particularly the young, were withdrawn, and running through those conversations was a streak of nihilism. I found the recklessness troubling.

This was best dramatized by a question Shuan asked me at one point in our talk, a query I have had to answer countless times in the Middle East: As an American with Lebanese grandparents, what was my religion? Christian, I said half-heartedly, expecting a few lines about how much we had in common with Muslims, or how nothing should prevent us from living together peacefully.

Instead, Shuan exclaimed, "Thank God!" and then went on to declare with a smile of almost adolescent guilt: "I'm an apostate."

That, I thought, was the most unusual answer I had ever heard from any Muslim in the Middle East. In the secular West, apostasy means little more than atheism, an inclination that although often frowned upon is not necessarily unacceptable. We see it as an expression of our freedom of religion or as one of the rights we usually take for granted as individuals. Under Islamic law, however, apostasy, or *ridda* as it is known in Arabic, is a capital offense. To renounce one's faith in God would bring the death penalty from an Islamic court, and it is a blasphemous idea that, until then, I had never heard uttered or, even worse, joked about. That I had heard it in the Islamic Republic, in its capital, made it even more jarring. Shuan, like other young Iranians, was tempting fate, his alienation so severe that he would recklessly flout a concept so dear to the religion, and, by default, to a government that saw itself as a guardian of that faith. By challenging belief itself, he seemed to have found a measure of freedom.[27]

I encountered the youthful idea of the forbidden becoming desirable throughout Tehran. The writing, in fact, was literally on the wall. Along with official slogans about the sanctity of the veil or praise of God was scrawled "Just do it!" in big red letters in north Tehran. Along Kordestan Street, there were a few more surprises: a peace symbol in black and the spray-painting of an electric guitar superimposed over other graffiti that had already been scrubbed out, washed off or painted over. Youthful energy seemed to me to be going everywhere and nowhere at the same time.

In nearly all Muslim countries I visited, the frustration of youth was fertile ground for Islamic activists. They point to corrupt regimes, brutal police and the misery bred by mismanaged economies and offer hope through slogans promising justice and a moral order under God. In Iran, however, young people had no ideology to articulate their frustrations. Islam here symbolized a government that was ineffectual at best, repressive at worst, and more often than not the target of their frustration. To Shuan and others, religion meant nothing and politics did not matter. By making the West, its music, its movies and its imagined way of life so forbidden, the authorities had instead made all these things more intriguing. This is the paradox of the Islamic Republic's attempt to reproduce Islamic citizens. Rather than creating a generation faithful to the revolution, it depoliticized it, giving rise to anger without vision and opposition without inspiration. In the worst case, it led to a dangerous cynicism. When repressed needs and pent-up demands exploded—as they did in students' protests at Tehran University in 1999—they failed to coalesce into a coherent movement.[28] The protests became action without a goal, a movement in search of a list of demands and definable cause.

As in much of the Muslim world, the young have little to inspire them about the future. It was no different in Iran, where economic hardship added to the palpable alienation and isolation. The economy was a mess, salvaged only by dwindling oil revenues that allowed it to muddle along without drastic or painful reforms. On average, Iranians earned two-thirds of what they did before the revolution and inflation, for a time, was running at 50 percent. Unemployment figures disguised underemployment and the fact that some people were forced to take on second and third jobs to make ends meet. The one bright spot, as noted, was an improvement in income distribution, but with incomes dropping across the board, this gain in social justice had little tangible impact.

In south Tehran, which is inhabited by the poor on whose behalf the Islamic government promised to speak, I met Ali Najjar, a twenty-seven-year-old student in accounting at Tehran University. His blue shirt was buttoned to the top, a sign I took for modesty or perhaps conservatism. His glasses subdued only somewhat his fierce black eyes, which left an impression of slow-burning, frustrated anger. He complained to me that money had become everything in Iran today, and it was something of which he had precious little.

"The morals have gone and been replaced by money," he said. "The social values and the principles are not there anymore."

It later came out that he was having trouble paying for medicine his mother needed for her heart condition, and I sensed that his inability to care for her was a source of great shame, that somehow he as a man had failed his family. It was a question of honor, and it again pointed to the danger in monopolizing the truth. If Islam as an ideology was the only solution to a nation's problems—political, economic, social, and, of course, moral—who was to blame when that same ideology brought misery? Ali saw himself as a good Muslim, yearning for justice and what he called "religious values," but the very proponent of those values was the source of his plight. Someone or, more appropriately, something had to be blamed, and increasingly the government's exclusive identification with Islam brought the faith inexorably into a no-win situation.

More troubling to youth than economics, however, were the intrusions that defined Iranian life, the interference that a government considered its right if it was to enforce a moral order. At my hotel, a few feet away from a sign that read "Death to America," I spent an afternoon chatting with an intelligent young couple with masters' degrees in English literature who were now working as instructors. Both thirty years old, they were just children when the Shah was forced to leave Iran, so they had lived most of their lives under the Islamic Republic. They told me a tale of threat and rebellion, a battle for privacy that was played out again and again on a very personal level.

"It's not a revolution, it's an institution," the husband, Daryush, told me when I asked what the revolution meant. "It's a part of our life because it's constantly intruding in our life. We have to think about it, we have to talk about it."

Both Daryush and Tahmineh saw their individuality at stake, which was especially galling to Tahmineh. To a degree not shared by Christianity, Islam recognizes the desire and passion of men, even celebrating it. Often, that recognition leads to sexually frank discussions among men that might shock a Westerner and an American, or leave them fumbling for words. But that same appreciation of desire condemns women in strict Muslim states to perpetual harassment. Their seduction, it is believed, must be controlled, blunted and channeled into marriage and motherhood, the highest callings of a good Muslim woman. The attachment to honor is one way to beat back temptation. The veil stands as another way to ensure that men are not led astray. Sometimes, however, even those restrictions fail, leading to occasionally surreal warnings. In Afghanistan, I heard a prayer leader insist with trembling anger that the voice of a woman could inexorably lead a man to adultery. What should be done about that? I wondered.

Iranian women have avoided the specter of Afghanistan. They run their own magazines, move freely in the streets and fill half the positions in the government bureaucracy. A woman serves as vice president and others have been elected to municipal councils and Parliament in numbers comparable to their American counterparts, although they cannot stand for president.[29] Women are prominent in medicine and thought to comprise more than half of practitioners. They can drive and vote, unlike women in Saudi Arabia, and they are fighting battles to amend divorce laws, bring about changes in child custody laws, receive payment for housework and be allowed to serve as judges. For more traditional women, in an unintended benefit, the conservative public environment fostered by the government has allowed them, in substantial numbers, to enter the workplace without fear of losing their identity as good Muslims. In comparison to the secular West, however, their repression in daily life remains pronounced, particularly for young women in public places like university campuses.

Tahmineh studied at a university in southern Iran, an experience that she does not recall fondly. Talking to a young man was dangerous, unless he was your husband or your brother. Classes were segregated. And every morning, she had to pass a woman standing at the gate, checking female students for makeup and making sure their head-to-toe chadors—always in somber colors of gray, brown, black or dark blue—were long enough so that their legs were hidden. Occasionally, she remembered, the woman would ask her to wipe her lips with a tissue to make sure she was not wearing lipstick.

"I wore the dark uniform, that dark covering, but I wore red socks, too," she said.

As a married couple, the intrusions were somewhat reduced, but still sufficient to regulate their lives in maddening ways. Even more frustrating, they said, was not knowing what those regulations were, a complaint I heard often.[30]

"There's no definition for something Islamic," Daryush said. "Tomorrow, I will go with jeans. The day after, I don't know. I don't know whether it will be approved.

"There's no definition of un-Islamic sunglasses. It always depends solely on the person who intrudes on you," he said.

"When you faced fixed rules, you know how to act. But when the rules are not fixed, you face something constantly changing," Daryush said, the frustration in his voice growing. "I have to accept it just to get by and that's the worst part of it."

"The government and its people hide behind Islam, but this is not Islam," Tahmineh said, interrupting her husband.

Daryush added, "This is vulgarized Islam."

Again, there was the question: What does that do to faith in God? Through his frustration, I saw the effect on the faith by its association with the regime, an identification so close as to blur the lines of distinction between the two. The government justified its rules, its regulations and its vision of a moral order through Islam or, more appropriately, through the one interpretation of Islam that it transformed into official ideology. There was no room for dissent; devotion to Islam meant devotion to the state since—in the government's eyes—they were one and the same. It was the metamorphosis Eshkevari feared and Faezeh despised. For Daryush and Tahmineh, like the couple I met for dinner who felt they had lost part of their culture and heritage, it meant they had to search for spirituality and solace elsewhere. Their friends, they said, were interested in transcendental meditation, Buddhism, or maybe even surrendering everything for an unspeakable atheism, both as an act of personal fulfillment and rebellion. Their statement was extreme. Most Iranians I met were not opposed to an

Islamic government per se; they only wanted an Islamic government that respected their rights and departed from the ideological rigor it had imposed on religion. Disengagement from politics, though, ran the risk of preventing that reform. For many Iranians, citizenship and the responsibilities it entailed had lost their meaning. The society, at the time, seemed gripped by a form of government-cultivated agoraphobia—a fear of public decisions, public participation and popular engagement in civic life.

In a phenomenon that was widespread, Daryush and Tahmineh did not care about politics. They retreated to their homes, to their satellite dish, to books and to music that the government could not stamp out. They created their own space, a lonely refuge that was removed from Islam, the revolution and the government. There, they could escape from menacing unpredictability and the opaque nature of oppression. Their existence seemed so depressing as to be almost hopeless. Always, there was the threat of young thugs bursting into theaters to find unmarried couples sitting together or raiding parties at homes. In the streets, a girl might nervously glance behind her after laughing boisterously. When she left home, she might worry that she was wearing too much color.

It was, at that time, a perpetual revolution, or more appropriately, revolution for the sake of revolution. Without institutions and without rules, nothing was certain, even in good times, and I came to believe that the government was possessed by a mentality that seemed to feed off chaos. Perhaps that was the legacy of Khomeini, who remained a revolutionary to the end. He thrived on the ideas of reshaping, redefining and remaking, always seeking to keep the energy produced by that disruption funneled into a revolution that he saw as sacred. Once the revolution died, he seemed to believe, his Islamic government would pass as well. The disorder, agitation and confusion were not viable, though. In Khomeini's wake, faith and revolutionary fervor were replaced, all too often, by a measure of fear and a menacing unease cloaked in moral order.

As one writer put it to me, "We have completely consumed our illusions."[31]

Iran today, in all its complexity, stands on the verge of post-Islam, a condition in which the appeal, energy and symbols of Islam are exhausted.[32] In its place are emerging ideas of democracy, an indigenous conception of human rights and a focus on individual freedom and choice. The ferment itself comes amid a growing perception among Iranians—as evidenced by conversations with clergy such as Eshkevari, intellectuals like Faezeh and the young academic couple—that Islam does not have the answers to all societies' problems, that alone it cannot handle every challenge Iran will confront. That recognition, one only now emerging, will prove crucial to the viability of Islamic movements everywhere. In Iran, it means a search for a new system and a rethinking of the Iranian Revolution are under way, a questioning brought about by the disillusionment and disenchantment that is frank, fresh and invigorating. The force behind that is another cleric who studied in Qom, Seyyed Mohammad Khatami, who was elected in a landslide as Iran's president in 1997.

The president of the Islamic Republic is a compelling figure in Iranian politics, a throwback to the refined, cultured clergyman of a now forgotten Iran. As a reformer, moreover, he wields the authority and stature of challenging the very institution from which he comes. Khatami was born in 1942 into a middle-class clerical family in Ardakan, a town in the central Iranian province of Yazd. He left his birthplace at the age of nineteen to study in Qom, where Ayatollah Khomeini's son was a classmate and a close friend. His time there began an eclectic and, at times, independent education that would take him to Isfahan to study philosophy, Tehran to study education and then Qom again to renew his religious scholarship. According to his official biography, he became politically active as a student leader during those years and was arrested by the Shah's secret police. In 1978, on the eve of the Iranian Revolution, he was chosen to lead the Iranian-sponsored Islamic Institute in Hamburg, Germany, where he had his first sustained contact with the West.

Khatami, a handsome, urbane man who traces his lineage to the prophet, was no outsider. He served as a deputy in Iran's postrevolutionary parliament, then was appointed to head the Ministry of Culture and Islamic Guidance, an institution with decisive influence over the country's intellectual and artistic life. He served as minister for ten years, most of his tenure falling during the war with Iraq when government persecution was at its peak (in some speeches, he has acknowledged the repression of those years, stopping short of apologizing for measures that he seems to believe were a political necessity). Books were banned and systematically censored, publishers had their licenses revoked and newspapers in the good graces of the government received the scarce and subsidized newsprint.[33]

A new style emerged after the war. Khatami presided over a relative flowering of Iranian culture, in particular cinema, which gained an international reputation in the 1990s for an evocative, simple style that stressed absolute values and a sense of justice and morality.[34] Writers found that they could appeal government decisions directly to Khatami or his deputy, and a press arbitration council was set up to deal with complaints against journalists and writers charged with violating occasionally obscure moral and political codes.[35] There seemed to be a sense of camaraderie between some intellectuals and Khatami, who clearly considered himself a scholar and thinker. (He speaks English, Arabic and German, can converse on the works of Alexis de Tocqueville and Immanuel Kant and has published two books, one of them a study of Western political thought.) Those years of his tenure, however, upset hard-line elements within the government who considered him too liberal and lenient, and he was forced from office in 1992. From there, he became the head of Iran's national library, a position of little consequence but one that allowed him to conceive his campaign for the presidency.

Khatami's election victory in 1997—he won with a stunning two-thirds of the electorate over a conservative candidate favored by the clerical establishment—was ensured by the votes of women and youth, and the festivities over the outcome reminded many in Iran of the heady days of the revolution itself.[36] Supporters danced in the streets, cars put on their headlights and youths handed out candy, a traditional Iranian gesture of celebration. What they marked was an occasion in which the people did not vote against the revolution but instead—in a remarkably democratic way—decided what direction their government should take. Khatami, who set up a Web site to elaborate on his ideas, promised to answer that call. He pledged to strengthen the institutions of a civil society and encourage open debate in a polity that would accept other views.[37] It was as politically perfect a convergence of popular demands and campaign promises as possible. He also put forth a new style, eschewing honorifics for a simple "Mr. President" or "Mr. Khatami," and promoted an image that bordered on the avuncular.[38] Every portrait seemed to picture him smiling, and he was not averse to flashes of humor, in striking contrast to the dour, forbidding visage of Khomeini. Some even remarked on the president's sex appeal—a first, I thought, in the Islamic Republic.[39]

Khatami brought intellectual force to his ideas, as well. As a religious thinker, he is fiercely devoted to his faith and Iran, but at the same time, he attempts to realistically appraise both of their places in the modern world. He asks the question posed by so many other Islamic thinkers: How can a society whose identity is religious guarantee freedom, democracy and social justice? To Khatami, the solution is not Islam in itself. Alone, as an ideology of government, it cannot solve the problems of a world that, for better or for worse, is dominated by the West. In one lecture, he declared bluntly, "We Muslims once had a dominant civilization and were shaping human history in a way that we are no longer capable of today. We want to regain our place in history and, if possible, build a future that is different from our present and even our past, without rejecting those who are different from us, and without ignoring scientific thought and the practical achievement of humanity."[40] If the revolution solely sought a return to an earlier Islamic civilization, a golden age, then it failed because that civilization, in Khatami's eyes, is an anachronism. It no longer exists in practical terms and, if it did, it could no longer meet the needs of the modern era. In that argument, he makes a subtle but compelling distinction between Islamic traditionalists who seek a return to what Islam once had and Islamist activists in Iran and elsewhere who seek to progressively reshape the faith into a viable, modern approach to government and society. The latter, he believes, is the only option, and he envisions it as the true legacy of the revolution. "If (Islamic civilization) had maintained its dynamism, relevance and ability to provide answers to people's problems," he said, "that civilization would have endured."

The problem then, he argues, is a static society, one that can no longer meet the psychological, material and social needs of the people but, even more dangerous, obstinately refuses to acknowledge its failings. Iran, he suggests, falls into that category, and the dangers posed by it could undo the vision of a religious society. Dynamism must be a goal. "Our society's fabric is strained by vice; economic and political difficulties loom large, and we suffer from the diluted identity of Westoxication—neither ourselves, nor Western," Khatami said. "In practical matters, as we have depended on theology to give order to the individual and social worlds, we face serious inadequacies. This can only mean that our theology must evolve to meet the demands of the revolution and also the practical needs we have today."

Khatami is a skillful politician. He recognizes that he is venturing into uncharted territory, calling for religious reform that could only come from a cleric who speaks the language of the educated clergy. Often, he uses selective quotes from Khomeini to bolster his position. In one passage, Khomeini asserts that in Islamic government, "there should always be room for revision. Our revolutionary system demands that various, even opposing viewpoints be allowed to surface. . . . It is here that traditional religious leadership prevalent in our seminaries will not suffice." The words echo Khatami's promises but, even then, it is difficult to imagine an ardent revolutionary like Khomeini endorsing the pragmatism and appeal for tolerance and understanding that the Iranian president represents. (In fact, Khomeini's successor and ideological heir as spiritual leader, Ali Khamenei, kept an uneasy distance throughout Khatami's tenure, skeptical of the direction in which the president's policies were leading, but fearful of the popular mandate he enjoyed.) The context of Khatami's argument—the sources of legitimacy he seeks—offers perhaps a greater insight in that it speaks to the prestige Khomeini still commands in postrevolutionary Iran. There remains the need, particularly in religion, the most delicate of issues in the Islamic Republic, to frame arguments within the context of the revolution's vision and its most esteemed institutions, Khomeini among them.

To create the flexibility in theology that Khatami pursues means to break the clergy's monopoly on religious interpretation, a right held by the *ulema* in Shiite Iran to a far greater extent than that possessed by their Sunni counterparts elsewhere in the Muslim world. Despite their theological disputes, the Shiite clergy have historically considered themselves the spiritual guardians of the community, and that spiritual prestige was the foundation on which Khomeini built the Islamic state. Khatami, though, sees a danger in that same prestige, the prospect of a single, infallible interpretation, made even more formal when it becomes an ideology of government. In essence, he proposes doing away with the clergy's unique right. In taking that step, he brings the revolution full circle. The fall of the Shah was one incarnation; the fall of an infallible clergy the second. Since the sixteenth century, the Shiite clergy had ruled with the monarchy, first the Safavid dynasty, then its successors. The clergy gave temporal supremacy to the monarchs but kept the right to be the unique interpreters of Islamic law. The struggle between those institutions for the soul of Iran was an integral part of society's fabric and a pervasive theme of the country's modern history. Yet, if Khatami was to create a society in which a multiplicity of views was the norm, the right of interpretation, at the very least, had to be broadened, perhaps even redefined. To do so, Khatami relies on an argument that other scholars have advanced, namely that every interpretation depends on man's inherently fallible reason, and therefore must be considered critically, even skeptically.

As Khatami said, "Given the multiplicity of views of religion over history, we must ensure that we do not think that our view of religion is the only one. . . . True, these are sacred matters, but our interpretations of them are human. Only through this realization will humans open their minds to the experiences and innovations of others."

In another address, he urges people not to follow the dictates of the clergy blindly, pointing out that even Khomeini himself is not infallible. Again and again, he remarks on the danger posed by "unenlightened religious dogma"[41] and, in a way, puts forth his own eclectic education, one both religious and secular, as a model. "A moral person who is a moving encyclopedia but lives outside his time," he said, "for whom the most pressing problems are for example the second and third Islamic centuries, cannot solve even the smallest of today's problems, for today's problems do not interest him."

Dogma, in particular, worries him and he scolds his fellow clergy: "We should all avoid considering our own understandings and interpretations as absolute, which can only be attributed to the Book and the Divine Revelation itself," he said. If interpretation remains absolute, Khatami suggests that Iranian society will experience the same dislocation, disruption and strife that came with the fall in the Middle Ages of the Catholic Church's hegemony over western European intellectual and political life. The church sought to maintain a monopoly on thought and to keep the sole right to interpret truth and falsehood; its persistence in defending that eventually obsolete prerogative was its undoing. The theme defines much of Khatami's thinking, and often, he seems implicitly to compare Iran to Rome:

> It is true that the inability of the culture of the Middle Ages to offer answers to human curiosity and needs, and resorting to physical and psychological force to suppress those questions and needs, led to an

intellectual and social explosion which caused the rule of the Church and feudal overlords to crumble. . . . [T]he harsh restrictions imposed by the Church and feudalism were instrumental in bringing about a reaction in the opposite direction. The Church had given its practices a sacred façade such that its excesses led Westerners not only to overturn the extant social order, but to doubt the whole validity of religion and spirituality.

Where next, then? Khatami sees religion—in Iran's case, the framework for society and government—as open to an interpretation that changes with time and place. And in today's world, time and place are clearly and overwhelmingly dominated by the West. Although he is critical of the materialism of Western society, its economic and cultural domination and its record of exploitation in colonial and postcolonial times, Khatami nevertheless sees its accomplishments as awesome and urges that it be reckoned with in a balanced, rational way. Muslims, he says, should neither be dogmatically and blindly opposed to it nor captivated by its appeal. Rather, they should draw from it.

"We must understand the peculiarities of our era and treat Western civilization as our era's ultimate manifestation and symbol," he said. "This means understanding the values and tenets of Western civilization and freeing ourselves from the equally harmful extremes of either hating it or being completely taken in and entranced by it."[42]

What the West does offer Iran, he believes, are some of the institutions that have made it so successful—individual rights, democracy, freedom, plurality of opinion and the rule of law, the very basis of modernity—and Khatami consistently urges the "judicious acquisition" of them. Those concepts and Khatami's endorsement of them in the framework of an Islamic civil society, I felt, spoke directly to the fear and unease I ran across so often in Iran, the mentality that had long fed off chaos.

At a rally in 1998 at Tehran University marking the anniversary of his election, Khatami elaborated his vision of that civil society, a concept blending West and East that he has returned to time and again. The ideas of democracy, human rights, freedom and choice echo through it. In such a society, Khatami said, the government "will guarantee freedom within the framework of law," a freedom that extends to all its citizens, including the opposition. "The art of government is not to eliminate the opposition from the arena," he said.

"The art of government is to compel even its own opposition to behave within the framework of the law."[43]

That vision was a conscious departure from the rule of the revolution, the codified anarchy that it seemed to instill. It meant, too, a retreat from the atomization and isolation that have marked Iranian society. Citizenship, thus, took on new meaning. As Khatami put it on another occasion, "establishment of the rule of law is an Islamic, revolutionary and national obligation, and an absolute imperative, which requires a conducive and enabling environment as well as legal means and instruments coupled with public involvement and assistance."

In his speeches, Khatami, like other Islamic thinkers discussed in the next chapter, draws on Islam's earliest days for inspiration. His Islamic civil society is not a slavish imitation of its Western equivalent. It instead stands as an Islamic alternative, relying as others have on the days of the prophet in the city of Medina, where Islam first held sway—an Islamic Athens of sorts. And in that Athens, Khatami sees a Muslim identity that transcends narrow-minded nationalisms, a community in which the rights of non-Muslims are respected, even guarded, and a society in which its citizens are protected by law, not threatened by the whims of a despotic ruler or the passions of a revolution.

In 1997, he delivered that idea before twenty-eight heads of state, prime ministers and crown princes of Muslim countries gathered for an Islamic summit under the snow-capped Alborz Mountains in Tehran. Khamenei, the supreme leader, talked of the "money, gluttony and carnal desires" of the West, but Khatami spoke of a civil society that would learn from the West. It would borrow Western ideas of political parties, social associations and an independent, free press, yet speak to the Islamic identity of Iranians and other Muslims. In a telling juxtaposition of two revolutions, he and Khamenei disagreed on almost every point: a dialogue of civilizations as opposed to a clash of cultures, adoption of what is good in the West as opposed to a disavowal of everything that is Western. As I watched the two men deliver their speeches, two visions of Iran's future were being laid out before much of the Muslim world. After my visits to the country, in interviews and conversations, I felt Khatami's prescription of an Islamic civil society was the only one viable.

In the civil society that we espouse, although centered around the axis of Islamic thinking and culture, . . . personal or group dictatorship or even the tyranny of the majority and elimination of the minority have no place. In such a society, man, due to the very attribute of being human, is venerated and revered and his rights are respected. Citizens of the Islamic civil society enjoy the right to determine their own destiny, supervise the governance and hold the government accountable. The government in such a society is the servant of the people and not their master, and in any eventuality, is accountable to the people whom God has entitled to determine their own destiny. Our civil society is not a society where only Muslims are entitled to rights and are considered citizens. Rather, all individuals are entitled to rights, within the framework of the law and order. Defending such rights ranks among the important fundamental duties of the government.[44]

Khatami's ideas inspired a sea change in Iranian politics, not only in adherence to the rule of law, effectively redefining the revolution and its sway over civic life, but also in the way politics, the interactions among Iranians and their relationship to the government were conceived. The *umma* remains a potent symbol in Islamic thought—at best, it can express a powerful idea of unanimity of identity and consciousness. *Fitna*, rebellion against an established authority and order, poses a threat to the *umma*, bringing impending anarchy, faction and division. For the revolution, vigilance against *fitna* was a prerequisite, particularly when Iran was under siege at home and abroad, and the cohesion of the *umma*, of the polity, stands as a powerful theme in the discourse of Iranian leaders. As Khamenei said, "When a nation and a society know that the enemy lies in wait, they set aside small differences. But when they lower their guard against the enemy, differences grow large, individuals start fighting and factions form."[45] In Khatami's vision, diversity is not *fitna* but instead the makings of his civil society. In a time of war and emergency, measures can be taken to stifle dissent. Survival is at stake. In peace, he suggests, there is no room for arbitrary oppression. Tolerance and plurality—or in another incarnation, faction and division—become the keys to society's survival, as long as they are regulated by the rule of law. At heart, they are signs of a vibrant, rich political life. As Khatami put it, "Destroying the atmosphere of peace in the name of freedom and destroying freedom in the name of religion and national interest represent two sides of the same coin, both symptomatic of the historical ailment that we suffer from due to centuries of despotic rule which has shaped our temperament to become irreconcilable with freedom."

⎯

Khatami was not alone. He was joined by other thinkers, in particular Abdol-Karim Soroush and Mohsen Kadivar, a popular university professor and middle-ranking cleric who was sentenced to eighteen months in prison in April 1999 after openly advocating the separation of political and religious institutions.[46] Like Khatami, neither thinker believed in doing away with religion in civic and political life. They were not against the idea of an Islamic Republic. But like others, they wanted to blend it with democracy, individual freedom, civil society and tolerance, and, by the end of the 1990s, they had drawn many of the revolution's staunchest defenders to their ranks. They included men and women involved in the defining moment of the revolution, the takeover by students of the American Embassy in downtown Tehran: Ibrahim Asgharzadeh, who was elected to Tehran's city council;[47] Abbas Abdi, cofounder of *Sobh-e Emrouz*, a pro-Khatami newspaper; Vice President Massoumeh Ebtekar; and Mohammad Musavi Khoeiniha, a cleric and former publisher of *Salam*, a newspaper whose banning led to the student protests in 1999.[48]

In Khatami's first years in power, substantial changes had begun to take place within Iranian society, reflecting his government's policies as well as pent-up popular demands and the progress of a nascent reform movement. A vibrant newspaper culture emerged that, in the absence of political parties, acted as a platform for the views of divergent political and social currents. Its precarious growth and vitality demonstrated the best of Khatami's vision and, more dangerous, the perils that the opponents of his reforms still posed. The tribulations of *Jameah* newspaper in 1998 were the best example. The trials of that newspaper became the news and reflected, in a microcosm, the trenchlike struggle between the two sides. *Jameah* began publishing in February 1998, an event that marked the beginning of a daily press that was independent of official institutions. It adopted a free and independent course, billing itself as representative of civil society rather than the state, and soon enjoyed spectacular popularity, its circulation surging to 230,000 with an occasional peak of 300,000. Its style was bold and irreverent. Its cartoons and drawings poked fun at political leaders, including Khatami (although not Khamenei). It criticized the military, demanded a multiparty system, freedom for trade unions and freedom of expression for all political currents, including communists and Marxists.[49] Not surprisingly, it ran afoul of the authorities and a court order, alleging fabrications and libel, closed it down in June. Two days after it was shut down, however, it came out, with the permission of Khatami's Ministry of Culture and Islamic Guidance, under the name *Tous*. Its first 100,000 copies were sold out in a few hours. Claiming, rightly, that it was identical to *Jameah* in format and staff, the judiciary closed it down. It then appeared the following day under yet a third name, *Aftab-e Emrouz*, with the permission again of the Ministry of Culture. The judiciary retreated and reinstated the license of *Tous*. Its respite was short-lived. In September, Khamenei ordered the judiciary to get tough with newspapers he said abused press freedom, and *Tous* was shut down for good. Soon after, other newspapers were closed as well. Finally, in the last skirmish in February 1999, the same group launched *Neshat*, another successor to *Tous*, which enjoyed the same popularity until it was banned in September 1999.

The battle seemed to pit two sides groping in the dark, each exploring strengths and weaknesses that neither could yet gauge. Pointedly, Mashallah Shamsolvaezin, chief editor of *Tous* who was sent to prison in April 2000 for two years for insulting Islam, described the precarious new freedoms enjoyed by him and his colleagues as shaky, "like a gelatin." In a memorable phrase, he said, "We have freedom of expression in Iran. But the problem is freedom after expression."[50]

The word *after* takes on a new meaning in the Islamic Republic. What comes *after* the revolution? What comes *after* the war with Iraq? What comes *after* Khatami's victory in the election? Iran's recent history is the story of epic conflicts and tragedies, cataclysmic wars and, at times, heroic struggles. A generation after the revolution, nothing was taken for granted in Iran; everything remained in a precarious flux. The question of what comes *after* had to be asked because no one in Iran had experienced what came *before*. The uncertainty colored much of Khatami's presidency. Newspapers and magazines helped create a vibrant forum for intellectual debates, political awareness and, a first in postrevolutionary Iran, a free and fierce exchange of open information. No sooner had that occurred then the imminent crackdown stifled most of the media's most prominent representatives. The maddening, oscillating periods of repression gave way to a more relaxed atmosphere in which women and youths were no longer routinely harassed by the *basij*, volunteer squads that once enforced a government-ordained public morality. Then, it emerged that elements with the government's Intelligence Ministry had murdered at least five Iranian dissidents in 1998 in death squad–style slayings.[51] After Khatami appointed prominent reformers to his cabinet, Tehran's mayor, a Khatami ally, was imprisoned after a public trial and his interior minister, a prominent and popular cleric, was impeached.

Yet, as Khatami's presidency went forward, it was an inescapable fact that although the *after* and the *before* seemed so precarious, Iranians were far more aware of their present. Iranian society, in fits and starts, had democratized. Municipal elections in February 1999 increased the number of elected officials from less than 400, concentrated in Tehran, to nearly 200,000 spread out across the country. In elections for Parliament in February 2000, voting lists were available and information was exchanged about the candidates, through newspapers and even at the voting stations themselves, a poignant gesture in defiance of politics that had doggedly remained nebulous and obscure. The political life Khatami envisioned had begun to take shape, and the questioning it entailed was becoming institutionalized, rather than treated as a luxury.

The vitality seemed fitting to me. The Islamic government in Iran did not emerge from a strong Islamic movement. Although Islam provided a powerful means to mobilize, the revolution itself was amorphous and opaque, and in its early days, many felt a leftist government might even come to power. The idea of *velayat-e faqih,* rule of the clergy and the constitution were all imposed from above, in the fashion of a vanguard, once the religious wing of the revolution won out over its nationalist and leftist rivals. Khatami's liberalization, in effect, was finishing a discussion cut short by revolutionary necessity and the war with Iraq. What is an Islamic government? And what are its rights and obligations?

I asked Ibrahim Yazdi, an Iranian opposition leader who had been foreign minister in the short-lived government of Mehdi Bazargan,[52] about the relationship between that Islamic government and the revolution that made it possible. He was a thoughtful man still faithful to the revolution, but seemed tired by the harassment and the hassles that his job brought. Nearly every sentence was tinged with a righteous anger that seems to come with the belief that you are on the side of truth.

"People very clearly draw a line between the revolution and the present authorities," Yazdi told me in his downtown office.

"The revolution is popular," he said. "People like it, they still are loyal and bound to its aspirations—liberty, independence and the Islamic Republic."

Does the same go for the government, I asked? He paused, then seemed to hedge.

"Before the revolution, it was very easy. What do you want? Islamic government. Now, everybody asks me what is Islamic government," he said. "There is a rewriting of some of the basic elements. Nowadays, they are talking about the interaction between religion and the state. Where do you draw the line? In the past, before the revolution, it seemed very obvious and nobody cared to analyze very critically the question. But now because of this experience after the revolution, many Iranian intellectuals are talking about what is the relation between religion and state."

"There is no end to this debate," Yazdi went on to say. "Society is continuous, like a running river. When you feel that you are through with one issue, there is another issue and another issue. These issues must continuously be debated."

The debate itself is crucial. In Iran, two faces of a revolutionary vision still resonate in the lives of its people. There is the failed revolution, the attempt to transform an insulated Islam into an ideology that could provide the answers for all matters of life, be they economic, political, educational, even artistic. As an ideology, it corrupted itself, repelling the faithful it sought to guide and discrediting the institution that sought to safeguard it. Islam, in Iran, was not the solution, and Khomeini's rule by the clergy—and the perpetual revolution to keep it beyond reproach—had failed.

Yet the other face of Iran's revolution provides a potentially more influential alternative. The generation that emerged toward the end of the 1990s championed the concept that a religious government could adhere to those institutions thought to belong to the Western tradition: dissent, democracy, human rights and basic freedoms. The vision of Khatami and others was not a crude imitation of Western democracy; it was a society that drew on the still powerful role of faith and history, but shaped it with the plurality and tolerance of a changing, dynamic polity. They did not seek to disavow the revolution or to bring an end of the Islamic Republic. They sought its maturity. How that society takes shape is the task that a new generation of thinkers across the Muslim world is addressing, including the most prominent among them, Abdol-Karim Soroush, an Iranian ideologue of the country's new Islam.

7

~

From West to East

A New Generation of
Thinkers and the Search for
Common Ground

LIKE NO OTHER COUNTRY in the Muslim world, revolutionary Iran experimented with political Islam, looking to a reinvigorated faith to solve modern-day problems that have bedeviled so many Third World societies. But the political Islam unleashed by the Iranian Revolution, with its monopoly on truth, failed spectacularly. The intolerance, narrowness of vision and rigidity were its undoing. As in Sudan, the failure did not go unnoticed at home or abroad. As important, neither have the successes secured under President Mohammad Khatami's reformation. Much of the discussion in Chapter 2 centered on the fault lines between democracy and Islam, the way in which the two intersected and mingled, diverging in their moral and theoretical underpinnings and finding commonalities in their aims and ambitions. Thinkers like Sheikh Mohammed al-Ghazali and Sheikh Yusuf al-Qaradawi drew a distinct line between democracy as a means to govern and democracy as a product of a Western heritage. They saw it as the former—a way to protect against abuses of power, prevent arbitrary rule and institutionalize the abstract Islamic concept of *shura,* or consultation and deliberation. A subversive current ran through the thoughts of those men and others. With varying degrees of vehemence, they urged a restructuring of religious authority, in effect a democratization of the right to interpret religion, a privilege the *ulema* had jealously guarded for centuries. Their arguments provided a pivot for the emergence of democratic movements across an arc of the Muslim world seeking to redefine the relationship between Islam and politics.

Today, another generation of intellectuals and scholars in Egypt, Turkey and elsewhere are seeking to elaborate on those same ideas and, often, take them a step further. They also look for intersections, and their work is crucial in bringing intellectual force to the movement of reform. Like Khatami, they seek neither to demonize nor romanticize the West, but to borrow from it, adapting its attributes to govern an indigenous society that is democratic yet remains religious. They, too, have rebelled against traditional religious authority, which they blame for Islam's perceived stagnation. Many of them were molded by a secular education, speaking a Western language, and some have a long history of involvement in its once most popular politics: socialism, Marxism and, most potent, nationalism. They have since returned to Islam, molding it into a voice of opposition and dissent. En route, they have also sought to reform the faith and popularize it. Their aim is to bring pluralism to interpretation, tolerance to divergent beliefs and a flexibility that will allow concepts grounded in the faith to address questions of modern governance. Although they seek to create models of society inspired by Islam, most of them do not advocate a reactionary return to a seventh-century Islamic golden age that probably never existed.[1] Rather, like Khatami, they seek a modern Islamic polity. As important, they attempt to ask the right questions, even if they cannot provide the necessary answers: What does the Quran mean in the modern world? What is the importance of the clergy? How do we define an Islamic society? How do we make that society and its government viable in the modern world? And, in practical terms, what do the faith and its heritage bring to plurality and democratic politics?

Fittingly, many of those questions are being asked in Iran, where the reformation, despite its influence throughout the Muslim world,[2] remained precarious years into Khatami's presidency. At the forefront of the critique is Abdol-Karim Soroush, a lay philosopher and one-time ideologue of the revolutionary government whose work I found in great demand at the downtown bookstores near Tehran University.

It was a sign, I thought, of the intellectual commotion—both excitement and dissent—that his thoughts had generated. Soroush is the flip side of Khatami, the intellectual equivalent to the president's political persona, and his writings have helped shape the ideas of post-Islam, a blending of religion and modernity, that have begun to take hold in Iran. That same influence has brought him notoriety among those who fear that reform and change, however gradual, could undermine the Islamic identity of Iran's government and society.

Abdol-Karim Soroush is the pen name for Hossein Dabbagh. Born in the capital Tehran in 1945, after an Anglo-Russian invasion of Iran and nearly a decade before Mohammad Reza Shah's rise to power, he was raised in a religious environment not uncommon to Iranian youths of modest means after the war. His parents were religious, by all accounts, and he studied at the Alavi secondary school in Tehran, which broke the mold of traditional education by teaching a combination of the modern sciences and religious studies.[3] He was the first of his family to attend university. As a young scholar, he soon grew intellectually close to an emerging group of Islamic thinkers, men like Ayatollah Murtaza Mutahhari and, in particular, Ali Shariati, whose writings served as an early salvo in the revolution that erupted soon after his death. Shariati was a daring thinker. Influenced by both East and West, he argued that Islam, rather than being a conservative, fatalistic creed or merely a personal belief, was in fact a revolutionary ideology that could fight oppression, exploitation and social injustice, themes shared by many Third World struggles looking for an alternative to Western capitalism and Soviet socialism. Interestingly, Shariati also saw the need for an enlightened Muslim intellectual to provide a reinterpretation of Islam and to make it compatible with what he considered the original aims of the faith, namely to create a just and progressive social order.[4] It is a role not unlike the one Soroush, an admirer of Shariati, has begun to serve, though his modesty would prevent him from claiming that was the case.[5]

Soroush studied pharmacology in Iran and the history and philosophy of science in England, returning to Tehran as the revolution gained momentum. A supporter of Ayatollah Ruhollah Khomeini, he went on to hold a high-ranking position on the Committee of the Cultural Revolution, which was charged with bringing university curriculum in line with government-approved Islamic precepts. The universities had been closed as part of the campaign, and the committee's

work ruined or sidetracked the careers of many scholars whose credentials were insufficiently revolutionary or religious. Soroush held
the job until 1987, when he resigned amid disagreements over its aims
and effectiveness, although some still bitterly resent his association
with the committee's work. Critically, unlike Khatami and other religious reformers, Soroush was never educated as a cleric. His instruction was thoroughly secular, even Western, and his training has
emerged as a clear factor shaping his ideas.

After his resignation, Soroush, a slight man whose glasses and
trimmed beard suggest an image of both a revolutionary and a scholar,
became a prolific writer and sometimes controversial speaker.
Cassette recordings of his talks circulated among Iranian students,
and he gained a fervent, often youthful following through his lectures
at mosques, seminaries and universities. To each setting, Soroush,
whose name in Farsi means "angel of revelation," brought a mix of
revolutionary credentials and association with the revolution's key
thinkers, academic training and a thorough knowledge of Islam. All of
this ensured him a listening audience and, as important, a platform
from which to speak with an authority few other religious intellectuals could claim.

Soroush also attracted a growing audience through his bold and
often controversial columns in *Kiyan,* a magazine founded in 1991 by
young Iranian thinkers, who were searching for a more dynamic relationship between Islam and society.[6] Its editors and contributors,
some of them former revolutionary militants, advocated respect for
human rights and argued that the separation of religion and state
would preserve the sanctity of Islam.[7] Understandably, Soroush's popularity and the magazine's assertiveness brought down the ire of the
clerical government, sensitive as it was to any question of its religious
legitimacy. *Kiyan* remained open, but its publisher was banned from
traveling abroad, and the lurking threat of closure hung over its staff
for years, particularly before Khatami's presidency.

To understand Soroush's thought is to begin with the Quran. Unlike
the Bible, it is considered the actual word of God delivered in Arabic
through the Prophet Mohammed. Throughout the Muslim world, cassette tapes of men chanting verses that still inspire awe circulate
across continents, some of the readers becoming stars in their own
right. Everywhere, Muslims are careful not to dirty the text or discard
it. In Afghanistan, near fighting on the front line, I met young soldiers

who insisted on placing their Qurans in a green, wooden artillery box that was then hoisted on top of a lonely mud bunker. They said they wanted to make sure the books would rest in the loftiest place possible.

For many Islamic traditionalists, the words themselves are immutable and unchangeable, their meaning frozen in the time they were delivered to the prophet. Soroush, however, has brought a mildly unorthodox idea to that tenet, in that he believes Quranic interpretation will evolve. Because knowledge changes and develops in any era, he says, the understanding of the Quran itself must change. The view of a modern scholar, for instance, would differ from that of a medieval scholar. To allow for that, the Quran's commands must be reinterpreted. Such a flexibility ensures that its teachings remain relevant in a dynamic world. As Soroush said in a lecture:

(The Quran) is immutable and changeable at the same time. It has been revealed to the heart of the prophet, and so it should be kept intact and nobody is permitted to tamper with it. At the same time, there is the interpretation of the text. That is changeable. No interpretation is without presuppositions. These presuppositions are changeable since the whole knowledge of mankind is in flux. It is age-bound, if you like. . . . This is how I express the situation: the text is silent. We have to hear its voice. In order to hear, we need presuppositions. In order to have presuppositions, we need the knowledge of the age. In order to have the knowledge of the age, we have to surrender to change. So we have here the miraculous entity that is changing but at the same time is immutable.[8]

For ideas swathed in the garb of intellect and academia, they have inspired a virulent response worthy of a barroom brawl, and Soroush has often found himself in danger. He was physically assaulted while giving a speech at Isfahan University in July 1995. Three months later, angry students prevented him from entering a classroom at Tehran University. In one extraordinary scene, thousands attending a university lecture by Soroush in Tehran in 1996 were joined by members of Ansar-e Hezbollah, a vigilante group that harasses dissidents and regularly breaks up speeches and lectures deemed un-Islamic. One of those men carried a noose. It was message enough for Soroush to slip out the door and flee the campus.[9] He abstained from lectures for more than a year, but after he returned, the same pattern of harassment continued. In November 1997, as his car approached the gates to Amir Kabir University in Tehran, where he had been invited to give a lecture, he was again attacked and prevented from entering the campus. As he left, vigilantes on motorcycles pursued him, yelling insults at him and pounding the sides of his car.[10]

Why the anger? Soroush comes from within the revolution's ranks and often conceals his strongest points in abstractions, as religious writing is prone to do. Yet in a dangerously clear manner, his arguments threaten Iran's *ulema*, a stratified, deeply institutionalized class of scholars who even before assuming power through the revolution enjoyed more prestige as interpreters of religion than did their Sunni Muslim counterparts. In effect, Soroush argues that the *ulema* have little basis to insist that their understanding of religion is somehow superior or infallible. Since all religious knowledge is human and thus potentially wrong, he argues, the clergy have no more right to interpret Islam than any other group in society or, for that matter, any individual. He stresses a key point: Knowledge gained from religion should not be confused with religion itself. Some interpretations may be more learned and even more authoritative but they do not automatically command more legitimacy. "There is no official interpretation of Islam. There is no authoritative interpretation. Extrareligious debates must be viewed as worthy, useful exchanges in Islamic society," he said.[11]

The repercussions of that argument are sweeping. Soroush is, in so many words, contending that the clergy, the underpinning of the government, cannot justify their role as the self-proclaimed shepherds of Iran's political system.

The threat he poses to the Iranian status quo becomes more apparent as Soroush develops the argument into a criticism not just of religious interpretation but of religious ideology itself. An obvious example of that ideology is Ayatollah Khomeini's *velayat-e faqih*, a concept of clerical government enshrined in Iran's constitution. Soroush believes that religious ideology assumes there can be an official and permanent form of our religious understanding. He has argued that is impossible. No interpretation is immutable, and all understanding is human, reliant on the conditions and circumstances specific to that era. Yet to make it an ideology means that, by definition, it is cast into an unchanging mold. Although ideology might serve the temporary purpose of overthrowing an oppressor or combating repression, once it becomes official, it assumes the permanence that Soroush denies can exist. In that form, he sees it as oppressive and detrimental to the faith, solely serving the government and legitimizing it at the expense of its own spirituality.[12] In doing so, it forsakes religious qualities that go beyond ideology: spirituality, devotion and love, the faith's mystical and esoteric nature.[13] More dangerous, it creates an official class of ideologues—in Iran's case, the *ulema*—who become government-sanctioned interpreters of religion. Their interpretation becomes the one true version of the faith—already a reality in Sudan and Iran.

Implicit in his argument is a critique similar to that made by President Khatami. In the last chapter, Khatami warned the Muslim clergy against making their own understandings and interpretations absolute. Defending a right to maintain a monopoly on truth would be disastrous. In the end, he suggested, it would lead to a fate similar to that of the Roman Catholic Church in the Middle Ages, whose authority over European society buckled under its own institutional inflexibility. Soroush, too, believes the clergy must avoid making their interpretations of truth and falsehood somehow sacred. An ongoing, unbridled process of religious reinterpretation, with clerical authority no longer a given, is the only way to maintain the faith's viability in a changing world. Interpretation must be opened up and put in the hands of the lay and the clerical, creating dialogue and diversity and reorienting religion to contemporary issues. Khatami has never mentioned Soroush publicly, and the two men still differ over the legitimacy of the *velayat-e faqih*.[14] Yet their beliefs, at a basic level, reach the same conclusion: Society must accept a plurality of views within religion and, thus, a tolerance of dissent.

As part of that argument, Soroush takes up the task of reconciling democracy, Islam and human rights. His ideas are again controversial. In a contention that would infuriate many Islamic activists, Soroush argues that there is a conception of justice that goes beyond the Quran. Although religious justice and *sharia* can be derived from the holy book, Soroush insists that justice consists, too, of a conception of man, of what it means to be human, and of what rights man enjoys. Essentially, he argues, these rights go beyond the religious texts.[15] That argument, of course, could just as easily serve as an endorsement of a Western, secular conception of human rights, a value Soroush partly upholds. "We do not draw [our conception of] justice from reli-

gion," he said, "but rather we accept religion because it is just."[16] For
the same reason, however, it angers Islamic traditionalists, many of
whom consider the application of *sharia* their highest calling.[17] To
them, not applying the law derived from God's word is tantamount to
blasphemy. Some Islamic thinkers, men like Egypt's Sayyid Qutb,
have taken the idea a step further. Qutb argued that failing to fight a
government not enforcing *sharia* and *sharia* alone was itself apostasy.
Soroush diverges drastically from Qutb and his singular focus on
sharia. To him, there is a secular component to a religious ethos, a
concept that fits a reinterpreted notion of democracy

Soroush believes that democracy is the only viable and just way to
rule. He dismisses the critiques of some Islamic thinkers, who insist
that democracy is a Western invention and therefore alien to Muslim
societies. Instead, he says, democracy and the rights it bestows to the
individual and community are universal principles appropriate to several cultures, including Islam. Since democracy reflects the will of the
people, it can therefore reflect their culture, their beliefs and their
morals. Taken a step further, he argues, democracy can ensure that a
government protects both the rights of man and religion, since democracy will, in large part, reflect the sentiments of a faithful Muslim people. A religious people will naturally make their society religious and,
in a democracy, the government will best reflect that religious society.
As people's religious sentiments change over time, the government
itself must change, providing a flexibility that allows the faith to
remain relevant. Similarly, if the people become less religious, Islam
must adapt or risk becoming obsolete. In that, it keeps a dynamism
that many feel it has lost over the centuries. Soroush's argument is, in
a way, the philosophical heart of Khatami's vision of an evolving,
viable Islamic polity.

The argument also strikes at the heart of the issues of identity that
were explored in Chapter 1 and the politics of engagement—movements that work within their communities, address their needs and
reflect their concerns—that were explored in Chapters 3 and 4.
Although he does not state it in so many words, Soroush charts a path
for electoral success of groups that seek to represent faith's powerful
appeal to identity, answering questions of unease in the modern world
through religion. In Soroush's reasoning, they will express popular
will and thus best represent a religious society. The same goes for
movements such as Hezbollah in Lebanon or the Virtue Party in

Turkey, which are politically engaged in their communities, with an overarching allegiance to religion but a distinctly indigenous program of action. Those movements are involved in social welfare and grass-roots activism that create the popular support necessary for political success. In broad terms, Soroush's argument returns to a common theme in contemporary Islamic politics: the conflict between revolution from above, as in Sudan, and democratic change from below, as is emerging in Egypt, Lebanon, Palestine, Turkey and elsewhere. Sudan has already proven a prescription for failure; the movements elsewhere can help weave the fabric of a democratic, religious society.

As Soroush puts it, "In an ideological society, the government ideologizes the society, whereas in religious societies, the society makes the government religious. In an ideological society, an official interpretation of ideology governs, but in a religious society, [there are] prevailing interpretations but no official interpretations. . . . [N]o personality and no *fatwa* is beyond criticism. And no understanding of religion is considered the final or most complete understanding."[18] It is a formula for activism from the ground up.

Naturally, Soroush's argument leads to the lingering contradiction of Iran's Islamic state—a government of religious autocracy that functions with democratic institutions. The question becomes: Does the government's legitimacy come from God or does it come through the representation of popular will? Conservative clergy in Iran would argue the former; Khatami, Soroush and reformers grouped around them believe the latter. Their vision of government is one that reflects popular opinion, whatever form or shape it takes. In a religious society like Iran's, it leads then to a religious government, one imbued with fragmented authority and the pluralism and debate that brings. The government draws its legitimacy from the people it represents, and power remains in their hands. To argue otherwise—that the government's authority comes from God—would assume the infallibility of religious interpretation, which Soroush believes is impossible.

The argument has proved explosive in Iran, upsetting large segments of the country's clergy and their lay supporters, for an obvious reason: If society is to accept Soroush's argument that all religious knowledge can be understood differently and therefore no official interpretation can exist, what then is the role of the *faqih,* or the jurist, who Khomeini insisted should have ultimate authority in the Islamic Republic? Soroush is effectively arguing that the authority of the *faqih* should be questioned. If he is fallible, why must he be obeyed? Although he would stop short of making the argument directly, Soroush suggests that the *faqih*, at least as the position is defined in Khomeini's *velayat-e faqih*, is essentially an undemocratic institution. His knowledge must be questioned, and his interpretations are never absolute. To be viable, the *faqih* would have to receive his authority from the people—and thus democracy, including the checks and balances it provides—rather than drawing his legitimacy from God. As Soroush put it in an interview, "I am for a democratic rule and the *velayat-e faqih* is based on a divine right of the ruler."[19]

That suggestion questions the very tenets of the Islamic Republic, ideas that are so potentially revolutionary that it becomes clear why some would consider it necessary to disrupt his lectures. The flip side, though, is that Soroush has provided a justification for a democracy that is faithful to religion and a conception of human rights that is ground in the faith—a potential course of reform for Iranian society. That reform, in many respects, had already begun even as Soroush faced the hangman's noose.

—

The currents of thought in Iran speak to a specific instance of history and politics. They were definitively shaped by the Shah's repression, the revolution's tumult, the country's Shiite Muslim faith, war against Iraq and a popular movement for change. Yet in a telling sign of Islam's transcendent nature, those same currents can be read by Muslims as universal. Indeed, other modern scholars have endorsed the same idea of the versatility of interpretation of the Quran, Islamic law and the faith's traditions. They believe such an interpretation is a crucial element in religious reform of their own societies. Two of those thinkers are Nasr Hamid Abu Zeid and Hassan Hanafi in Egypt who, in circumstances not unlike those Soroush faced, found themselves in trouble with religious authorities for their ideas and writings. It is all the more remarkable that it occurred in a country, Egypt, which many in the West would view as far more tolerant, democratic and supportive of free speech than Iran. In its treatment of those men, it was not.

Abu Zeid, a professor of Arabic language and literature at Cairo University, was denied tenure in 1992 on the grounds that he was a heretic and a *kafir*, an apostate. Like Soroush, Abu Zeid argued that the Quran should be interpreted in the historic and linguistic setting of the time and that those interpretations would thus be applicable and relevant amid social change. (The argument, incidentally, was not unlike that put forth by Islamic reformers in the nineteenth century.) As part of his contention, Abu Zeid suggested that Quranic imagery like genies, angels and the throne of God were metaphors, to be interpreted in context, and that they were not meant to be taken literally. That led to charges of blasphemy. To some traditional religious scholars in Egypt and elsewhere, the idea of a changing Quran—one that was not literal—was tantamount to heresy. God's word, in their view, cannot change. It is eternal. Doubting that concept would be akin to questioning a Christian's belief in Jesus' divinity. The dispute over Abu Zeid's writings led to a celebrated trial in Cairo in 1995 in which the scholar was actually declared an apostate by a court and divorced from his wife—against both their wishes. The grounds for the court's ruling was a stipulation in traditional Islamic law that a Muslim woman cannot marry a non-Muslim (although the reverse is acceptable).

There was a sense of surrealism to the case, even instances of the bizarre. After the court order against Abu Zeid, I interviewed the chief plaintiff, a sententious sheikh named Yusuf al-Badri who had preached in mosques in Paterson, New Jersey, and Jersey City in 1992 and 1993. Familiar with American journalists, he typically asked television crews to pay him $100 for an interview, upping his price when he judged the crew more prominent. (A colleague and I apparently made a poor impression; the sheikh never required us to pay.) I visited Badri at his house in the Cairo neighborhood of Maadi, which, oddly, was home to many of the country's American expatriates, a fact that he seemed to ignore. His small flat was decorated with religious kitsch: a rug hanging on the wall embroidered with an image of the Great Mosque in Mecca, a clock inscribed with the word *Allah*, seven framed posters of Quranic verses and, looking displaced, a rustic river scene redolent of Europe. When I entered, Badri escorted me through his apartment, waving his hand like a wand over dusty books stacked from floor to ceiling, a library that he said numbered 4,000 volumes and testified to the traditional, centuries-old education of a Muslim sheikh. Here is Islamic jurisprudence, he told me; there, Quranic interpretation; over here, sayings of the prophet; and along that wall, dictionaries and bibliographies. There was even a Bible, he proudly pointed out. "You should know that I'm well-educated," he proclaimed, with no suggestion of modesty. "When I speak, I speak with education."[20]

What Badri proceeded to tell me was why he thought Abu Zeid was a *kafir.* He needed no prompting. That man is "guilty, guilty!" he shouted at me. "He is an apostate, really. He knows that." (Abu Zeid, who considers himself a good Muslim, called Badri "a crazy man.") When I asked the sheikh about the next target of his lawsuits, he smiled and pointed to the ceiling of his apartment. "God knows best," he said softly. He paused, then shot back, "Perhaps you!"[21]

Despite the sheikh's bombast, the case to divorce the couple was, in the end, successful. Although the judgment was eventually overturned on appeal, after a byzantine track through Egypt's courts and their ambiguous mishmash of Islamic tradition, French law and colonial-era British regulation, Badri succeeded in what he had set out to do: silence one of the country's preeminent intellectuals. With a possible bounty on his head as a perceived apostate, Abu Zeid left Cairo in July 1995 with his wife, Ebtehal Younis, for Leiden University in the Netherlands. They have been teaching there since, a permanent exile with which Soroush never had to contend.[22]

The other thinker, Hassan Hanafi, made a similar argument and he, too, incurred the wrath of traditional clergy. I met him at his house in a Cairo suburb, a white stucco, two-story dwelling decorated in a distinctly Arabesque style. Wood latticework graced the windows and low-slung furniture was adorned with Eastern, geometric designs of inlaid bone and glossy mother of pearl. His office had paper everywhere—on the table, on small stands, on the arms of chairs and on the floor. Hanafi, a philosophy professor at Cairo University, greeted me with what I thought was one of the oddest gestures of hospitality from a religious man. He offered me 7-Up, tea and then added, "There is beer if you'd like." The hospitality soon took a turn for the worse, though. Hanafi, a man of very formidable intellect, had a healthy disdain for journalists. He suggested they were guilty of "intellectual tourism," visiting one country after another and leaving with only a superficial understanding, if that. He told me that he had agreed to speak with me solely because I was of Arab origin and spoke the language but he adamantly refused to let me tape the interview. "That is journalism," he said, shaking his head. Our conversation, nevertheless, was enlightening, a window on the way in which ideas cross borders, divided by language and culture but united by faith. His thinking and its similarities to Soroush were a testament to the powerful concept of an Islamic *umma*.

Hanafi, like Abu Zeid, urged an interpretation of the Quran "without any restrictions from the tradition." "In a progressive theology," he wrote, "interpretation does not begin from the text but from reality,"[23] a contention much like Soroush's. Hanafi made a similar point in our interview, taking the idea of unrestricted interpretation to its logical conclusion. "There is no universal theology for all time and all places," he told me. "There is a theology compatible with different levels of society." A poor man, he said, would see God as poor, a rich man would see him as rich. In each case, God—his spiritual meaning—is interpreted according to a person's circumstances and, by default, the era in which the person lives. Hanafi did not disagree with comparisons of his thoughts to those of Abu Zeid, but suggested that their goals and approach were different. In fact, I felt that Hanafi's aims and background were closer to Soroush's. Both men were steeped in the religion, coming of age during a time of upheaval and change—Egypt in the 1950s and Iran in the 1970s—and were seeking a faith that was amenable to social change and tolerant of pluralism. The project to achieve that, Hanafi said, had begun in the nineteenth century with the writings of Jamal al-Din al-Afghani and Mohammed Abdo (see Chapter 2), but in the end, their work was turned back by institutional and clerical inertia.[24]

Like Abu Zeid, some disapproved of Hanafi's writings. In 1997, the head of a committee of traditional and conservative Muslim scholars known as the Al-Azhar Scholars Front said that Hanafi had called into question divine revelations in the Quran. Among them was the *isra'a wal mi'raj*, a mysterious journey during which Mohammed is said to have visited Jerusalem and then Paradise. Hanafi never addressed the charges in public and never engaged his critics in debate. Unlike Abu Zeid's case, the dispute eventually died down, leaving Hanafi to teach and write. Insecurity remained, though. During our conversation, an armed guard sat behind a rickety desk outside his front door. Hanafi later told me that the government had posted twenty-four-hour sentries at his home since April 1997. The protection the government believed that he needed was a powerful reminder of the sensitivity surrounding the ideas those men broached.

Yet those ideas also provide a framework for a pliant rethinking of political Islam. Only a fraction of the Quran is dedicated to an Islamic vision of a political system. As was seen in Chapter 1, the prophet left his followers no government, and no particularly Islamic code to administer the community emerged from the Quran. Beyond the loose concept of *shura*, there was no dictate or procedure to choose rulers, hold them accountable or remove them from power. To today's thinkers, that lack of direction allows and, in fact, warrants reinterpretation that can correspond to both time and place. In response to tradition, codified in centuries of interpretation applicable to the time in which it was considered, thinkers must now bring their own intellect to bear on issues of modern society, namely the state and the way it rules. That can only occur if interpretation is free and unfettered, effectively the argument of Abu Zeid, Hanafi and Soroush.

As Mohammed Salim al-Awa, a prominent Islamic thinker in Egypt, said, "Even the very early generation of Muslims, the prophet's companions, introduced new measures, means and methods that were not known during the time of the prophet himself. It is only natural that Muslims should respond to changes and developments at all times and in all circumstances."[25]

—

Who are the intellectuals responding to those changes? Unlike Soroush, who is seeking to reform a religious state that already exists, these thinkers are typically defined by a far different historical experience—namely, decades in opposition, often in the face of repression at the hands of authoritarian states that answer to their militaries. They see in Islam a language of opposition, similar to that espoused by movements explored in Chapters 3 and 4, and have undertaken the task, similar to Soroush, of exploring the faith's relationship to democracy, pluralism and even other political currents—in their case, from the outside looking in. They share the agenda of many opposition groups barred from participation: the right to elect their governments, to dissent from those governments and to be guaranteed individual rights and civil liberties. Often, they are also willing, even eager to borrow from the West if it achieves those aims. Finally, like Soroush, they resist traditional religious authority, which they view as an impediment to reform. Although the clergy in the Sunni Muslim world enjoy far less prestige and authority in political affairs than they do in Iran, the thinkers in this movement still view them at best as an obstacle—as in the experiences of Hanafi and Abu Zeid—and at worst as a vassal of the authoritarian governments they oppose, Egypt being a good example.[26]

As a group, they are fascinating in themselves. From Turkey to Egypt, their ranks are filled by former Marxists and communists, activists who even today are probably more familiar with *Das Kapital* than the intricacies of Islamic law. Like Soroush, they escaped immersion in medieval scholarship in hallowed institutes like Cairo's Al-Azhar[27] or the Iranian seminaries of Qom for a secular education and all that entails: a foreign language, fluency in Marx and Weber and a respect, if not jealousy, for Western prowess and achievement. They speak the language of the Western academy, yet often have a love-hate relationship with its civilization. They define themselves in opposition to its culture but are enticed by its institutions. Typically, they have in common a road-to-Damascus experience that revolves around the defeat in the 1967 war with Israel.

The conflict, as seen in an earlier chapter, transformed the political and intellectual landscape of Arab countries and, by default, much of the Muslim world, a cataclysmic climax to disillusionment that had been building for years. There were other sources of disenchantment at the time. Many of those countries were subjected to a heavy-handed culture of surveillance that still lingers; economies led by the public sector that had languished, dashing hopes for rapid and comprehensive development; and repression, often arbitrary, that seemed the most effective way for governments to secure popular acquiescence. The war, however, was the emblematic moment of the era, the *coup de grace* to an imminent failure. I once spoke with Sadiq Jalal al-Azm, a philosophy professor, about its impact. Azm remained an ardent secularist. He opposed the direction the revival had taken, disagreed with what it sought to create and resented what he considered its stifling effect on intellectual life throughout the Arab and Muslim world. To him it was "a reactive rather than an active movement."[28] But he had a keen insight into the revival's dawn, and even today, stood in awe of the havoc the war wrought on his generation, shattering in a matter of days both militaries and myths.

"Had Arab nationalism, Nasserism, secular nationalist ideologies, even leftism and communism, had they been more successful, I doubt we would have had the reaction," Azm told me as we sat in his well-endowed library of English and Arabic texts. He paused for a moment, seeming to search for the proper sweep. "1967 discredited all the major galvanizing ideas that ruled Arab social, political and cultural life since the end of the Second World War. The idea of Arab unity, Arab socialism, the liberation of Palestine, building strong patriotic armies, cooperation with the Soviet bloc. In one stroke, '67 discredited all this."

Azm lived in Damascus. The city, an uneasy hybrid of ancient mosques along cobblestone streets and gray, utilitarian architecture indebted to socialist realism, is the capital of Syria, a country that, more than three decades on, is still ruled by the Ba'ath Party. Its ideology is an anticolonial, avowedly socialist brand of Arab nationalism— and throwback to another era—that promised a renaissance of culture and ideas. (Today, Ba'athism is perhaps best known as a symbol of cruelty and injustice, employed to legitimize the spectacularly oppressive governments in Syria and Iraq.) To Azm, the ideology that still held sway over his life seemed no more than an anachronistic relic from a debacle that left in its wake no secular alternative. "The defeat was so devastating," he said, shaking his head, "that sometimes you wonder how it took people so long to lose their illusions."[29]

Adel Hussein was one of those who lost their illusions. A thin man with wispy hair, Hussein is the secretary-general of Egypt's Islamic-oriented Labor Party, which enjoyed a brief period of prominence in the 1980s when it joined forces with the Muslim Brotherhood but has since, like other Egyptian opposition parties, effectively been barred from power. I met him at the party's headquarters in the rough-and-tumble Cairo neighborhood of Sayyida Zeinab. His office was sparse and dusty, as most are in the city. On his wall was a painting of the Dome of the Rock, a familiar symbol of Muslim Jerusalem and a rallying point for nearly every Islamic activist. On his desk was the clutter of a week's worth of Arabic newspapers, which gave the appearance of having been read and reread. Hussein, who had been jailed most recently in 1994 and was released after three weeks only because his frail heart had become weaker, measured his words, often looking down. But he spoke forcefully and persuasively, as if he had undergone a religious conversion that gradually became more fervent.

"I started as a Marxist-Leninist to be precise, because there are differences, then I turned to be a Nasserite, which represented radical nationalism, and radical nationalism in the '60s and '70s was quite influenced by communism. Then afterward, I started to understand," he said, "and to be part of the Islamic trend.

"It was not an arbitrary decision. It is a process, a long process for an intellectual and a politician to change the way of action, way of thinking," he told me. As always, Hussein spoke more like an academic than a politician, a role he seemed to prefer. I had the sense his work at the party was more an obligation of activism than a pursuit of political prominence.[30] "I am still committed to independence," he went on to say, "I am still committed to comprehensive development, I am still committed to democratization, and I am still committed to social justice, but now I interpret all these differently."

I visited Hussein again a few weeks later, this time at his house in the Cairo suburb of Heliopolis. Spacious by the standards of Cairo's destitute intellectuals, it was tastefully decorated, but as I looked around the room, I felt that it was maybe most remarkable for what was not there. The looping, sweeping Arabic inscriptions of the Quran so popular among Islamists elsewhere were nowhere to be found. Nor were the pictures of worshipers in Mecca or, as in his office, the panorama of the Dome of the Rock. The decor, in fact, evoked an African motif, its wood carvings and paintings speaking, perhaps, of a now-forgotten Third World solidarity, a time of heady optimism hailing from defiant struggles against Western colonizers. The bookshelves against the wall of his sitting room were striking, too. Titles like *Socialist Integration, On Communism, The Economics of Socialism* and *Planning in the USSR* spoke more of class struggle than the hand of God. The authors themselves—G. Sorokin, for instance—suggested Politburo-era politics rather than a source for religious ideas and inspiration. For years, Hussein was one of Egypt's more prominent leftist thinkers, particularly in economics, and he still can hardly speak of the government—its ministers and its officials, its president and its policies—without a tinge of resentment and an edge in his voice that conveys well the disgust it inspires in him. He also felt the anger during his years as a Marxist and an Arab nationalist, a resentment that continues to tie him to the past. He has never been reluctant to address that element of his heritage.

"I respect the Marxist tradition and I admit it was quite stimulating and enriching. And, accordingly, I cannot deny that certain aspects of Marxist thought were quite important," he told me, with a slight hint of nostalgia. "I benefited from the Marxist experience in both theory and practice and also I benefit from other Western schools of thought. But now, for me, Islam is my starting point and my framework.

"The fight in the south against inequality in the world and Western domination, all this was under communist banners in one way or another. Young people who were ready to sacrifice their lives for this independence in Arab countries were communists. Now you have another era, the fight in the south is led by Islamists."

The year 1967 has overshadowed the hope and fervor that preceded it. But the ideologies of which he spoke were more than academic exercises. They prompted passion and hope, sacrifice and devotion. Ryszard Kapuscinski, a Polish journalist, once captured the optimism of that time, when nationalists and leftists like Sekou Toure, Kwame Nkrumah and, of course, Gamal Abdel-Nasser seized the popular imagination. In a memorable passage, he wrote, "A rally in Africa is always a people's holiday, joyous and full of dignity, like a harvest festival."[31]

The witch-doctors cast spells; the imams read the Koran; the orchestras play jazz. The wind snaps the colourful crepe, women vendors sell rattles, and the great ones talk politics from the rostrum. Nasser speaks tough, forceful, always dynamically, impulsively, imperiously. Toure banters with the crowd, winning it over with his good cheer, his constant smile, his subtle nonchalance. Nkrumah is turgid, intent, with the manner retained from his days preaching in the American black churches. And then that crowd, carried away by the words of its leaders, throws itself in exultation under the wheels of Gamal's car, lifts Sekou's car off the ground, breaks ribs trying to touch Kwame's car. Meteoric careers, great names. The awakened Africa needs great names. As symbols, as cement, as compensation.

The peak of those passions helps explain the depth of pathos 1967 caused. Nasser and the myths and memories to which he gave rise— from the battle at Faluja in 1948 to the union with Syria a decade later—came to an end. The new reality made way for an alternative moral and political vision to emerge. The vision was, in part, a withdrawal into culture. Hussein knew that and he saw the continuity.

"Some people think that when we speak about Islamist programs that we are inventing something that is very unique in the sense that it has no relation with previous efforts for developing the country. But to me," he said, "the Islamic revival represents the highest phase of the national liberation movement in our countries."

As he spoke, the Muslim call to prayer began from what seemed like the neighborhood's thousand mosques, drowning his last words. After even a few weeks in Cairo, the call to prayer can fade into the background and go unnoticed, its beauty lost amid the city's turbulence. Hussein, for one, seemed oblivious. This time, though, its melancholy struck me. It seemed to float, the muezzin's tinny voice carried by a breeze, deposited, willfully or not, in every labyrinthine alley. Invariably, it was joined by others, some voices resonant, some muffled by indolence, some brittled by age. At times, through the cacophony came a recognizable phrase, "God is most great." The voices submerged, tumbling over one another in confusion, then came up for air: "There is no god but God." Then they converged, for a fleeting moment, to testify, "Mohammed is the messenger of God."

The prayer, coming as Hussein spoke, gave me pause. As I listened to both, I had the sense of the force Hussein's political conversion carried. It was historically rooted, encompassing not only a political program but also an answer to questions of identity and independence. It brought a recognizable morality and spirituality to his politics, unscathed by the failures of 1967 or the more recent examples of Iran and Sudan, experiences he saw as exceptional. Some might see in his choice opportunism, a charge heard often in Egypt and elsewhere; he told me himself that he considered Islam—through its ability to persuade people and mobilize them—as the best tool to achieve the same goals that he espoused as a Marxist or nationalist. Yet I saw no reason to consider his faith insincere. Through Islam, he could dismiss products of the West that seemed to alienate and confuse so many in his country: sexual promiscuity, consumerism and materialism, moral decadence, and even nationalism. They are the sins of the West, and these thinkers—and, by extension, the activists who propagate their ideas—find resistance in a historical, collective memory shaped by Islam. They see in the faith a language that enunciates morality and expresses grievances. They see in its heritage the vitality not only to confront the challenges but also to construct the answers.

I always felt that pull of history and identity in the Cultural Park for Children, a revered experiment in Islamic architecture in Cairo built on a wasteland once inhabited by drug dealers, petty criminals and the destitute in the neighborhood of Sayyida Zeinab.[32] From a tower inside the park, two views of the city are visible. Outside its walls lies chaos; beggars crowd the streets, lead-laden smoke hangs over the neighborhood, blaring horns announce the approach of packed buses and misery marks the face of Cairenes occupied by a quest to survive. Inside the park, though, is an image that entices. Stone paths wind across a stream and through trees in an attempt to bring together the elements of nature—a motif repeated time and again in Islamic architecture from Spain to Central Asia. Domes, arches and the wood latticework known as *mashrabiyya* adorn buildings constructed in what the architect Abdel-Halim Ibrahim Abdel-Halim, a visionary in his own right, describes as "Islamic modernism." Inside those stone buildings, fresh-scrubbed children seemingly oblivious to the hardships outside study computers or read books with religious themes. It was, I thought, the Islamic conception of modernity—or, perhaps more appropriate, a historically rooted alternative vision to the West.

The park has long fascinated me, as has Abdel-Halim himself. Fifty-five years old and trained in the United States, he considers himself "free, authentic and local." A handsome man with a beard, glasses and thick gray hair, he exudes the confidence of an architect who knows his work elaborates a vision, as well as exuding the frustration of one who knows his vision is not yet understood. For him, the park, both in the inspiration for its design and the architectural symbol that it created, was a rediscovery.

"We have taken the heaps of dirt away from things and we came across something that has been there for centuries and it's going to continue to be there," he told me in his office, which was crammed with maps, drawings, diagrams and pictures.

As he spoke, his words reminded me of a passage I had read from Naguib Mahfouz, the Egyptian Nobel laureate who has a singular knack for conveying the sentiments of a generation. He was writing about what he considered a typical Cairene Muslim, his condition confused by contradictions and paradoxes inculcated by secularization, a relentless process at work in Egypt for arguably 200 years after Napoleon led his conquering army ashore at the Mediterranean town of Agami. He questioned his identity—to which world did he belong? I came across that process of soul-searching in conversation after conversation with Hussein and his ideological colleagues, men grounded in the West but seeking an alternative to it. It was a conflict with which I could identify. I had always felt more Arab in America, more American in the Arab world, never giving myself to either. As Mahfouz wrote:

> He leads a contemporary (i.e. 'modern') life. He obeys civil and penal laws of Western origin and is involved in a complex tangle of social

and economic transactions and is never certain to what extent those agree with or contradict his Islamic creed. Life carries him along in its current, and he forgets his misgivings for a time, until one Friday he hears the imam or reads the religious page in one of the papers, and the old misgivings come back with a certain fear. He realizes that in this new society he has been afflicted with a split personality: half of him believes, prays, fasts and makes the pilgrimage. The other half renders his values void in banks and courts and in the streets, even in the cinemas and theaters, perhaps even at home among his family before the television set.[33]

Abdel-Halim, too, was troubled by the dual nature of life. He seemed overwhelmed by the power and persuasion of the West, where he completed his graduate work at the University of Oregon and the University of California at Berkeley. There was an alienation in his words that reminded me of Eid Rabia, the trashman in Cairo who looked to Islam as a buffer against a future that made him uneasy and uncertain. There was also a struggle to reclaim something that made him Egyptian and Muslim, that element of his personality that, as he put it, made him authentic. The park was not a copy of a mindless imitation of an Islamic masterpiece. Reclaiming history, for Abdel-Halim, did not mean mimicking it. He looked to the Islamic heritage for artistic inspiration, a way to overcome the pervasive alienation. His words echoed Hussein.

"We are completely drowned with impositions of theories or doctrines or images or perceptions, to the point where even the most enlightened, the most alert intellectual will not see it. We are completely drowned with these kinds of impositions. I wouldn't even call it domination because it has come to the point where you don't see dominance, you are just swimming in it," he told me, his voice tinged with exasperation.

"You go about drinking, about eating, about speaking, about everything in your life as if your existence locally and what makes you Egyptian, or Arab or Muslim is not there. Nobody can say that someone is dominating me, I'm just completely unconscious, completely unaware and this awakening is very difficult. Every aspect of life as such is structured around the perpetuation of this state of half sleep. We are half asleep," he said. "So for us, the park encountered that decay, the decay that is happening physically, socially, economically,

also the decay of consciousness, the decay and deterioration of alert-
ness, the state of sleep that we are all in."

Days after my conversation with Abdel-Halim, I met up with Abdel-
Wahab Elmessiri, another of Hussein's fellow travelers. An Egyptian
writer and academic, Elmessiri earned his master's degree at
Columbia University in New York, then went on to complete a doctorate at Rutgers University in English and American poetry. A former
Marxist, he is now a retired professor from Ain Shams University, one
of Egypt's largest, and a proponent of what he describes as a new, still
somewhat undefined Islamic discourse. I met him at his Heliopolis
apartment. Its walls were decorated with Islamic art and its furniture,
hugging the floor with subtle wood carvings that had an eastern hint,
exuded a modernist interpretation of Arabesque. Elmessiri had a tendency toward the abstract and wandering tangents, but he, too, had a
story of his ideological conversion, from Marx to Mohammed.

"If anyone would have told me that I would be a Muslim thinker, I
would have laughed. I would have laughed," he told me, relishing the
irony. "And when I converted, some of my friends fainted or laughed.
They couldn't believe it."

But, Elmessiri said, he and the others brought a vitality to tradition-
laden Islamic thought that was not there before. They brought an altogether different perspective.

"You have, in fact, for the first time, Islamic thinkers who can speak
the language of the modern world," he told me.

Traditional Islamists, scholars that hailed from al-Azhar, for
instance, did not have the training to operate in a changing society, he
said, and their teaching and intellectual leadership had lost relevance.
Had they impeded reform, I asked him? Were they, in fact, detrimental? "Harmful would be too strong a word," he told me. "Let us say it
is more like a fossil standing in the way. The modern Muslim has
problems that they don't understand and they don't have a comprehensive view of things. You ask them and they say everything is in
Islam. This is quite true, but it needs to be operationalized. They don't
understand international law, they don't understand international
economics, they don't understand the power of the media, the power
of literature, all of these things. And therefore, they are, in a sense,
pathetically irrelevant."

The vacuum had to be filled by people like Adel Hussein,
Mohammed Salim al-Awa and Tariq al-Bishri, another religious

thinker and former leftist, men, he said, "who came back to Islam, people who understand its value, its relevance to modern man but at the same time feel that there is a crisis in the West, that to import the West wholesale is no solution." Through them could come a reinterpretation unfettered by tradition, he said, one that looks both East and West.

This is, perhaps, the irony of their emergence. Elmessiri, Hussein and even Abdel-Halim exude a syncretism. These thinkers both resist the West and intersect with it, displaying a mix of envy and repulsion, admiration and loathing. For us, the West as an idea represents who we are, our very identity—social freedom, political liberty, the comforts that many of us enjoy and the achievements that we often take for granted, such as in technology and medicine. To them, the West is an aggressor, a society and culture so powerful and forceful that it shapes and defines, makes irrelevant and declares obsolete, in ways it is not even conscious. They find its influence distasteful, in that they see it creating a consumer mentality and encouraging a flaunting of wealth that is enjoyed, at best, by a select few. Those few can be understood as the rich north (as opposed to the poor, more populous south) or as the privileged, Westernized elites that have grown up in their midst in countries like Egypt. Their power and prosperity rise during times of scarcity for most—poor housing, little opportunity for work and a government that has abandoned its subsidies and support for the destitute.[34] In Islam, these thinkers see an answer: an alternative vision and a morality that is rooted in their culture and heritage.

Yet at the same time, they are products of that very same West. They have shared in its intellectual heritage and they have admired its political system, in particular the rights, freedom and liberty it assures. They have shared, too, in its ideologies and doctrines— Marxism and socialism, for instance. In essence, they have a foot in each world, the secular and the religious, West and East, and they consciously employ both to shape their vision. In that space is, for the first time, room for interaction and dialogue, particularly within the political arena of their own countries. They acknowledge that point, in a clear and compelling departure from the past.

For Hussein, his Islam is not the Islam of the Iranian Revolution or Sudan's Islamic Bolshevism, a belief that the faith, by itself, can answer every challenge the modern Muslim world faces. Instead, it is an Islam that looks for connections with other trends of thought, with other activists and with secular and western ideologies, the same ones that he once espoused. Through a common heritage, he sees common ground and the potential for "a historic compromise" between secularists and Islamists. His party, he said, supports democratization, greater political participation and social justice, campaigns against corruption and maintains a deep skepticism of American intentions and its steadfast support for Israel. Those ideas are shared by virtually every opposition party in Egypt and, for that matter, the Arab world.

"Personally, as a politician and an intellectual, I really see that such a compromise is quite possible and that compromise doesn't mean stagnation but means that different partners would accept coexistence for a fairly long time and exchange views and interact through this long process of coalition," Hussein told me. "Perhaps we differ with others on what democratization in our country means but still we're against the present authoritarian way of government, against the dictatorial ways of ruling the country. There are major points of agreement and that's why it is quite possible that we can make a compromise."

It is an idea that will prove critical in the following chapter, where ideas of coalitions and joint political work have become a reality in several Muslim countries. Among these thinkers, it helps illustrate their path to prominence. Like so many in the Muslim world, they draw on the faith's heritage and its meaning for their identity, both personally and politically;[35] through their intellectual background—a typically secular education—they bring a dynamism to political Islam. They may resist the West, yet borrow from it. They may speak the language of faith, yet are cognizant of other currents, other ideologies and other platforms. They are the intersections that are necessary for pluralism, tolerance of dissent and coalitions—the makings of a more democratic society.

—

The Egyptian thinkers speak of an ongoing struggle for independence against domination by the West—be it political, cultural, even economic. They see in the West both what they desire and disavow. Their often secular, diverse background makes room for compromise and flexibility, yet their religion frames their critique. The West serves as a theme in the writings of other Islamic thinkers, too, in particular an influential group of Turkish Islamists. They ask the question: How do you compete with such an awesome force? The issue weighed heavily on Chinese and Japanese thinkers in the nineteenth century as the West loomed over their destiny. They struggled with the possibility of taking Western technology—the instruments, they believed, of its ascent—but not Western culture. The Turkish Islamists, centered around Ismet Ozel, a former Marxist poet, and Ali Bulac, another leftist turned Islamist with a background in sociology, have struggled with the same question today. They offer a utopian, unorthodox answer, and, in its criticism, it is far more sweeping than the prescription offered by Hussein and others. They seek to comprehend the West then, as Soroush did in Iran, determine in what capacity and from what perspective their own societies should borrow from it. Their answers are indirect yet, in the end, they bring an additional perspective to the pluralism other thinkers have envisioned. On another level, their criticism illustrates one more intersection of Western philosophy and Islamic ideals, shedding light on the new trends of thought that have emerged from it.

Like their Egyptian colleagues, the Turkish Islamists are, at least in part, products of the West.[36] Most of them have a secular education, know a European language, have knowledge of Western literature, philosophy and social history, write in a contemporary, accessible language and follow trends in Western political thought, drawing on them extensively in their writings.[37] Their criticism of the West echoes their one-time Marxist critique reinterpreted through the lens of an idealized Islam.

Ali Bulac and others argue that modern life is alien and has removed man from the setting in which God conceived he should live.[38] They see modern life as essentially a product of Western civilization and, to them, it encompasses both Western technology and culture. The two cannot be separated since they are essentially one and the same: Once you adopt the technology and industry of the West, you inescapably adopt the civilization that is created by them. According to these thinkers, that civilization deifies technology, and science serves as a new idol. Just as primitive men worshiped the moon, the sun or pagan gods, modern men worship science.[39] That subservience extends to technology and the market that drives it, defining our needs, our values and, critically, our lifestyle. As Ozel said, "Commodities are sacred; brands and designer names have a special spiritual force; advertisement has replaced prayer."[40] Their argument is not the traditional

dichotomy of Islam versus the West. Rather, they put forth a comprehensive vision of a conflict between an Islamic concept of society and
the reality of modern civilization.[41]

What then is the response? Loosely, they say, the alternative is a
return to God. Yet as a utopian vision, they dedicate little time outlining the practical means to achieve that goal. Instead, they seek to offer
an ideal, and the essence of that ideal—the solution to the loss of faith—
is a vision of a reinterpreted *umma*, or Islamic community. A similar
idea has emerged in the thoughts of other Islamists trying to conceive of
a religious society that is democratic and pluralist, an issue of concern
to everyone from Khatami and Soroush in Iran to the activists of the
Center Party in Egypt. The writings of the Turkish Islamists add another interpretation to *umma*. Bulac believes that an Islamic society existed only from the advent of Islam through the rule of the first four
caliphs, collectively known as the *rashidun*, or rightly guided. The goal
of any Islamic movement, then, is to recapture the essence of that time
when society was guided by the prophet himself or his companions,
men who had firsthand experience with the revelations of the Quran
and his example. That contact is most important, overshadowing the
trouble that followed among his temporal successors.

Bulac was influenced, in particular, by the Medina Document, the
seventh-century agreement the prophet reached with the Jews and
other communities living at the time in Medina, the city in which he
first gained political authority. Under the pact, the other communities
were protected and allowed to live in accordance with their own laws,
and their relations were regulated with Muslims on the basis of mutual respect and understanding. Bulac believes today that different
groups can enjoy that same autonomy. In its modern reinterpretation,
the community would preserve their rights and provide for their
accommodation, answering the reservations that so many express
about the status—and sometimes poor record—of minorities under
Islamic law. Different groups within that community would develop
their own economic relations and institutions of law, education and
culture.[42] In Lockean fashion, the community would designate its
rulers and make a pact to obey them as long as they acted within the
tenets of Islam and adhered to its preferences. There is little room for
the clergy in his conception. Bulac believes an individual has the right
to interpret his religion and should be free to decide how to and even
whether to practice it at all. Like other Islamists, he criticizes the

claim of the *ulema* to monopolize the interpretation of God's will.[43] In practice, Bulac says, the clergy have assumed authority without consent, a relationship that he considers un-Islamic.

The key element in his argument is that society is not organized by the state—what Bulac considers an imitation of the West—but through the Islamic notion of *umma*. Some Islamists, although acknowledging its utopian element, see in the theory a potential recipe for pluralism. It is not a stretch to consider the implications for those ideas in solving, for instance, the campaign of Kurds in southeast Turkey for self-determination. The Turkish government resists a separate ethnic identity for Kurds because of its implications for the ardent Turkish nationalism that has underlined the state since Ataturk. However, in a community of dispersed authority, with different elements living under their own laws, diversity can be assured. It would bring new meaning to the idea that politics are local. Again, Bulac and the others offer no blueprint for action, and such a radical reinterpretation of *umma* will never be realized. Yet the ideas are important, demonstrating a search for the meaning of pluralism, individual rights, identity and spirituality. These thinkers seek to elaborate those concepts in a distinctly Islamic context. Their arguments are one theoretical perspective—an Islamic justification—for the practical pluralism that Hussein and others in Egypt and Iran espouse.

That creates yet another intersection. Across the spectrum of Islamic thought today, some currents are shared, despite the divide of culture, language, history and even divergent practices and beliefs within the faith itself. Soroush and the others seek an end to the authority of the *ulema*, most notably in Iran, where they exercise the greatest prestige and power. Through the democratization of religious authority, a flexibility can emerge that remains open to ideas of democracy and individual rights, concepts that may have arisen in the West but that can be borrowed and adapted, even reinterpreted within an Islamic context. The thinkers often share an experience of education abroad or a familiarity with the politics and currents of thought in the West. For some, like Bulac, that background is instrumental in formulating a bold, incisive critique of the West and, by default, their own societies. He sees a reconstructed *umma* as the answer. For others, like Hussein, the breadth of experience is a means for a new style of politics. The vanguard of the Muslim Brotherhood acting alone, for instance, gives way to a search for coalitions between secular and religious groups on the basis of points on which they agree. Together, they are the intellectual foundation for the emergence of movements within political Islam that have eschewed the exclusivist, sometimes violent politics of Iran and Sudan for a new style that places them firmly within a society of competing interests and conflicting demands. Islamists' rights are protected when those of others are protected in a wide-open playing field. That style is representative of a new pivot in political Islam. The shift is making possible a radically different, more democratic Muslim world that has already started to emerge.

8

The Changing Legacy

New Politics, New Interpretations, and the Onset of Islam in Democracy

It is a remarkable feature of the Muslim world that a region divided by histories and geographies, languages, cultures, governments and, occasionally, a common faith can, in the case of political Islam, share so much. From soldiers on the front line in Afghanistan to Eid Rabia and the trashmen clinging to centuries-old traditions in Cairo's changing, Westernizing neighborhoods, its symbols and memories have intertwined in a gut, visceral appeal to identity in an unfamiliar world. As a movement, it has shaped a language of opposition and dissent, heeding often legitimate grievances of those facing misery, arbitrary authority and occupation. It has engaged those communities, changing society from below in lieu of political participation and creating popular support through welfare and social activism that, to a degree unmatched by other movements, has addressed people's wants and needs. The movement has weathered the failures of Sudan and Iran, emerging with a maturity that has given rise to new interpretations of democracy, of pluralism, of dissent and of individual rights. These ideas have often been encapsulated in a notion of *umma*, a concept that dates to the ministry of the Prophet Mohammed and has now emerged, in the minds of many Islamic thinkers, as a viable framework for modern society. Within the currents is a subversive force, too. A resistance to traditional religious authority and outdated interpretations of the Quran and Sunna has allowed a new generation of thinkers, lay men and women raised with a secular education and working as engineers, lawyers, academics and bureaucrats, to personalize Islam. In the process, they have reinterpreted the faith and sought to make sense of it in a world they are seeking to change. Often they ask: How can Islam be democratic? How can it justify a pluralist society in which rights are protected? How can it express culture and traditions and, at the same time, serve as a framework for government and society?

For more than a decade, I have traveled to the Middle East as a journalist and student. I have always felt tied to the region by a distant heritage, my Lebanese grandparents leaving a village in the East for the promise of a better life in the West, and I called Cairo, one of the region's greatest capitals, my home for nearly five years. As a Westerner, though, I visited those locales with the lingering fears and anxieties of a society that, from a distance, seemed aggressive and alien, a faith inclined to intolerance and a culture resistant to change. All too often, I had seen Islam used to justify galling acts of violence, the slaughter of tourists in Egypt just one example. On nearly every trip, almost without exception, I left with a far different and unexpected impression: I saw a compelling search for identity, a reinterpretation of Islam and the emergence of democratic movements.

Time and again, those elements have come together in the idea of *umma*, the notion of an Islamic community created when Mohammed's disparate followers began to look beyond their clan and tribal affiliations in Arabia to see themselves foremost as Muslims. Today, as with many traditional Islamic concepts but to a greater degree, *umma* still resonates among the faithful. To many, it suggests the brotherhood of Muslims that transcends borders, sect, nationality and ethnicity, providing Eid Rabia, for instance, a sense of security amid the alienation and dislocation of an unfamiliar Cairo. For those same Muslims, it can also mean the body politic, the blueprint for a religious community that is democratic and pluralist. The Turkish thinker Ali Bulac saw a radical interpretation of *umma* as the basis of an idealized society—a community whose very nature assured individual rights, self-determination, identity and spirituality. To him, legitimacy sprung from the community, and the community was the final arbiter of all authority. The reinterpretation has not been confined to thinkers, either. In grassroots politics, a variation of *umma* seemed to me to define many Islamic movements and their day-to-day approach to society. Always, they have identified themselves with the community, be it Hezbollah in Lebanon, Hamas in Palestine or emerging democratic currents in Egypt and Turkey. They have eschewed the lonely and hollow ramblings of the exiled militants in Afghanistan or Europe, removed as they are by distance and experience from the struggles at home. Rather, these new activists have placed themselves squarely within the *umma*, insisting that community action is both a religious obligation and a successful political program. By nature, that action has been a democratizing force, drawing its legitimacy and vitality from the community rather than imposing itself from above.

The sweep of that force represents a change as important as any in the religion's modern history. It is at the heart of a democratic transformation under way today in Islamic politics, most notably in parties that are offering a platform that appeals to the faith and increasingly pragmatic policies that ensure their broader support in the community. In the electoral arena, these parties, despite setbacks, have found sometimes striking success in Lebanon, Turkey and Jordan. In Egypt, where the first organization for Islamic political activism was created, thinkers have reconciled democracy and Islam and a party has emerged to promote that synthesis, drawing directly on the notion of a modern *umma*. Some of the militants in Egypt, meanwhile, who saw a rebirth of the faith through the assassination of Anwar Sadat and a vengeful insurgency along the Nile, have looked for change through a different venue: at the head of political parties engaged in the occasionally mundane bargaining of a democratic society. Inside these movements, an equally telling shift has emerged: greater democracy within the parties themselves, a moderation that can take place regardless of the regime's tint. These twin forces of democracy—a changing relationship to society and internal reform—promise a better future for a region that has become an increasingly lonely outpost for dictatorship and authoritarianism. At the heart of that vision is a new ideal of community.

In Cairo, I found the struggle between old and new most poignantly expressed in a shabby government office overlooking a stretch of the Nile that wandered through one of the city's busiest districts. Across the river stood the five-star Meridien Hotel, offering a telling contrast of Cairene life: luxuries housed in steel, stone and glass catering to the rich and foreigners, the dinginess of the government's titanic bureau-cracy serving the rest. It was 1997, and I was there for a court hearing. Such hearings before a magistrate were not unusual in Egypt, where lawsuits, some of them frivolous, have become a pastime.[1] This one stood out, though. On one side, it pitted a young group of Islamist reformers (and, surprisingly, a Christian) who were seeking to estab-lish a political party known as Hizb al-Wasat, or the Center Party, which seemed to promise a new style in Egypt's moribund political landscape. In announcing its formation, the reformers pledged to wel-come women and even Christians into their ranks and, in an unusual step for a religious group, to consider coalitions with secular parties. On the other side was the Muslim Brotherhood, the group founded by Hassan al-Banna in the Suez Canal town of Ismailiyya in 1928 whose name has since become synonymous with the political activism of Islam. During the Brotherhood's troubled history, it also has become as well known for its rigid hierarchy, iron discipline, clandestine style and intolerance of dissent, all qualities that hailed from its years of struggle with the Egyptian government.

The two groups were a study in contrasting styles. The young reformers with the Center Party were accessible, media savvy and pre-pared to play the political game. They had even tipped me off to the court hearing, suspecting that, as a journalist, I would enjoy seeing a confrontation between two faces of the Islamic movement. They were quick, too, to pledge their allegiance to a government that had subject-ed the Brotherhood to varying degrees of repression over more than a half-century of undulating conflict. Most of the Brotherhood represen-tatives, on the other hand, were of another generation. Many of their leaders were in their seventies, having come of age during the reign of Gamal Abdel-Nasser. Prison time, to them, was still a badge of honor; more time behind bars conveyed more respect, authority and status within a movement that extolled sacrifice and suffering. At times, it courted those qualities.

There was little love lost between the two groups either, an animos-ity that only a divided family can know. Most of the Center Party activists were former Brotherhood members. And they were not just the group's foot soldiers. Some, like Abul-Ela Maadi, were among the movement's youngest, brightest and, as the battle between the govern-ment and the Brotherhood dragged on, most impatient. In 1996, without seeking the leadership's approval first, Maadi and those activists petitioned the government to form the Center Party (in Egypt, the state must give permission). The move drew interest from Islamic activists across the region. The petition, though, infuriated the Brotherhood, which rightly sensed a threat to its vaunted unity—a quality that had taken on more importance during its long years underground. In the ensuing months, the fight quickly became personal when accusations were traded in Arabic newspapers and magazines. The Center Party activists called their former mentors out-of-touch dinosaurs; the Brotherhood leaders dismissed them as upstarts craving publicity and scolded them for not first seeking their permission. The conflict reverberated through the organization's ranks. Dozens of prominent Brotherhood members resigned in protest of the group's treatment of the nascent party, and Brotherhood activists abroad in London and elsewhere warned their colleagues in Egypt to go easy—to no avail.[2]

That conflict was the genesis of the court hearing in 1997. The two sides had come before the judge to debate the Center Party's application to be recognized by the government as a political party. The Brotherhood, siding with the government, wanted the recognition denied. It was more than a legal dispute, though. Its roots went back fifty years to the Brotherhood's conflict with Nasser, and its subsequent resurrection under Sadat. To understand the hearing's impact is to understand the history that made possible the contest between these two generations, a struggle whose repercussions would be felt in Egypt and, in time, much of the Muslim world.

I met Mamoun al-Hodeibi, the septuagenarian spokesman of the Brotherhood and son of the movement's second leader, a few days before the hearing. Even then, he was irate, and he could barely hide his disgust at former members he considered traitors. "If you want to know something about the Center Party, then you go ask them," he told me curtly, in stern tones that sounded like the judge he once was.[3] "Neither I nor the Muslim Brotherhood has anything to do with them."

Hodeibi and I spoke at an office in a run-down neighborhood that Cairenes refer to as *shaabi*, an Arabic word that suggests working-class and crowded, somewhat akin to a Mexican barrio. I went into the meeting, my first with him after two years as a correspondent in Egypt, with a distinctly poor impression. I had expected Hodeibi to be

brooding, hackneyed and remote, filled with anger and bitterness over
a political career that was marked all too often by jail and torture,
arrests, harassment and exile. Instead, the Brotherhood spokesman
charmed me, exuding a paternalism that I found good-hearted, if at
times overbearing. He carried himself like a doting grandfather and,
less endearing, liked to lecture from the all-knowing perspective of
age. He was quick to smile, talked as though he enjoyed himself and
tried earnestly to persuade me of the rightness of his cause. He followed his answers, which often tended toward the pat, by nodding his
head then letting out a low, rumbling laugh, as if to suggest that he
was a man who has seen it all. He had seen much—a successful career
as judge and prosecutor in Cairo, followed by six years in prison beginning in 1965 and then, like many other Brotherhood members, self-
imposed exile in Saudi Arabia for more than a decade.

Those years under Nasser shaped Hodeibi, who still clearly remembered life on the run. Nasser's government, which came to power in a
military coup of junior officers in 1952, feared the movement's
strength and appeal. In its turbulent first years in power, it was only a
matter of time before the government acted to end the influence of its
only real challenger. Using the pretext of an assassination attempt on
Nasser himself in the Mediterranean city of Alexandria, the government launched a terrifying crackdown, arresting legions of its activists
and imprisoning many of them in Tura Prison in Cairo's southern suburbs. The conditions, equivalent to a concentration camp, were horrific. The men were tortured and sometimes killed. In June 1957, in one
of the worst episodes, a group of Brotherhood members locked themselves in their cells, fearing they might be killed by vengeful guards if
they reported to work. Armed soldiers eventually broke into the cells
and massacred twenty-one of them, leaving the wounded to die. The
government said it had put down a rebellion.[4]

With Nasser's death in 1970 and Anwar Sadat's succession, a new
chapter began. The Brotherhood openly renounced violence, and Sadat
encouraged the movement's growth as a counterbalance to the left,
which seemed to pose a greater threat at the time. The reemergence
continued under President Hosni Mubarak and, by the late 1980s, the
Brotherhood enjoyed its greatest prominence since the movement's
early years. To some in Egypt, it had become too powerful to take on.
As it soon learned, it was not. In 1995, weeks after I arrived in Cairo,
the government sensed it had the upper hand and initiated a devastat-

ing, sophisticated crackdown, one that would continue for years. Ending the Brotherhood's influence was not enough. In time, the government campaign felt like a vendetta. Mubarak seemed to have a seething dislike for Islamic groups, both violent and otherwise. He was present in the viewing stand at the military parade where Sadat was gunned down in 1981, and he himself was the target of at least three assassination attempts by Islamic militants. He had voiced fear, too, that an Algeria-style bloodbath could visit Egypt if Islamic activists were not checked. Mubarak, I felt, had bided his time patiently until he could strike.

The government began arresting dozens of Brotherhood members, eventually sentencing fifty-four to prison terms of up to five years, in the biggest crackdown since Sayyid Qutb was executed in 1966.[5] More military trials followed, but the first batch of sentences proved to be the most debilitating. In effect, the government removed the Brotherhood's junior leadership, the cadres responsible for its student activism in the 1970s, its later forays into party politics in the 1980s and its success in taking control of most of Egypt's powerful professional unions from the 1980s on. They were an intellectual force, as well. Among other innovations, they were credited with the Brotherhood's declaration in 1994 that women had the right to work, vote, engage in political activism and hold public positions. The stand was in contrast to more traditional scholars who argued their place was at home as wife and mother.[6] The loss of the junior activists, figures like Essam al-Iryan,[7] fractured the organization, removing respected up-and-comers who could link the septuagenarian leaders with the rank and file.[8] The Brotherhood never recovered, effectively withdrawing from political life and, in a marked sign of weakness, taking pains to avoid provoking the government.[9] Gloom pervaded the organization, which in the wake of the crackdown appeared more ossified than ever. It was in that climate that the younger Brotherhood activists went on their own in the attempt to gain government recognition for the newly conceived Center Party.

As I spoke with Hodeibi in an office made frigid by air-conditioning, he echoed the hopelessness, as if he had surrendered to the government's will. Neither angry nor bitter, he seemed more at a loss. "I want to ask you," Hodeibi said, shrugging his shoulders in incredulity, "are there really any parties in Egypt, religious or nonreligious? To have parties means to alternate power. Parties compete in elections, real elections, people vote for something and they change something. Can that happen here? It is not an issue of religious parties or nonreligious parties. It is an issue of policy—there are parties present, but they are parties in name and they have no effect. They don't have the ability to do anything. We have fourteen parties but no one knows their names. It is inevitable that if a trend, group or individuals have strength among the people, they will never be permitted. What is present now—and I don't want to mention names or individuals—it is all merely decoration. They won't do anything."

Neither would he, I thought as I listened to him speak. I didn't disagree with Hodeibi. Egypt was, without question, an authoritarian country. Its most flagrant excesses—torture made routine in its police stations and jails, the detentions of thousands of political prisoners and an effective ban on new political parties—were largely ignored abroad by virtue of Egypt's importance as a political and military ally of the United States. More troubling, the victims were nearly always Islamists, and they generated less concern as victims of human rights abuses in a West inured to an Islamic threat. More than twenty years after Sadat's assassination, the government was still ruled by emergency law, allowing the president to send suspects to military courts and giving his security forces the right to detain suspects without charge or trial. (In one of the more Orwellian statements, the government's chief parliamentary spokesman called the three-year extension of the law in 2000 a means to "exercise democracy.")[10] Its crackdown on the Brotherhood, meanwhile, appeared excessive and unending. Five years after the arrest of Iryan and the others, scores of other influential members were detained from provinces across Egypt. Some of them were ordered to stand trial before military courts, whose swifter, more draconian sentences can be appealed only to the president. He is rarely forgiving. The timing of those arrests seemed intentional, as if to say: We're still watching.

Hodeibi, though, spoke to a defeatism pervading the Brotherhood that was born, oddly, of the movement's strength. In his eyes, the conflict with the government would always be zero-sum. One side won, and one side lost. To him, there was no middle ground, and there was no room for compromise. The Brotherhood was thwarted now, and it had no choice but to wait it out, be it in prisons or on the political sidelines. Its strength was that it could do that. With a patience bred of long stints behind bars, the Brotherhood counted time in decades, not years, and another trek through the wilderness did not daunt its aging leaders, many of whom might not be around to see its imminent resurrection. They remembered the prison years. Some even darkly romanticized them as a time of heroism and martyrdom. For Hodeibi, the group forged its unity and discipline in Nasser's era, and when Sadat rehabilitated them, they emerged stronger than ever, again becoming the country's premier opposition force. The next generation, he suggested, could do the same.

"In the prisons there will be a period of training and study," Hodeibi told me, as we sipped sweet, scalding tea. "In the long run, it will be useful."

His patience was more than rhetoric or a tactic. The Brotherhood conceived of its political activism in the same terms. Muslims would be changed from within, over years, even generations. Once they were reformed, once they themselves had returned to the faith through the *da'wa* of the Brotherhood, then society would naturally follow. From that perspective, the success of a party or the latest government crackdown were not pressing concerns. It was the morality of man that mattered. The question, ultimately, was the direction of society, not its share of parliamentary seats, coalitions with secular parties or an evolving ideology with appeal to a different time and place.

I asked Hodeibi about the Brotherhood today and whether its doctrine and ideology had changed. What made it still relevant to other Muslims fifty years after Banna was felled by an assassin's bullet? What did they offer?

"Its people live correct and upright," he told me earnestly. "They are not violent, they are not perverted, they don't have perverted thoughts and they don't blaspheme."

In short, he said, they were good Muslims. It was an answer that could have been uttered fifty years ago, even earlier. Hodeibi's sincerity was not in doubt. He believed in the Brotherhood's mission of reform, in bringing about a Muslim society. The leadership's belief that it was right, regardless of the criticism from within and without, was virtually an article of faith. The group's *murshid*, or guide, Mustafa Mashhour, said as much. The Brotherhood saw no reason, he declared, to adapt its vision to the next century. Although the Brotherhood might change the means of implementing its ideology— the creation of a Muslim society—it would be done "within the framework of what God ordered."[11] The statement itself was interesting, reminiscent of an absolute certainty that was fading among other Islamic movements. Unlike Soroush, Khatami and some of the Egyptian and Turkish Islamist intellectuals, Mashhour suggested that the Brotherhood could actually *know* God's will and therefore wield an authority that was unquestioned. (Those writers, on the other hand, insisted that any interpretation is fallible, making for a society in which various interpretations of God's will are equally valid and, hence, one where tolerance is requisite.) If the interpretation is infallible, then the program, at least as envisioned by Hodeibi, need not have evolved since Banna's death. Context mattered less than the mission, and the Brotherhood still saw itself as the agent of change, the only agent of change. To serve in that capacity, though, it had to maintain the discipline of its followers to the vision—the concept of absolute obedience that was known from Banna's time as *al-sama' wa'l-ta'a*, literally hearing and obeying. In that sense, the Center Party proved a threat. It was a danger both to the Brotherhood's leadership and to its adherence to an outdated, untenable ideal of the 1930s.

The Brotherhood seemed blinded by its anger, and it was determined to do everything to stop the Center Party's emergence. From 1996 on, it threatened to expel members who sided with the Center Party and, in one instance, forced a follower out of his job at a school in Alexandria over his support.[12] The struggle finally came to a head in the court hearing at the dreary government office, where the battle of two generations and two approaches finally emerged into the open.[13] The contest made for harsh rhetoric and a startling, bewildering alliance. A government committee had already rejected the Center Party's application for approval in 1996. The party appealed that decision. Sensing weakness, the Brotherhood got involved in the deliberations. In reality, it was more than involvement. In a step that demonstrated the Brotherhood's desperation, it began working in court with the very government that had set out to crush it. The Brotherhood's lawyers proceeded to bring evidence that dozens of the Center Party's original founders had withdrawn their support. Government lawyers conveniently used that evidence to make their own arguments for rejecting the appeal.[14] In the end, after two years of hearings, the Center Party lost.

At the hearing I attended in February 1997, in a dusty room packed with lawyers and cigarette smoke, the attorney for the Center Party, Essam Sultan, promised to press forward, despite the opposition. If some supporters had withdrawn their names, Sultan said, they would find new ones who were less constrained by Brotherhood pressure.

Throughout the hearing, he and his colleagues barely acknowledged the Brotherhood lawyers. There was smoldering anger, the resentment inspired by the worst of sectarianism. I had the sense the Brotherhood representatives themselves were embarrassed by an alliance that they had to detest from afar. Finally, as Sultan finished his address to the judge, he turned to the Brotherhood lawyer, Mamoun Masir, acknowledging his presence for the first time.

"I will prove that the members were pressured to leave the party," Sultan told him.

Masir looked down, saying nothing. The silence appeared to anger Sultan even more. Pointing his finger, he warned Masir that the Brotherhood "would not be forgiven by history" for either of its actions: its steadfast opposition to the party and its opportunist alliance with the government.

Masir finally spoke. "God has to forgive us," he said, "not history."

As I listened to Masir, I thought to myself it was neither God nor history that would forgive them. It was the future that would leave the Brotherhood behind.[15]

—

Why were the Brotherhood and the government so concerned with an organization that, although influential, had not yet entered an election, put forth candidates or even organized a political rally? In essence, the Center Party represented a threat to both of them, endangering the very premise on which they had done business for decades. For the Brotherhood's leadership, the Center Party charted a retreat from the iron discipline and unity that was fostered by a generation of repression. To the Center Party's young activists, those qualities meant something else: secrecy, suspicion and a rigid hierarchy. Each of those was anathema to the party's preeminent goal, which was a more prominent role in civic life and, in a more democratic environment, electoral success. Without flexibility and openness, the party believed it could not adapt to the demands of a changing landscape. Secrecy, it said, was for a time of war. Those ideas seemed to bewilder the Brotherhood. Its elderly leaders in decline and its younger generation in jail, disenchanted or on its way out, the group had neither the will nor the capacity to give up an organization and an agenda that had

served it since Banna began preaching along the Suez Canal. Its leadership was still infused, even proud of the prison psyche: It remained
distrustful, suspicious and, most important, secretive simply because
it believed it should.

With the ardor of converts, the Center Party relentlessly made the
point that it differed from the Brotherhood not only in approach but
also in organization. One of its founders, the young lawyer named
Essam Sultan, conceived that shift as a historic mission. "The Muslim
Brotherhood has inherited the enmity between it and the ruling
regime, from the era of Nasser until the present day," he told me.[16]

It doesn't believe in the democratic process, whether it concerns the
state if it took power or the internal movement within the Muslim
Brotherhood itself. The opinion of the leader is the opinion that is followed. Listen and obey, absolutely, without discussion. You should
listen and obey. Listen and obey. The truth is that the most important, the clearest difference between the Center Party and the
Muslim Brotherhood is faith in these matters—faith in pluralism,
faith in democracy, faith in freedom, faith in freedom of opinion, freedom of thought, freedom of creativity, relations with other currents.
The Muslim Brotherhood isolates itself from other political currents
because they are outside the group's religious framework. In relation
to us, the Center Party, we consider the other political currents part
of the national framework. We must and we have to interact with
them. It is not possible to bring about a renaissance for the future
nation without joining forces with these other groups in society.

The government, like the Brotherhood, faced a similar threat from
the Center Party. To recognize the group, it had to forgo the assumption that, barring brief periods of necessity, had defined Egyptian political life since the monarchy was overthrown in 1952: An Islamic current was, by nature, subversive.[17] In a way, the government was
possessed by the same outlook of the Brotherhood: a zero-sum game in
which one side wins and the other loses. At a deeper level, the attitude
spoke to a more far-reaching perception of what the government saw
itself representing. Countries like Iran and Sudan were not alone in
preaching an exclusivist ideology that proclaimed to possess a monopoly on ideas and their interpretation. There was a secular counterpart,
most visible in Ataturk's campaign of relentless Westernization of

Turkey's Muslim society. Other countries experienced it to a lesser degree: Syria and Iraq's Ba'athism, the avowed Marxism of former South Yemen, and Moammar Qadhafi's quixotic blend in Libya of socialism, Islam and populism. The Egyptian government was no exception.

Like many states in the Third World, it had searched for an ideology—a set of beliefs and a program to carry it out—through the thirty years in which Nasser and Sadat ruled. The first leader promised a sprawling project of nation-building—industrial development, land reform and social justice—that would be led by a military in the service of the country. Unity and solidarity were required. As Nasser frequently said, parties would not be tolerated because that meant dividing the body politic. That, to him, was unacceptable.[18] Nasser's answer was a social contract that revolved around satisfying the needs of workers and peasants. Implicit in its provisions was the temporary suspension of political freedoms and democratic participation for the greater good of the nation. Sadat, his successor, envisioned a new compact in the 1970s, a reorientation of the economy toward the West, social and political liberalization and an emphasis on Egyptian pride over Nasser's Arab nationalism, which had fallen victim to defeat and disillusionment. Sadat, in the end, did not deliver. Many Egyptians were left without a safety net as the state-led economy embraced the market. Demands for greater political freedoms, meanwhile, were largely unmet, particularly as government repression peaked in the months before Sadat's assassination. Yet the programs of both men, sweeping in their vision, lended themselves to the larger-than-life reputations the leaders still enjoy. They also gave little room for alternative visions. To acknowledge the legitimacy of another ideology, current of thought or political program would somehow suggest that the government, never lacking in paternalism, was unsure in its course. At all times, the state had to project a vision of the future, generate popular support for that vision and persuade the public, even in an undemocratic environment, that it could achieve it.[19]

Mubarak inherited both the best and the worst of his predecessors. A former air force chief of staff who was considered a hero in the 1973 war for planning Egypt's defenses against Israel's vaunted air force, he never escaped the image of a diligent but uninspired soldier carrying out his duty. Always, he eschewed the dramatic gestures of Nasser and Sadat for the tedious: He envisioned a country that had outgrown its days of sacrifice, war and heroism—and the disappointment those brought—and was instead ready for the stability that, as Egypt's longest-serving president, only he could bring.

That promise posed a threat, as well. In his day, there was no crusade to build a state that had thrown off the yoke of colonialism, no campaign to bring political freedom to a country that had weathered a generation of repression. As a counterbalance, Mubarak never seemed to offer anything except for his ill-defined *ingazat*, or achievements (a potpourri of new telephones lines, bridges and other renovated infrastructure) and a slew of economic reform that brought growing, occasionally ostentatious wealth to a segment of Egypt's people. Throughout his tenure, he was at a loss to say what he actually represented and, particularly in times of economic trouble, he seemed vulnerable in the face of a more sweeping ideology. In Mubarak's case, that vulnerability came from the political Islam that reemerged as a potential alternative in the 1980s. I sensed that the ferocity of his crackdown on the Brotherhood stemmed from that insecurity. As I watched the arrests and imprisonments unfold, I realized that Mubarak and the Brotherhood would probably never reach an understanding. There was too much bad blood, and too much history, both raised on the lesson that only one could emerge victorious.[20]

There was a different way to read Mubarak's vulnerability, though. Unlike Nasser and Sadat, Mubarak was not bound by ideology. His lack of a competing vision meant that he had no vision to protect. In that environment, currents of politics and ideas that did not threaten the state but that instead sought to compete within it need not be automatically disqualified. A revolution, wars and an insurgency behind it, Egypt under Mubarak finally had room for pluralism and dissent.

Regrettably, the government, throughout Mubarak's tenure, never provided the space for effective opposition, and it remained wedded to the ideal of zero tolerance for real and potential threats. The inertia of the past was ironic, and it persisted even as the government's lack of ideology offered the prospect of a more diverse political life. With little hope for success, the Center Party attempted to seize upon the potential opportunity, however remote. It broke with the past that others could not surrender and offered a way to end the stalemate: It presented politics without an exclusive program and an agenda that did not pose a comprehensive alternative. Instead, it envisioned itself as one party among many.

Abul-Ela Maadi, an engineer with a long history in Egypt's Islamic movement, was the strategic force behind the party. He joined the Islamic Group in the 1970s, in the years before that militant organization took up arms, at the university in Minya. The city was in one of southern Egypt's poorest regions, the birthplace of Khaled al-Islambuli, who assassinated Sadat, and Karam Zuhdi, a prominent militant leader still in prison for his role in the assassination. Maadi never went in that direction, although like other activists, his affiliation with the Islamist current alone landed him repeatedly in jail. (He emerged relatively unscathed from his four stints, never staying longer than seven months.) Maadi left the Islamic Group in 1979 to join the Muslim Brotherhood, quickly rising as one its young, dynamic activists who, along with Iryan, Abdel-Moneim Abul-Futuh and Ibrahim al-Zaafarani, helped reshape the party's activism, in particular by playing a more prominent role in Egypt's professional unions. Maadi himself became a member of the engineers' union in 1984, then its deputy secretary-general. His defection from the Brotherhood to form the Center Party ended the career of one of its emerging stars.

A stocky man in his early forties with a well-trimmed, raven beard, Maadi was imbued with an infectious enthusiasm. His persistence in pursuit of a political party bordered on zealotry; his optimism came across, at times, as naive. On nearly every occasion I saw him, he displayed a politician's passion to curry favor, but his expansive personality was tempered by a sharp mind and the sometimes overwhelming dedication of a reformer, who senses, even before he has achieved his aims, that his ideas will long be remembered. (Each time that I spoke with him, Maadi, always wearing a green suit, would show me binder after meticulous binder stuffed with articles chronicling the Center Party's contest with the Brotherhood and its attempt to gain government recognition.) Maadi believed a turning point in Islamic politics in Egypt and elsewhere was under way, and he was determined to help shape its direction and success.

"We know that the hardest choice is moderation, and the easiest choice is extremism. We have opted for the former," Maadi once said to a doubting public, which had seen only occasional examples of officially recognized Islamic parties taking part in Egyptian political life.[21] "The state should know that we do not want to be an alternative to the system; rather, we seek to form a part of Egypt's political landscape in the coming century. In other words, we want to be viewed as an opposition force and not as a resistance movement; the opposition

is part of the system whereas the resistance seeks to overthrow it—
this is precisely what we do not want."

In my first interview with him, Maadi put it to me in similar terms:
"Our idea is to make change, not to take power then make change.
The traditional way is to take power and then make change, but for
us, it is not an issue of power," he told me at his office along Kasr al-
Aini Street, a chaotic thoroughfare that runs through a crowded
stretch of downtown Cairo.[22] "We want change from the inside, not
from the outside."

Sometimes intentionally, and sometimes not, Maadi brought
together the ideas of Soroush and Khatami in Iran, echoed Hussein
and other Egyptian thinkers in both their skepticism and admiration
of the West and espoused the argument for a more aggressive, modern
reinterpretation of Islam. Like Bulac and other Turkish intellectuals,
he elaborated a forceful idea of an inclusive Islamic *umma*, which he
and his party considered a modern, religious alternative to the West's
notion of a secular civil society. He also credited Sheikh Mohammed
al-Ghazali and Sheikh Yusuf al-Qaradawi and their writings on
democracy for helping shape the party's philosophy.

The name Maadi and the others chose for the party was a play on
those ideas. Above all, the party considered itself an instrument of
moderation, a means to break the impasse between a government that
had refused to tolerate a potential alternative and an Islamic movement that, to varying degrees, had questioned the government's legitimacy to rule. The Center Party explicitly recognized the government,
its institutions and its laws and it considered the state its field of
action. It believed it could best influence the government by working
from inside, forcing the regime peacefully to adhere to a code of laws
and a system of rule that, on paper at least, provided hope. (That was
in contrast to the Brotherhood's traditional thinking, in which political action was discouraged so that organizing and activism could focus
on the gradual, incremental reform of society from below.) As part of
the Center Party's approach, it sought compromise with other opposition parties, making overtures to Egypt's liberal and leftist groups as
well as parties that represented the legacy of Nasser, the Brotherhood's
historical nemesis. At all times, it placed itself squarely within
Egypt's still emerging political life, envisioning itself as part of an
inclusive community.

More striking, in its public pronouncements, it tried to draw a line
between Islam as a faith and Islam as a civilization, a line of thought

not all that unlike ideas espoused by thinkers in Iran and Turkey. The belief that Islam is *din wa dawla*, religion and state, is a powerful idea among traditional Islamic activists. The slogan is a critique of the West's division between the two as well as an expression of Islam's all-embracing, comprehensive nature. In their eyes, it can never be considered merely a set of beliefs. The Center Party's division between faith and civilization was a subtle turn of that phrase. The faith, they said, was for Muslims. They shared the civilization, though, with Jews and Christians, all of whom helped build it over centuries and had in common its culture, traditions and historic memory. The religion might be universal, yet it was also inclusive.[23] In line with that, the party recruited nineteen women and three Coptic Christians as part of its formal membership of 100.[24] Their role illustrated an important point. To be inclusive, the party had to be pluralist as well, and it could not limit its ranks to the like-minded or loyalists to a political line of thought. It was a clear sign the party had broken with the exclusivist ideologies of the past in places such as Sudan and Iran. By encouraging dissent, tolerance and a multiplicity of views, the party's leaders echoed ideas that were emerging a continent away with figures like Soroush and Khatami.

"It is a mistake for us to say that a certain system represents an Islamic system," Sultan, the lawyer, told me in his immaculate office, decorated by a sprawling Japanese painting behind his desk and remarkably absent of Islamic adornment.

> The ruling system in Sudan represents its understanding of Islam. Like Iran. The ruling system in Iran represents its understanding of Islam. We differ with these understandings of Islam, but it is not possible for any of us to claim that this is not Islam. This is a mistake and this is dangerous. No, I am not able to say—no one in the Center Party is able to say that the program of the Center Party, this is Islam. But I can say that the program of the Center Party is my understanding of Islam. My understanding is the understanding of man. It is possible for you to agree or to disagree with me about it. If you agree with me, *ahlan wa sahlan*, welcome. If you disagree with me, you are not a *kafir*, an apostate.

The notion itself was liberating. The Center Party leaders freely admitted that they were one of several trends of thought that *together* had to address Egypt's problems. Although Islam was a comprehensive religion, Maadi said, that did not mean the organization itself had to be comprehensive and that it alone had the answer to society's ills. No group could do everything.[25] Like other thinkers, that newfound flexibility allowed them to look cautiously to the West for guidance.

"When we couldn't change the Muslim Brotherhood, we left the organization," Maadi told me.[26] "They think about the old community—the Ottomans, the Omayyads.[27] We have a different vision—a modern community with Islamic values. We need a modern community, modern cities, modern people, modern systems. We need cooperation. We know the West. The West is the most important thing: its administration, its organizations, thinkers, artists, human rights groups. So you should relate with the West, not clash with it. To cooperate with it, actually, as Mr. Khatami said. I accept this."

Ever the engineer, he put a number on it for me. He found 95 percent of the West acceptable. With the rest, he said grinning, there might be problems. Indeed, like Adel Hussein and other Egyptian intellectuals, he still saw a danger in losing identity. It was the same current of alienation and dislocation in the face of Westernization so common in much of the Muslim world. The West, he readily acknowledged, was a great civilization, yet it was a different civilization. Despite the need to borrow from it and interact with it, some of its qualities remained alien—and should remain alien—even today.

"We need to rediscover our Islamic identity, while cooperating with another culture, another civilization. We can accept some things from another culture but not all," he said. "Like morals. We have differences in ethics. Like family. In the West, the community depends on the individual, the one person, but in our culture, it is the family."

How did the Center Party arrive at its different conclusions? The party took the thoughts of Soroush in Iran and Abu Zeid and Hanafi in Egypt another step, making their notion of interpreting the Quran in its own time and place a means for political reform. Maadi was a radical proponent of this: Islam provided principles, but it was up to the umma—the people and their representatives—to determine what they mean.

"Some Islamic groups," he told me, "refuse the constitution and the law, all of it. They say the law is the Quran only. But what is the law in the Quran? The Quran has principles, not laws. The laws are the people, and the people make the laws. They will make the law according to their culture and according to their background. Through that, they will determine what is acceptable to the people, not what should be imposed on them."

To him, that meant virtually everything beyond the rituals of the faith was up for debate: the necessity of wearing the *hijab*, or veil, the idea of women and Christians serving as judges, even the payment of interest. The interpretation in one country, he said, might differ from that in another, and the debates would be fierce over what was right and wrong.

Maadi saw my very visible surprise at his remark and shook his head, smiling. "Not everyone agrees with this," he admitted.

I found statements like that one of Maadi's strong points. Unlike Islamists in Sudan, who habitually said one thing in English to the West (that they supported democracy, that they sought coexistence with the Christian world and that they saw religion as having no role in the war in the south) and another thing in Arabic to their own people (that Islam was the answer, that the Christian world hated us because Islam threatened it and that the war in the south was a *jihad*), Maadi and his colleagues spoke one language, be it English or Arabic. Always the terms were the same: pluralism or *ta'adudiyya*, moderation or *a'itidaal*, freedom or *huriyya*.

In the party's platform, I was struck by a point that seemed to capture the new direction those phrases envisioned. The party argued that Islamic groups in the past had employed very visual religious rituals, such as beards and the veil, and slogans—"Islam is the solution," for instance, or *din wa dawla*—as a means to define themselves. That held true especially in Egypt, an insecure society that was alienated from its own government, threatened by the West's political, economic and cultural influence and nostalgic for a romanticized time of brotherhood and community. The slogans and outward appearance were, by nature, defensive: on one side were those who embodied them, demonstrating their identity as Muslims, their devotion to God and their belief in Islam as a comprehensive answer; on the other side were those who did not. The struggle was to remain Muslim. Protecting that identity was sufficient in itself and, in the end, substituted for programs, agendas and action. The argument reminded me of a remark Hodeibi, the Brotherhood spokesman, once made to me. On Friday, the Muslim sabbath, he said, you could walk through the streets of Cairo and see crowds of people praying, the mosques literally overflowing into the streets. Many of those worshipers bore the *zabiba*, the darkened, quarter-size scar some Muslim men wear on their forehead as a sign of diligent praying. To him, that was a measure of the Brotherhood's success. People were becoming more religious, he seemed to say, so what more need the organization do? To the Center Party, that was the crux of the problem. Leaving activism in the realm of ritual and belief condemned society to a stagnation that would eventually be its undoing. Simply put, prayers were not enough. Now, the party said, it was time for Islamic activists to turn those slogans into programs, to move from their "role in defending the *umma* to a role in awakening the *umma*."[28]

The *umma*, the Muslim community, was a pivotal concept in the Center Party's thoughts, and it drew on it as its idealized vision of a society. To the party's activists, the *umma* was inclusive, drawing together all faiths under the notion of a shared Islamic civilization. As with Ali Bulac in Turkey, the role of the state was subservient to that community. The Center Party believed that in modern Egyptian history, helped by bureaucracy, technology and repression, the government had become all-powerful. As an authoritarian institution that ruled effectively beyond the law, there was little room for dissent or political participation. Policies were imposed and order was enforced through a culture of surveillance backed by the military and security forces. The community's will or consent was, more often than not, irrelevant. The party's answer to that powerlessness was support through political, grassroots action for the emergence of a civil society modeled on a reinterpreted, modern *umma*. The *umma* would be an inclusive polity in which the community's will was expressed democratically and freely through representatives in, for instance, a national legislature. Democracy would then become more than a goal in itself; it would become the means to restore the authority of the community.[29] Within that system, issues of importance to some Islamists—a ban on alcohol, for instance, or censorship of literature, art and film deemed irreverent or blasphemous—would be debated in the open. As in President Khatami's vision in Iran, such a society could only exist in an environment that endorsed tolerance and pluralism. Ideology—a monopoly on truth and interpretation, be it in a religious or secular setting—was anathema to that ideal.

The Center Party thus arrived at a program that drew its legitimacy from one of Islam's oldest concepts, the *umma*, but looked remarkably Western and democratic. To ensure the authority of the community, the party called for free and fair elections, freedom of religion, speech and expression, the right to establish political parties without government interference, an independent judiciary and the right to strike—all means to build their conception of a civil society.[30] Through that, they reached a synthesis of Islam and democracy, a development also being realized in Turkey, Jordan and Lebanon. In Egypt, though, its fate remained in the hands of the still skeptical government.

—

The Center Party's program, although far-reaching and influential, remained stymied by an Egyptian government clinging to a style of authority that mimicked the military that gave rise to its leaders: arbitrary authority, obedience and an intolerance of dissent. So far, the Center Party's promises have remained that, untested in the venue of meaningful politics in which real authority is at stake. Not all Islamic parties have met that fate, though. When a government has accepted its former adversaries into the political system, those groups, in turn, have typically supported that system. Fierce bargaining may take place over divergent goals and programs but limits are adhered to, sometimes forcing formerly militant groups to moderate or forgo a more ambitious, overarching mission of changing society.

One insight into that process, I felt, was in Lebanon, where Hezbollah, a group almost synonymous with the idea of an irrational Islam with a penchant for bloodshed, had become a political party accepted by the government and tolerated—although not supported—by the vast majority of Lebanese. It had gained legitimacy through its extensive and effective social welfare—like the *da'wa* of groups in Palestine, Turkey and Egypt. As important, it transformed itself through politics and war into a national movement—in some ways, as Lebanese as it was Islamic. The breadth of its transformation was remarkable, and the path it took was still visible.

Growing up in America in the 1980s, I was met with two reactions when I told someone that my grandparents were from Lebanon. The first was a nostalgic recollection of the country's beauty as a Switzerland of the Orient, a foreign country that, in hindsight, did not seem all that foreign. They would reminisce about its terraced mountains and eastern Mediterranean beaches, its legendary food and vibrant nightlife. The second reaction usually dealt with the morning's headlines—stories of anarchy, massacres, and warring militias—a Hobbesian state of nature.

My first trip to Lebanon came in 1990, months after the war ended, to visit relatives whom I had never met. It remains a poignant memory: My aunt and uncle—a brother and a sister—had lived the fifteen-year war on opposite sides of the Green Line,[31] a burned-out, gutted no-man's-land that separated Beirut's west from its largely Christian east. Between those two neighborhoods was an apocalyptic stretch of rubble, dust and weeds that was once part of the mortar and brick of Lebanon's former commercial and financial hub.[32] My uncle, never a man of risk, wisely avoided crossing it whenever possible, as did his sister. A few miles apart, they were strangers in the same city.

In later years, I traveled often to Lebanon, mainly as a reporter, and on every visit, I was in some way taken back to the tortured country I had heard about as a youth—a story of a massacre, glimpses of the cavernous, skeletal buildings that still stood, or a retelling of a conspiracy, in one version or another, of how the war started. Never did the war seem more vivid than during drives through the suffocating dreariness of Beirut's southern slums, swaths of misery inhabited by Shiite Muslims, the disenfranchised of Lebanon. It was in those tattered, tedious buildings that dominate the suburb's skyline where some of the more than fifty Americans, Frenchmen, Britons, Germans and other foreigners were held during the war's grimmest days. From those poor neighborhoods sprung the men who bombed U.S. embassy buildings twice—in 1983 and 1984—killing seventy-two people, including the CIA's then top Middle East expert, Robert Ames, and several of his aides. Most notoriously, it was the place where the suicide truck bombings were organized against U.S. Marines and French paratroopers in Beirut in October 1983. Those attacks, spectacular in their devastation and blood-drenched success, killed 300 men, searing images of horror into the minds of many Americans.

In Beirut, a city barely standing, Hezbollah matched the bombings, the hijackings and the kidnappings with a zeal for smashing up bars in free-wheeling neighborhoods and, on the beaches, for trying to enforce what it considered an Islamic dress code: the less skin the better. In southern Lebanon, they closed down coffee shops, banned the sale of alcohol in stores and restaurants and prohibited parties, dancing and loud music. Popular weekend retreats on the coast became ghost towns in the 1980s and mixed swimming was forbidden.[33] Even card-playing at cafés was declared un-Islamic. In all, the fervor bolstered the group's already robust image as a collection of religious fanatics, its bearded militants inspiring a menacing and unpredictable fear. In those years, to most people, Beirut meant anarchy, and Hezbollah meant terror.

When I arrived after the war, the streets were still dreary, winding past bland, bleak concrete buildings more reminiscent of Cairo's *shaabi* neighborhoods than Beirut's ritzy Christian suburbs, where nightclubs, restaurants and chic cafés exude a flashy materialism and a veneer of prosperity. The banners of clenched fists and Kalashnikovs still fluttered over the mishmash of wires cobwebbed together to provide electricity during the war's almost constant blackouts. And the slogans still echoed the revolutionary fervor of Shiite Islam: the martyrdom of Hussein in the seventh century, the sacrifice at Kerbala, where he died, and the undying loyalty to the militant Iran of Ayatollah Khomeini.

Times, however, had changed, an impression almost immediately made on me in one of my first interviews in the country. Like most journalists, I paid my respects at an office that served as the Hezbollah press center. There, in the same south Beirut of the civil war, I was told, in so many words, no hard feelings.

"We don't have any problem establishing contacts with the American people," said Hajj Nayef Kraim, the Hezbollah spokesman who looked the picture of moderation as he sat in a Western jacket behind a desk cluttered with workaday papers. Indeed, he told me earnestly, such contacts were "a required task."

"They will help improve the perception of each other and, at the same time, the perception of the American people," Kraim said.

The Hezbollah I encountered, in fact, resembled the group of yesteryear in little more than name. Its leaders had gone from issuing religious edicts declaring the Lebanese government criminal to running candidates in elections for its parliament. It had neither the desire nor the ability to shed its image as a religious party representing Shiite Muslims, Lebanon's largest sect and a growing force in the country, but its leaders routinely spoke out against unemployment and the spiraling cost of living, complaints voiced by unions, other opposition parties and grumbling Lebanese across a landscape still fractured by religion. In Parliament, its representatives attacked government repression and presented themselves as champions of the oppressed. Its deputies rarely focused on Islamic issues.[34] Most striking, perhaps, was the image Hezbollah created for itself, one that stood in stunning contrast to its once fearsome visage. From years of secrecy and shunning outsiders, be they foreigners or Lebanese, the group began running a sophisticated information office, its well-dressed functionaries carrying cellular phones. It owned television and radio stations and published a weekly newspaper. And it used its grassroots activism and work in hospitals, schools and clinics to gain widespread legitimacy, entering the mainstream of political life and, in contrast to its one-time reputation as an Iranian proxy, assuming a distinctly Lebanese, nationalist identity. Hezbollah seemed to have learned the lesson of electoral success everywhere: Politics is always local.

Perhaps the oddest business card I have ever received was handed to me at the Hezbollah office during my interview with Kraim. In a corner was the group's symbol—a Kalashnikov propped atop the soaring Arabic script that spells "Party of God." Below it in Arabic and English was the office's address in south Beirut, a telephone and fax number, an e-mail address and its Web site: www.hizbollah.org, naturally.

The decade-long transformation of Hezbollah from a shadowy band of militants into Lebanon's most formidable popular movement stands as a stunning example of political Islam's entry into the democratic fray. More important, its success will likely point the way for other Islamic groups like the Center Party—long barred from political life or kept safely at its margins—to integrate themselves in Muslim societies, forgoing violence for potentially more effective politicking. The pattern it set—a roadmap available to any Islamic party—was both simple and effective: a vision grounded in the faith that resonated among its constituency and an increasing moderation that made its message more appealing. For governments like Egypt, Hezbollah's evolution provides the lesson that Islamic movements can reform themselves and compete in a relatively free political life without threatening the government's legitimacy or endangering its stability.

The transformation of Hezbollah, oddly, was woven into the war it fought to dislodge an Israeli army that occupied the valleys and escarpments of Lebanon's south for more than twenty years, controlling the lives of nearly 100,000 Lebanese and one-tenth of the country's territory. The region, one villager once told me, was a "burning ground." By the end of the 1990s, the Islamic Resistance, the movement's formidable military wing, had won the battle to drive Israel out of that territory, a stunning defeat for one of the world's most powerful armies. The war served the aims of Syria, which considers Lebanon its protectorate and views Israel as its pre-eminent threat, and the guerrillas' growing sophistication was already noted. But the conflict over the years brought an additional benefit to the movement—its resilience gained it respect, an admiration that flowered as Hezbollah transformed its own war into a war for the nation. The conflict was instrumental in the movement's shift: The war, in essence, helped Hezbollah become Lebanese.[35] When the last of the hundreds of Israeli soldiers passed through the Fatima Gate crossing in May 2000, ending the occupation, it was the entire country that celebrated what it viewed as a victory for Lebanon.

I saw that change in the war's identity in the words of villagers who heard the scream of Israeli jets overhead almost every day and in the sobs of elderly women whose sons were killed in the fighting. It was not a war between Israel and Hezbollah, they said, it was a war between Lebanon and Israel, one that Hezbollah had grounded in faith, but one that remained intensely local and had become increasingly Lebanese.

Hajja Awatif, a veiled, elderly mother of eleven wizened by grief, was one of those voices, a veteran of the conflict. One of her sons, seventeen-year-old Assem, was in an Israeli prison in Ashkelon as a suspected subversive. (He was like a blossoming rose, she told me, "then someone came along and picked it.") The leg of another son, thirty-three-year-old Abbas, was ripped apart in Israeli shelling. As if to mock her fate, Awatif's house was destroyed, too, in one of Israel's frequent bombings. "This house was totally destroyed, my son was taken, my other son's leg was amputated and he has a family. Who's going to feed his family?" she said, her voice wandering from sobs to shouts. "Is all this because of Israel? Yes, it's because of Israel."

To her, Hezbollah was the only one willing to fight. "In the beginning we hated the resistance," Awatif said, nodding her head. "But when Israel started harassing us, raiding and destroying our homes, we began to like those who defend us. We only have the resistance to protect us. The resistance is awake all night."

That is a powerful message, one that comes in the context of generations of disappointment. A latent insecurity pervades much of the Arab and Muslim world, a once-great civilization that has found itself shackled by decades of humiliating colonialism. Defeat in wars with Israel followed independence, a metaphor for failed dreams of development, grinding poverty and dependence on a West that remains dominant in nearly every respect. In Egypt, the sense of inferiority even has a name—'uqdat al-khawaga, a foreigner's complex, a feeling that someone from abroad, more specifically the West, is by nature superior. One of the few places I visited in the region where I did not sense that lack of confidence was Lebanon. Timur Goksel, the spokesman for the UN forces in Lebanon since 1979 who had stayed on during the civil war and then the fight against the Israeli occupation, noticed it as well. He saw it as part of Hezbollah's transformation.

"Many Lebanese see Hezbollah as the savior of their dignity," he told me.[36] "All these years, they're fighting against very heavy odds. They say you must leave our land and they never deviated from that and they kept losing men because of it." The respect only grew in 1997, he said, when the seventeen-year-old son of Hassan Nasrallah, Hezbollah's secretary-general, was killed in the fighting. Many in Lebanon, regardless of their religion, were moved by the sacrifice.[37] "The Lebanese feel, sometimes grudgingly, that they are the only guys still fighting. It comes again to dignity, to having face," Goksel said. "There has been a transformation in Hezbollah. They have become much more Lebanese and by doing that they've been able to garner much more support."

Nowhere was that message clearer than Qana, a picturesque village near hills of cedars and olive groves dominated by so many shades of green that, with its ominous, overcast skies, reminded me strangely of Ireland. It was the site, too, of tragedy, home to a UN peacekeepers' post shelled by Israeli forces on April 18, 1996, at the height of one of the more savage bouts of fighting between Hezbollah and Israel. Today, next to the post, sits the mass grave where the more than 100 victims of the shelling—those that could be pieced together—were buried under gray marble bordered with black. In glass cases at the cemetery, pictures of the dead—children, teenagers, even infants—stare blankly out. In one, a box of tissues is propped next to flowers, a symbol for those who come to cry. Two tattered black flags flutter at the gate. At the back of the cemetery, a vivid painting of reds and blacks, shrouded bodies, charred limbs and burned corpses depict the horror of the massacre, a Lebanese version of Pablo Picasso's Guernica. The simple cemetery, no bigger than a swimming pool, has become a national monument, and April 18 a day of remembrance. For Hezbollah, it speaks to its tragic success in making the war in the south, and its very identity, synonymous with a fight for the country.

As I stood at Qana on a rainy day, when cold winds lashed the rolling hills, I wondered how conscious Hezbollah's leaders were of the group's change from a onetime Iranian puppet to a legitimately national movement. Was it what they intended? Every leader, I found in time, saw their future tied up in that transformation.

"You can go anywhere among the Lebanese and you will see the popularity of the Islamic resistance," Sheikh Naim Kassem, Hezbollah's deputy leader, told me a few days later in an office in south Beirut adorned with flags both of Lebanon and Hezbollah. A slogan emblazoned on a plastic replica of the Dome of the Rock sitting on a nearby table read, "The resistance is your glory and your pride so support it."

"Today, it is rare to hear a voice raised against the resistance in all of Lebanon." He paused, then added with a hint of bravado: "We in Lebanon fight to liberate our land."

More interesting to me, though, was what Kassem said afterward. "I think that the role of Hezbollah after the Israeli withdrawal, God willing, will be stronger than now. Hezbollah has become part of the Lebanese fabric, and it has a part in the political and social reality," he said. "Its role is not limited to the resistance to the occupation only."

In that, I could only agree. With financial support from Iran, which remains Hezbollah's spiritual guide, the movement spent tens of millions of dollars a year to run nine schools and three hospitals, provide drinking water to Beirut's Shiite Muslim slums and rebuild homes damaged in the war. It was the same helping hand that Hamas and activists in Turkey, Egypt and Jordan have employed to such great success—the very groundwork of their political campaign in any election.

More important, though, Hezbollah complemented that work, a powerful source of its popularity, with a subsequent moderation, a recognition that an Islamic state, particularly an Iranian-style Islamic republic, was not imminent in a country of eighteen religious sects still scarred by communal war. Hezbollah has acknowledged Lebanon's patchwork political system, and eight of its members sat in a 128-member parliament it long denounced as a sham. It took pains to avoid threatening the sovereignty of the nation or the supremacy of its institutions—a state whose historic raison d'être was the preservation of Lebanon's Christian minority. Like other Islamic movements, it pressed an image of cleanliness amid the mind-boggling corruption and cronyism that defines Lebanon's fiercely aggressive capitalism. Yet its members did not insist on a ban on alcohol or the segregation of classrooms, issues atop the agendas of other Islamic activists not yet tested inside a democratic cauldron. Like other movements—the Center Party, for instance—it had disavowed a monopoly on right and wrong.

"We don't ignore reality," Kraim told me. "The reality in Lebanon is that it has geographic borders, Christians and Muslims participate in it. We say that if the Lebanese people, Christians and Muslims, adopt the choice of an Islamic state, this is something excellent. But if the Lebanese people, Christians and Muslims, do not want to adopt the choice of an Islamic state, it is not possible to impose this choice on them by force. We won't carry on a war between them and us, we will rely on dialogue with them. If through this dialogue we cannot persuade them to establish an Islamic state, then it is possible to have a dialogue on the shape of the state that we want, on the shape of the regime that we want, and we can live together with them within this regime."

The movement's secretary-general made a similar point, one reminiscent of the Center Party's call for dialogue and coalition. He eschewed the idea of a universal ideology that would threaten the state. The government came before the movement, and Hezbollah would compete within its parameters—a promise the movement, a decade after the civil war's end, had followed through on. "Hezbollah affirms the importance of maintaining national unity, social peace and stressing that the Lebanese people should never return to internal fighting under any circumstances. Any differences should be resolved by political means and dialogue," Nasrallah said.[38] "We believe in building a state with a strong institutional basis and that peaceful coexistence should be the basis of interaction among Muslims and Christians of all sects, parties and groupings. Participation by all Lebanese is needed in the building and running of state institutions."

Hezbollah comes from a far different background than the Center Party. It arose from the historically underprivileged Shiite community, making its name in the Lebanese civil war, then in its campaign to oust Israeli forces from southern Lebanon. It had to shed its militant image to enter Lebanese politics, and once there, it preached pluralism and tolerance, dialogue and participation. The Center Party, on the other hand, was a product of the Muslim Brotherhood, a Sunni

Muslim movement that preached a universal Islam, one that in time would reform Muslim societies gone adrift. The Center Party, too, sought to shed an image: Unlike the Brotherhood, it endorsed pluralism and political participation. And, like Hezbollah, it pledged its loyalty to the state and its institutions. Its entry into Egypt's political life, however, was still barred.

Those movements were not the only ones to witness a transformation. In their twelve months in power in 1996 and 1997, Turkey's Islamists demonstrated similar changes before they drew the anger of the country's military, the self-appointed guardian of secularism. They backed away from onetime calls for eternal conflict with the Christian world or signing Turkey up for an Islamic currency. The Refah Party rested more on its appeal to the faith and the alienation it answered, its relatively clean image amid Turkey's corruption and its record in the streets—the can-do image it fostered in Istanbul and Turkey's other big cities. Once in charge, its moves were mainly symbolic: attempting to allow female civil servants to wear scarves at work, changing working hours during the month of Ramadan, when Muslims fast from dawn to dusk, and pushing for a mosque in Taksim Square, which in some ways symbolizes the seedier side of Istanbul. Remarkably, Refah also accepted the development of ties between Turkey and Israel, despite the harsh anti-Zionist rhetoric of its past. Under its watch, the two countries consolidated a free-trade agreement, took part in military maneuvers and oversaw a flurry of reciprocal state visits.[39] Taken together, its rule represented an agenda instead of a vision. Rather than an Islamic force ready to overtake the regime and dramatically alter Turkey's course, it more resembled a coalition that brought together Islamist, nationalist, even Kurdish currents— and all the competing ideas and programs that they separately endorsed. At all times, the party accommodated fully a strictly secularist political system.[40]

The party's experience also pointed to another direction for Islamic politics that in the 1990s had become more and more visible in Turkey, Egypt and elsewhere: internal democratization, a complement to the entry of the movements into the arena of elections. The Refah Party, then its successor, the Virtue Party, pressed for a more democratic Turkey. As vociferously, its members urged greater tolerance for dissent within the parties. They were successful to a degree. In contrast to the past, internal debate was more visible and members openly expressed their unhappiness with the Virtue Party's leader, Recai Kutan. The choice of the next leaders—once imposed from above— may well be imposed from below, democratically and transparently.[41]

That process is at work elsewhere in the Muslim world, in particular with other descendants of the Muslim Brotherhood. In Jordan, like with the Center Party in Egypt, activists have retreated from the group's iron discipline and unity. A little-noticed but telling example of the divergence came during the drawn-out debate among opposition parties over participation in Jordan's parliamentary elections in 1997. The resulting boycott, I thought, was not as important as the process itself. The traditional Brotherhood acted first, announcing that its 120-member consultative council had voted unanimously against taking part in the election. All eyes were then cast on the Islamic Action Front, the political party that had emerged from the Brotherhood in Jordan and, in many ways, represented the new generation of Islamic politics. For the Brotherhood, at least, there was no question about what the Front's decision would be. The movement had made up its mind.

Abdul-Majid Thneibat, the Brotherhood's spiritual leader, put it bluntly. The group's decision, he said, was "binding for all our members, whether in the Brotherhood or in the Front." He added that the Brotherhood was prepared "to take all necessary measures against violators," steps that he said would include expulsion from the movement in Jordan.[42] But to the Brotherhood's chagrin, the party waffled on its own stance. When the vote was counted, eighty members of the Front's consultative council abided by the decision, but sixteen voted against it, and twenty-four took no part in the vote. Members spoke openly of sharp disagreements within the organization, and a ranking leader promised that the decision to boycott the election was not final if the government compromised on some points of a new electoral law that Islamic activists found unpalatable. Airing such a rancorous, fierce internal debate would have been unheard of within traditional Brotherhood circles. But the new generation of activists had adopted a new style, similar to their Center Party colleagues in Egypt. They resisted the Brotherhood's withering grip and searched for a different, more effective direction.[43] In 1999, a more moderate wing inclined to cooperate with the relatively tolerant monarchy decisively won an internal Brotherhood election, marking yet another step in the reform of the group and making possible its reentry into Jordanian politics. It found electoral success the same year in municipal elections, sweeping the board in all of Jordan's bigger cities.[44]

It was another example of change crossing borders. The Brotherhood had succumbed to a new style of politics in two countries, Jordan and Egypt. In one case, it had taken steps to reform itself, adapting to an environment that would tolerate it. In the other, it was left isolated on the margins, a new generation charting a different example. The fate of that example was now in the hands of the Egyptian government.

———

Kamal al-Said Habib's résumé reads like a rap sheet. His first arrest came at the age of twenty-four on October 16, 1981, ten days after a small band of assassins had gunned down Anwar Sadat as he watched military vehicles parade down a street on the anniversary of the 1973 Arab-Israeli war. Habib, at the time, was considered the deputy *emir*, or leader, of Jihad, the organization that plotted and then executed the plan to kill the Egyptian president. He won his freedom exactly ten years later, walking out of prison on October 16, 1991, looking grimmer and grayer than his thirty-four years would suggest. It would not be his last time behind bars, though. Less than two years later, he was jailed again, this time for forty-eight days, during one of the frequent crackdowns on Islamic militants in Cairo in the 1990s. As he remembers it, other detainees had told the *mukhabarat*, Egypt's intelligence services, that they had met him in the past. In those times of tension, association was the equivalent of guilt. It was the same story in 1994 when he was held for four days, picked up, as before, as a usual suspect. His last arrest came a year later after a suicide bomber rammed a truck packed with explosives into the Egyptian Embassy in Pakistan, killing seventeen people and wounding nearly sixty. The attack had followed, in quick succession, an assassination attempt on President Hosni Mubarak in Addis Ababa, Ethiopia, and the killing of an Egyptian diplomat in Geneva, sending a chill across the country. Held for ten days, Habib said the *mukhabarat* had picked him up as a precaution. His arrest was a good indication of his standing in their eyes.

I came to see Habib in 1999 in a miserable office in the Cairo neighborhood of Sayyida Zeinab that housed *Al-Shaab*, an Islamist newspaper. The ever-present cacophony from Cairo's streets poured into the dark, musty and claustrophobic halls, which suggested to me a Soviet-style bureaucracy gone bad. The floor was chipped with soiled splash-

es of paint strewn across it, the walls were peeling and the already tattered furniture was starting to literally crumble: the leg of a chair
here, an arm over there. When I made it to the room in which Habib
worked as a journalist, I was told by a group of men to have a seat in
another room and wait. A burly man with a gray beard and *zabiba* on
his forehead was inside, kneeling on a red, blue and white carpet. His
soft, mumbled prayers were audible across the room. From the corner
of his squinting eye, he saw me enter, but paid no attention, bringing
practiced patience to a ritual he had performed tens of thousands of
times. He finished after a few minutes, and I asked him if he knew Mr.
Kamal Habib. "Who are you?" he responded, more curious than concerned. I told him I was a journalist, why I had come and what I wanted to speak about: democracy and Islam. He nodded his head slowly, "I
am Kamal."

Habib, I soon learned, considered himself a democrat and despite his
initial coolness, he was eager to talk about a movement that he
believed was only now beginning to take shape, in Egypt and other
Muslim countries. The violence of his younger days had given way to
the maturity of his adulthood and, he said, he was by no means alone.

"There is something new that is trying to storm and overcome old,
traditional ideas and play a political and social role in society," he told
me.[45]

The violence of past years, Habib said, was understandable,
although not necessarily justified. The government had left no room
for compromise and no room for political activity that it did not sanc-
tion. In his eyes, Sadat was a tyrant, making a mockery of his own
promises for greater democracy, most egregiously when he ordered the
arrests of more than 1,500 people—both his secular and religious
opposition—in the month before he was gunned down. Sadat had visited Israel, he said, then made peace with it. In that confused environment, when truths and lies seemed so fluid and the impetuosity of
youth held sway, the movement saw violence as its only recourse.

"Our goal," Habib told me, "began to focus on the idea of carrying
out a strong and decisive strike against the political regime." In the end,
that proved short-sighted. Through violence, the movement had hoped
to secure a path to power. "Of course," he said, "that's not possible."
The government would not fall, and the violence would not win the
movement new adherents. Eventually, the attacks "hurt not only the
Islamic movement but also Islam itself as *da'wa* and as a religion."

In prison, he and others serving time for violence in the name of religion began interpreting the Quran on their own. Their goal remained a greater role for Islam in political life. But to achieve that, they had to decide among themselves "what to take, what to leave, what to build on and what to add to."

Their new focus, he said, became the creation of a political party.[46]

By the late 1990s, through repression and exhaustion, Egypt's insurgency had come to an end, its symbolic climax the massacre before the Temple of Hatshepsut near Luxor of fifty-eight foreign tourists and four Egyptians. Their deaths in November 1997 shook the country, and as popular revulsion over the bloodshed built, hints by Islamic militants of their willingness to enter into an unconditional cease-fire with the government gained momentum over the ensuing months. In 1999, the Islamic Group, Egypt's main militant opposition, had declared definitively that it was ending all attacks, both in Egypt and abroad, and the country enjoyed a period of quiet it had not witnessed in nearly a decade.[47] At the same time, the relaxed atmosphere gave rise to a striking political trend. Just three years after the Center Party announced its formation, two more Islamic groups sought government permission, both of them grouping together men like Habib: former militants once the scourge of governments who sought to bring about change through democracy rather than violence.

Habib's group, known as Hizb al-Islah, or the Reform Party, and Hizb al-Sharia, or the Islamic Law Party, both applied for government permission in 1999. The parties saw their steps as more idealistic than practical, each acknowledging that the government was sure to reject their applications. Still, they considered the initiative a crucial step in showing that the cease-fire of that same year was not an end in itself. Rather, they said, it reflected a new trend.[48]

"We are the sons of the Islamist movement who struggled against and clashed with the government in 1981," said Mamdouh Ismail, who served three years in prison after Sadat's assassination.[49] "We have been through a violent clash between the state and members of Islamist groups and saw the negative consequences of this violence. We have learned from bitter experience that we must reorder our priorities."

Neither Habib nor Ismail was an American-style democrat. Both believed that *sharia* should be the law of the land, and both opposed relations between Israel and the Arab world. Christians, they said, could live under their own laws as an autonomous community, and the responsibility of women was first and foremost in the home.[50] Beyond that, their proposals were what might be expected from activists who espoused a conservative religious agenda and who have endured a checkered, usually troubled past with the government. In its platform, the Islamic Law Party asked that all political prisoners be released, that the government end its rule by emergency law and that jails under the control of the Interior Ministry be transferred to the more independent Justice Ministry. It called for an end to all political violence but, it added, "We should not bury our heads in the sand like ostriches and intentionally ignore the real reasons for the eruption of this violence and its continuity." It blamed emergency law and an authoritarian government for blocking channels of communication, "limiting the means of the people to express their opinions and beliefs in a peaceful way."[51] Habib's Reform Party had a similar agenda, if somewhat broader. It urged the government to stop intervening in religious affairs, a response to the government's campaign in the 1990s to bring mosques independent of the state under its control by appointing preachers and monitoring their sermons. The faith of God, the party said, was above "narrow-minded political goals." It urged more religious material on television and in radio and an end to the wholesale import of Western films and music.[52]

Few in the West would agree with their goals. Some seem intolerant, others overly traditional, even regressive. But their platforms raise an important question: What is the danger in proposing those ideas? More important, is the alternative envisioned by the government—rejecting their applications for official status and harassing their members—a better alternative?[53] Is it more democratic? And a question we in the West must ask ourselves: Can people only be democrats when they believe what we in a different society and different culture believe? The Egyptian government had given its answer. It had already denied permission to the Center Party, a more liberal version of the Reform and Islamic Law Parties. In 1996, it arrested Abul-Ela Maadi, one of its founders, and put him before a military court on the charge of attempting to form a front for the outlawed Muslim Brotherhood. His intention, of course, was the opposite—he sought a peaceful alternative to the Brotherhood that pledged its loyalty to the state. Years later, though, he remained undaunted.

"They have authority, they have the power, they have money, they have everything and they don't want to change anything, of course," Maadi told me after the government first rejected the Center Party. "History won't accept that. When, I don't know. After one year, after ten years, but it will happen in the future."

Maadi has reason to be optimistic. The goals of a more pluralist, democratic society—a modern *umma*—can begin to evolve, influence and mature even without government permission. In the contemporary world, one that is increasingly tied together by technology, the Center Party's ideas electrified Islamic activists everywhere, unquestionably influencing other currents in Egypt and elsewhere in the Middle East. The party and its program were mentioned to me in interviews from Iran to Britain by activists who saw similarities to their own situations or were enchanted by the new, bold uses and reinterpretations of political ideas and vocabulary. As religious authority fragments—the traditional sheikhs losing their authority—more voices of disparate backgrounds like the Center Party will arise, bringing a plurality to thoughts that mingle and interact. Abu Zeid in Egypt resembles Soroush in Iran; Khatami speaks a language not all that unfamiliar to the Center Party. Their ideas and platforms cross borders. They reorient themselves to vastly different environments—a war against an occupation in Lebanon, for instance, or the precarious reform movement in Iran—and influence movements that are as different as Hamas in Palestine and the Virtue Party in Turkey.

At another level, political activism cannot be defined solely as electoral participation, particularly in environments in much of the Middle East where a ballot is more a means of conveying a cover of legitimacy than in serving as an instrument to bring about change. Maadi's Center Party, as well as the newer entrants in Egypt's political life, do not expect to be putting forward candidates in any election soon. Yet they see their work taking other forms—organizing and action within professional associations, labor unions, students and women's groups, human rights organizations, seminars and universities. In countries like Egypt, a political life has begun to evolve without government encouragement, even without its consent. In recognition of this, some of the Center Party's leaders took to calling themselves the Center Current. Their idea, they told me, was democracy by stealth: a visible role in the country's social, economic and political life in preparation for the day when free and fair elections at any level might open the door for an effective role in government. As always, their goal remained a greater role for Islam in people's lives.

Nevertheless, the reality that they are forced to pursue that course of action raises a deeper, perhaps more troubling question. Islamic activists from across the Muslim world have, to one degree or another, done their job. Thinkers have rethought the relationship between religion and democracy, opened the faith to more tolerant interpretations, searched for a viable and modern role for the religion in the lives of an already devout people and rethought attitudes to a West that, from the Crusades to colonialism, has little to be proud of in the Middle East. Movements have recognized failures in Sudan and Iran. As alternatives, they have sometimes evolved into grassroots movements bettering societies for which governments are unwilling or unable to provide. In some cases, they have looked to transform societies in the communities in which they live; in others, they have employed social activism as a legitimate means to win influence and power through elections (and, in the case of Turkey, then be forced out through undemocratic means). From Egypt to Lebanon, activists whose names were synonymous with horrific violence have emerged as political movements that seek to work with governments rather than overthrow them. Yet, in the final analysis, what has been the response?

No Arab head of state, outside Lebanon, has changed by truly democratic means for a generation.[54] Often those countries, Egypt in particular, have raised the threat of Islamic militancy to justify a lack of democracy. (The Egyptian government, for one, has rejected the applications of dozens of political parties over the past twenty years.) Turkey's military, sensing an undefined and, to many, nonexistent threat to the country's secularism, plotted Refah's removal from power and succeeded in banning the party's leader from politics for five years. The political landscape of those countries, though, is no longer what it was twenty years ago. The majority of Iranians were not alive for the revolution that toppled the Shah. The same goes for Egyptians and Sadat's assassination. Outside Algeria, no country in the Muslim world is seriously threatened by an Islamic insurgency. The greatest danger, it seems, is that the currents that operate within the framework of religion, looking to Islam to address their social, political and economic concerns, are the ones most likely to draw the broadest support. The threat is not to the governments' ideologies.

The threat is to their monopoly on authority, and only a handful today—Jordan and Lebanon among them—have accepted partners in power. As Fahmi Howeidi, a newspaper columnist and Islamic thinker in Cairo, once remarked to me, "The problem in Egypt is not between the government and the Islamists, it is between the government and democracy."

I left Cairo for the last time a few days after my interview with Habib, the former militant who served time for Sadat's assassination. As most are, it was an odd goodbye. In many ways, after nearly five years, Cairo felt as much like a home to me as any place I had lived in America. My friends lived there, and my work was there. Even my daily routine, that sign of familiarity, had become mundane: I had coffee every morning at the same café, I chatted with the fruit vendor, the butcher and the young boy at the newspaper kiosk and, week after week, I saw the same friends on the same days. Yet Egypt was a country of Muslims and I was not one of them. Language and heritage aside, I had the valuable perspective of an outsider, an eye on the society that was at once alien and observant. That perspective provided perhaps an insight. I had visited Tehran, Khartoum and Kabul, spent time in those cities as a reporter and traveled through them as a foreigner. Each time I returned home, though, I realized that Cairo was, by far, the most religious of cities—its people to me seemed the most devout, and the faith itself seemed ever-present, ordering life through its morals and its history, its people sharing a pride and a powerful sense of identity. It was a conception that went beyond our notion in the West of faith and nation. As I drove to the airport, through a city once said to have a thousand minarets, I thought to myself that a reckoning would have to occur in Egypt and countries like it. Faith, the temper of society, could not be ignored, a sentiment Cairo powerfully pronounced. One side, the Islamic movement, had taken the first step; the governments, in time, would have to reciprocate. As Habib told me in his dingy office, the splendor of Cairo's chaos outside, "Islam is a force that you cannot resist in an Islamic society. You have to try to search for an arrangement, an alternative to violence so that its presence can be legitimate."

Epilogue

IN THE INTRODUCTION to *Legacy of the Prophet*, I suggested that researching and writing the book, on one level, constituted a personal journey for me. In the United States, I had felt the disenchantment and, at times, resentment that so many hyphenated Americans of Middle East origin do: Stereotypes and prejudices against Arabs and Muslims always seemed to hit home. Yet I was often as puzzled by those same two identities—the Arab world from which my ancestors came and the religion, Islam, which shapes and defines that world's cultures, traditions, politics and memories, for Christians, Muslims and Jews alike. Those questions and conflicts made the book, in the beginning, a search for my own identity, potentially providing answers about my relationship to both my country of birth and the place of my ancestors.

As I look back on the turbulence, confusion and anger since the events of September 11, I have a different sense of that search. Reflecting on my interviews and conversations, my research and travels, I feel that my fractured identity has, in fact, given me a small chance to see the long-standing conflict between East and West in a different light. To many, a generation after the Iranian Revolution, the shot heard around the Muslim world, the sense of animosity and enmity between the two persists unabated, deepened dangerously by the attacks on New York and Washington. Islam, at least in the West, comes across as unyielding, blinded by its anger and inspired by vengeance. Many Muslims see the West as equally inflexible. Both seem short on understanding. Yet by default and through luck of birth and circumstance, I spent much of my time in the Middle East outside that relationship that was loosely "us" versus "them." I typically fell into a gray area, comfortable with neither but, as a journalist, interested in both. At times consciously, more often not, I tried to step outside the traditional equation. In hindsight, I was looking for the alternatives to what we have come to believe as truths—that Islam is one way, the West another and that religion can represent one immutable standard.

The years I spent in the Middle East represent a turning point in the region's history. Broadly, both faith and politics are changing. Far removed from the *jihad* of Osama bin Ladin, their relationship to each other is being reinterpreted, and many of the people whose lives are guided by them are asking bold, far-reaching questions that, in time, will have to be answered. In day-to-day life, Islamic political movements are using the faith and its appeal to Muslims' roots and identity, powerful forces in an uncertain world, to frame their political, social and economic programs. The goal is to create an alternative in a landscape colored by despotism and repression and gripped by war and a perceived clash of cultures. Although each locale has its own specific conditions—one of Islam's strengths, of course, is its adaptability—essential ideas are being shared: democracy, the right to religious interpretation, the role of religion in politics and the notion of *umma*.

Umma, perhaps, is the most powerful of those ideas. The Islamic concept of community and people seemed to play a permanent role in the lives of the individuals I met, from soldiers to activists to scholars. Mirza Khan, on the lonely plains of Afghanistan, found in it a mission. Eid Rabia, the trashman in Cairo, found security. To him, *umma* meant the community of Muslims, of Egyptians, of Cairenes, of the group of men who spent time with him in a café drinking tea sweetened just right. In it was his answer to Cairo's bewildering, mystifying changes, a language of resistance and, as important, his moral reference. In a way, I thought, it was his utopia of mind.

To me, Eid was the personal side of Islamic politics. His desires and his memory represented what was once termed "*the reactivation of tradition,*" a gut response to a changing world cloaked in faith. Eid looked to Islam for salvation and security and, in that, he defined his own *umma*. The community meant what he wanted it to mean, a definition probably different than that conceived by all the others sitting next to him in the shabby café tucked away in the otherwise wealthy Cairo neighborhood of Zamalek. In any incarnation, though, the community was defined loosely by Islam, drawing on a culture, traditions and collective memory. That flexibility and breadth provided the faith its powerful appeal to Eid and others. The meaning of faith was divergent but it shared an idea, providing a momentum in precarious times for its emergence politically.

Islam as a political force proved far more successful than the secular ideologies it once confronted after World War II and in the heady days of independence, even though it often shared their aims and their protests. Shielded from the setbacks that devastated those movements, most notably the Arab-Israeli war in 1967, political Islam endured as an ideology. It was reshaped by the thoughts of Islamic modernizers of the nineteenth century, redefined this century by the Muslim Brotherhood and its ideologues, primarily Sayyid Qutb, and then redirected by a new generation that has sought to reconcile Qutb's focus on the state with the potential of democratic activism. New currents of thought have emerged—from Iran to Turkey to Egypt—providing an impetus for change and an intellectual framework for democracy. As with Eid Rabia, those thoughts typically center on a reinterpreted *umma*, a justification for a democratic polity that stands as an alternative to Western tradition. Often, that reinterpretation has come at the expense of theological scholars known as the *ulema* and their traditional, centuries-old centers of religious thinking.

The intellectual currents have gained influence through their practical application. The rhetoric and exploits of wandering militants like bin Ladin, while appealing to a small segment of a Muslim world disenchanted to the point of hopelessness, rings hollow to the overwhelming majority. The realities of war and the promises of revolution are distant—both in physical terms and in the sense of their relevance. The real force of Islamic politics is represented by movements that have incorporated the new currents of thought with the persuasive and successful application of *da'wa*, an Islamic brand of welfare and social activism. These movements can be in opposition, as with Hamas in Palestine, or a complement to those in power, as with Hezbollah in Lebanon. In their most mature form, they can take on the visage of electoral politics, as with Islamists in Turkey. At the level of the polity itself, though, the effect of these movements, across the region, is remarkably uniform: In all cases they engage the general population, not in seeking intangible goals in some far-off future but in making a better life in the here and now—at the local level, where *umma* can be felt, seen, and even *used* profoundly.

These movements stand in contrast to the now-discredited revolution from above, which was practiced most visibly in the 1990s in
Sudan. There, a clique of visionaries blinded by promise sought to
implement one brand of Islam on a country too diverse to tolerate it.
They failed to reform the country or, in the face of failure, their program of action. In the end, Hassan al-Turabi and his following never
grasped the success of the grassroots movements elsewhere that took
note of the failures in Sudan. Those groups were anything but elite.
Instead, they drew their support from below, adapting their ideas and
programs to the very local conditions in which they worked. The independence of movements like Hamas and Hezbollah was their success,
a clear sign that political Islam is a rebelliously nonmonolithic movement. They represent one element of many Islams, all responding and
shaping the milieu from which they grew and now work.

Yet although the shape and pace of politics in individual countries
may diverge, one can still point to a general trend across the Islamic
political spectrum. Many states share a history of colonialism as well
as postcolonial disappointment, as succeeding governments were no
more just or democratic than their imperial predecessors. Typically,
those governments are best remembered for their failures: the 1967
war, Stalinist-style repression and economies that ridicule promises of
prosperity. The most vibrant response today to that disappointment
comes in the form of politicized religion as it is taken up by Islamic
intellectuals, movements like Hezbollah and the Center Party in
Egypt, political parties such as the Islamic Action Front in Jordan and
even governments in the throes of change like Iran under President
Mohammad Khatami. Together, they have broadly abandoned tradition to help reform the faith, giving it a legitimate role—both practically and potentially—in the political life of their countries. These
currents share their belief in Islam as the framework of action, looking
to religion in one way or another to address their social, political and
economic concerns. More often than not, they are the ones most likely to draw the broadest support from a public resentful over inequities,
injustice, chronic weakness and the slavish imitation of the West by
indigenous elites. These movements see in Islam and its resonant
symbols their legitimacy; they see in its non-Western concepts—
umma, for instance—an alternative, independent rationale and framework for an Islamic polity. And across the region, they see within the
faith a justification for a democratic, progressive region that is cur-

rently neither. All of them appeal to Islam as an overarching institution and ideology, even if their specific goals and programs are diverse and, at times, contradictory.

Will these movements find success? Yes, but gradually. In coming years, many of the governments in the Middle East—Egypt, Palestine, Turkey and countries in much of North Africa among them—will be forced to compromise with the Islamist elements in their midst. Simply put, the groups command too much popular support and represent too important a political current to be indefinitely neglected or, even worse, repressed. The alternative is insecurity and instability, the dread of all authoritarian governments. The survival of these governments will require a degree of transparency—and the reform that requires—if they are to engage economically and politically with the rest of the world. In a landscape without superpower rivalry and knit tighter together, for better or worse, by a neoliberal vision of the future, bureaucratic authoritarianism will in time prove less acceptable, even if in the short term it finds its repression sanctioned under the pretext of the emergency that followed the events of September 11. Through that inevitable future, I believe a window of opportunity will open, however slightly, making possible a compromise between the states and their Islamist opposition.

Although I admit being less certain than when I finished the book in 2000, I still remain hopeful for this scenario. My reason is this: I suspect that the future Middle East—in terms of its relationship between Islam and the state—will eventually witness a degree of the political transformation that Western Europe underwent during the twentieth century. There, Soviet-style socialism underwent a long metamorphosis to the social democracy of today. It was both a tactical and an ideological shift, dictated to a large extent by political survival. The parties and currents of the left were incorporated into the European political system without threatening its survival. Eventually, through political necessity, the same will go for Islamic parties. Already, a coming moderation on the part of Islamists is evident in the departure of the Center Party from the Muslim Brotherhood, President Khatami from his revolutionary antecedents and the Virtue Party in Turkey from its more militant predecessors. The changes reflect a broader trend toward integration rather than the past practice of offering an alternative. Somewhat metaphorically, the evolution of Kamal Habib and his cohorts in Egypt is a microcosm of that shift. From an impera-

tive to assassinate Anwar Sadat to a plea for the government to accept
his idea for a political party, Habib made a very conscious practical
and theoretical choice. In time, again with survival at stake, the
Egyptian government will see his choice as an opportunity rather than
as a threat, although that realization will likely have to wait for the
departure of President Hosni Mubarak and his seemingly permanent
vendetta against the country's Islamic opposition. Egypt may be a late-
comer to the new politics of Islam, since already a coming acceptance
of an Islamist opposition on the part of governments is evident, to one
degree or another, in Yemen, Kuwait, Jordan, Lebanon and occasionally Turkey and Palestine. Their choices are often motivated by a simple
desire for stability.

What about the United States? This question has assumed even
more importance in light of the campaign declared by the United
States against militant Islam in Afghanistan and elsewhere. While
the merits and dangers of that specific battle are better argued elsewhere, the breadth of U.S. policy toward the Muslim world is a concern, one that is becoming increasingly vital. Now, more than ever, I
believe a rethinking is in order, however difficult it may be to con-
template in a martial atmosphere that tends to claim a monopoly on
righteousness. For two decades, the U.S. government has been
unremitting in its hostility toward Iran, at times with justification. It
ostracized Sudan, criticizing it for a human rights record that, while
woeful, is not incomparable to the track records of governments in
Egypt and Saudi Arabia, among America's closest allies in the region.
Meanwhile, U.S. policy toward Israel—unflinching in its backing—
has created a reservoir of anger in all quarters of the Muslim world.
The one exception to the rule—American support for the *mujahideen*
against Soviet troops in Afghanistan in the 1980s—was a disastrously
opportunistic move that had a hand in creating Osama bin Ladin and
other borderless militants whom the United States sees as its greatest
threats today.

The rethinking should be ordered around two poles—stability and
democracy. Much of the Muslim world remains one of the last out-
posts of defiantly undemocratic rule—from tyranny to benign authoritarianism. With myriad examples before us, it is clearly evident that
such a system is anything but viable. In the short run, the all-powerful
parties, monarchies and dictatorships that have ruled the countries of
the region since independence have pledged their loyalty to the United

States. But the more lasting repercussions of their rule are becoming increasingly clear: a disenchantment among their people that has given rise to the very currents of militant Islam we now seek to destroy. To chart a new path, one that is squarely in U.S. interest, we must encourage popular participation as a means to a more democratic, stable government in countries the United States deems crucial to its interests. It becomes both a practical and principled approach. Rather than sanctioning repression in countries such as Egypt, most often through silence, the United States must encourage them to enact the reforms for a democracy that it espouses itself. Beyond that, both in practice and policy, the United States must avoid making distinctions between acceptable and unacceptable Islamists—support, for instance, for the Center Party, but not the Islamic Law Party in Egypt. If those groups pledge to adhere to limits of the system, they should be accepted and encouraged. It cannot be up to the West to determine good democrats and bad democrats—only democrats. Ultimately, if the goal is stable, humane and legitimate regimes in the countries with which the United States interacts, the governed must choose those who govern them. Washington's role will occasionally be that of bystander, although it should never eschew dialogue and constructive debate with the new parties.

The risk of such a policy to the United States—a move away from the black and white of the past and toward the more nuanced gray of the future—is obvious. Many of the movements that enjoy the greatest popularity in these countries are the least likely to bow to American wishes on Israel, Iraq, Iran or the Persian Gulf. The people have long memories and the United States rarely appears as a friend. Creating the alliance that fought the Gulf War in 1991, for instance, would have been impossible if the countries in the region had democratically elected governments expressing popular opinion, which, to varying degrees, sided with the Iraqi government of Saddam Hussein. It was no coincidence that Jordan, Yemen and Algeria—countries with hints of democratic rule—were the most critical of U.S. policy during the crisis. Memories, too, remain. Americans will never forget the televised images as the towers of the World Trade Center collapsed, an attack blamed, to one degree on another, on Islam. Iranians, in no less painful terms, still recall the U.S. role in 1953 in overthrowing the country's popular prime minister, Mohammad Mossadeq, and then its sustained, indulgent backing of the dictatorial Shah.

Not seeking an alternative, though, is clearly untenable. Repression has already failed in Iran and is soon to fail in the Persian Gulf and in countries like Egypt, where time and again the government has tried in vain to stamp out the substantial support political Islam enjoys. The status quo will only accentuate hardship and suffering. The benefit, meanwhile, is a potential turning point in the region's history. Greater democracy will bring about a more humane political life in bleakly authoritarian countries, greater stability in a region that produces the world's oil, an effective weapon against the scourge of terrorism that feeds off discontent and disillusionment and an effective way to begin ending a cultural conflict, whose roots extend as far back as the Middle Ages.

However difficult it is to suggest today, such a rethinking will also represent a much-needed step toward mutual respect—and the beginning of the end to the "us" versus "them" that characterizes relations between the West and much of the Muslim world. Sustained and consistent support for the emergence of democratic regimes will bring an entirely different hue to the way in which we perceive parties—Islamist and otherwise—that participate within the system. It is a path that offers us a way out of the bloodshed that will only mount amid the cries for war celebrated by both sides. In that, we face a choice, a rare moment to decide our common destiny. Our future is already at hand.

Notes

Introduction

1. I traveled to Egypt as a correspondent for the *Boston Globe*. At the time, I was based in the newspaper's Washington bureau, covering the diplomatic side to the story of the September 11 attacks on New York and Washington. I joined the *Globe* in December 2000 after more than ten years with the Associated Press. Much of the book is based on my experiences as an AP reporter in Cairo from 1995–1999, when I had the opportunity to travel to Turkey, Iran, Afghanistan, Pakistan and most of the Arab world.

2. John L. Esposito, *The Islamic Threat: Myth or Reality?* (Oxford: Oxford University Press, 1992), 4.

3. Robert Malley, *The Call from Algeria: Third Worldism, Revolution and the Turn to Islam* (Berkeley: University of California Press, 1996), 231. Malley sees Islamism as distinct from Islamic fundamentalism. While there is considerable overlap, fundamentalism concerns itself more with questions of morality. Islamism, on the other hand, is dedicated to an overarching approach to modern society. He points out that Islamism is far from traditional, since its political instruments, activities and goals are often influenced by European and American culture. Olivier Roy, in *The Failure of Political Islam* (Cambridge: Harvard University Press, 1994), uses *Muslim* to designate what is fact—a Muslim country, a Muslim intellectual. *Islamic*, he says, signifies the result of an intention—an Islamic state bases its legitimacy on Islam, and an Islamic intellectual is one who consciously organizes his thought with Islamic concepts. Throughout, I have borrowed the framework of both authors in using the terms *political Islam, Muslim* and *Islamic*.

4. Esposito, *Islamic Threat*, 23.

5. Sami Zubaida, "Islam and the Politics of Community and Citizenship," *Middle East Report* 221 (winter 2001): 21.

6. Essam Sultan, interview by author, Cairo, 6 July 1999

Chapter One

1. Most Afghans belong to the Pashtun, Tajik, Uzbek, Hazara, Turkmen, and Aimak ethnic groups. As Olivier Roy notes in "Rivalries and Power Plays in Afghanistan: The Taliban, the Shari'a and the Pipeline," *Middle East Report* 202 (winter 1997): 37–38, Pashtuns long dominated Afghanistan's political life. They lost influence during the war against the Soviet Union, which was carried out mostly in the north from 1979 to 1988. But they have returned to prominence with the success of the Taliban, a largely Pashtun movement. Amir Shah was Hazara, most of whom are Shiite. The Pashtuns are Sunni, and relations between the two groups are very poor, with both sides accusing the other of a series of massacres. Human Rights Watch, quoting aid workers, reported in September 1998 that thousands of Hazaras were killed when the Taliban took the northern city of Mazar-e Sharif a month earlier.

2. The United States helped the campaign of the *mujahideen* in the 1980s with its biggest, most elaborate and most expensive covert operation, and the *mujahideen*, in time, emerged as one of the most successful insurgencies in history. In Afghanistan, though, the story was different. After they overthrew the Soviet-backed government of Najibullah in 1992, their popular support soon faded as they turned their guns on each other, effectively destroying Kabul.

3. United Nations Development Programme, *Globalization with a Human Face*, Human Development Report, 1999, 246.

4. In the months after the Taliban took Kabul, almost nightly edicts were handed down on Radio Shariat, the Taliban station whose broadcasts many Afghans came to dread.

5. In fact, the little humor I found in Afghanistan came from Amir Shah, the driver. I met him soon after arriving in Afghanistan and within minutes of greeting each other, he had recited to me a long list of the photographers and journalists with whom he had worked. Numbering in the dozens, it was an impressive résumé, testament to Amir Shah's knack for winning people over. In time, I would learn that Amir Shah had the ability to be all things to all people, his method of survival in trying times. When I asked him whether he was an orthodox Muslim or a member of the minority Shiite branch, he answered with another question: "Which is better?" With his Turkic, Central Asian looks, he usually tried to pose as a Japanese at the Pakistani border, which was notoriously unfriendly to Afghans, hoping for better treatment. At checkpoints, he would weave intricate tales of bringing emergency relief to starving Afghans or try to pass off a Western journalist as an important diplomat or visiting dignitary. It sometimes worked.

6. United Nations Development Programme, *Globalization*, 246.

7. Olivier Roy, *The Failure of Political Islam* (Cambridge: Harvard University Press, 1994).

8. A *madrasa* is an Islamic school that, according to Richard Bulliet in *Islam: The View from the Edge* (New York: Columbia University Press, 1994), dates back to the late eleventh century and is of Iranian origin. They were devoted to the study of Islamic law as well as hadith (words and actions attributed to the Prophet Mohammed) and Quran reading. Many of the Taliban's cadres come from the rural *madrasas*, particularly in southern Afghanistan, which is dominated by Pashtun like Khan.

9. United Nations Drug Control Programme, *Capacity Building for Drug Control*, Afghanistan Project Summary, 1997, 1.

10. W. Montgomery Watt, *Muhammad: Prophet and Statesman* (Oxford: Oxford University Press, 1961), 40.

11. Ibid., 48–49.

12. As the revelations continued, though, he eventually came to see himself as the last in the long line of God's prophets that began with Abraham and continued through Moses and Jesus.

13. John L. Esposito, *The Islamic Threat: Myth or Reality?* (Oxford: Oxford University Press, 1992), 28.

14. Medina is short for Medinat al-Nabi, or City of the Prophet.

15. Watt, in *Muhammad*, 89, says the residents of Medina were more inclined to accept him as prophet because they were influenced by the concept of a messiah propagated by the Jews who lived among them.

16. Watt, *Muhammad*, 100.

17. Ibid., 204–5.

18. Ibid., 218–19.

19. The description of the rally came from two articles: "A New Age of Martyrs," *Economist*, 28 June 1997, and Jay Reeves, "Thousands Rally in Support of Judge's Ten Commandments Display," *Associated Press*, 12 April 1997.

20. Throughout the book, I use interchangeably the terms "Islamists" and "Islamic activists" to denote those who consciously approach society and its problems with Islamic concepts. They seek to revive and modernize religion so as to provide a blueprint for dealing with modern society. The only possible distinction between the two terms is that "Islamists" can include individuals who are not necessarily political. For instance, a religious scholar at Al-Azhar in Cairo might be considered an Islamist but not an Islamic activist, particularly if his work did not extend beyond the walls of the institution.

21. Adel Hussein, interview by author, Cairo, 1 July 1996.

22. Gilles Kepel, *The Revenge of God: The Resurgence of Islam, Christianity and Judaism in the Modern World* (University Park: Pennsylvania State University Press, 1994), 11.

23. Ibid., 2.

24. In contrast to the proliferation today of McDonald's, Pizza Hut and others, there was just one fast-food locale in Cairo twenty-five years ago, a lone Wimpy.

25. Timothy Mitchell, "Dreamland: The Neoliberalism of Your Desires," *Middle East Report* 210 (spring 1999): 32.

26. National Population Council. *Egypt Demographic and Health Survey 1995* (Cairo, 1996), 23.

27. Stella was long a butt of jokes, and I always thought the Westernization of Cairo, in a superficial way, could be measured by the change in its quality. The jokes have nothing to do with the subject at hand, but one is probably worth mentioning: An American chemist takes a sample of the beer home with him. He turns it over to a laboratory, which after a week delivers its finding: His camel has diabetes.

28. Stephen Keefer, in an interview by author, Cairo, 10 February 1999. "There's basically not a beer culture here. The whole point was to introduce these products because there's a vacuum in the market," said Keefer, the spokesman for the recently privatized Al-Ahram Beverages Company, which effectively had cornered the Egyptian market. "They like beer but they can't drink alcohol."

29. National Population Council, *Egypt Demographic and Health Survey 1995*, 23.

30. Eric Denis, "Urban Planning and Growth in Cairo," *Middle East Report* 202 (winter 1997): 9.

31. "Go to Dreamland, Forget the Mosques," *Economist*, 17 August 1996.

32. Max Rodenbeck, *Cairo: The City Victorious* (Cairo: The American University in Cairo Press, 1998), 197–203. Much of the history of Cairo in this chapter draws from Rodenbeck's book, a fascinating and entertaining look at the city's evolution.

33. The flip side was the alienation some of Cairo's Westernized population felt for their own society. At the American University in Cairo, located in the heart of the city's downtown, a group of women hanging out on a stairwell told me they felt comfortable only inside the campus walls. "I can't walk like this outside the university. It would be a disaster," said Nadine, a twenty-one-year-old in a sleeveless black shirt with a silver clasp around her bicep and a ring on every finger. "I wouldn't wear a miniskirt in the streets." Her friends earnestly nodded their heads in agreement. "You can wear what you want here and people won't stare," another woman, Yasmin, insisted in flawless English. The alienation extended to their own language. The women felt more comfortable in English, the university's language of instruction, than Arabic, the language of the country. They found reading particularly difficult. I asked Yasmin if her lack of literacy in her native tongue frustrated her, making her country somehow less accessible. She nodded her head, befuddled. "Speaking is something you do twenty-four hours a day," she told me. "But reading and writing, you just sit and read and write by yourself."

34. Rodenbeck, *Cairo*, 122.

35. The discussion of the trash collectors is based on an article by Ragui Assad, "Formalizing the Informal? The Transformation of Cairo's Refuse Collection System," *Journal of Planning Education and Research* 16 (1996): 115–26. Other information came in an interview by author with Assad, Cairo, 7 March 1999.

36. Albert Hourani, *A History of the Arab Peoples* (Cambridge: Harvard University Press, 1991), 452.

37. Robert Malley, *The Call from Algeria: Third Worldism, Revolution and the Turn to Islam* (Berkeley: University of California Press, 1996), 167.

38. Dale F. Eickelman and James Piscatori, *Muslim Politics* (Princeton: Princeton University Press, 1996), 9.

Chapter Two

1. Khaled Mohieddin, interview by author, Cairo, 9 March 1998.

2. Egypt's union with Syria, perhaps the most serious of many attempts by Arab countries to erase colonial and often arbitrary boundaries, lasted just three years. The nationalization of the Suez Canal, its control by the British long a lightning rod for Egyptian nationalism, led to the 1956 attack by Britain, France and Israel aimed at retaking the waterway, which links the Red and Mediterranean Seas. President Eisenhower forced their withdrawal from the Sinai, and Nasser claimed the retreat as a victory.

3. Albert Hourani, *A History of the Arab Peoples* (Cambridge: Harvard University Press, 1991), 407.

4. The struggle with Israel consumed vast amounts of Egypt's national resources, undermining one of the projects that propelled the Free Officers to take power in the first place: development of the country. Nasser once said his goal was for a *fellah*, or peasant, to command a higher rate for a day's work than did the *gamoosa*, or water buffalo. At his death, they still did not. The *fellah* cost fifty-eight cents a day; the *gamoosa*, sixty-nine cents. From "Nasser's Legacy: Hope and Instability," *Time*, 12 October 1970.

5. Palestinian nationalism was a notable exception. If anything, the war provided an impetus to its struggle, marking the emergence of the Palestine Liberation Organization and its leader, Yasser Arafat.

6. Taken from Alan Richards and John Waterbury, *A Political Economy of the Middle East: State, Class and Economic Development* (Boulder: Westview Press, 1990), 359, and *Historic World Leaders*, Gale Research, 1994.

7. Richard W. Bulliet, *Islam: The View from the Edge* (New York: Columbia University Press, 1994), 4. He goes on to add: "By contrast, answers that purport to be rooted in Islamic tradition . . . have a much stronger likelihood of winning the questioner's confidence and loyalty."

8. Quoted in Richard P. Mitchell, *The Society of the Muslim Brothers* (Oxford: Oxford University Press, 1969), 30. Mitchell's book, which ends with Nasser's crackdown on the Brotherhood in 1954, remains the preeminent account of the movement's early years, its organization and ideology.

9. Ibid., 55–58.

10. Ibid., 99. As Mitchell said: "Their shared experiences in battle, especially at the siege of Faluja, established for some and reinforced for others shared attitudes about things related and unrelated, especially about those responsible for the humiliation suffered in Palestine."

11. Ibid., 104.

12. Ibid., 328.

13. Ibid., 151. Three days after the assassination attempt, Nasser vowed that "the revolution shall not be crippled; if it is not able to proceed white, then we will make it red."

14. See Olivier Roy, *The Failure of Political Islam* (Cambridge: Harvard University Press, 1994), 110–12, for a discussion of the Brotherhood's reach and shifting identities.

15. Mitchell, *Muslim Brothers*, 321, "In that sweep of developments in the Arab world beginning with the movement of the Wahhabiyya in the late eighteenth century, the Society of the Brothers emerges as the first mass-supported and organized, essentially urban-oriented effort to cope with the plight of Islam in the modern world." The Wahhabiyya was an austere, revivalist movement in the Arabian Peninsula that rose in the eighteenth century and eventually found common cause with the al-Saud family, later the rulers of modern Saudi Arabia.

16. Hourani, *A History of the Arab Peoples*, 317.

17. Quoted in Mitchell, *Muslim Brothers*, 5.

18. David Sagiv, *Fundamentalism and Intellectuals in Egypt, 1973–93* (London: Frank Cass, 1995), 30.

19. Quoted in Mitchell, *Muslim Brothers*, 8, from the Brotherhood's own account. Mitchell said their actual words cannot be verified, whether it was spontaneous or rehearsed, but argues that what is claimed is said is worth noting as an accurate summation of the inspiration and spirit of the movement and an insight into the group's strength: the relationship between the leader and the led.

20. Quran 13:12.

21. Afghani (1839–1897), Abdo (1849–1905) and Rida (1865–1935), known as Islamic modernists, were concerned with the decline of Islam as a faith and a civilization, the causes of it, how to bring about a renaissance and how to confront the growing social, intellectual, economic and military power of Europe. Abdo, in particular, saw in Europe the inspirations and

the challenge needed to arrest Islam's decline. All three stressed the concept of *ijtihad*, or personal reasoning, in reinterpreting Islam so that it was compatible with a modern world. As Hourani notes in *A History of the Arab Peoples*, 308, summing up their task, "When circumstances change they too should change; in the modern world, it is the task of Muslim thinkers to relate changing laws and customs to unchanging principles, and by so doing to give them limits and a direction."

22. The code of Islamic law known as *sharia* is based on the Quran and Sunna, the example of the life of the prophet and his companions. Traditionally, it has been elaborated and upheld by the *ulema*, the class of men who serve roughly as a clergy in Islam but with far less structure, authority and hierarchy than their Christian equivalent. Since the 1970s, the demand to reintroduce *sharia* as the code of law has been a common denominator of Islamic activists across the region. The exact application of that law is still fiercely debated by the same activists, even if its core concepts are largely shared.

23. Gehad Auda, "The 'Normalization' of the Islamic Movement in Egypt from the 1970s to the Early 1990s," in *Accounting for Fundamentalisms*, ed. Martin E. Marty and Scott Appleby (Chicago: University of Chicago Press, 1994), 376–77.

24. Robert Malley, *The Call from Algeria: Third Worldism, Revolution and the Turn to Islam* (Berkeley: University of California Press, 1996), 200–201. Malley's book provides a fascinating discussion on the way in which the banner of Islam has filled the void left by the demise of Third World, postcolonial and anti-imperial struggles, a phenomenon that was very visible in Nasser's Egypt.

25. Banna quoted in Asef Bayat, "Revolution without Movement, Movement without Revolution," *Comparative Studies in Society and History* 40 (January 1998): 163. Italics added by author.

26. Quoted in Mitchell, *Muslim Brothers*, 103. In fact, in his later years, Hodeibi wrote *Preachers, Not Judges*, a book that stood as a critique of revolutionary Islam. Preaching, he said, was the task of the Brotherhood and its success would lead to an Islamic society.

27. Mitchell, *Muslim Brothers*, 300.

28. Ibid., 297.

29. The killings were part of a long-running contest for authority between elements of the movement and an Egyptian monarchy that was becoming increasingly unstable in the wake of the disastrous war in Palestine, mounting political violence inside Egypt and persistent anger over the British presence.

30. Hassan Hanafi, "The Relevance of the Islamic Alternative in Egypt," *Arab Studies Quarterly* 4 (spring 1982): 60–61.

31. Some accounts say he was born in the village of Qaha.

32. The account of Qutb's early life comes from Sagiv, *Fundamentalism and Intellectuals*, 36–42, and William E. Shepard, "Islam as a 'System' in the Later Writings of Sayyid Qutb," *Middle East Studies* 25 (January 1989): 31–32.

33. Gilles Kepel, *Muslim Extremism in Egypt: The Prophet and Pharaoh* (Berkeley: University of California Press, 1985), 40–41.

34. Cited in Sagiv, *Fundamentalism and Intellectuals*, 37.

35. Sayyid Qutb, *Milestones* (Indianapolis: American Trust Publications, 1990), 119.

36. Kepel, *Muslim Extremism*, 41.

37. Cited in Kepel, *Muslim Extremism*, 42. Ghazali visited Qutb's two sisters regularly and, through this link, Qutb sent his writings to activists outside prison.

38. Qutb, *Milestones*, 8.

39. Ibid., 118.

40. Ibid., 48.

41. The discussion of Qutb's thought is taken from the book itself. I also relied on Kepel, *Muslim Extremism*; Auda, "'Normalization' of the Islamic Movement"; and Ibrahim M. Abu-Rabi, *Intellectual Origins of Islamic Resurgence in the Modern Arab World* (Albany: State University of New York Press, 1996). The three authors would not necessarily agree with my analysis.

42. Hassan al-Turabi, interview by author, Khartoum, 21 May 1996.

43. Turabi's reference to traditional, sectarian Islam is an indirect criticism of Sufi orders in Sudan, which were instrumental in the spread of the faith and later became the country's dominant political parties. Through much of his career, they amounted to his most formidable political opposition.

44. Essam Sultan, interview by author, Cairo, 6 July 1999.
45. Kamal Habib, interview by author, Cairo, 14 July 1999. Habib is a compelling figure. He spent ten years in prison for membership in Jihad, the group that assassinated Sadat. He pursued an academic career afterward, earning a doctorate in politics, and began working as a journalist. In 1999, he floated the idea of forming a political party of former Islamic militants. His attempt is discussed further in another chapter.
46. Tariq al-Bishri, interview by author, Cairo, 10 July 1999.
47. Najib Ghadbian, *Democratization and the Islamist Challenge in the Arab World* (Boulder: Westview Press, 1997), 75.
48. "The Islamic understanding of democracy is with an Arab and Islamic identity, far from the dregs of secularism and European culture." Abul-Ela Maadi, "Al-Haraka al-Islamiyya wa al-Dimocratiyya: Darasat fil-Fikr wa al-Mamarasa," Cairo, 18 September 1999.
49. Qutb is perhaps the most famous of the Brotherhood leaders radicalized by his time in prison. According to Hisham Mubarak, the late Egyptian human rights activist, Qutb witnessed the massacre of twenty-three of his colleagues in Tura prison in 1957, when prison forces opened fire on detainees who had staged a sit-in and refused to work in quarries. Those and other incidents hardened his attitudes.
50. Quoted in Maadi, "Al-Haraka al-Islamiyya wa al-Dimocratiyya."
51. Quoted in Metin Heper, "Islam and Democracy in Turkey: Toward a Reconciliation?" *Middle East Journal* 51, no. 1 (winter 1997): 38.
52. Roy, *Political Islam*, 10–11.
53. Khomeini, true to his nature as a revolutionary, responded in 1988 to a sermon in which the country's president suggested *sharia* was binding on Iran's Islamic government. Khomeini issued a strong refutation. He declared that the Islamic government can abrogate *sharia* principles if it is acting in the interests of the Muslim nation. He said it could forbid even the most basic pillars of the faith like prayer, fasting and *hajj*. Sami Zubaida, "Is Iran an Islamic State?" in *Political Islam: Essays from Middle East Report*, ed. Joel Beinin and Joe Stork (Berkeley: University of California Press, 1996), 107.
54. Ghadbian, *Democratization and the Islamist Challenge*, 76–78.
55. Rachid al-Ghannouchi, head of Tunisia's Islamic movement, is another prominent thinker on religion and democracy. He argues that democratic procedures such as elections and majority rule are universal and do not contradict Islam. Some of his thoughts are remarkably progressive. For instance, he supports affirmative action to increase women's representation in legislative bodies. Both he and his movement have run afoul of the government, in part because of their popularity. He lives in exile in London.
56. Ghadbian, *Democratization and the Islamist Challenge*, 78.
57. Ibid., 79.
58. Glenn E. Robinson, "Can Islamists Be Democrats? The Case of Jordan," *Middle East Journal* 51, no. 3 (summer 1997): 378–79.
59. Maadi, at times, seems to enjoy taking jabs at the Brotherhood. When a Christian member of his party resigned in 1999, Maadi said he respected the decision and added that his group "does not follow the principle of listen and obey," the old Brotherhood hallmark. Mohammed Salah, "Al-Qibti al-Wahid Yansahib min La'ihat Mu'asisi al-Wasat al-Masri," *Al-Hayat* (London), 11 June 1999.
60. Gudrun Kramer, "Islamist Notions of Democracy," *Middle East Report* 183 (July-August 1993): 8.
61. Abul-Ela Maadi, interview by author, Cairo, 22 January 1997.
62. Essam Sultan, interview by author, Cairo, 6 July 1999.
63. Dale F. Eickelman and James Piscatori, *Muslim Politics* (Princeton: Princeton University Press, 1996), 159.
64. Ibid., 112–13.
65. Mitchell, *Muslim Brothers*, 212.
66. Quoted in Eickelman and Piscatori, *Muslim Politics*, 43.

Chapter Three

1. Karam Zuhdi, a militant leader in southern Egypt, was reported to have said during a court hearing that the pamphlet amounted to no more than a series of quotations by various *ulema*.

2. The five recognized pillars of Islam are *tawhid,* or the oneness of God, which is expressed by the creed, "There is no god but God and Mohammed is his prophet"; prayer, which is required of Muslims five times a day; alms, which must be given to the poor annually; fasting, which is required of Muslims during the holy month of Ramadan; and the pilgrimage to Mecca, which Muslims who can afford it and are physically able must make once in a lifetime.

3. John L. Esposito, *The Islamic Threat: Myth or Reality?* (Oxford: Oxford University Press, 1992), 96–97.

4. The most notable was Shukri Mustafa, who formed the Society of Muslims in the early 1970s. They fled briefly into exile in the mountains but returned to poor neighborhoods ringing Cairo and other Egyptian cities. They were later crushed by Egyptian security forces after kidnapping and killing Egypt's minister of religious endowments in 1977. A short time later, Shukri was arrested, sentenced to death and executed.

5. Gilles Kepel, *Muslim Extremism in Egypt: The Prophet and Pharaoh* (Berkeley: University of California Press, 1985), 193.

6. Ibid., 194.

7. The event was a "victory parade." In October 1973, Egypt launched a surprise attack on Israeli forces occupying the east bank of the Suez Canal. At the same time, Syria launched an attack on the Golan Heights. (Both the Sinai Peninsula and the Golan Heights were captured by Israel six years earlier in the 1967 Arab-Israeli War.) Egypt quickly crossed the canal, driving Israeli forces back, and Syria soon found similar success. In the ensuing days, however, Israel counterattacked, helped in part by massive shipments of American arms. Its forces crossed to the west bank of the Suez Canal and drove the Syrians back, as well. At best, the war ended in a draw, with a cease-fire brokered by the United States and the Soviet Union. Still, the initial success of the Egyptian army—a credit to planning and determination, skills not demonstrated in the earlier wars with Israel—is celebrated as a victory in Egypt and the Arab world.

8. A study of 303 political prisoners from the group arrested after the assassination showed that one-third were students, 10 percent were university graduates and 6 percent were high school students. There were doctors, educators and military personnel but not a single cleric or peasant, long thought to be the stronghold of the disenfranchised and disinherited. R. Hrair Dekmejian, *Islam in Revolution: Fundamentalism in the Arab World,* 106, in Olivier Roy, *The Failure of Political Islam* (Cambridge: Harvard University Press, 1994), 212.

9. The account of the assassination is drawn from several sources, primarily Kepel, *Muslim Extremism,* 210–15.

10. Kamal Habib, interview by author, Cairo, 14 July 1999.

11. Mohammed Salah, "Ali al-Rashidi: al-Shurti al-Masri alathi Mahad al-Tariq lil-Afghan al-Arab fi Afriqiyya," *Al-Hayat* (London), 30 September 1998.

12. Mark Huband, *Warriors of the Prophet: The Struggle for Islam* (Boulder: Westview Press, 1998), 3.

13. Hisham Mubarak, "A Tragedy of Errors," *Cairo Times,* 22 January–4 February, 1998.

14. Arabic has no letter "p" so a word like Panjshir would be transliterated as Banshir.

15. U.S. officials have strongly denied suggestions that Afghan Arabs were involved in fighting against American forces in Somalia.

16. Mohammed Salah, "Al-Qahira: Qa'id al-Afghan al-Arab Qutila fi-Dowla Afriqiyya," *Al-Hayat* (London), 11 June 1996.

17. Roy, *Political Islam,* 117–18.

18. Mansoor Alam, interview by author, Cairo, 17 June 1996.

19. Tal'at Fu'ad Qasim, "What Does the Gama'a Islamiyya Want? An Interview with Tal'at Fu'ad Qasim," interview by Hisham Mubarak, *Middle East Report* 198 (January-March 1996): 46.

20. Some accounts say his mother was Saudi.

21. Faiza Ambah's profile "Saudi Militant's Wish: To Die Fighting America," *Associated Press,* 29 August 1998, stands as one of the best, most succinct tellings of his personal history.

22. Scott MacLeod, "The Paladin of Jihad," *Time,* 6 May 1996.

23. Khaled al-Fawaz, interview by Associated Press special correspondent Charles J. Hanley, London, 15 January 1997.

24. Ambah, "Saudi Militant's Wish."

25. Mubarak, "A Tragedy of Errors."

26. Western accounts have put his fortune at $250 million. That seems exaggerated. His share of his family's empire was frozen in 1992 and he lost an investment of $150 million when he was forced to leave Sudan in 1996. No accurate figure that I know of exists for his actual wealth.

27. The United States consistently accused Sudan of harboring men it considered terrorists and made no secret of its desire to see him denied sanctuary there. In an interview, Turabi denied bin Ladin left in 1996 as a result of U.S. pressure. Somewhat unbelievably, he said bin Ladin made the decision on his own, choosing not to risk worsening already tense relations between Sudan and Saudi Arabia.

28. Hassan al-Turabi, interview by author, Khartoum, 24 August 1996.

29. Ambah, "Saudi Militant's Wish."

30. Olivier Roy, "Fundamentalists Without a Common Cause," *Le Monde Diplomatique* (Paris), 2 October 1998. The parentheses are in the original. The bracketed material was added by the author.

31. Graham Usher, *Palestine in Crisis: The Struggle for Peace and Political Independence after Oslo* (London: Pluto Press, 1995), 8.

32. Donna Abu-Nasr, "Prison a Turning Point in Life of One Suicide Bomber," *Associated Press*, 29 January 1995.

33. Ibid.

34. Hamad family, interviews by author, Gaza, 12 July 1996.

35. Usher, *Palestine in Crisis*, 7–9. The Oslo peace agreement was the result of a series of fourteen secret meetings between PLO officials and Israeli advisers and academics that began in late January 1993 and stretched over eight months. The agreement in itself was not new, dating back to proposals put forth in the Camp David accords signed by Menachem Begin and Anwar Sadat in 1978. Under the accords, Palestinians would receive "limited authority" over parts of the West Bank and Gaza Strip, beginning with an Israeli withdrawal from Gaza and the West Bank town of Jericho. It also made provisions for a Palestinian police force and elections for a Palestinian Council that would have authority over education and culture, health, social welfare, direct taxation and tourism. Israel would retain control of external relations and foreign affairs. After two years, Israel and the Palestinians would start negotiations on a permanent settlement and address such issues as Jerusalem, Jewish settlements in the West Bank and Gaza and the fate of refugees from the 1948 war. Those negotiations and the Israeli withdrawal were delayed time and again by successive Israeli governments, particularly after suicide attacks or following episodes in which Israel claimed that Arafat had not provided security in exchange for peace.

36. Known as "the engineer," the twenty-nine-year-old Ayyash taught his few but fiercely devoted followers how to make bombs. He was No. 1 on Israel's most-wanted list and, after going underground in 1992, narrowly eluded death for years, sometimes disguising himself as a Jewish settler or a woman. His death in January 1996 unleashed an orgy of bloodshed in which Palestinians took their lives and those of fifty-nine others in suicide attacks in February and March in revenge for Ayyash's death.

37. Ibrahim Rashed, interview by author, Nablus, 11 July 1996.

38. The Israelis were not alone in their casual use of repression. Once in Palestine, Arafat's security forces quickly grew adept at detentions without charges, mass arrests and, according to Amnesty International, severe beatings, burnings by cigarettes, prolonged sleep deprivation and other torture. At a police station in Gaza, I sat across the desk from a mid-ranking officer. In another room, a man was beaten for fifteen minutes. After each slap, he would scream. The officer did not acknowledge the yells, despite the obvious impression it was leaving on me. In other instances, Palestinian prisoners have spoken to their Palestinian guards in Hebrew, a poignant statement of the role they thought the guards were playing.

39. It is a statement repeated over and over in the West Bank and Gaza. Violence is usually wrong, but Palestine is a special circumstance, goes the refrain. "It is difficult for people in the West to understand, but it is not difficult for us," Ghazi Hamad, a Hamas leader in Gaza, told me. "They want to fight, they want to struggle against the occupation and when they die, they become martyrs."

40. Napoleon, who invaded Egypt in 1798, was defeated at al-Baroud, near the southern Egyptian city of Qena, and the British had no posts in Upper Egypt. Mamoun Fandy, "Egypt's Islamic Group: Regional Revenge?" *Middle East Journal* 48 (autumn 1994): 611.

41. Upper Egypt generally includes all of the country south of Cairo along the Nile River, home to about a third of Egypt's 65 million people. In Arabic, it is referred to as the Sa'id. The division of Egypt into upper and lower halves is derived from their location on the Nile, which unlike most great rivers, flows from south to north. Thus, the Nile first runs through Upper Egypt before branching into the delta of Lower Egypt and flowing into the Mediterranean Sea. As for the statistics used in this section, I relied on two reports: Institute of National Planning, *Egypt: Human Development Report*, Cairo, 1995, and National Population Council, *Egypt Demographic and Health Survey 1995.*

42. Fandy, "Egypt's Islamic Group," 607.

43. Ibid., 611.

44. See Kepel, *Muslim Extremism,* 134, for a discussion on the role of Muhammad Uthman Ismail, the governor of Asyut province in the 1970s. He was considered the "godfather" of the Islamic Group, encouraging its blossoming to battle the "communists," who were especially active in 1972–1973.

45. John L. Esposito, *The Islamic Threat: Myth or Reality?* (Oxford: Oxford University Press, 1992), 94.

46. Ibid., 98.

47. Census information in Egypt must be viewed skeptically, particularly as it relates to religious minorities, since data can be manipulated to bolster or discredit calls for greater political representation. Nevertheless, the figures indicate that the biggest Christian minorities live in Asyut, Minya and Sohag, three provinces that saw the fiercest strife during the insurgency in the 1990s. More important, those three provinces are the only ones in Egypt in which Copts are predominantly rural: 66 percent in Asyut, 71 percent in Sohag and 74 percent in Minya. For census numbers, see E. J. Chitham, *The Coptic Community in Egypt: Spatial and Social Change* (Durham: Centre for Middle Eastern and Islamic Studies, 1986).

48. For a discussion on land and conflict in Egypt, see Timothy Mitchell, "The Representation of Rural Violence in Writings on Political Development in Nasserist Egypt," in *Peasants and Politics in the Middle East,* ed. John Waterbury (Miami: Florida International University, 1991), 235–36. "The fields that villagers own or rent, labor in or supervise, sell or seize control of are the crucial site for constructing rural power relations."

49. Most Egyptian jokes are at the expense of Sa'idis and usually start with "Marra wahid Sa'idi," or "Once, an Upper Egyptian." As with the stereotypes, they cast them as country bumpkins.

50. Hosni Mubarak, statement read on state television, 19 November 1995.

51. Qasim, "Interview."

52. Unconfirmed reports at the time suggested he was captured by U.S. agents and handed over to Egyptian intelligence on September 22. He was said to have been taken to intelligence headquarters in the Nile Delta town of al-Mansoura, then transferred to Cairo in early October. He was among the individuals accused of terrorism who had their assets frozen by President Clinton in 1995.

53. The figures are from a count kept by the Associated Press in Cairo.

54. Anthony Shadid, "Five Years, 1,100 Dead, Egypt Alone in Winning Against Islamic Insurgency," *Associated Press,* 9 August 1997.

55. In 1997, Interior Minister Hassan al-Alfi said 4,392 Egyptians had been detained for terrorism. Human rights groups put the figure at more than four times that.

56. Jailan Halawi, "Extradition Put Off," *Al-Ahram* (Cairo) *Weekly,* 24 February–1 March 2000.

57. Mohammed Ali, a renegade Ottoman officer of Albanian descent, invited twenty-four Mamluk lords of Egypt to a dinner. Afterward, as they left, his guards trapped them and killed the lords and their 400 escorts. His guards then hunted down 3,000 more Mamluks in one of Egypt's bloodiest episodes, consolidating his rule and ending their hold on a society that had remained, until then, distinctly medieval. Max Rodenbeck, *Cairo: The City Victorious* (Cairo: The American University in Cairo Press, 1998), 160–61.

58. Mohammed Salah, "Misr: Qadat al-Jama'a al-Islamiyya Yaqarirun Waqf al-Amaliyyat," *Al-Hayat* (London), 5 July 1997. Previous appeals for a truce had included conditions for a truce: implementation of Islamic law, release of Islamic Group prisoners and the end of military trials. The others signing the July declaration were Ali al-Sherif, Hamdi Abdel-Rahman and Fouad al-Dawalibi.

59. Mohammed Salah, "Misr: Qiyadiyan fi al-Jihad Andaman ila Alaan Waqf al-Amaliyyat," *Al-Hayat* (London), 10 July 1997.

60. In a statement faxed to journalists, expatriate members of the groups issued statements suggesting the declaration was made under police pressure. "The regime is trying to shake the (Islamic Group's) image and to create the impression that there is a retreat in our declared struggle and that there is a division within the group's ranks. But the (Islamic Group) will continue its policy against the regime until it responds to our declared demands. . . . The Islamic Group affirms confidence in its leaders behind bars but does not exclude the possibility that this declaration is a government-inspired trick."

61. Jihad was similarly divided over the prospect of ending its violent campaign. Its longtime leader, Ayman al-Zawahiri, was reported in February 2000 to have resigned from the group. At the same time, Osama Sadiq Ayoub, a Jihad leader with asylum in Germany, announced that the group would end all violence in Egypt and abroad so as to "focus all our energies on the realization of our greatest cause, which is the liberation of al-Aqsa Mosque" in Jerusalem. Diaa Rashwan, "Life after El-Zawahiri," *Al-Ahram* (Cairo) *Weekly*, 17–23 February 2000.

62. Zayat himself was held for seven months in 1995 on charges of belonging to banned organizations, communicating with militants abroad and concealing information about attacks on political figures, for which he could have been sentenced to death.

63. Montaser al-Zayat , interview by Scheherezade Faramarzi, Cairo, 10 February 1998. As for his own reaction to Luxor, Zayat said, "I didn't leave my home for three days. I had shut off my mobile phone because I was ill, I was frustrated, I was exploding. What could I say? How could I justify such an incident? How could I defend it? I was in shame. I was furious." Rifai Ahmed Taha, the Islamic Group leader, left Egypt in 1988 and was sentenced to death in 1992. Taha was reported in December 1999 to have fallen out with other leaders in the group, another sign of the organization's disarray. Mohammed Salah, "Misr: al-Jama'a al-Islamiyya Multazama Waqf al-Amaliyyat wa Juhud l-Ihtiwa'a Bayn Rifai Ahmed Taha wal-Akhreen," *Al-Hayat* (London), 6 December 1999.

64. Bassem Mroue, "Egyptian Militant Group Declares Cease-Fire," *Associated Press*, 26 March 1999.

65. Mohammed Salah, *Al-Hayat* (London), September 19, 1999.

66. Kamal Habib, interview by author, Cairo, 14 July 1999. The Feast of the Sacrifice, or Eid al-Adha, marks the end of the *hajj*, the annual pilgrimage to the holy city of Mecca in Saudi Arabia.

Chapter Four

1. Community work has not always been carried out in opposition to a government. In Lebanon, welfare networks have actually worked in place of the state, providing water to war-wrecked parts of Beirut where the government was unwilling or unable to go. Under the Israeli occupation, Islamists in the West Bank and, in particular, Gaza were allowed at times to set up services with the implied consent of the authorities. Even today, the Palestinian authority has occasionally looked the other way, acknowledging the needs the services meet. More often, though, the role is contrarian. The Palestinian authority has often deemed the networks a threat that undermined its influence. In times of strife, Palestinian police have moved to shut down even the most conventional: women's groups and clinics serving the poor.

2. The Muslim Brotherhood began providing welfare in Egypt soon after its founding, conceiving social activism as one of the most important elements of its program. Hassan al-Banna, the group's founder, made sure that every new chapter included a school, a workshop and a sporting club. In the 1970s, Musa al-Sadr, an influential Lebanese Shiite religious figure, promoted a similar approach among Lebanon's traditionally neglected Shiite population. His legacy is still evident in the work of Hezbollah.

3. Dale F. Eickelman and James Piscatori, *Muslim Politics* (Princeton: Princeton University Press, 1996), 35.

4. Ibid., 36.

5. Algeria, too, saw a sophisticated Islamist welfare network in the 1980s.

6. The group makes clear that the camp is designed to make the young adept at using computers in their daily lives—"to transfer the most important aspects of modern developments." Technology has a special place among Islamists. Contrary to an image as medieval, they often display an almost obsessive concern with learning new technology, attempting to borrow the West's science without being influenced by its culture. It is another aspect of the movement's perception of itself as inherently, distinctively modern.

7. Hisham H. Ahmad, *Hamas: From Religious Salvation to Political Transformation, the Rise of Hamas in Palestinian Society* (Jerusalem: Palestinian Academic Society for the Study of International Affairs, 1994), 75.

8. Graham Usher, "What Kind of Nation? The Rise of Hamas in the Occupied Territories," *Race & Class* 37 (1995): 66.

9. Yassin, a quadriplegic with lung, eye and ear problems, spent ten years of a life sentence for ordering the killing of Palestinians who collaborated with Israel. He was released from an Israeli jail in October 1997 as part of a prisoner swap with Jordan for two Israeli operatives after a failed assassination attempt on Khaled Mashaal, the head of Hamas's political bureau in Jordan.

10. The Brotherhood's message is, by now, familiar. It emphasized change from below, reforming society rather than taking power. As Hisham H. Ahmad, *Hamas*, 17, said, "The 'liberation of Palestine' in the mind of the Brotherhood was to be considered only after liberating the people socially, or only after returning them to the 'right path' of Islam."

11. *Fedayeen* translates as "men of sacrifice."

12. The figure was provided in an interview on July 15, 1996, with Ziad Abu Amr, a Gaza-born academic who has studied the rise of political Islam in Palestine. According to his research, the number of mosques in the West Bank rose from 400 to 750 over the same period.

13. According to Usher, "What Kind of Nation?" 74, "The bulk of Hamas's support in the territories is drawn from socially conservative sectors for whom the ideology of 'secular nationalism' remains an apology for the rank materialism, corruption and moral permissiveness of the region's ruling regimes, including the PLO. Such strata are the legatees of the MB's [Muslim Brotherhood] old culturalist tradition."

14. Khalil Shikaki, interview by author, Nablus, 14 July 1996. Iyad Barghouti, a Palestinian sociology professor at al-Najah University in the West Bank city of Nablus, makes a similar point. "[A]mong young people, Hamas has a lot of popularity. Not much of this, in my opinion, is tied to religion. Rather, people are discouraged by the failure of the more established groups to achieve serious political changes and they look to Hamas as an alternative. Much of Hamas' support is in effect a critique of other groups rather than support for Islamist politics." From Iyad Barghouti, "The Islamist Movements in the Occupied Territories: An Interview with Iyad Barghouti," interview by Lisa Hajjar, *Middle East Report* 183 (July-August 1993): 9.

15. Qassem was killed by British troops in the hills around Jenin in November 1935.

16. Hamas's covenant, a document of thirty-six articles released in August 1988, calls the liberation of all of Palestine a duty, playing to more radical elements within Palestinian society and to the refugees abroad who were forced out of their homes inside present-day Israel in 1948. "When an enemy occupies some of the Muslim lands, *jihad* becomes obligatory for every Muslim. In the struggle against the Jewish occupation of Palestine, the banner of *jihad* must be raised." Quoted in Ahmad, *Hamas*, 54.

17. Graham Usher, *Palestine in Crisis: The Struggle for Peace and Political Independence After Oslo* (London: Pluto Press, 1995), 31.

18. The phrase was borrowed from Dan Tschirgi, a lecturer in political science at the American University of Cairo. He used it to describe the appeal of the Islamic Group in Egypt and the Zapatistas in southern Mexico, movements that he argued had much in common.

19. "[T]he movement's ideology equates Jewishness with enmity. To them, all of Palestine belongs to Allah. No human being can decide the destiny of that which belongs to Allah and henceforth to all Muslims. One cannot miss such precepts in Hamas' ideology as contained in its leaflets and other publications." From Ahmad, *Hamas*, 114.

20. Sayyid Abu Musameh and Ghazi Hamad, interview by author, Gaza, 13 July 1996.

21. Many in those generations were hostile to Arafat's Palestinian authority as well. In Gaza, I spoke to a twenty-five-year-old whose family was involved with Hamas. He talked of his cousin's torture by Palestinian police and his anger toward the Israeli occupation in the same breath. Authority seemed to be losing its identity. Palestinian or Israeli, it was oppressive. "The authority is working day and night," he told me. "They're not sleeping. They're working harder than the Israelis. Slowly, slowly, you see the people and (Arafat's) leadership growing apart." As for the occupation, "it moved from us to the border, that's it. If you want to leave, you leave by Moshe, if you want to work, you work by Moshe. Moshe is still everywhere."

22. Barghouti, "Islamist Movements," 11.

23. Bassam Jarrar, "The Islamist Movement and the Palestinian Authority," interview by Graham Usher, *Middle East Report* 189 (July-August 1994): 29.

24. Sara Roy, "Professionalization versus Politics: The Transformation of Islamist NGOs in Palestine," *Middle East Report* 214 (spring 2000 upcoming).

25. Jews returned to Hebron in 1968, a year after Israel's capture of the West Bank, when a group led by Rabbi Moshe Levinger checked into the city's Park Hotel and refused to leave.

26. John Kifner, "Alms and Arms: Tactics in a Holy War," *New York Times*, 15 March 1996. Support for Hamas increased after the Gulf War when Arafat supported Iraq, alienating the Gulf countries that felt threatened by Saddam Hussein's ambitions. The support was seen as a way of bolstering Hamas and, as a result, damaging Arafat's position. In addition, the governments and individuals in those countries see a certain piety in supporting through *zakat*, or alms, an Islamic movement in Palestine, still a name that resonates among nearly all Arabs and Muslims. Because they are the richest, they give the most.

27. Ibrahim al-Yazouri, secretary-general of the society, interview by author, Gaza, 18 July 1996. According to Khalil Shikaki, the Palestinian academic, "Hamas was able to mobilize financial and other resources to facilitate its ability to bring a very impressive civilian infrastructure which was many folds more effective, influential and widespread than the military infrastructure. The military infrastructure is very small in terms of people, in terms of money, in terms of activity."

28. According to Robert Malley, "It is not the financially strapped Palestinian National Authority but the religious movement that provides free health clinics, summer camps, and kindergartens, offers courses in computer science, electrical repair, and sewing, distributes meat to forty thousand families during religious holidays, sponsors sports teams, and runs eighty percent of the mosques. The Palestinian state has yet to see the day, and already its rival-to-be is taking over its putative role." From *The Call from Algeria: Third Worldism, Revolution and the Turn to Islam* (Berkeley: University of California Press, 1996), 201.

29. Roy, "Professionalization versus Politics." She estimates that 65 percent of educational institutions below the secondary level are Islamic.

30. The din from the call to prayer in Cairo, often amplified by loudspeakers, became so deafening at one point that a parliamentary committee came up with recommendations to cut down on the noise. Among the proposals: keep the amplifiers inside the mosque, ban competition between muezzins to broadcast the loudest prayer and choose muezzins for the quality of their voice rather than its pitch.

31. Asef Bayat, "Revolution Without Movement, Movement Without Revolution: Comparing Islamic Activism in Iran and Egypt," *Comparative Studies in Society and History* 40 (January 1998): 155–56.

32. Ibid., 164.

33. Algeria's Islamic Salvation Front responded similarly after an earthquake hit that country in 1989.

34. Stephen Hubbell, "Fault Line," *The Nation*, 2 November 1992.

35. Vickie Langhor, "Do Clients of Clinics Become Cadres? Critiquing Some Assumptions About Islamist Social Welfare," research paper, unpublished.

36. Salim Nasr, "Roots of the Shi'i Movement," *MERIP Reports* 133 (June 1985): 12.

37. Ibid., 12. The community's transformation was also aided by a process during those years that saw a large Shiite migration to Beirut, the emergence of a radical intelligentsia and the influence of Shiite businessmen who emigrated abroad, particularly to West Africa and the oil-rich Persian Gulf, and sent money back, usually to southern Lebanon.

38. The word is also an acronym of *Afwaj al-Muqawama al-Lubnaniyya*, or the Lebanese Resistance Detachments.

39. Hala Jaber, *Hezbollah: Born with a Vengeance* (New York: Columbia University Press, 1997), 13–14.

40. "Insecurity Zone," *Economist*, 22 February 1997.

41. The SLA was once a mainly Christian militia, but as economic conditions deteriorated in southern Lebanon, the $350 monthly wage of a militiaman drew more local Shiites into its ranks.

42. Jaber, *Hezbollah*, 149–50.

43. Anthony Shadid, "From Militia to Movement, Hezbollah Faces Uncertain Future," *Associated Press*, 7 June 1998. Also see Jaber, *Hezbollah*, 155–56.

44. "Hizbullah in Politics," *Economist*, 7 September 1996.

45. Laura King, "On South Lebanon Battlefront, Village Backing Aids Guerrillas," *Associated Press*, 12 March 1999.

46. Rodeina Kenaan, "Hezbollah, Lebanese Government Start Process of Rebuilding South," *Associated Press*, May 31, 2000.

47. Hajj Nayef Kraim, a Hezbollah spokesman, told me in an interview in south Beirut in May 1996, that "there aren't specific numbers in this regard. The movement spends as a movement of donations."

48. Jaber, *Hezbollah*, 152.

49. Interviews by author, Beirut, March and May 1998.

50. "Amin Aam Hezbollah al-Sayyid Hassan Nasrallah Yahawar 'Al-Afkar' bi Kul Shafafiya," *Al-Afkar* (Beirut), 20 March 1998.

51. Jaber, *Hezbollah*, 148.

52. Paul Geitner, "Religious Parties Paint Quake as Divine Retribution," *Associated Press*, 25 August 1999.

53. Selcan Hacaoglu, "Islamic Groups Bypass Government, Build Support During Quake," *Associated Press*, 9 September 1999.

54. Tracy Wilkinson, "Islamists Strive for Firmer Ground," *Los Angeles Times*, 27 August 1999.

55. Selcan Hacaoglu, "Authorities Freeze Bank Accounts of Islamic Aid Groups," *Associated Press*, 27 August 1999. Egypt's government reacted to the success of Islamist aid organizations in a similar fashion. After the 1992 earthquake, a presidential decree ordered that disaster donations be first approved by the Ministry of Social Affairs, allowing the government to monitor their activity. Mona el-Ghobashy, "The Doctor Is Out: Will Prison Credibility Enable Essam el-Eryan to Breathe New Life into the Muslim Brothers," *Cairo Times*, 9–22 March 2000.

56. Nilufer Gole, "Secularism and Islamism in Turkey: The Making of Elites and Counter-Elites," *Middle East Journal* 51, no. 1 (winter 1997): 49–50. In 1928, in one of the most extreme examples of secularization, the government set up a commission at Istanbul University and charged it with looking at ways to reform Islam. The commission came up with the suggestion of putting pews in mosques for the performance of prayers and introducing classical Western music at the services. The suggestion was not accepted, although it gives an idea of the secular fervor of the time. Binnaz Toprak, "Islamist Intellectuals: Revolt Against Industry and Technology," in *Turkey and the West: Changing Political and Cultural Identities*, ed. Metin Heper, Ayse Oncu and Heinz Kramer (London: I. B. Tauris, 1993), 240.

57. According to Nilufer Narli, a professor at Marmara University, "There's a nostalgia for the glories of the Ottoman past. Within the last ten years, there has been more emphasis on this Ottoman past, the glorious Ottoman past, and there is more interest in understanding Ottoman history and interest in Islamic art during the Ottoman period. This is one of the factors explaining the increased influence of Islamist movements, this nostalgia for the glorious Ottoman past and rediscovering this Ottoman identity." My interviews in Turkey were conducted in August 1996.

58. Ertugrul Kurkcu, "The Crisis of the Turkish State," *Middle East Report* 199 (April-June 1996): 5.

59. Sami Zubaida, "Turkish Islam and National Identity," *Middle East Report* 199 (April-June 1996): 11.

60. Kurkcu, "Crisis of the Turkish State," 7.

61. Zubaida, "Turkish Islam," 11.

62. *Gecekondu* means "built in the night," recalling an Ottoman law that said no one could tear down a house begun at night and completed before dawn.

63. Zubaida, "Turkish Islam," 12.

64. Veiling is another example of Islamists' reappropriation of space, often signifying a very conscious decision by women to assume a specifically Muslim identity. In contrast to the stereotype of veiled women as docile and passive, Muslim women activists in Turkey are politically active and very visible. At a fundamental level, they project a modernist alternative to the country's secularism: A woman can still be an activist, study and work but maintain her identity as a devout Muslim. The equation they seek to project is the upholding of morality *and* a movement in support of social change. In that sense, as Olivier Roy points out, the veil is a modern adaptation of traditional dress: It signifies a new place for women in modern society. Selami Caliskan, interview by author, Istanbul, 24 August 1996.

66. A survey found that 41 percent of those who voted for Refah declared themselves *laik*, a Kemalist identification. Ferhat Kentel, "L'Islam, carrefour des idenites sociales et culturelles en Turquie: Le cas de Part de la Prosperite," *Cahiers d'etudes sur la Mediteraneee orientale et le monde turco-iranien (CEMOTI)* 19 (Jan-Juin 1995), 211–27, quoted in Zubaida, "Turkish Islam."

Chapter Five

1. Donald Petterson, *Inside Sudan: Political Islam, Conflict and Catastrophe* (Boulder: Westview Press, 1999), 20.

2. Ghazi Salah al-Din al-Atabani, interview by author, Khartoum, 21 April 1996. At the time, he was head of the government's National Congress, a body that oversaw Turabi's vision of grassroots politics. In 1998, he became minister of information and culture.

3. In 1990, Sudan and Libya signed a declaration calling for an alliance between the two countries. The pact went nowhere, but Libyan leader Moammar Qadhafi for a while provided the Sudanese with subsidized oil. Those shipments came to an end in 1993 amid fear in Libya that Sudan was seeking to spread its brand of Islamist politics beyond its borders. Turabi spoke openly about his belief that Islamists in Libya would eventually displace Qadhafi. Petterson, *Inside Sudan,* 41–42.

4. The other countries are North Korea, Libya, Syria, Cuba, Iran and Iraq. Of the seven, five are predominantly Muslim countries and four are in the Arab world. The list has always seemed motivated more by politics than by a human rights standard uniformly applied to all countries.

5. The name is said to derive from the thin split of land at the convergence of the two rivers.

6. Petterson, *Inside Sudan,* 5.

7. The Ansar and Khatmiyya are the two most important of those orders. Both transformed, in part at least, into political parties that guided Sudan's brief periods of parliamentary life.

8. The term was coined from *suf,* the Arabic word for wool, a reference to the coarse woolen garments worn by mystics as part of their ascetic practices.

9. Mark Huband, *Warriors of the Prophet: The Struggle for Islam* (Boulder: Westview Press, 1998), 141–42.

10. Ibid., 142.

11. Rudolf Slatin, one of Gordon's governors who had been captured by the Mahdi's men, was shown Gordon's severed head. Instead of shock, he replied laconically, "What of it? A brave soldier, who fell at his post. Happy is he to have fallen. His sufferings are over." *Historic World Leaders,* Gale Research, 1994.

12. Huband, *Warriors of the Prophet,* 144.

13. In one famous episode, the Mahdi sent a letter to Queen Victoria, inviting her to become a Muslim.

14. Christians represent just a fraction of southerners, probably less than 5 percent, but their influence is far greater than their numbers would suggest.

15. John L. Esposito, *The Islamic Threat: Myth or Reality?* (Oxford: Oxford University Press, 1992), 89.

16. Sadiq al-Mahdi's Umma Party won the largest number of seats, ninety-nine, followed by Osman al-Mirghani's Democratic Unionist Party with sixty-three seats. The NIF won fifty-one seats.

17. Martha Wenger, "Sudan: Politics and Society," *Middle East Report* 172 (September-October 1991): 6.

18. Ibid., 6.

19. Human Rights Watch/Africa, *Behind the Red Line: Political Repression in Sudan* (New York: Human Rights Watch, 1996).

20. Ibid.

21. For some, the university is part of Sudan's national mythology. Abdallahi al-Naim, a former law professor there, described it in its heyday from independence through Nimeiri's rule as a bastion of dissent and debate. "It was wonderful in terms of academic freedom, of public engagement, as a model for the role of the university in the intellectual and political life of the community. We had debates, student activities, student politics incomparable to anything known in the region anywhere. None of the Egyptian universities or Middle Eastern universities or East African universities could compare in academics or public engagement." Other Sudanese universities like Nilein and Gezira shared Khartoum's reputation for political activism and rigorous academics.

22. Ali Abdalla Abbas, "The National Islamic Front and the Politics of Education," *Middle East Report* 172 (September-October 1991): 24.

23. Anthony Shadid, "Sudanese Battle Over Islam in Once-Independent Universities," *Associated Press*, 24 June 1996.

24. The government, in typical fashion, dismissed the complaints. In an interview in April 1996, Ghazi Salah al-Din al-Atabani, the head of the National Congress, said the criticism came from self-absorbed university staff and students who overestimated their importance. "Khartoum University did play a magnified role in politics in the past because it was the only university then and because a demonstration in the streets of Khartoum in the 1960s would topple a government. It would not do such a thing right now. That's why they feel weakened, but that's a natural evolution of things." He added later, "I am a graduate of Khartoum University and we've got this grandiose feeling that Khartoum University is the center of the universe. I used to have that feeling at one time."

25. Abdallahi al-Naim, interview by author, 6 November 1997.

26. His criticism, in a 1997 interview, was a strong comment even by his standards. "Religion always has a concept of the devil and an angel. You know it, of course, and someone must incarnate the devil and someone must incarnate the angel. America incarnates the devil for Muslims. When I say Muslims, I mean all the Muslims in the world, whether in Russia, in China, in Indonesia, in Morocco or inside America itself. And Islam is spreading in America."

27. Donald Petterson, the American ambassador from 1992 to 1995, refers to Turabi's "ingratiating smile." Overall, though, I was impressed with Petterson's description of their conversations: "I appreciated his discourse on political Islam in different parts of the Muslim world, for example. Too often, however, he focused on pet themes and lashed out intemperately on such things as the evils of the West, the stupidity of those in the Arab world who resisted change, and the hopelessly ignorant Americans and other benighted enemies of Sudan." Others were more flattering. Milton Viorst, who interviewed him for his book *In the Shadow of the Prophet: The Struggle for the Soul of Islam* (New York: Anchor Books, 1998), calls Turabi "a man of winning ways." "Though rather small and slim in build, he has handsome dark features and delicate hands, which move gracefully when he speaks. His voice is soft, and he smiles easily. He has poise. His presentation, without being pompous, is confident and self-assured." Others, even those criticizing his policies, make note of his personal charisma.

28. Virtually everyone recognized his role as the real power in Sudan, particularly his opponents. He was the target of a bizarre assassination attempt in 1992 when a Sudanese assailant trained in martial arts attacked him at the Ottawa airport in Canada. He survived but was beaten unconscious, and rumors began to circulate that he had lost some of his mental agility in the attack.

29. Hassan al-Turabi, "The Islamic State," in *Voices of Resurgent Islam*, ed. John L. Esposito (Oxford: Oxford University Press, 1983), 241. Italics added by author.

30. Ibid., 241.

31. Like many of his attacks, his resentment seemed personal: "I'm not a sheikh," Turabi told me in 1996. "People don't come and kiss my fingers or give me money to pray for them. I don't claim to have a monopoly on access to God. God is accessible to all people, even if they are corrupt."

32. At a government-orchestrated rally after the U.S. bombing in 1997, the opposition parties came in for as much criticism as the Americans. The sign of one protester read, "No to the lackeys." Nearby were pictures of former prime minister Sadiq al-Mahdi and Mohammed al-Mirghani, the titular leaders of the two parties. Across the pictures were blue Stars of David, the symbol of Israel. "There are those who are much worse than Clinton," President Omar al-Bashir told the crowd. "And they are Sudanese."

33. Turabi, "Islamic State," 245.

34. Ibid., 244.

35. According to Egypt's Middle East News Agency, Sadiq got out word at the wedding that he was too sick to attend. Later, he donned horse-riding gear and fooled security men into thinking he was going for a ride. He then fled with his son east to the border, a six-hour drive. "Even his children were not aware of what their father was intending to do," Sara al-Fadil, one of Sadiq's wives, told a Sudanese newspaper.

36. Suleiman was another symbol of a sometimes incestuous elite. He opposed the government but, as the lawyer of the plant's owner, Salah Idris, he opposed the attack and indirectly had to defend the government. As a dissident, he had been arrested several times, as recently as four months before the U.S. strike; his brother, Badr el-Din Suleiman, served as Sudan's industry minister. Suleiman never seemed to mince his words, even during times of tension. "The government uses Islam just like a machine gun—to protect its interests," he told me in August 1998, a few days after the attack. "This government has no future. It has failed to solve the problems of the Sudanese people. If they have any blood in their veins, they would be ashamed of what they are doing to the country."

37. Other opposition figures said that although they did not doubt the government was trying to build chemical weapons, they believed the United States had hit the wrong plant. They thought the real target should have been a military-industrial area about forty miles south of Khartoum.

38. Huband, *Warriors of the Prophet*, 152. Iran, after the revolution, set up a similar counterbalance to the traditional military, the Islamic Revolutionary Guard Corps, which has hundreds of thousands of men in arms and its own air force and weapons industry.

39. In an interview by author in 1996, Ghazi Salah al-Din al-Atabani, the head of the National Congress and later the information minister, predicted the south would eventually become Muslim. "I say that as an intellectual, not as a politician. I have no doubt that ultimately—and I don't say this out of religious vehemence or adherence or a bigoted feeling toward my religion but as a matter of fact when you study the pattern of the spread of Islam over the past 1,000 years or the past 500 years in Sudan—ultimately, people in southern Sudan will totally accept Islam and will even claim an Arab ancestry. This is part of the process which has taken place in the Sudan. Now the majority of Sudanese will tell you that they are Arabs. They are not genetic Arabs as such, but they became Muslims and they found some pride in saying that they were Arabs." He added later: "Islam appears to be quite appealing to the African intellect. That is why Islam has never faced resistance in Africa as it did in Europe or in Asia. Ultimately, I predict that Islam will become the dominant religion in Africa."

40. "Some 63,000 Students Have Undergone Military Training," *Associated Press*, 6 October 1997.

41. Human Rights Watch/Africa, *Behind the Red Line,* 202. The numbers in the militia varied. Diplomats in Khartoum told me that they believed the militia had 15,000 active members with 60,000 reserves.

42. Anthony Shadid, "Religious Militia Could Make or Break Sudan's Islamic Government," *Associated Press,* 5 February 1997.

43. Anthony Shadid, "Despite Repression, Women Fight Unpopular War in Sudan," *Associated Press,* 28 August 1998.

44. The women had tried to deliver a statement to the United Nations Children's Fund, known as UNICEF, that read, in part, "We appeal to you to stand by the women of Sudan who, notwithstanding all forms of oppression, continue the struggle to save Sudanese children from being forcibly brainwashed, traumatized or incinerated in a brutal, unjust and unnecessary war of destruction."

45. I asked Ghazi Salah al-Din al-Atabani, who was information minister at the time, about the protests. He dismissed them. "It is a natural response from parents to a new routine in their life, a new demand on their children and their households. It is very natural."

46. Bashir justified his move by claiming that Turabi had tried to act as Sudan's actual ruler and that his policies over the past ten years had led to Sudan's isolation and ruined relations with its neighbors. Mohamed Khaled, "Bashir-Turabi Confrontation Escalates," *Al-Ahram* (Cairo) *Weekly,* 23–29 December 1999.

Chapter Six

1. Hasan Yusufi Eshkevari, interview by author, Tehran, 9 August 1996.

2. Ali Banuazizi, "Iran's Revolutionary Impasse: Political Factionalism and Societal Resistance," *Middle East Report* 191 (November-December 1994): 5.

3. Security forces arrested Eshkevari in August 2000 on charges of acting against national security and publishing articles that defamed Iranian officials and criticized the government. His detention came upon his return to the country after attending a conference in Berlin on Iran's parliamentary elections. Several other delegates were also arrested.

4. Asef Bayat, "The Coming of a Post-Islamist Society," *Critique* (fall 1996): 45.

5. I owe this phrase and idea to Bayat from his article in *Critique,* 45–46.

6. Ervand Abrahamian, *Iran: Between Two Revolutions* (Princeton: Princeton University Press, 1982), 526.

7. The October 1971 celebration of the 2,500th anniversary of the Persian monarchy was a telling symbol of the Shah's extravagance, excess and insensitivity. More than $200 million was spent to gather dignitaries from around the globe at Persepolis, the uninhabited pre-Islamic capital of Persia. Weeklong celebrations featured a feast catered by Maxim's of Paris that included 25,000 bottles of wine. John L. Esposito, *The Islamic Threat: Myth or Reality?* (Oxford: Oxford University Press, 1992), 104–5.

8. Abrahamian, *Iran,* 529.

9. Michael M. J. Fischer, "Imam Khomeini: Four Levels of Understanding," in *Voices of Resurgent Islam,* ed. John L. Esposito (Oxford: Oxford University Press, 1983), 151.

10. Ayatollah is an honorific title for high-ranking Shiite religious authorities. One earns the title through acceptance by existing ayatollahs and by popular acclamation.

11. Abrahamian, *Iran,* 425.

12. Ibid., 425. *Gharbzadegi* is often translated as "Westoxification," a term coined by the Iranian writer Jalal al-Ahmad, who criticized the imitation of the West among his generation. As for his sense of popular discontent, he once stated a maxim as persuasive to the masses as any: "For that is your Islamic duty, to take from the rich and give to the poor," quoted in Fischer, "Imam Khomeini," 159.

13. Fischer, "Imam Khomeini," 157. Khomeini admitted that there was no specific justification for *velayat-e faqih* in the Quran or sayings and examples of the prophet. Instead, he argued it was logical and self-evident from the nature of Islam. Its lack of a specific religious justification and its implications for autocracy are among the reasons the concept became such a point of contention among clergy and laymen in Iran following Khomeini's death.

14. I owe this idea to Fischer in "Imam Khomeini," 160.

15. Ibid., 162.

16. Ibid., 168–69.

17. Khomeini's imposing tomb on the outskirts of Tehran always seemed to me an odd tribute to the man. It was anything but ascetic and far from subtle. The cavernous hall was decorated in lavish green marble with chandeliers. It offered little testament, I thought, to the man's personality.

18. Abrahamian, *Iran*, 476.

19. Sami Zubaida, "Is Iran an Islamic State?" in *Political Islam: Essays from Middle East Report*, ed. Joel Beinin and Joe Stork (Berkeley: University of California Press, 1996), 109–11.

20. Azadeh Niknam, "The Islamization of Law in Iran: A Time of Disenchantment," *Middle East Report* 212 (fall 1999): 19.

21. The Parliament seated on June 1, 2000, had 290 deputies.

22. Olivier Roy, "Tensions in Iran: The Future of the Islamic Revolution," *Middle East Report* 207 (summer 1998): 39.

23. Burton Bollag, "20 Years After the Islamic Revolution, Iran's Campuses Begin to Loosen Up," *Chronicle of Higher Education*, 10 March 2000.

24. Bayat, *Critique*, 49–50.

25. In Iran today, Khomeini is often referred to as "Imam." His acquiescence in the use of the title unsettled some, particularly among the clergy. One ayatollah called it close to blasphemous. Fischer, "Imam Khomeini," 164.

26. Bayat, *Critique*, 50.

27. I found the same youthful recklessness at the Alvand Pizza Parlor, a popular locale that had gained an element of notoriety in recent years. On any night, teenagers gathered in its parking lot or searched, usually without success, for a seat inside. Waiters might be wearing a baseball hat or a beret, and women threw their veils fashionably far back on their head, letting their hair fall free. I met Sanaz and Sara there, two sisters who were up-front about their reason for coming: to see the boys. Sanaz was a pretty twenty-year-old with brown hair, hidden just barely by a gray scarf. The loose-fitting cape that she wore over her clothes was a wild mishmash of green, purple and white stripes. Sara, her eighteen-year-old sister, wore jeans and a green scarf propped precariously over bleached hair. Her cheerfully round face was set off by ruby red lipstick. "We don't have any place for fun," Sara told me, keeping an eye peeled for the police. "That's why we come here." Freedom to them was embodied by America, they said, a place where people can think, say and do what they want. "Here, we get nervous because we cannot do anything and we get mad," Sara told me. "We get crazy!" When not at the pizza parlor, they told me they might go to a friend's house, where three or four people could get together and listen to their favorite music—Pink Floyd, Metallica and Guns n' Roses—or watch Western music videos and movies broadcast on illicit satellite dishes that are often tucked behind clotheslines, hidden by mattresses or hastily put up once the sun has set. Inside, they could also avoid the patrols of religious police that hassled them about their lapsing veils. If caught, a rare occasion in later years, their parents had to pay a fine so that they could escape a lashing. "We do everything in hiding. The boys and girls meet at each other's houses and no one can control them," Sanaz said. "But in the open we must be very, very careful."

28. I borrowed the phrase from Kaveh Ehsani in *"Do-e Khordad* and the Specter of Democracy," *Middle East Report* 212 (fall 1999): 11.

29. Scheherezade Faramarzi, "Women in Iran, Qatar, Yemen Can Vote but Not Dress as They Please," *Associated Press*, 17 May 1999.

30. The constantly changing modes of conduct and norms of acceptability often were played out in bizarre episodes that inspired equally innovative subversion and resistance. In one instance, recounted by Ehsani in *"Do-e Khordad,"* the Ministry of Culture and Islamic Guidance had banned publishing James Joyce's *Ulysses* in Persian for years. The contention was over the book's racier passages, and the translator refused to publish the book without them. One possible compromise was publishing them in a foreign language within the Persian text, but the ministry vetoed English since many people would actually be able to read them. They finally settled on including them in Italian.

31. The same writer remarked on the isolation and alienation that I had heard in other interviews. "Everyone lives on a small island," he told me. "There are a lot of Robinson Crusoes here."

32. Asef Bayat uses the term to describe a phase in which the appeal and legitimacy of Islamism are exhausted. In its place is the idea of fusing Islam as a personalized faith with individual freedom and choice, creating an environment in which the values of democracy and aspects of modernity are compatible with the religion.

33. Shaul Bakhash, "Iran's Unlikely President," *New York Review of Books*, 5 November 1998.

34. It is interesting to note that Russia, after its own war and revolution, produced a similarly cutting-edge, artistically courageous cinema, *Battleship Potemkin* among the films.

35. Morad Saghafi, the editor of *Guftugu* (Dialogue), a secular journal launched in 1992, said maintaining editorial independence and keeping censors at bay involved continuous bargaining. He visited officials at the Ministry of Culture and Islamic Guidance once a week for a chat over tea that could last anywhere from five minutes to an hour. Sometimes the magazine or its articles were barely mentioned, with the talk dwelling on Tehran's maddening traffic jams, but he considered the constant contact necessary to keep lines of communication open. "Sometimes it is very, very hard. Sometimes I've said to myself just stop it. Don't go and talk with anyone. And if they want to close the newspaper after all this, they should close it. You will be much more free to travel and to do what you want, to read books and things like this, what I like. But we should exist, so we try to keep the dialogue going."

36. In Iran, anyone over the age of fifteen is eligible to vote.

37. At a rally at Tehran University to mark the anniversary of his election, tens of thousands of adoring students poured into the campus to hear him speak. They were not disappointed. When a clique of hard-line students began shouting "Death to America!"—the mantra of more revolutionary days—Khatami uttered words that brought cheers from the other students. "In this gathering," the president told the crowd, "I prefer that we speak about life, not death." Afshin Valinejad, "Iranians Celebrate Anniversary of Khatami's Election," *Associated Press*, 23 May 1998.

38. Khatami, who is married with three children, lives modestly in a two-story yellow-brick townhouse in north Tehran.

39. Scheherezade Faramarzi, in a December 28, 1998, article for the Associated Press, recounted a conversation with a seventeen-year-old woman who said she broke down in tears when she found herself standing next to Khatami at a book fair. "I felt I was under a tremendous force . . . an attraction," she said. Others carried his photo in their wallet. Khatami himself seems to bring a certain fastidiousness to his appearance. His graying beard is trimmed, his shoes are shined and his well-pressed clerical robe carefully matches his flowing cloak. Asked in an interview in spring 1997 with *Zanan*, a Tehran-based women's monthly, about his reputation for being attractive and chic, he answered, "I value order and beauty. A moderate person needs these, and Islam approves. As far as possible, I try to be so, without allowing this to get in the way of my main tasks. Well, I am not sure how people interpret this."

40. This and other quotes, unless otherwise noted, were taken from two books of Mohammad Khatami's lectures: *Hope and Challenge: The Iranian President Speaks*, New York: Institute of Global Cultural Studies at Binghamton University, 1997, and *Islam, Liberty and Development*, New York: Institute of Global Cultural Studies at Binghamton University, 1998.

41. Interestingly, Khatami praises Ali Shariati, an influential Iranian sociologist who tried to synthesize socialism with traditional Shiism and adapt theories of Marx, Fanon and others to his prerevolutionary Iranian environment. Shariati, who died in 1977 at the age of forty-three, was criticized by some clergy who suggested he had a poor grounding in Islamic thought and accused him of propagating anticlerical views. In hindsight, some of his thoughts have an obvious overlap with Khatami's writings. Shariati spoke out against clerics demanding blind obedience from their congregations, retaining a monopoly over the religious texts and preventing the public from gaining access to a truer Islam. Ervand Abrahamian, "Ali Shari'ati: Ideologue of the Iranian Revolution," *MERIP Reports* 102 (January 1982): 28.

42. Khatami by no means disavows Iran's Islamic past. In one passage, he argues that "dismantling aspects of tradition must be based on indigenous models, not imported and artificial. Indeed, Westerners at the dawn of modernity were awakened by delving deeply into their tradition. Thinkers revisited the artistic tradition of the Greeks and the social traditions of Rome. Religious believers returned to what they considered to be the most authentic aspects of Christianity, and hence the Reformation. And these returns to tradition and reappraisals ushered in the new epoch."

43. Valinejad, "Iranians Celebrate."

44. The speech was delivered by Khatami at the eighth summit of the Organization of the Islamic Conference in Tehran on 9 December 1997.

45. Bakhash, "Iran's Unlikely President."

46. Kadivar argues that "the political and cultural struggle between proponents of religious democracy and those of religious autocracy has become the most important issue in Iran." Azadeh Kian-Thiebaut, "Political and Social Transformations in Post-Islamist Iran," *Middle East Report* 212 (fall 1999): 14.

47. Asgharzadeh, one of the former student leaders, created a stir when, at a rally in November 1998 marking the embassy's seizure, he invited the American hostages to return to Iran as guests. The embassy, a twenty-seven-acre compound, is now used as a school for the Islamic Revolutionary Guards Corps.

48. Christopher de Bellaigue, "The Struggle for Iran," *New York Review of Books*, 16 December 1999.

49. Zarir Merat, "Pushing Back the Limits of the Possible: The Press in Iran," *Middle East Report* 212 (fall 1999): 34.

50. Scheherezade Faramarzi, "Iran's Press is Battleground for the Country's Future," *Associated Press*, 13 December 1998. Shamsolvaezin's quote comparing freedoms to gelatin was from an unpublished version of the article. Also see Bakhash, "Iran's Unlikely President."

51. Two newspapers, *Khordad* and *Sobh-e Emrouz,* forced the government to admit that government agents were involved in the killings of the five: Mohammad Jafar Pouyandeh, Mohammad Mokhtari, Majid Sharif, Daryush Foruhar and his wife, Parvaneh. After the disclosure, Khatami obtained the resignation of Intelligence Minister Qorbanali Dorri-Najafabadi, replacing him with Ali Yunesi, the military judge who had helped investigate the crimes.

52. Bazargan, named prime minister by Khomeini, resigned less than a year after the revolution to protest Khomeini's refusal to end the occupation of the U.S. Embassy.

Chapter Seven

1. After Mohammed's death, four of his companions were chosen by the community as caliphs and they are commonly referred to as the *rashidun,* or the rightly guided. The twenty-nine-year period, though, was wracked by dissent, assassination and even civil war. There was first a dispute over succession. Followers of Ali ibn Abi Talib believed that Ali, as a representative of Mohammed's family, should succeed him. They believed the choice was sanctioned by the prophet. Omar ibn al-Khattab, the second caliph, was murdered for private vengeance; an insurrection in Medina, supported by soldiers from Egypt, led to the murder of Othman ibn Affan, the third caliph; and Ali, who became the fourth caliph, was assassinated. Classical scholars were far less defensive about this period than modern advocates of an Islamic golden age who have often put forth a romanticized notion of harmony and religious consent. As with all movements, myths assume a certain importance. As'ad AbuKhalil, "The Incoherence of Islamic Fundamentalism: Arab Islamic Thought at the End of the 20th Century," *Middle East Journal* 48, no. 4 (autumn 1994), 680–82.

2. Adel Hussein, an Islamist thinker in Egypt discussed in this chapter, once told me the reforms instituted by Khatami would have an impact in the Arab world, even though Iranians speak a different language and follow a different sect of Islam than most Arabs. "There are new, evolving trends out of Iran," he said. "And these positions will give a push to innovative Islam throughout the region."

3. Valla Vakili, "Debating Religion and Politics in Iran: The Political Thought of Abdolkarim Soroush," Studies Department Occasional Paper Series 2 (New York: Council on Foreign Relations, 1996): 8–9.

4. Abdulaziz Sachedina, "Ali Shariati: Ideologue of the Iranian Revolution," in *Voices of Resurgent Islam,* ed. John L. Esposito (Oxford: Oxford University Press, 1983), 197.

5. "I'm just a writer putting forward my ideas. This may seem dangerous to some people," Soroush said in a 1997 interview in New York with journalist Josef Federman.

6. The magazine has published translations and interviews with Karl Popper on science, Paul Ricoeur on Christianity, Emmanuel Levinas on Judaism, Mohammed Arkoun on Islam, Leszek Kolakowski on Marxism and Claude Lefort on human rights. Zarir Merat, "Pushing Back the Limits of the Possible: The Press in Iran," *Middle East Report* 212 (fall 1999): 33.

7. Ibid.

8. Robin Wright, "Two Visions of Democracy," *Journal of Democracy* 7 (April 1996): 69.

9. Anwar Faruqi, "Amid Change in Iran, Dissident Thinker Gets Acclaim—and Threats," *Associated Press*, 13 July 1997.

10. Human Rights Watch/Middle East, "Human Rights Watch Appeals to Iranian Government to Guarantee the Safety of Embattled Scholar Abdol Karim Soroush," New York, 26 November 1997.

11. Abdol-Karim Soroush, interview by Federman, New York, 1997.

12. Most of the discussion of Soroush's ideas comes from Vakili, "Debating Religion and Politics in Iran."

13. Soroush counts the thirteenth-century Sufi poet Jalaluddin Rumi as an influence. Like Rumi, Soroush often speaks of a lofty, personally liberating Islam.

14. "Mr. Khatami is an intelligent man. I believe he has read my writings. He is familiar with what I say," Soroush said. Interview by journalist Scheherezade Faramarzi, Tehran, 13 April 2000.

15. For Shiite Muslims, the religious texts include the Quran and *hadith.* Unlike Sunnis, they also rely on the teachings of the imams that followed the prophet.

16. Quoted in Vakili, "Debating Religion and Politics in Iran," 18–19. Bracketed material in the original.

17. In Chapter 6, Khomeini contended that the government, acting in the interests of the Islamic state, could abrogate principles of *sharia,* itself an unorthodox view of Islamic law. His argument, though, was grounded in a religious justification. Soroush's argument is effectively secular—he is seeking to safeguard the rights of man, not the rights or survival of the state.

18. Quoted in Vakili, "Debating Religion and Politics in Iran," 16–17.

19. Abdol-Karim Soroush, interview by Faramarzi, Tehran, 13 April 2000.

20. Yusuf al-Badri, interview by author, Cairo, 31 January 1996.

21. One of the sheikh's next campaigns was to initiate a case to force the government to abolish the Ministry of Education. It should be left up to religious authorities, he said. "Yusuf al-Badri Yatalib Bilgha' Wizarat al-Taalim," *Al-Hayat* (London), 30 June 1998.

22. The ruling alarmed even orthodox Islamic thinkers. Fahmi Howeidi, a columnist in Egypt's *Al-Ahram* newspaper, was dismayed that an intellectual issue like Abu Zeid's writings was brought before a family court. He called it symptomatic of a breakdown of society. Nobody debates anymore, he said, and "only two channels are left, guns and judges." "Egypt: Bad Law," *Economist*, 10 August 1996. Abu Zeid made a similar point in an interview with me in January 1996: "Islam has been used and manipulated by most of the political powers, not only in Egypt but in the whole Islamic world, and this is exactly the manipulation of Islam, whether by a specific political group or by some governments, it is exactly this kind of manipulation that I am against," he said angrily. "I think we need a lot of courage not to be afraid of this silly accusation of apostasy because this is silly, this is stupidity. Someone is unable to discuss with you, to debate with you and the only way is to kill you by declaring you an apostate by way of a court decision."

23. Hassan Hanafi, *Religious Dialogue and Revolution: Essays on Judaism, Christianity and Islam* (Cairo: Anglo Egyptian Bookshop, 1974), 209–10.

24. Hanafi, in a lighter moment, held himself up as an example of a diversity of beliefs. "Some imams in Saudi Arabia consider me a *kafir,* others use my writings in their sermons," he told me in the interview in July 1999. "I am considered by conservatives as a disguised secularist, a disguised atheist, a disguised Marxist. If you ask the secularists, they will label me a fundamentalist and an Islamist. If you ask the state, well, they have filed me under 'communist Muslim Brotherhood.'"

25. Muhammad Salim Al-Awa, "Political Pluralism from an Islamic Perspective," in *Power-Sharing Islam?* ed. Azzam Tamimi (London: Liberty, 1993), 73.

26. The *ulema* exercise limited independent authority in Egypt, in particular al-Azhar. Although still powerful, it came under increasing government control during the reign of Gamal Abdel-Nasser, who took power with other junior officers in July 1952. In later years, al-Azhar could be counted on to support government policies from Camp David and the denunciation of Khomeini to the regular condemnation of militant Egyptian groups. Its judgments tended toward the conservative. John L. Esposito, *The Islamic Threat: Myth or Reality?* (Oxford: Oxford University Press, 1992), 136. Even then, some preachers in Egypt could wield substantial influence, more than the government would probably prefer. Two such preachers were Sheikh Mohammed Mutwali Shaarawi and Sheikh Abdel-Hamid Kishk. Shaarawi, who died in June 1998, gave a popular religious lecture on Egyptian television on Fridays, attracting audiences with his use of colloquial Egyptian Arabic and his everyman approach to Islamic principles. Across Egypt, his books, videotapes and cassettes were available at bookstores and sidewalk stalls. He stayed in the government's good graces, even though some of his opinions went against government policies: He supported female circumcision (over the protests of women's groups), condemned organ transplants and opposed paying interest on bank deposits. Kishk was more controversial. I found his tapes on sale at a mosque in Gaza (his supporters said they were available from the Persian Gulf to Morocco). As a preacher, he had an emotional style carried by a stentorian voice, seamlessly moving from Egyptian slang to formal Arabic. His low-brow, swaggering approach mixed humor and everyday experience. Always, he stayed political, often angering the government (he was imprisoned twice, in 1965 and 1981). In one taped sermon I heard, drawing on age-old prejudices, he declared, "What is between the Jews and us is only a truce and as soon as they can, they will break this truce. . . . I expect that the Jews are preparing for a decisive strike. They will not make a concession with either their maps or their plans, whether we treat them as guests or whether we shake their hands." Before he died in 1996, the Egyptian government had banned him from preaching.

27. Al-Azhar, built in the tenth century by the Fatimids, the same dynasty that founded Cairo, was originally designed as a seminary to teach their brand of Shiite Islam. With their departure, it became one of the greatest centers of Sunni Muslim scholarship and, for centuries, the main congregational mosque of the city. Today, it is part of a modern university system, enrolling 125,000 students and offering programs in agriculture, pharmacology and medicine, in addition to traditional religious studies.

28. Sadiq Jalal al-Azm, interview by author, Damascus, 7 May 1996.

29. Tariq al-Bishri, a former judge and a prominent Islamic thinker in Egypt, made a similar statement to me in an interview in Cairo in July 1999: "In the 1960s, there was the idea of independence, the idea of unity, the idea of social and economic development, building the state and its institutions, then 1967 happened and we asked, 'Where was the mistake? What was it? What was the problem? Why couldn't we defend ourselves? Why didn't we succeed in building strong institutions that were capable of protecting the security of our society?' That was the question we faced after 1967.'"

30. Adel Hussein, interviews by author, Cairo, 9 June and 1 July 1996.

31. Ryszard Kapuscinski, *The Soccer War*, trans. William Brand (New York: Vintage International, 1992), 48–49.

32. Abdel-Halim Ibrahim Abdel-Halim, "The Cultural Garden in Sayyida Zeinab: An Expensive Toy," interview by Fayza Hassan, *Middle East Report* 202 (winter 1997): 13.

33. Sadik al-Azm, "Islamic Fundamentalism Reconsidered: A Critical Outline of Problems, Ideas and Approaches," *South Asia Bulletin: Comparative Studies of South Asia, Africa and the Middle East* 13, nos. 1 and 2 (1993); 14, no. 1 (1994). Azm quoted Mafhouz from a prior source: Hisham Sharabi, *Neopatriarchy* (Oxford: Oxford University Press, 1988), 8.

34. See Robert Malley, *The Call from Algeria: Third Worldism, Revolution and the Turn to Islam* (Berkeley: University of California Press, 1996), 224–5.

35. Mohammed Emara, another former leftist who had joined the Islamist current, told me in an interview in Cairo in June 1997 that, early on, secular philosophies "were like lightning. They enthralled the people." But even then, he said, the influence of the faith was inescapable. "Even a Marxist thinker cannot exit completely from the circle of influence of Islam because in Islam there is belief, there is law, there are morals, there are customs and traditions, there is a heritage, there is a method of education. Every person born in a Muslim

society can't help but be affected by Islam, even if a person is submerged in materialist, atheist philosophies like Marxism." We met in his apartment in Cairo, a cramped few rooms decorated with the taste of a scholar most concerned with his prized books. Volumes were stacked on shelves to the ceiling. On his dusty desk were piles of books four feet high. On the floor and atop ratty sofas and threadbare chairs were files bursting with paper. "If an intellectual is born in an Islamic country, lives in an Islamic country, is a citizen of an Islamic country, interacts with Muslims, he can't help but have a part—big or small—in adhering to Islam. Islam is the nature, the essence, the identity, the culture that prevails in society, so a person can't help but be influenced by Islam," he told me. "Even if he clashes in a fight with Islam, this struggle in fact makes him a partner with Islam."

36. Others include Rasim Ozdenoren and Ilhan Kutluer. Their backgrounds, almost without exception, were grounded in Turkey's republican secular education. Ismet Ozel was enrolled at the prestigious Political Science Faculty of Ankara University, then transferred to the French Language and Literature Department of Hacettepe University in Ankara, and after graduating from there, served as a French instructor at the State Conservatory. Ali Bulac graduated from the Higher Institute of Islam and later from the Sociology Department of Istanbul University. Kutluer graduated from the Philosophy Department of Istanbul University. Ozdenoren graduated from both the Journalism Institute of the Faculty of Economics and from the Law Faculty of Istanbul University. Binnaz Toprak, "Islamist Intellectuals: Revolt against Industry and Technology," in *Turkey and the West: Changing Political and Cultural Identities*, ed. Metin Heper, Ayse Oncu and Heinz Kramer (London: I. B. Tauris, 1993), 245.

37. Metin Heper, "Islam and Democracy in Turkey: Toward a Reconciliation?" *Middle East Journal* 51, no. 1 (winter 1997): 40.

38. Sami Zubaida, "Turkish Islam and National Identity," *Middle East Report* 199 (April-June 1996): 14. Zubaida notes that among the thinkers to which Bulac makes reference are Adorno, Marcuse, Horkheimer, Barrington Moore, Deleuze, Lyotard, Illich, as well as modern Iranian and Arab Islamists, including Shariati.

39. Much of this discussion is taken from Toprak, "Islamist Intellectuals," 246–57.

40. Ibid., 250.

41. There are elements of Sayyid Qutb in the critique as well. Qutb, in a bold reinterpretation, saw modern man living in *jahiliyya*, the state of ignorance in the Arabian Peninsula that preceded the divine revelation conveyed by Mohammed in the seventh century. The Turkish Islamists see a similar paganism. They believe today's subservience to technology and the market is a new dark age, a return to *jahiliyya*.

42. Zubaida, "Turkish Islam and National Identity," 14.

43. Heper, "Islam and Democracy in Turkey," 41.

Chapter Eight

1. In a 1995 lawsuit, two lawyers sued Yousra, one of Egypt's most famous actresses, for appearing in a silk negligee on a magazine cover. They called the picture scandalous. A court agreed, fining her the equivalent of $150, but the judgment was overturned on appeal in 1999. "Egyptian Actress Wins Appeal Over Negligee Photo in Magazine," *Associated Press*, 11 March 1999.

2. Mohammed Salah, "Bawadir Muwajha Bain Ikhwan Misr wa Ikhwan al-Kharij," *Al-Hayat* (London), 20 October 1996.

3. Mamoun al-Hodeibi, interview by author, Cairo, 16 February 1997.

4. Gilles Kepel, *Muslim Extremism in Egypt: The Prophet and Pharaoh* (Berkeley: University of California Press, 1985), 28.

5. Amnesty International called the defendants prisoners of conscience.

6. Mona el-Ghobashy, "The Doctor Is Out: Will Prison Credibility Enable Essam al-Eryan to Breathe New Life into the Muslim Brothers," *Cairo Times*, 9–22 November 2000.

7. Iryan was released in January 2000, many in the movement hoping that his return might bring a new vitality to the Brotherhood. Days after his release, he was already writing in opposition newspapers and welcoming well-wishers with mint candies at his office at the Doctors'

Syndicate, a professional union where he serves as assistant secretary-general. In prison, he said he read Nobel laureate Naguib Mahfouz, Charles Dickens and Shakespeare (in addition to the Quran). Ghobashy, "Doctor Is Out." Iryan disagreed with the view that his arrest proved debilitating to the Brotherhood. "The group never relied on one person or persons for that matter," he said after his release. Amira Howeidy, "'Too Early to Decide,'" *Al-Ahram* (Cairo) *Weekly*, 3–9 February 2000. The government welcomed his release by arresting nineteen more Brotherhood members the same day Iryan walked out of prison. Mohammed Salah, "Al-Qahira: Aatiqaal 19 min al-Ikhwan Yom Itlaq Essam al-Iryan," *Al-Hayat* (London), 23 January 2000.

8. In January 1997, I visited Kamal al-Helbawi, a Brotherhood spokesman in London who later resigned from the organization, to ask him about the group's future. He told me over a dinner of lamb, rice and salad at his apartment that the arrests had made "a mess, really." "If those men were out of prison," he said, "the problem would not have developed originally. There would have been no vacuum, and they would have covered the gap."

9. As late as 1999, after another wave of arrests, the Brotherhood was still urging its members to lay low, instructing them to avoid organizing protests over the new arrests. Mohammed Salah, "Misr: Qadat al-Ikhwan Yalja'un ila al-Tahdi'a wa Yatalabun min Anasirhum Adam Istifzaz al-Hukuma," *Al-Hayat* (London), 9 November 1999.

10. Salah Nasrawi, "Parliament Endorses Mubarak's Decision to Extend State of Emergency," *Associated Press*, 27 February 2000.

11. Omayma Abdel-Latif, "Brotherhood in Decline?" *Al-Ahram* (Cairo) *Weekly*, 25 November–1 December 1999. Yusuf al-Qaradawi, an Islamic scholar, warned about the repercussions of such thinking. "I welcome the idea of the Wasat Party, which may offer the Islamist movement an opportunity to break out of the isolation imposed on it. I fear, however, that the movement will seek to constrain its younger, freer thinkers, close the door to renovation and independent thought and insist on one mode of thinking that refuses to entertain an opposing view." Quoted in Mohamed Selim El-Awwa, "A Return to the Centre," *Al-Ahram* (Cairo) *Weekly*, 9–15 December 1999.

12. Mohammed Salah, "Istiqaalat Qiyaadi fi Jama'at al-Ikhwan," *Al-Hayat* (London), 10 August 1998.

13. The confrontation had been brewing for years. As Gehad Auda put it, "As a result of its involvement in every aspect of formal politics during the 1980s, the young generation acquired more prominence and influence in the structure of the organization. Sometimes this influence came at the expense of the old and middle generations, which signaled a change in the sources of leadership. Since 1929, loyalty to the organization and closeness to the general guide have been the main requirements for organizational leadership. Involvement in open politics added another requirement: the ability to win an election. This external requirement complicated the power game inside the Brotherhood for it expanded the influence of the younger generation and made some of them public celebrities. The need to curb the advancement of the younger generation was an operative factor—among others—behind the decision to boycott the parliamentary elections of 1990." Gehad Auda, "The 'Normalization' of the Islamic Movement in Egypt from the 1970s to the Early 1990s," in *Accounting for Fundamentalisms*, edited by Martin E. Marty and Scott Appleby (Chicago: University of Chicago Press, 1994), 389.

14. "Al-Hukuma al-Misriyya Tastakhdim Ijra'at al-Ikhwan li-Rafd Ta'asis Hizb al-Wasat," *Al-Hayat* (London), 9 April 1997.

15. The party's appeal was rejected on May 1998. The activists reformed the party under a different name, "The Egyptian Center," but its application for government recognition was rejected in September 1998 and its appeal in June 1999. In both cases, the government said the party did not offer anything new, its standard reason for dismissing new applicants. The party's activists promised to make a third attempt at recognition. "We have a project and we still believe that political life in Egypt needs it and that it can provide a way out of some of the crises that are harming society. The constitution and the law give us the right to form a party to express our ideas and our principles," said Abul-Ela Maadi, one of the party's founders. "Abul-Ela Maadi Yu'akid Khowd Muhawala Thalitha li-Ta'asis Hizb," *Al-Hayat* (London), 5 August 1999.

16. Essam Sultan, interview by author, Cairo, 6 July 1999.

17. Even with the Brotherhood a shadow of its former self and the government's more militant opposition crushed under a withering crackdown, the suggestion that the government's unquestioned authority would permit it to provide Islamic opposition groups political space was ruled out. The brief period of tolerance in the early 1980s "only gave them the chance to spread their extremist views and made them feel that they could take over the country," a security official said in a statement that seemed to reflect prevailing government opinion. "Now, these days are gone, and there is no way in the near future that supporters of these groups will be allowed to go public again." Khaled Dawoud, "Farewell to Arms," *Al-Ahram* (London) *Weekly*, 6–12 January 2000.

18. Alan Richards and John Waterbury, *A Political Economy of the Middle East: State, Class and Economic Development* (Boulder: Westview Press, 1990), 305.

19. Cassandra, "The Impending Crisis in Egypt," *Middle East Journal* 49, no. 1 (winter 1995): 18. Interestingly, Nasser and Sadat, like Mubarak, emerged from Egypt's lower middle class, a sprawling strata that also provides the traditional support for the country's Islamist movement.

20. Abul-Ela Maadi, one of the Center Party founders, similarly saw no resolution in the conflict between the Brotherhood and the government, mainly because the opportunity was missed in the very beginning. Speaking on the struggle that erupted after Nasser took power, he asked, "The question is who is responsible for this clash? And what if the clash had not happened? I believe both sides are responsible. The Brotherhood's leadership had the 'special apparatus' [its military wing] which wanted its men to seize control of the group and resort to revolution in confronting the new regime. . . . On the other hand, responsibility also falls to the revolutionaries, who wanted to take revenge for everything, eliminate any opposition and prevent any real plurality. I can say that if this clash hadn't happened, the face of Egypt and the region would have been different, and there would have been nothing to prevent the movement from merging with the new regime—working from within and supporting it rather than seeking to seize control of it or destroy it—and concentrating on the issues of development, construction, education and the confrontation with the nation's enemies." Abul-Ela Maadi, "Thawrat Julio wal-Ikhwan al-Muslimun fi Misr," *Al-Hayat* (London), 19 May 1999. Bracketed material added by author.

21. Abul-Ela Maadi, "'The Hardest Choice is Moderation,'" interview by Omayma Abdel-Latif, *Al-Ahram* (Cairo) *Weekly*, 16–22 December 1999.

22. Abul-Ela Maadi, interview by author, Cairo, 22 January 1997.

23. "Al-Wasat: Dalala Tarikhiyya," *Awraq Hizb al-Wasat* (Cairo: Hizb al-Wasat, 1996), 13.

24. One of the founders was a Christian named Rafiq Habib, the son of a prominent Protestant clergyman in Egypt. Habib, a social worker, often acted as the party's spokesman before leaving the group after its second attempt to secure government permission failed. Like others in the party, Habib believed that Arab Christians and Muslims share an Islamic culture, and that Christians need not be threatened by a state in which religious law applies. Muslims would live under *sharia*, he said, while Christians and Jews would live under their own religious law (that, of course, begs the question of what happens to those who do not believe in God; the question rarely arises, though, given Egypt's overwhelmingly religious nature). Habib believed such an arrangement would recognize the differences between communities. Hence, equality would give way to plurality. "I'm a Christian and Egyptian and Arabic and Islamic because no idea contradicts the other," he told me in an interview in July 1996. He admitted that his support for an Islamic state had surprised some of his fellow Christians, who probably make up about 10 percent of Egypt's population, although estimates vary widely. "Most of them don't understand what I do," he said.

25. Abul-Ela Maadi, "Abul-Ela Maadi: al-Tanzim al-Dowli lil-Ikhwan Wahm Kabir," interview by Talaat Ramih, *Al-Wasat* (London), 19 January 1998.

26. Essam Sultan, interviews by author, Cairo, 10 and 14 July 1999. He went on to praise Khatami's call for reform. "I am an admirer of Khatami. He is a religious figure who has power and progressive thoughts—the civil community, accepting the other, dialogue between civilizations, the role of artists."

27. The Ottoman Empire, one of Islam's greatest civilizations, emerged in the thirteenth century, ruling over much of the Middle East and parts of Europe and Asia for more than 600 years. For a brief period of the sixteenth century, the empire, its capital in Istanbul, was the

world's most powerful state. The Omayyad Empire, with its capital in Damascus, was the first great Muslim empire, ruling a territory that stretched from India to Spain from 661 to 750, when the Abbasid caliphate was founded in Baghdad.

28. *Awraq Hizb al-Wasat*, 15.

29. Ibid., 18.

30. Ibid., 28–29. As an Islamic group raised in an environment of government repression, it also urged the government to end emergency law, release political prisoners, ensure the right to due process and transfer the responsibility for security duties to a civilian authority.

31. Journalists covering the conflict in Cyprus are credited with bringing the term "Green Line" with them when they began reporting on the Lebanese civil war. The line originally marked the division between Greek and Turkish Cypriots after the Turkish invasion in 1974. It was said to have been drawn on a map with a green pen.

32. On that visit, in the still wrecked downtown, a billboard company's advertisement near an army checkpoint asked: "What do our boards have in common with the CIA? They're both all over the place."

33. Hala Jaber, *Hezbollah: Born with a Vengeance* (New York: Columbia University Press, 1997), 29.

34. Ibid., 210.

35. At Friday prayers in Haret Hreik, a Shiite Muslim neighborhood in Beirut, there was the sense that war was a national crusade. Young boys and men collected money for the fight, and others left donations in boxes propped in the back of a blue Volvo station wagon, which was equipped with two speakers blaring songs to celebrate the guerrillas' fight. "Support the Islamic resistance!" one man with a short gray beard called out as hundreds of worshipers, some carrying cardboard to shield their heads from the sun, filed into the mosque. Another man wore a yellow hat that read, "We are all the resistance, the entire nation is the resistance."

36. Timur Goksel, interview by author, Tyre, Lebanon, 26 March 1998.

37. By Hezbollah's count, more than 1,250 guerrillas had died fighting Israeli and allied forces in southern Lebanon between 1982 and 2000.

38. Nasrallah also echoed Kraim's point on ideology. "While it is true ideologically that we support the idea of an Islamic government, we are not trying to impose this notion on anyone. Lebanon has its own circumstances and diversity which have meant that there is no room for this idea." Hassan Nasrallah, "Determined to Fight On," interview by Khaled Dawoud, *Al-Ahram* (Cairo) *Weekly*, 16–22 December 1999.

39. Asli Aydintasbas, "The Malaise of Turkish Democracy," *Middle East Report*, no. 209 (winter 1998): 34. He quotes a remark by Israeli Prime Minister Binyamin Netanyahu on Refah and its leader, Necmettin Erbakan. "Contrary to all our fears and concerns," Netanyahu said, "today we are very pleased with Mr. Erbakan's government."

40. Ibid., 32–34.

41. The party held its first national congress in May 2000. A leading reformist, Abdullah Gul, challenged Kutan for the party leadership, running on a platform that concentrated more on social welfare policies and less on religion. Gul lost narrowly. Before the vote, he was condemned by some party leaders for entering the race. He dismissed their criticism. "If we want Turkey to move closer to democracy, we must be able to criticize ourselves." Quoted in Ayla Jean Yackley, "Turkey's Islamic Party Elects Leader Amid Internal Turmoil," *Associated Press*, May 14, 2000.

42. Jamal Halaby, "Muslim Brotherhood Calls for Boycotting Elections," *Associated Press*, 9 July 1997.

43. The Brotherhood won twenty-two of eighty seats in 1989. Four years later, the Brotherhood and its political wing, the Islamic Action Front, won seventeen seats. It boycotted the 1997 elections, although at least thirty Brotherhood members ran as independents.

44. "Abdullah's Little Revolution in Jordan," *Economist*, 16 October 1999.

45. Kamal Habib, interview by author, Cairo, 14 July 1999.

46. In a paper distributed by his party, Habib argued that while the rejection of political or social institutions because they are not Islamic was understandable on a social level, the Quran or *sharia* could not be used as a justification. He argued that the prophet obtained a stamp when he learned the Romans would not accept a message that was unsealed. Arabs, he

said, accepted traditions and customs of the countries they invaded and often relied on the existing institutions to administer their newly won domains. Military techniques evolved, as well. Thus, he argued, Muslims should look to elections, parliaments, political parties, the peaceful succession of power and respect of the majority's will without violating minority rights as devices that Muslims could use to build a better community.

47. Hani al-Siba'i, a leader of Jihad, acknowledged that the years of violence had harmed the organization. It was a prevalent opinion among many of the militants but somewhat remarkable coming from al-Siba'i, who was considered a top leader of a group blamed for the bombing of the Egyptian Embassy in Pakistan and, in Egypt, attempts on the lives of the prime minister and interior minister. Mohammed Salah, "Misr: Ayya Mustaqbal lil-Usuliyyeen ba'd Sanawat al-Jihad wal-Jama'a al-Islamiyya," *Al-Hayat* (London), 10 February 2000.

48. Amira Howeidy, "Any Old Reason," *Al-Ahram* (Cairo) *Weekly*, 23–29 December 1999.

49. Jailan Halawi, "Former Militants Seek Legal Party," *Al-Ahram* (London) *Weekly*, 19–25 August 1999.

50. Mohammed Salah, "Hizb al-Sharia Yuwaddah Nazaritu ila al-Aqaliyyat," *Al-Hayat* (London), 23 September 1999. One of the founders of the Islamic Law Party included a woman, Hanan Rashad, who said, "We are witnesses to the tragic confrontation between the government and the Islamic movements. Our religious and nationalistic conscience forced us to intervene. We know that the road to achieving our goals will not be paved with fragrant flowers, but requires perseverance." Scheherezade Faramarzi, "New Islamic Party Seeks Approval of Egyptian Government," *Associated Press*, 27 October 1999.

51. Mohammed Salah, "Hizb al-Sharia al-Misri Ya'ati al-Owlawiyya lil-Marja'iyya al-Islamiyya wa Muwajahit al-Tatbi'a ma'a Israel," *Al-Hayat* (London), 17 August 1999.

52. *Hizb al-Islah: al-Barnamaj al-Siyassi*, Cairo, 1999.

53. According to Ismail, one of the founders of the Islamic Law Party was arrested at his home and taken to a police station in the Cairo neighborhood of Imbaba, where he was pressured to withdraw from the party. At least two others faced similar treatment, he said. The party had also tried to organize a seminar titled "The Islamist Movement Between Government Restrictions and Open-Door Politics" at the luxury Shepheard's Hotel. When people arrived, they were told the meeting was canceled. The hotel, Ismail said, had denied permission for the meeting under pressure from the government. Mohammed Salah, "Misr: Aitiqaal Anaasir min Hizb al-Sharia," *Al-Hayat* (London), 22 November 1999.

54. When Egypt sent observers to oversee Palestinian elections in 1996, voters in Gaza joked that the winner was sure to be President Mubarak. "Arab Autocracy for Ever?" *Economist*, 7 June 1997.

Selected Bibliography

Abbas, Ali Abdalla. "The National Islamic Front and the Politics of Education." *Middle East Report* 172 (September-October 1991): 22–25.

Abdalla, Ahmed. *The Student Movement and National Politics in Egypt*. London: Al-Saqi Books, 1985.

Abdel-Halim, Abdel-Halim Ibrahim. "The Cultural Garden in Sayyida Zeinab: An Expensive Toy." Interview by Fayza Hassan. *Middle East Repor* 202 (winter 1997): 13.

Abdel-Latif, Omayma. "Brotherhood in Decline?" *Al-Ahram Weekly* (Cairo), 25 November–1 December 1999.

Abrahamian, Ervand. "Ali Shari'ati: Ideologue of the Iranian Revolution." *MERIP Reports* 102 (January 1982): 24–28.

———. *Iran: Between Two Revolutions*. Princeton: Princeton University Press, 1982.

———. *Khomeinism*. Berkeley: University of California Press, 1990.

———. *Radical Islam: The Iranian Mojahedin*. Society and Culture in the Middle East Series, ed. Michael Gilsenan. London: I. B. Tauris and Co., 1989.

AbuKhalil, As'ad. "The Incoherence of Islamic Fundamentalism: Arab Islamic Thought at the End of the 20th Century." *Middle East Journal* 48, no. 4 (autumn 1994): 677–94.

"Abul-Ela Maadi Yu'akid Khowd Muhawala Thalitha li-Ta'asis Hizb." *Al-Hayat* (London), 5 August 1999.

Abu-Nasr, Donna. "Prison a Turning Point in Life of One Suicide Bomber." *Associated Press*, 29 January 1995.

Abu-Rabi, Ibrahim M. *Intellectual Origins of Islamic Resurgence in the Modern Arab World*. Albany: State University of New York Press, 1996.

Ahmad, Hisham H. *Hamas: From Religious Salvation to Political Transformation, the Rise of Hamas in Palestinian Society*. Jerusalem: Palestinian Academic Society for the Study of International Affairs, 1994.

Ambah, Faiza. "Saudi Militant's Wish: To Die Fighting America." *Associated Press*, 29 August 1998.

"Amin Aam Hezbollah al-Sayyid Hassan Nasrallah Yahawar 'Al-Afkar' bi Kul Shafafiya." *Al-Afkar* (Beirut), 30 March 1998.

Anwar Faruqi, "Amid Change in Iran, Dissident Thinker Gets Acclaim—and Threats," Associated Press, 13 July 1997.

Arjomand, Said Amir. *The Turban for the Crown: The Islamic Revolution in Iran*. Oxford: Oxford University Press, 1988.

Assad, Ragui. "Formalizing the Informal? The Transformation of Cairo's Refuse Collection System." *Journal of Planning Education and Research* 16 (1996): 115–26.

Auda, Gehad. "The Normalization of the Islamic Movement in Egypt from the 1970's to the Early 1990's." In *Accounting for Fundamentalisms*, ed. Martin E. Marty and R. Scott Appleby. Chicago: University of Chicago Press, 1994.

El-Awwa, Mohamed Selim. "A Return to the Centre." *Al-Ahram* (Cairo) *Weekly*, 9–15 December 1999.

Aydintasbas, Asli. "The Malaise of Turkish Democracy." *Middle East Report* 209 (winter 1998): 32–35.

al-Azm, Sadik. "Islamic Fundamentalism Reconsidered: A Critical Outline of Problems, Ideas and Approaches." Parts 1 and 2. *South Asia Bulletin: Comparative Studies of South Asia, Africa and the Middle East* 13, nos. 1 and 2 (1993): 93–121; 14, no. 1 (1994): 73–98.

Bakhash, Shaul. "Iran's Unlikely President." *New York Review of Books*, 5 November 1998.

_____. *The Reign of the Ayatollahs.* New York: Basic Books, 1984.

Banuazizi, Ali. "Iran's Revolutionary Impasse: Political Factionalism and Societal Resistance." *Middle East Report* 191 (November-December 1994): 2–8.

Barghouti, Iyad. "The Islamist Movements in the Occupied Territories: An Interview with Iyad Barghouti." Interview by Lisa Hajjar. *Middle East Report* 183 (July-August 1993): 9–12.

Bayat, Asef. "The Coming of a Post-Islamist Society." *Critique* (fall 1996): 43–52.

_____. "Revolution Without Movement, Movement Without Revolution: Comparing Islamic Activism in Iran and Egypt." *Comparative Studies in Society and History* 40 (January 1998): 136–69.

_____. *Workers and Revolution in Iran.* London: Zed Books, 1987.

De Bellaigue, Christopher. "The Struggle for Iran." *New York Review of Books*, 16 December 1999.

Bollag, Burton. "20 Years After the Islamic Revolution, Iran's Campuses Begin to Loosen Up." *Chronicle of Higher Education*, 10 March 2000.

Bulliet, Richard. *Islam: The View from the Edge.* New York: Columbia University Press, 1994.

Cassandra. "The Impending Crisis in Egypt." *Middle East Journal* 49, no. 1 (winter 1995): 9–27.

Chitham, E. J. *The Coptic Community in Egypt: Spatial and Social Change.* Durham: Centre for Middle Eastern and Islamic Studies, 1986.

Dawoud, Khaled. "Farewell to Arms." *Al-Ahram* (Cairo) *Weekly*, 6–12 January 2000.

Dekmejian, R. Hrair. *Islam in Revolution: Fundamentalism in the Arab World*, 106. Syracuse: Syracuse University Press, 1985. Cited in Olivier Roy, *The Failure of Political Islam* (Cambridge: Harvard University Press, 1994).

Denis, Eric. "Urban Planning and Growth in Cairo." *Middle East Report* 202 (winter 1997): 7–11.

Diamond, John. "U.S. Intelligence Cites Iraqi Tie to Sudan Plant." *Associated Press*, 26 August 1998.

Donohue, John J., and John L. Esposito, eds. *Islam in Transition: Muslim Perspectives.* Oxford: Oxford University Press, 1982.

Ehsani, Kaveh. "*Do-e Khordad* and the Specter of Democracy." *Middle East Report* 212 (fall 1999): 10–11, 16.

Eickelman, Dale F., and James Piscatori, *Muslim Politics.* Princeton: Princeton University Press, 1996.

Enayat, Hamid. *Modern Islamic Political Thought.* Austin: University of Texas Press, 1982.

Esposito, John L., ed. *Islam in Asia: Religion, Politics, and Society.* Oxford: Oxford University Press, 1987.

_____. *Islam and Politics.* Syracuse: Syracuse University Press, 1984.

_____. *The Islamic Threat: Myth or Reality?* Oxford: Oxford University Press, 1992.

_____, ed. *Voices of Resurgent Islam.* Oxford: Oxford University Press, 1983.

Fandy, Mamoun. "Egypt's Islamic Group: Regional Revenge?" *Middle East Journal* 48 (autumn 1994): 607–25.

Faramarzi, Scheherezade. "Iran's Press Is Battleground for the Country's Future." *Associated Press*, 13 December 1998.

_____. "Iranian President Captures Hearts and Minds of Iranian Women." *Associated Press*, 21 December 1998.

_____. "New Islamic Party Seeks Approval of Egyptian Government." *Associated Press*, 27 October 1999.

_____. "Women in Iran, Qatar, Yemen Can Vote but Not Dress as They Please." *Associated Press*, 17 May 1999.

Fischer, Michael M. J. "Imam Khomeini: Four Levels of Understanding." In *Voices of Resurgent Islam*, edited by John L. Esposito. Oxford: Oxford University Press, 1983.

Flores, Alexander. "Egypt: A New Secularism?" *Middle East Report* no. 153 (July-August 1988): 27–30.

Gaffney, Patrick D. *The Prophet's Pulpit: Islamic Preaching in Contemporary Egypt.* Berkeley: University of California Press, 1994.

Geitner, Paul. "Religious Parties Paint Quake as Divine Retribution." *Associated Press,* 25 August 1999.

Ghadbian, Najib. *Democratization and the Islamist Challenge in the Arab World.* Boulder: Westview Press, 1997.

el-Ghobashy, Mona. "The Doctor Is Out: Will Prison Credibility Enable Essam al-Eryan to Breathe New Life into the Muslim Brothers." *Cairo Times,* 9–22 November 2000.

Gole, Nilufer. "Secularism and Islamism in Turkey: The Making of Elites and Counter-Elites." *Middle East Journal* 51, no. 1 (winter 1997): 46–58.

Gordon, Joel. *Nasser's Blessed Movement: Egypt's Free Officers and the July Revolution.* Oxford: Oxford University Press, 1992.

Hacaoglu, Selcan."Authorities Freeze Bank Accounts of Islamic Aid Groups." *Associated Press,* 27 August 1999.

_____. "Islamic Groups Bypass Government, Build Support During Quake." *Associated Press,* 9 September 1999.

Halaby, Jamal. "Muslim Brotherhood Calls for Boycotting Elections." *Associated Press,* 9 July 1997.

Halawi, Jailan. "Extradition Put Off." *Al-Ahram* (Cairo) *Weekly,* 24 February–1 March 2000.

_____. "Former Militants Seek Legal Party." *Al-Ahram* (Cairo) *Weekly,* 19–25 August 1999.

Halliday, Fred. *Islam and the Myth of Confrontation.* London: I. B. Tauris and Co., 1996.

Hanafi, Hassan."The Relevance of the Islamic Alternative in Egypt." *Arab Studies Quarterly* 4 (spring 1982): 54–74.

_____. *Religious Dialogue and Revolution: Essays on Judaism, Christianity and Islam.* Cairo: Anglo Egyptian Bookshop, 1974.

Heper, Metin. "Islam and Democracy in Turkey: Toward a Reconciliation?" *Middle East Journal* 51, no. 1 (winter 1997): 32–45.

Hitti, Philip K. *History of the Arabs.* New York: St. Martin's Press, 1970.

Hizb al-Islah: al-Barnamaj al-Siyassi. Cairo, 1999.

Hourani, Albert. *Arabic Thought in the Liberal Age, 1798–1939.* Cambridge: Cambridge University Press, 1983.

_____. *A History of the Arab Peoples.* Cambridge: Harvard University Press, 1991.

Howeidy, Amira. "Any Old Reason." *Al-Ahram* (Cairo) *Weekly,* 23–29 December 1999.

_____. "'Too Early to Decide.'" *Al-Ahram* (Cairo) *Weekly,* 3–9 February 2000.

Huband, Mark. *Warriors of the Prophet: The Struggle for Islam.* Boulder: Westview Press, 1998.

Hubbell, Stephen. "Fault Line," *The Nation,* 2 November 1992.

"Al-Hukuma al-Misriyya Tastakhdim Ijra'at al-Ikhwan li-Rafd Ta'asis Hizb al-Wasat." *Al-Hayat* (London), 9 April 1997.

Human Rights Watch/Africa. *Behind the Red Line: Political Repression in Sudan.* New York: Human Rights Watch, 1996.

Human Rights Watch/Middle East. "Human Rights Watch Appeals to Iranian Government to Guarantee the Safety of Embattled Scholar Abdol Karim Soroush." New York, 26 November 1997.

Huntington, Samuel P. *The Clash of Civilizations and the Remaking of World Order.* New York: Simon and Schuster, 1996.

Ibrahim, Saad Eddin. "Anatomy of Egypt's Militant Islamic Groups: Methodological Notes and Preliminary Findings." *International Journal of Middle Eastern Studies* 12 (December 1980): 423–53.

Institute of National Planning. *Egypt: Human Development Report.* Cairo, 1995.

Jaber, Hala. *Hezbollah: Born with a Vengeance.* New York: Columbia University Press, 1997.

Jarrar, Bassam. "The Islamist Movement and the Palestinian Authority." Interview by Graham Usher. *Middle East Report* 189 (July-August 1994): 28–29.

Kapuscinski, Ryszard. *The Soccer War.* Trans. William Brand. New York: Vintage International, 1992.

Keddie, Nikki R. *Roots of Revolution*. New Haven: Yale University Press, 1981.

Kedouri, Elie. *Democracy and Arab Political Culture*. Washington: Washington Institute for Near East Policy, 1992.

Kepel, Gilles. *Muslim Extremism in Egypt: The Prophet and Pharaoh*. Berkeley: University of California Press, 1985.

_____. *The Revenge of God: The Resurgence of Islam, Christianity and Judaism in the Modern World*. University Park: Pennsylvania State University Press, 1994.

Khaled, Mohamed. "Bashir-Turabi Confrontation Escalates." *Al-Ahram* (Cairo) *Weekly*, 23–29 December 1999.

Khatami, Mohammad. *Hope and Challenge: The Iranian President Speaks*. Lecture. Binghamton, New York: Institute of Global Cultural Studies at Binghamton University, 1997.

_____. *Islam, Liberty and Development*. Binghamton, New York: Institute of Global Cultural Studies at Binghamton University, 1998.

Kian-Thiebaut, Azadeh. "Political and Social Transformations in Post-Islamist Iran." *Middle East Report* 212 (fall 1999): 12–16.

Kramer, Gudrun. "Islamist Notions of Democracy." *Middle East Report* 183 (July-August 1993): 2–8.

Kurkcu, Ertugrul. "The Crisis of the Turkish State." *Middle East Report* 199 (April-June 1996): 2–7.

Langhor, Vickie. "Do Clients of Clinics Become Cadres? Critiquing Some Assumptions About Islamist Social Welfare," research paper, unpublished.

Lapidus, Ira M. *A History of Islamic Societies*. Cambridge: Cambridge University Press, 1988.

Laroui, Abdallah. *The Crisis of the Arab Intellectual*. Berkeley: University of California Press, 1976.

Maadi, Abul-Ela. "Abul-Ela Maadi: al-Tanzim al-Dowli lil-Ikhwan Wahm Kabir." Interview by Talaat Ramih. *Al-Wasat* (London), 19 January 1998.

_____. "Al-Haraka al-Islamiyya wa al-Dimocratiyya: Darasat fil-Fikr wa al-Mamarasa." Cairo, 18 September 1999.

_____. "'The Hardest Choice Is Moderation.'" Interview by Omayma Abdel-Latif. *Al-Ahram* (Cairo) *Weekly*, 16–22 December 1999.

_____. "Thawrat Julio wal-Ikhwan al-Muslimun fi Misr." *Al-Hayat* (London), 19 May 1999.

Malley, Robert. *The Call from Algeria: Third Worldism, Revolution and the Turn to Islam*. Berkeley: University of California Press, 1996.

Marty, Martin E., and Scott Appleby, eds. *The Fundamentalism Project*, vol. 1, *Fundamentalisms Observed*, 1991; vol. 2, *Fundamentalisms and Society*, 1993; vol. 3, *Fundamentalisms and the State*, 1993; vol. 4 *Accounting for Fundamentalisms*, 1994. Chicago: University of Chicago Press.

Merat, Zarir. "Pushing Back the Limits of the Possible: The Press in Iran." *Middle East Report* 212 (fall 1999): 32–35.

Mernissi, Fatima. *Beyond the Veil*. Bloomington: Indiana University Press, 1987.

_____. *Islam and Democracy: Fear of the Modern World*. Trans. Mary Jo Lakeland. Reading, Massachusetts: Addison-Wesley Publishing Co., 1992.

Mitchell, Richard P. *The Society of the Muslim Brothers*. Oxford: Oxford University Press, 1969.

Mitchell, Timothy. *Colonizing Egypt*. Cambridge: Cambridge University Press, 1987.

_____. "Dreamland: The Neoliberalism of Your Desires." *Middle East Report* 210 (spring 1999): 28–32.

_____. "The Representation of Rural Violence in Writings on Political Development in Nasserist Egypt." In *Peasants and Politics in the Middle East*, ed. John Waterbury. Miami: Florida International University, 1991.

Mottahedeh, Roy. *The Mantle of the Prophet*. New York: Penguin Books, 1985.

Mroue, Bassem. "Egyptian Militant Group Declares Cease-Fire." *Associated Press*, 26 March 1999.

Nasr, Salim."Roots of the Shi'i Movement." *MERIP Reports*, no. 133 (June 1985): 10–16.

Nasrallah, Hassan. "Determined to Fight On." Interview by Khaled Dawoud. *Al-Ahram* (Cairo) *Weekly*, 16–22 December 1999.

Nasrawi, Salah. "Parliament Endorses Mubarak's Decision to Extend State of Emergency." *Associated Press*, 27 February 2000.

National Population Council. *Egypt Demographic and Health Survey 1995.* Cairo, 1996.

Niknam, Azadeh. "The Islamization of Law in Iran: A Time of Disenchantment." *Middle East Report* 212 (fall 1999): 17–21.

Petterson, Donald. *Inside Sudan: Political Islam, Conflict and Catastrophe.* Boulder: Westview Press, 1999.

Pullapilly, Cyriac, ed. *Islam in the Contemporary World.* Notre Dame, Indiana: Cross Roads Books, 1980.

Qasim, Tal'at Fu'ad. "What Does the Gama'a Islamiyya Want? Interview with Tal'at Fu'ad Qasim." Hisham Mubarak. *Middle East Report* 198 (January–March 1996): 40–46.

Qutb, Sayyid. *Milestones.* Indianapolis: American Trust Publications, 1990.

Ranstorp, Magnus. *Hizb'Allah in Lebanon: The Politics of the Western Hostage Crisis.* New York: St. Martin's Press, 1997.

Rashwan, Diaa. "Life after El-Zawahri." *Al-Ahram* (Cairo) *Weekly,* 17–23 February 2000.

Richards, Alan, and Waterbury, John. *A Political Economy of the Middle East: State, Class and Economic Development.* Boulder: Westview Press, 1990.

Robinson, Glenn E. "Can Islamists Be Democrats? The Case of Jordan." *Middle East Journal* 51, no. 3 (summer 1997): 373–87.

Rodinson, Maxime. *The Arabs.* Chicago: University of Chicago Press, 1981.

Rodenbeck, Max. *Cairo: The City Victorious.* Cairo: The American University in Cairo Press, 1998.

Roy, Olivier. *The Failure of Political Islam.* Cambridge: Harvard University Press, 1994.

———. "Fundamentalists Without a Common Cause." *Le Monde Diplomatique* (Paris), 2 October 1998.

———. "Rivalries and Power Plays in Afghanistan: The Taliban, the Shari'a and the Pipeline." *Middle East Report* 202 (winter 1997): 37–40.

———. "Tensions in Iran: The Future of the Islamic Revolution." *Middle East Report* 207 (summer 1998): 38–41.

Roy, Sara. "Professionalization versus Politics: The Transformation of Islamist NGOs in Palestine." *Middle East Report* 214 (spring 2000 upcoming).

Sachedina, Abdulaziz. "Ali Shariati: Ideologue of the Iranian Revolution." In *Voices of Resurgent Islam,* ed. John L. Esposito. Oxford: Oxford University Press, 1983.

Said, Edward. *Covering Islam: How the Media and the Experts Determine How We See the Rest of the World.* New York: Pantheon Books, 1981.

———. *Orientalism.* New York: Vintage, 1979.

Salah, Mohammed. "Ali al-Rashidi: al-Shurti al-Masri alathi Mahad al-Tariq lil-Afghan al-Arab fi Afriqiyya." *Al-Hayat* (London), 30 September 1998.

———. "Al-Qahira: Aatiqaal 19 min al-Ikhwan Yom Itlaq Essam al-Iryan." *Al-Hayat* (London), 23 January 2000.

———. "Al-Qahira: Qa'id al-Afghan al-Arab Qutila fi-Dowla Afriqiyya." *Al-Hayat* (London), 11 June, 1996.

———. "Al-Qibti al-Wahid Yansahib min La'ihat Mu'asisi al-Wasat al-Masri." *Al-Hayat* (London), 11 June 1999.

———. "Bawadir Muwajha Bain Ikhwan Misr wa Ikhwan al-Kharij." *Al-Hayat* (London), 20 October 1996.

———. "Hizb al-Sharia al-Misri Ya'ati al-Ulawiyya lil-Marja'iyya al-Islamiyya wa Muwajahit al-Tatbi'a ma'a Israel." *Al-Hayat* (London), 17 August 1999.

———. "Hizb al-Sharia Yuwaddah Nazaritu ila al-Aqaliyyat." *Al-Hayat* (London), 23 September 1999.

———. "Istiqaalat Qiyaadi fi Jama'at al-Ikhwan." *Al-Hayat* (London), 10 August 1998.

———. "Misr: Aitiqaal Anaasir min Hizb al-Sharia." *Al-Hayat* (London), 22 November 1999.

———. "Misr: al-Jama'a al-Islamiyya Multazama Waqf al-Amaliyyat wa Juhud l-Ihtiwa'a Bayn Rifai Ahmed Taha wal-Akhreen." *Al-Hayat* (London), 6 December 1999.

———. "Misr: Ayya Mustaqbal lil-Usuliyyeen ba'd Sanawat al-Jihad wal-Jama'a al-Islamiyya." *Al-Hayat* (London), 10 February 2000.

———. "Misr: Qadat al-Jama'a al-Islamiyya Yaqarirun Waqf al-Amaliyyat." *Al-Hayat* (London), 5 July 1997.

———. "Misr: Qadat al-Ikhwan Yalja'un ila al-Tahdi'a wa Yatalabun min Anasirhum Adam Istifzaz al-Hukuma." *Al-Hayat* (London), 9 November 1999.

_____. "Misr: Qiyadiyan fi al-Jihad Andaman ila Alaan Waqf al-Amaliyyat." *Al-Hayat* (London), 10 July 1997.

Sagiv, David. *Fundamentalism and Intellectuals in Egypt, 1973–93.* London: Frank Cass and Co., 1995.

Schwedler, Jillian. "A Paradox of Democracy? Islamist Participation in Elections." *Middle East Report,* no. 209 (winter 1998): 25–29.

Shadid, Anthony. "Despite Repression, Women Fight Unpopular War in Sudan." *Associated Press,* 28 August 1998.

_____. "Five Years, 1,100 Dead, Egypt Alone in Winning against Islamic Insurgency." *Associated Press,* 9 August 1997.

_____. "From Militia to Movement, Hezbollah Faces Uncertain Future." *Associated Press,* 27 June 1998.

_____. "Religious Militia Could Make or Break Sudan's Islamic Government." *Associated Press,* 5 February 1997.

_____. "Sudanese Battle over Islam in Once-Independent Universities." *Associated Press,* 24 June 1996.

Sharabi, Hisham. *Neopatriarchy.* Oxford: Oxford University Press, 1988.

Shepard, William E. "Islam as a 'System' in the Later Writings of Sayyid Qutb." *Middle East Studies* 25 (January 1989): 31–50.

"Some 63,000 Students Have Undergone Military Training." *Associated Press,* 6 October 1997.

Tamimi, Azzam, ed. *Power-Sharing Islam!* London: Liberty, 1993.

Tibi, Bassam. *The Crisis of Modern Islam.* Salt Lake City: University of Utah Press, 1988.

Toprak, Binnaz. "Islamist Intellectuals: Revolt against Industry and Technology." In *Turkey and the West: Changing Political and Cultural Identities,* edited by Metin Heper, Ayse Oncu and Heinz Kramer. London: I. B. Tauris, 1993.

"A Tragedy of Errors." *Cairo Times,* 22 January–4 February 1998.

al-Turabi, Hassan. "The Islamic State." In *Voices of Resurgent Islam,* ed. John L. Esposito. Oxford: Oxford University Press, 1983.

United Nations Development Programme. *Globalization with a Human Face.* Human Development Report. 1999.

United Nations International Drug Control Programme. *Capacity Building for Drug Control.* Afghanistan Project Summary. 1997.

Usher, Graham. *Palestine in Crisis: The Struggle for Peace and Political Independence after Oslo.* London: Pluto Press, 1995.

_____. "What Kind of Nation? The Rise of Hamas in the Occupied Territories." *Race & Class* 37 (1995): 65–80.

Vakili, Valla. "Debating Religion and Politics in Iran: The Political Thought of Abdolkarim Soroush." Studies Department Occasional Paper Series 2. New York: Council on Foreign Relations, 1996.

Viorst, Milton. *In the Shadow of the Prophet: The Struggle for the Soul of Islam.* New York: Anchor Books, 1998.

_____. *Sandcastles: The Arabs in Search of the Modern World.* New York: Knopf, 1994.

Voll, John Obert. *Islam: Continuity and Change in the Modern World.* Boulder: Westview Press, 1982.

_____, ed. *Sudan: State and Society in Crisis.* Bloomington: University of Indiana, 1991.

"Al-Wasat: Dalala Tarikhiyya." *Awraq Hizb al-Wasat.* Cairo: Hizb al-Wasat, 1996.

Watt, W. Montgomery. *Muhammad: Prophet and Statesman.* Oxford: Oxford University Press, 1961.

Wenger, Martha. "Sudan: Politics and Society." *Middle East Report* 172 (September-October 1991): 3–7.

Wilkinson, Tracy. "Islamists Strive for Firmer Ground." *Los Angeles Times,* 27 August 1999.

Wright, Robin. "Two Visions of Democracy." *Journal of Democracy* 7 (April 1996): 64–75.

"Yusuf al-Badri Yatalib Bilgha' Wizarat al-Taalim," *Al-Hayat* (London), 30 June 1998.

Zubaida, Sami. "Is Iran an Islamic State?" In *Political Islam: Essays from Middle East Report,* ed. Joel Beinin and Joe Stork. Berkeley: University of California Press, 1996.

_____. "Turkish Islam and National Identity." *Middle East Report* 199 (April-June 1996): 10–15.

Index

War
in Afghanistan, 80–83
Arab-Israeli, 34, 44, 46–49, 78, 102, 237
Iran-Iraq, 87, 197, 232
in Lebanon, 272, 274–277
Persian Gulf, 87, 295
War, civil
in Lebanon, 133–135
in Sudan, 155, 159–161, 164, 177–178, 180–184
Waraqah, 21
Wasat Party. *See* Center Party
Waxman, Nachson, 97
Web sites, 140, 212, 274
West
attitudes toward, 51–53, 84, 217, 268
attitude toward Muslims, 2, 9, 28, 96, 133, 289
view of Islam, 74, 289
West Bank, 93, 117–119, 123, 126, 131
Westernization, 22, 30–36, 39, 145
attitude toward, 77, 85, 102, 246–250
resistance to, 190–191, 194, 241–243, 245
Western values
discredited, 65–66
use of, 216–217, 224, 237, 268
"When Worlds Collide," 35
White Revolution, 194

Women, 125, 183
in Egypt, 267, 269, 284–285
in Iran, 208–210, 212, 220
Muslim attire, 14, 272. *See also* Veils
and political parties, 254, 257, 267, 269, 279, 285
in politics, 5, 65, 194
rights of, 154, 173, 194, 198, 212
in Sudan, 178, 180–183
under Taliban, 14–15, 19, 208
in Turkey, 147–148
World Bank, 155
World Trade Center
bombing, 1993, 84, 107
terrorist attacks, 2001, 1, 295

Yassin, Sheikh Ahmed, 119, 121,129
Yazdi, Ibrahim, 221–222
Yemen, 47, 88
Islah Party, 69
Yilmaz, Murat, 144
Youth, 129, 204–210, 212, 220

Al-Zaafarani, Ibrahim, 265
Zabbaleen (trash collectors), 36–37
Zakzouk, Hamdi, 106
Al-Zawahiri, Ayman, 105
Al-Zayat, Montaser, 108
Zionism, 116, 121–123
Zuhdi, Karam, 101, 107, 265
Al-Zumur, Abboud, 78, 101, 107